Shojo Beat

We Were There

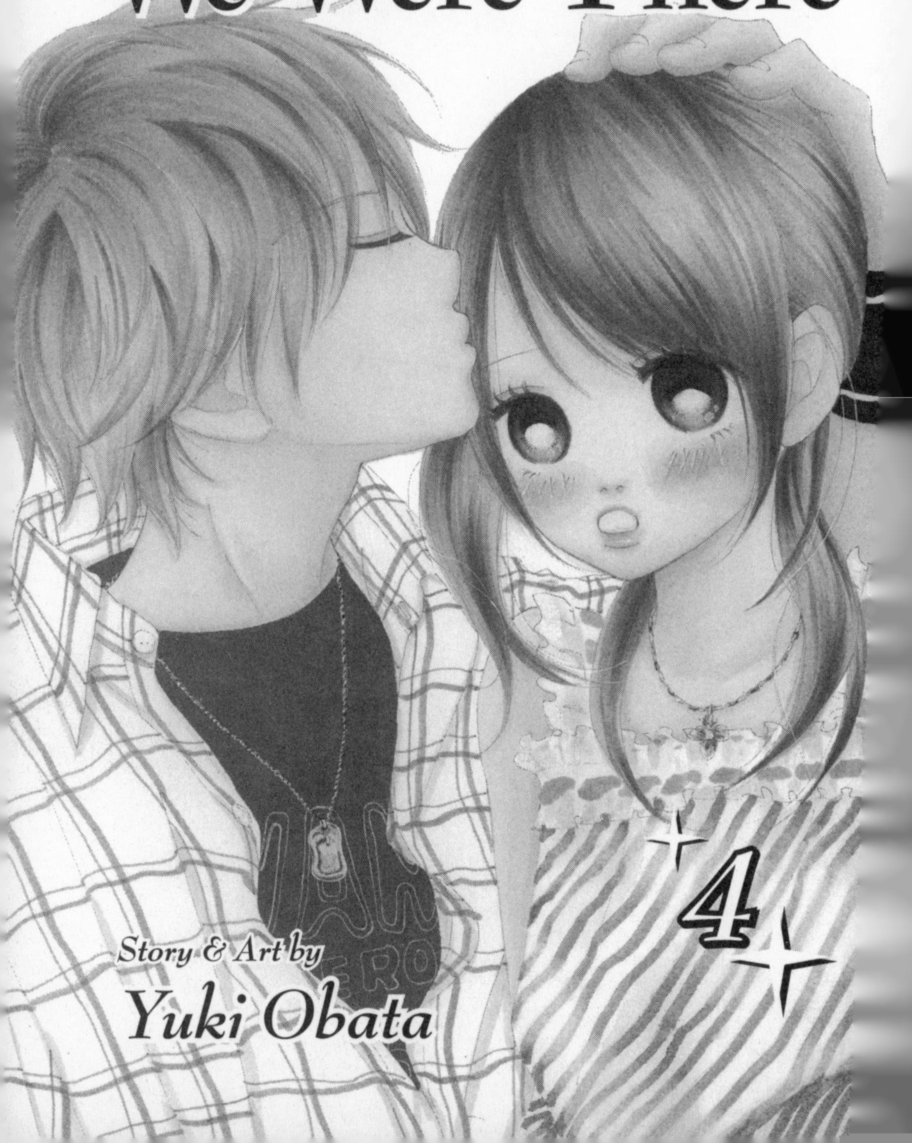

4

Story & Art by

Yuki Obata

Contents

Characters

Yuri Yamamoto
Nanami's classmate. Nana-san was her older sister.

Motoharu Yano
Nanami's popular classmate. His girlfriend Nana-san died.

Nanami Takahashi
She's earnest but a bit forgetful at times.

Story

Having fallen in love with the extremely popular Yano, whom she had disliked in the beginning, Nanami gradually begins to get the hang of being his girlfriend. She had been feeling insecure because of Yano's painful past, as well as the fact that he's her first boyfriend. But after getting in touch with her feelings, Nanami decides she's ready to have sex with him and tells him so...

Chapter 13

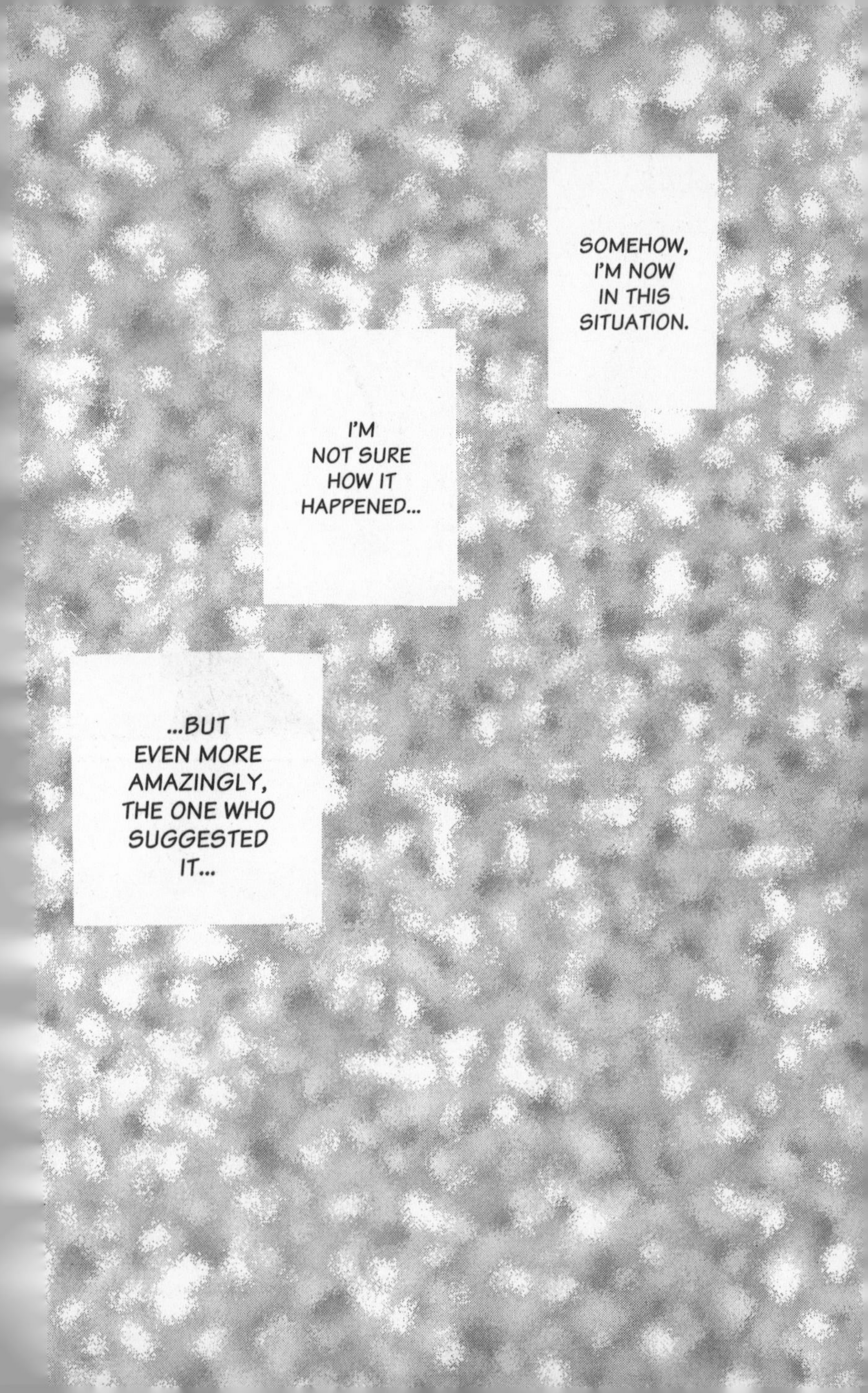
SOMEHOW, I'M NOW IN THIS SITUATION.
I'M NOT SURE HOW IT HAPPENED...
...BUT EVEN MORE AMAZINGLY, THE ONE WHO SUGGESTED IT...

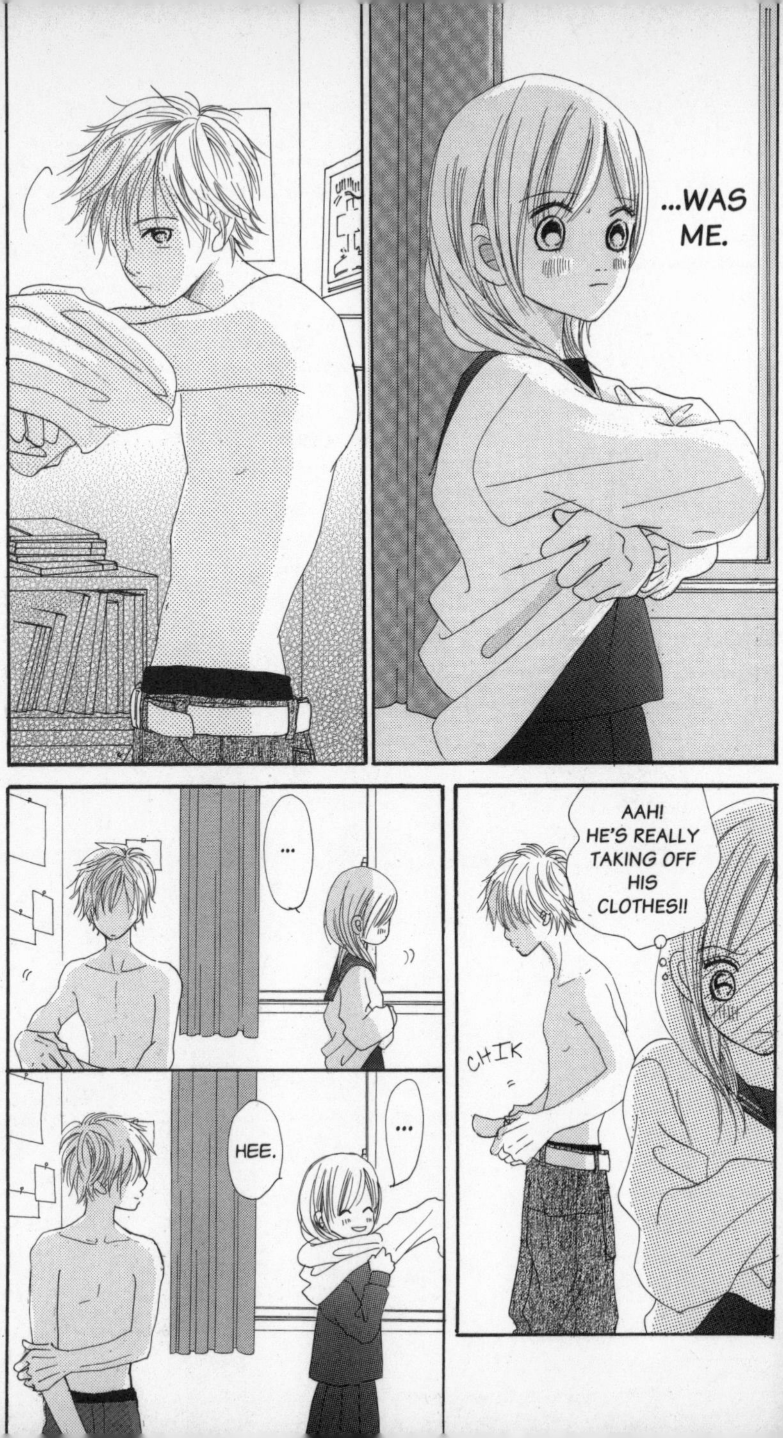
...WAS ME.
AAH! HE'S REALLY TAKING OFF HIS CLOTHES!!
CHIK
...
...
HEE.

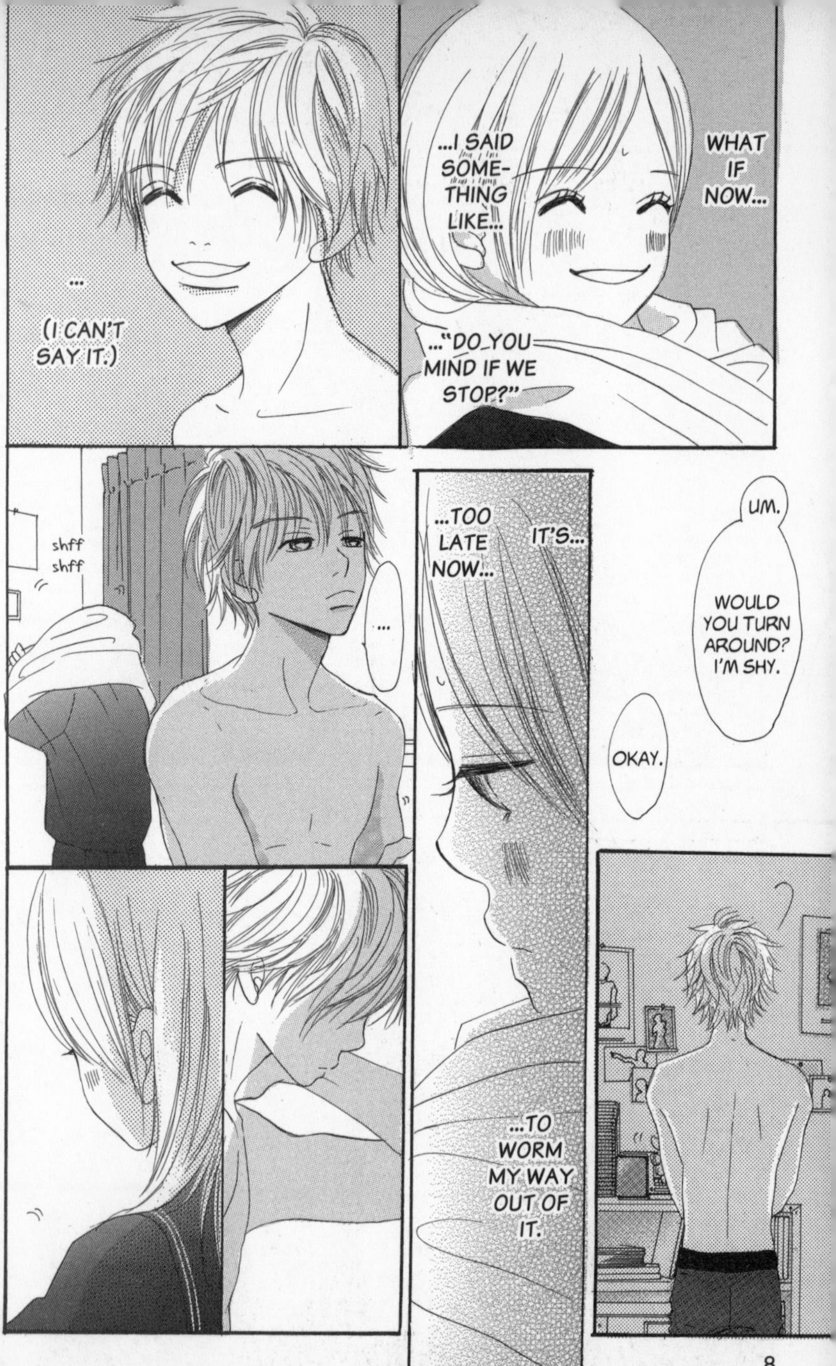
WHAT IF NOW...
...I SAID SOME-THING LIKE...
..."DO YOU MIND IF WE STOP?"
...
(I CAN'T SAY IT.)
UM.
WOULD YOU TURN AROUND? I'M SHY.
OKAY.
IT'S...
...TOO LATE NOW...
...TO WORM MY WAY OUT OF IT.
...
shff shff

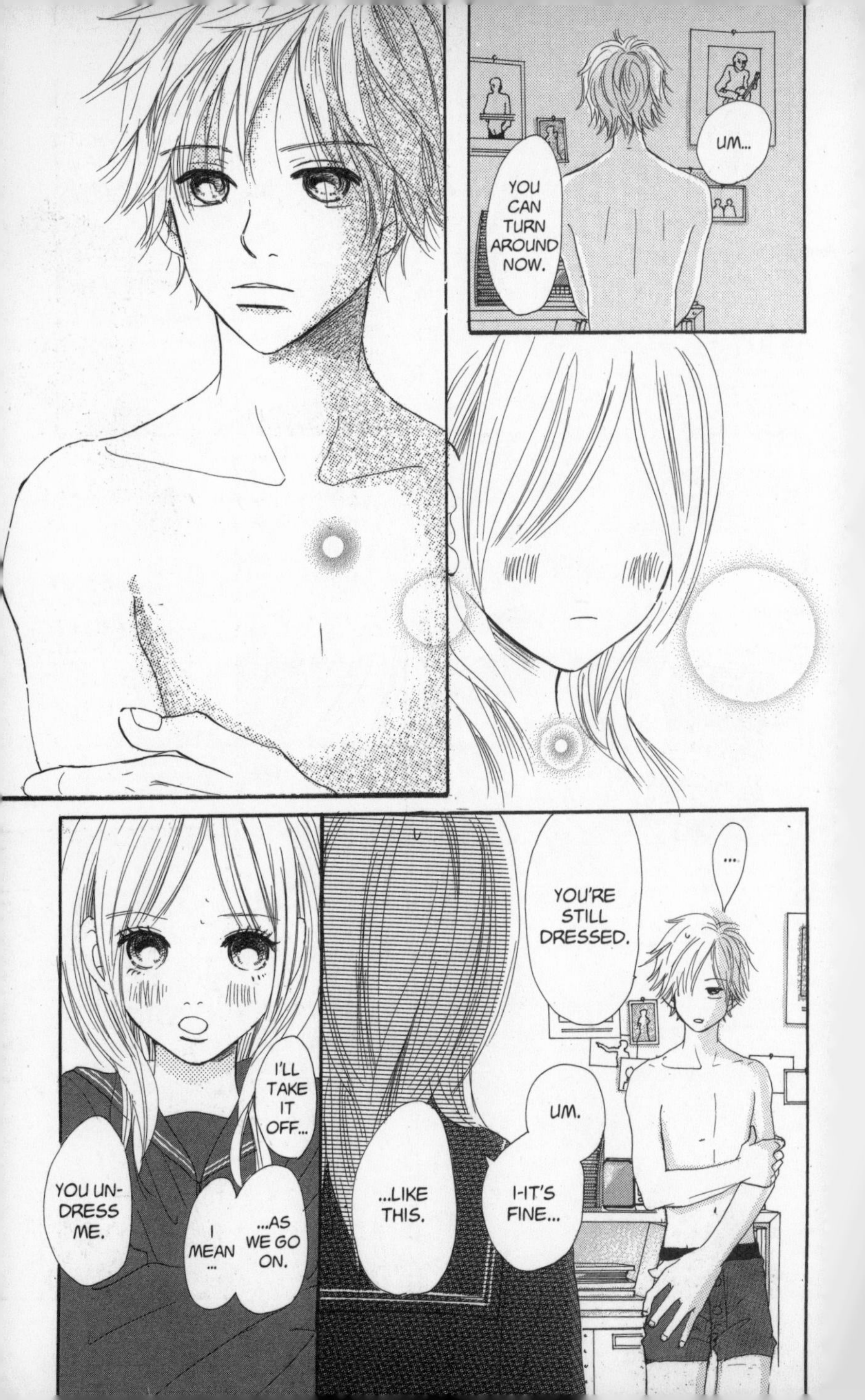
UM...
YOU CAN TURN AROUND NOW.
...
YOU'RE STILL DRESSED.
UM.
I-IT'S FINE...
...LIKE THIS.
I'LL TAKE IT OFF...
...AS WE GO ON.
I MEAN ...
YOU UN-DRESS ME.

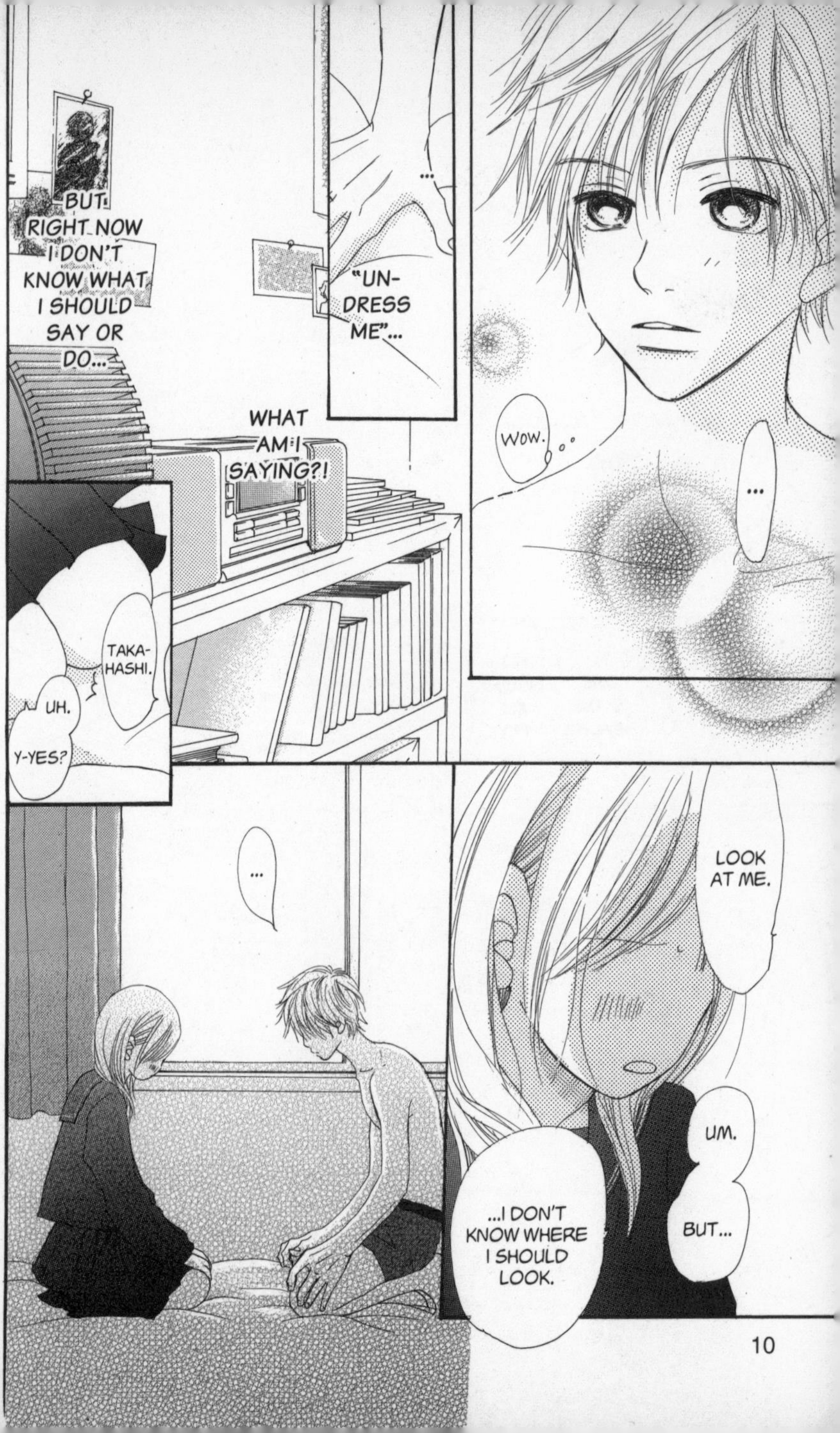
WOW...
...
...
"UN-DRESS ME"...
BUT RIGHT NOW I DON'T KNOW WHAT I SHOULD SAY OR DO...
WHAT AM I SAYING?!
TAKA-HASHI.
UH.
Y-YES?
LOOK AT ME.
UM.
BUT...
...I DON'T KNOW WHERE I SHOULD LOOK.
...

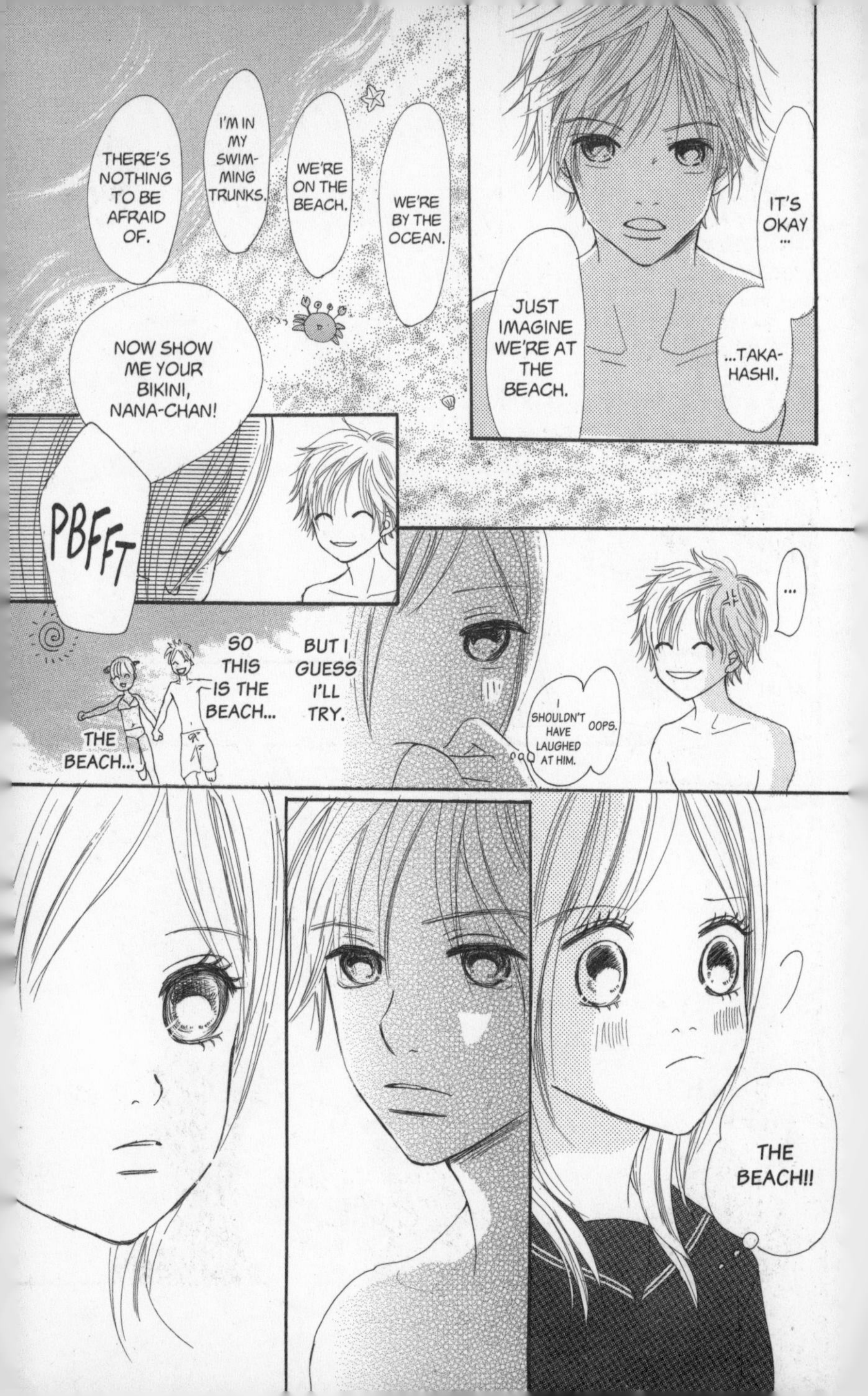

IT'S OKAY ...
...TAKA-HASHI.
JUST IMAGINE WE'RE AT THE BEACH.
WE'RE BY THE OCEAN.
WE'RE ON THE BEACH.
I'M IN MY SWIM-MING TRUNKS.
THERE'S NOTHING TO BE AFRAID OF.
NOW SHOW ME YOUR BIKINI, NANA-CHAN!
PBFFT
...
OOPS.
I SHOULDN'T HAVE LAUGHED AT HIM.
BUT I GUESS I'LL TRY.
SO THIS IS THE BEACH...
THE BEACH...
THE BEACH!!

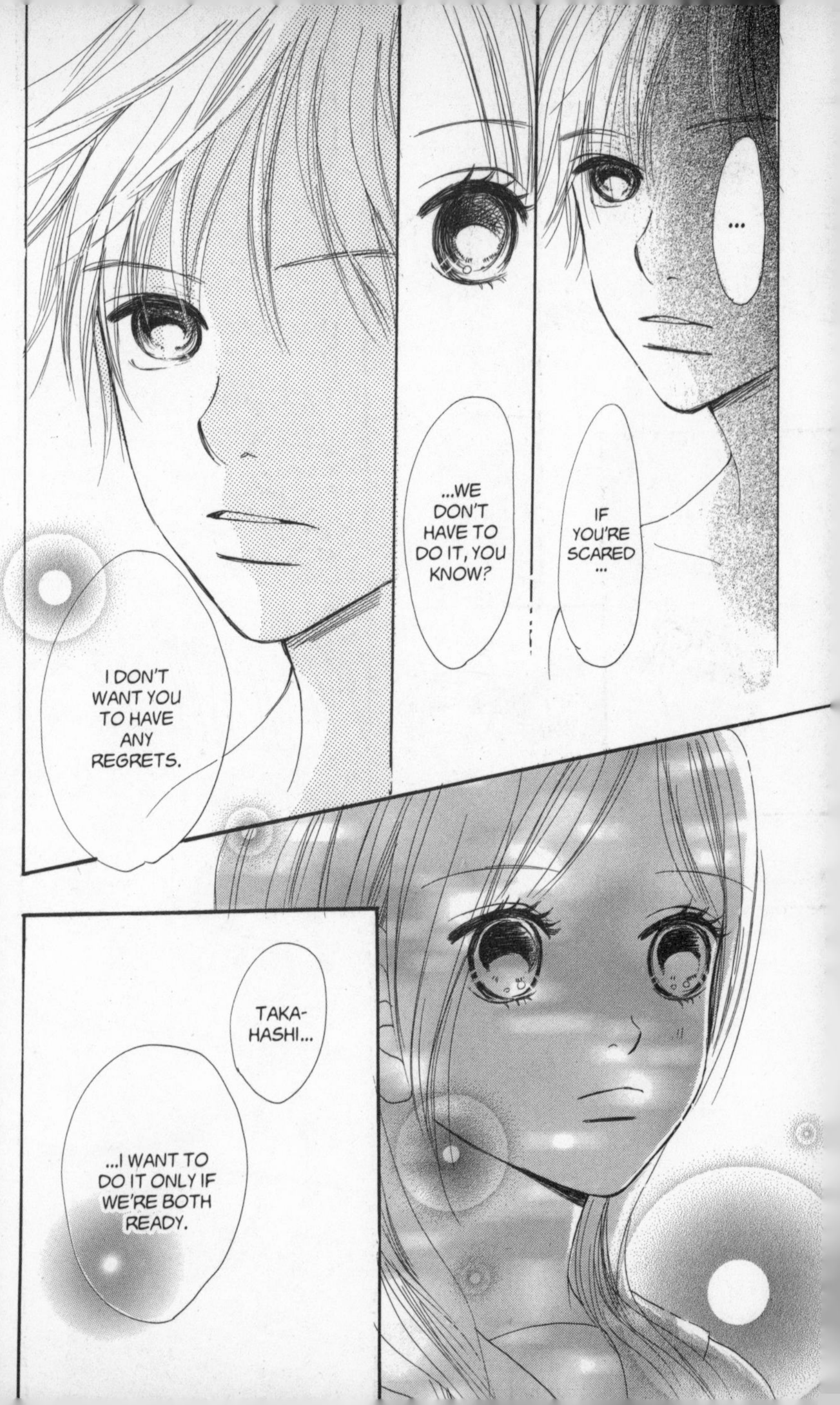
...
IF YOU'RE SCARED...
...WE DON'T HAVE TO DO IT, YOU KNOW?
I DON'T WANT YOU TO HAVE ANY REGRETS.
TAKA-HASHI...
...I WANT TO DO IT ONLY IF WE'RE BOTH READY.

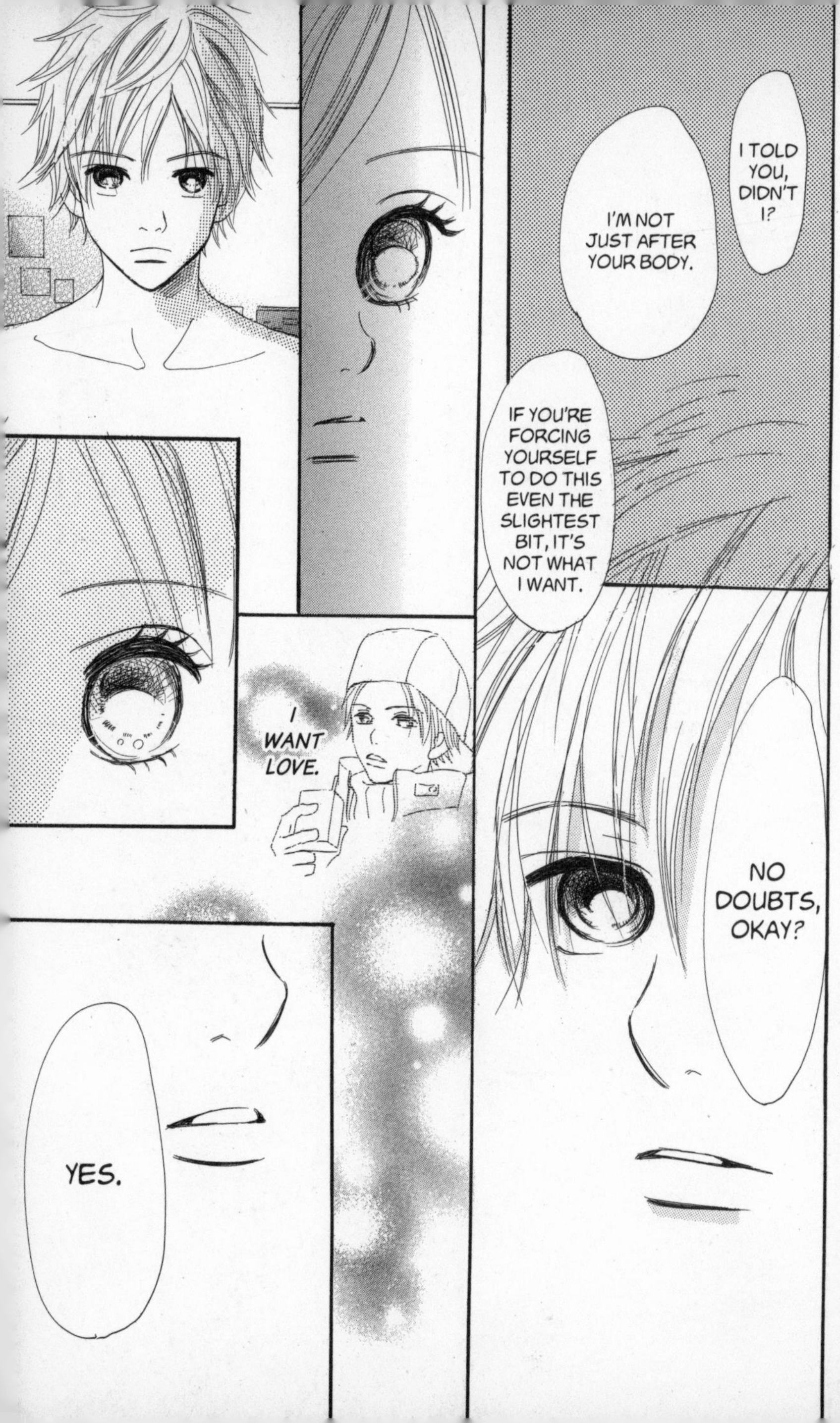
I TOLD YOU, DIDN'T I?
I'M NOT JUST AFTER YOUR BODY.
IF YOU'RE FORCING YOURSELF TO DO THIS EVEN THE SLIGHTEST BIT, IT'S NOT WHAT I WANT.
NO DOUBTS, OKAY?
I WANT LOVE.
YES.

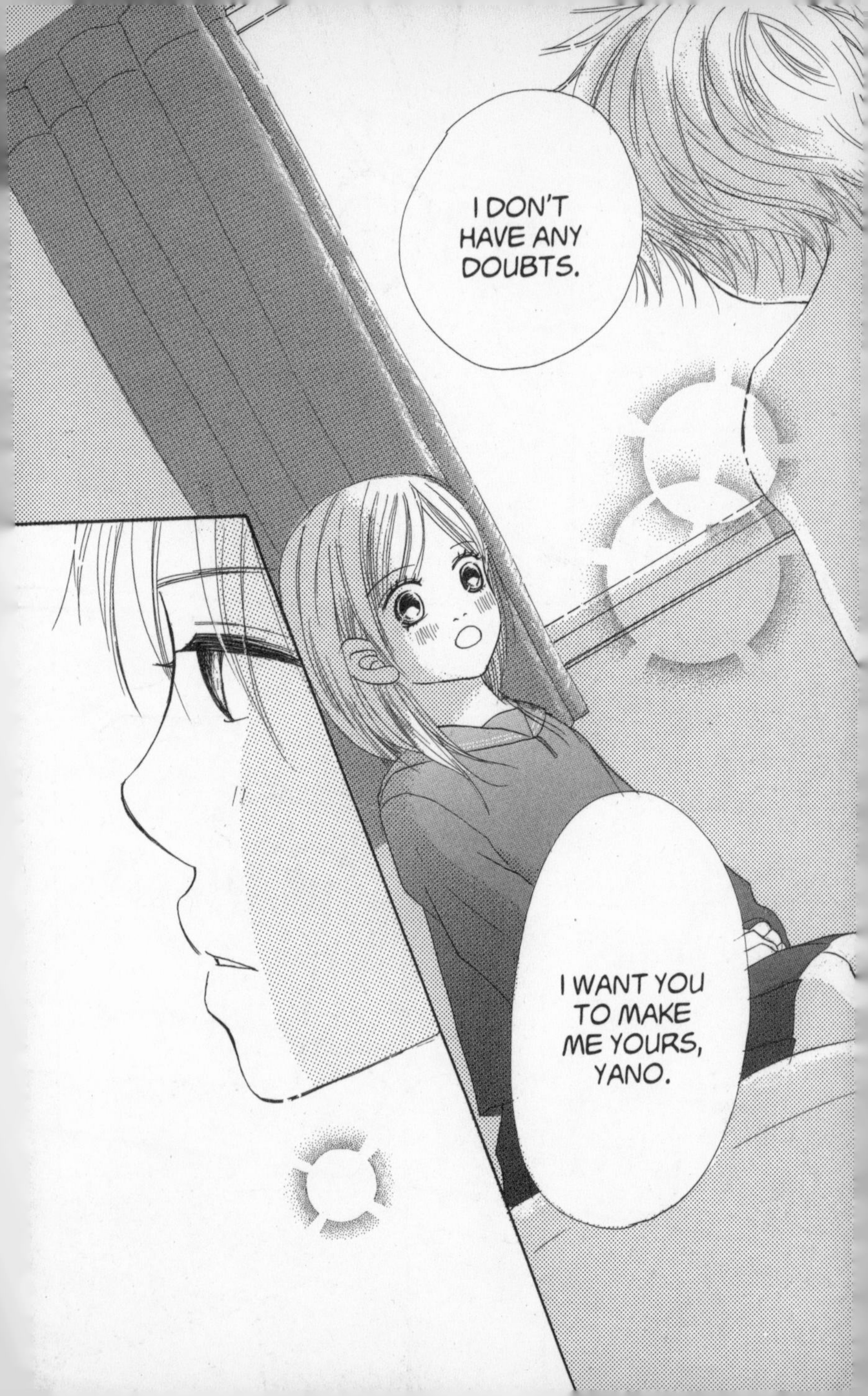
I DON'T HAVE ANY DOUBTS.
I WANT YOU TO MAKE ME YOURS, YANO.

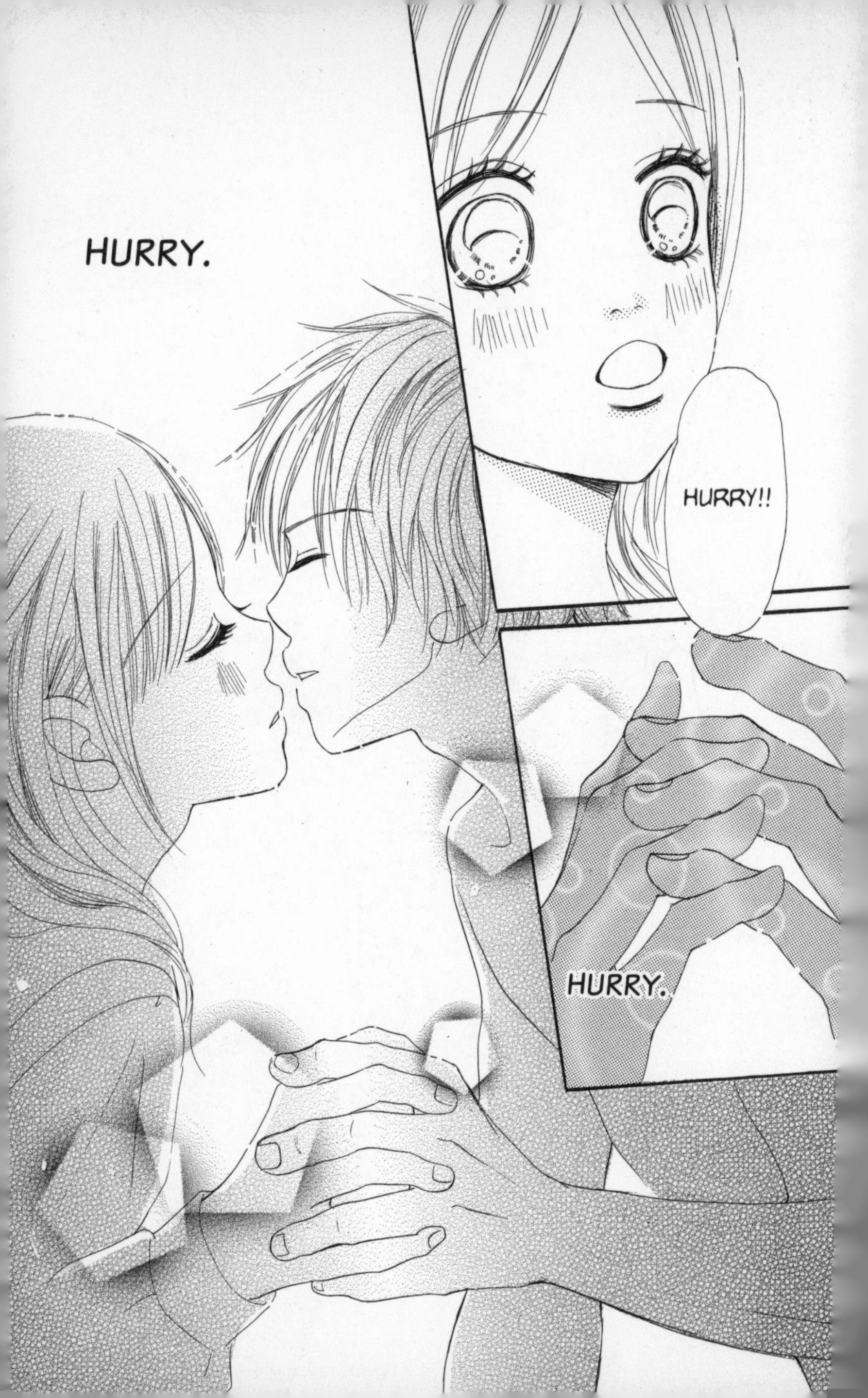
HURRY!!
HURRY.
HURRY.

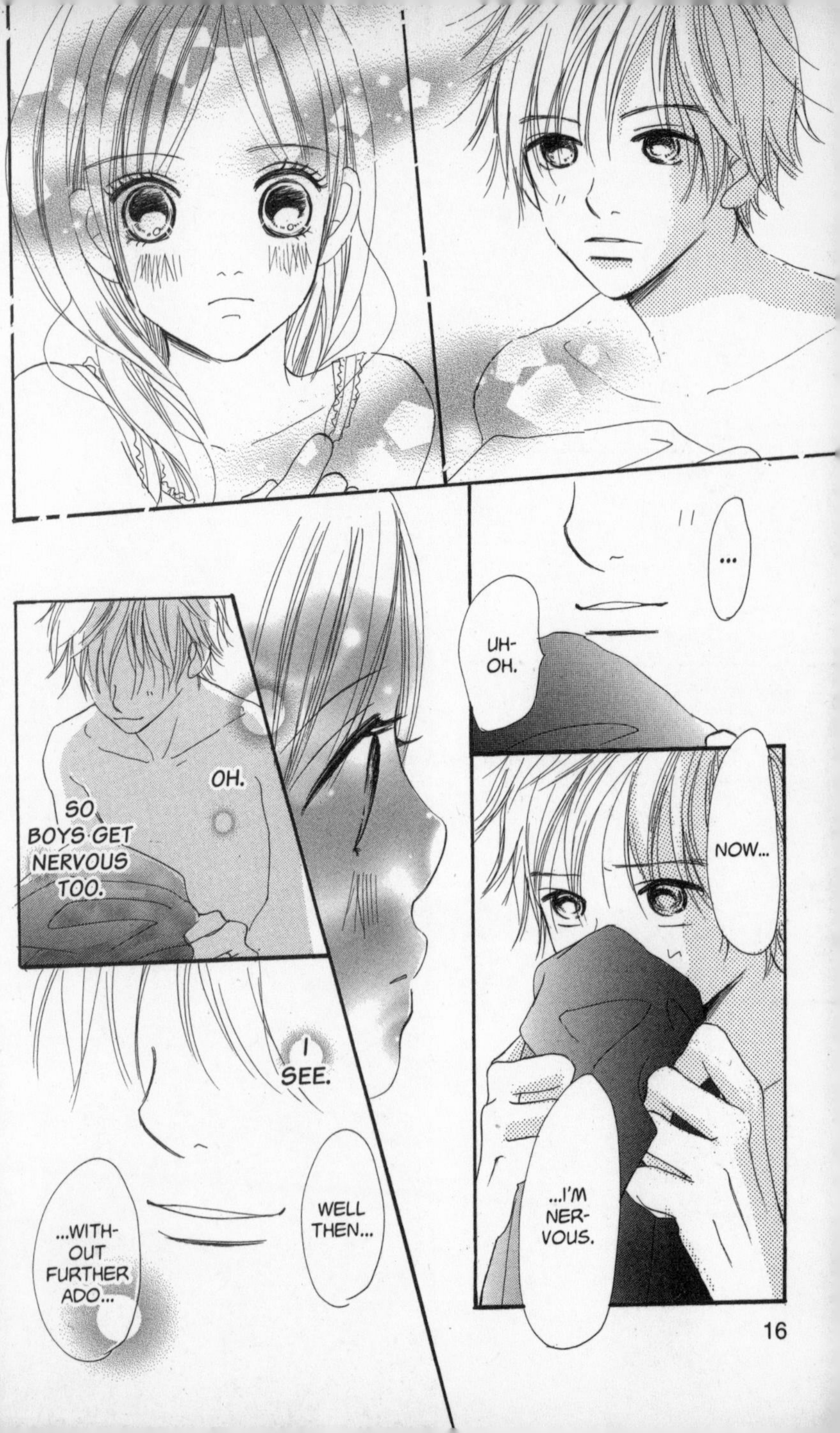
...
UH-OH.
NOW...
...I'M NERVOUS.
OH.
SO BOYS GET NERVOUS TOO.
I SEE.
WELL THEN...
...WITHOUT FURTHER ADO...

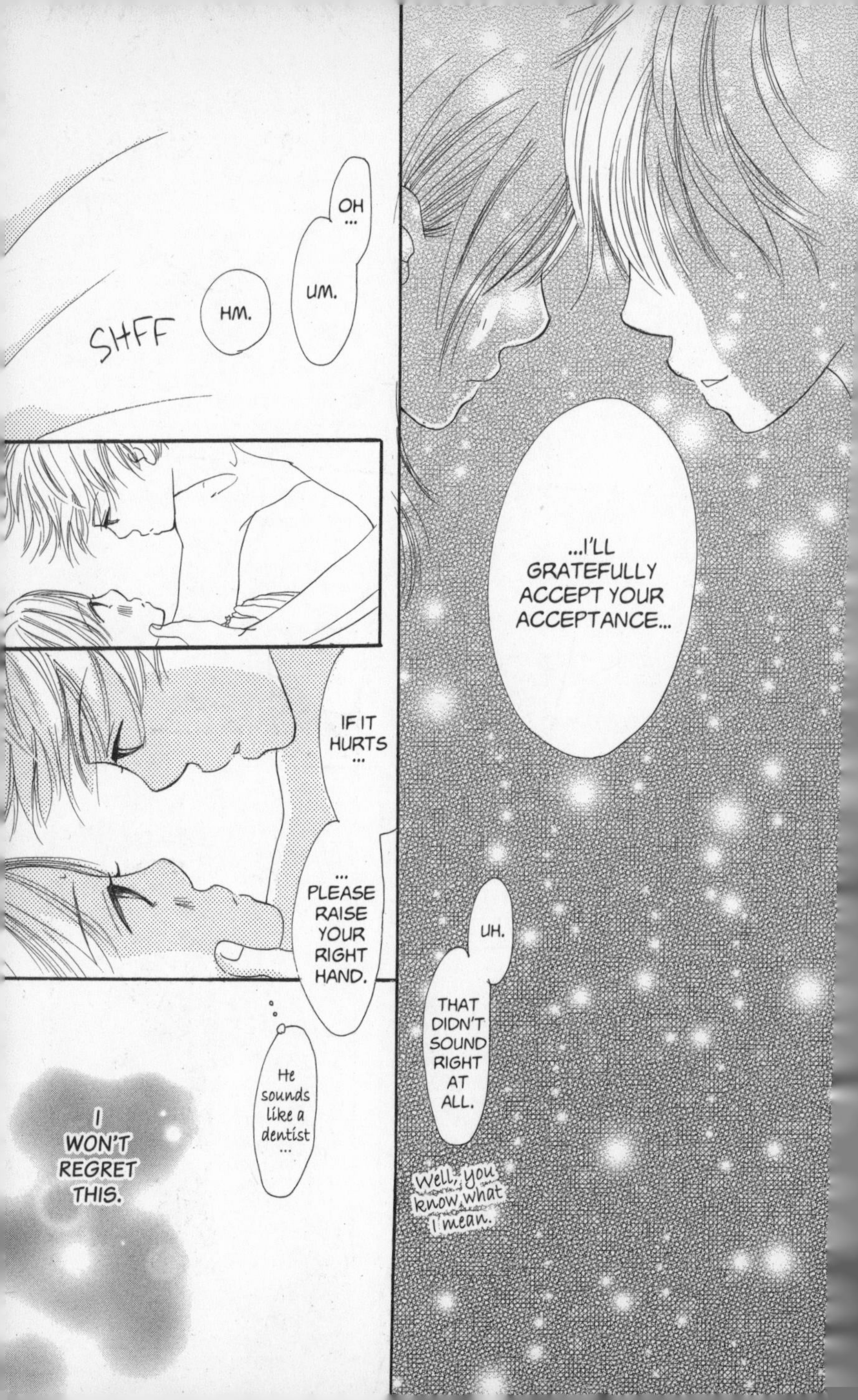
...I'LL GRATEFULLY ACCEPT YOUR ACCEPTANCE...
UH.
THAT DIDN'T SOUND RIGHT AT ALL.
Well, you know what I mean.
OH...
UM.
HM.
SHFF
IF IT HURTS...
...PLEASE RAISE YOUR RIGHT HAND.
He sounds like a dentist...
I WON'T REGRET THIS.

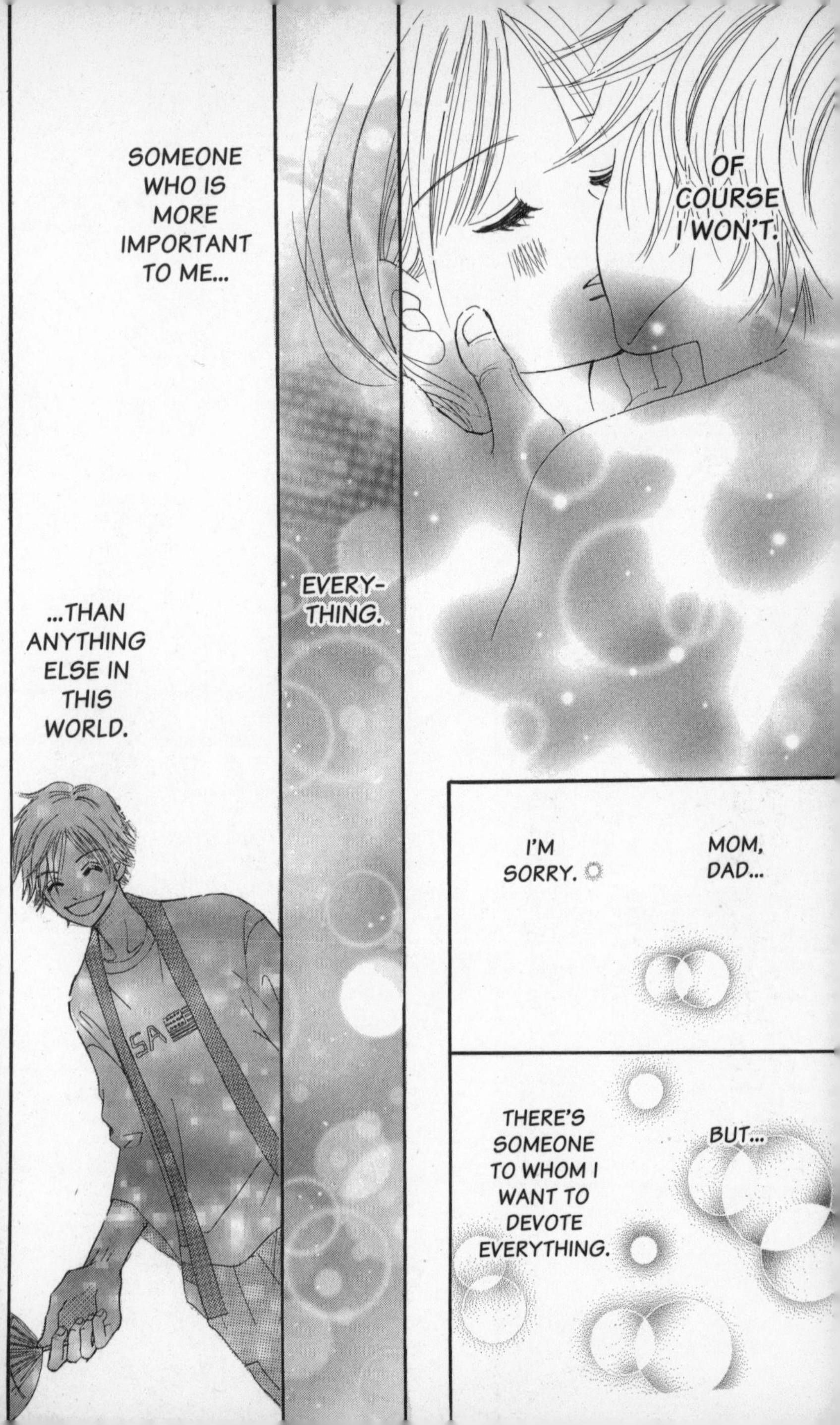
OF COURSE I WON'T.
MOM, DAD...
I'M SORRY.
BUT...
THERE'S SOMEONE TO WHOM I WANT TO DEVOTE EVERYTHING.
EVERY-THING.
SOMEONE WHO IS MORE IMPORTANT TO ME...
...THAN ANYTHING ELSE IN THIS WORLD.

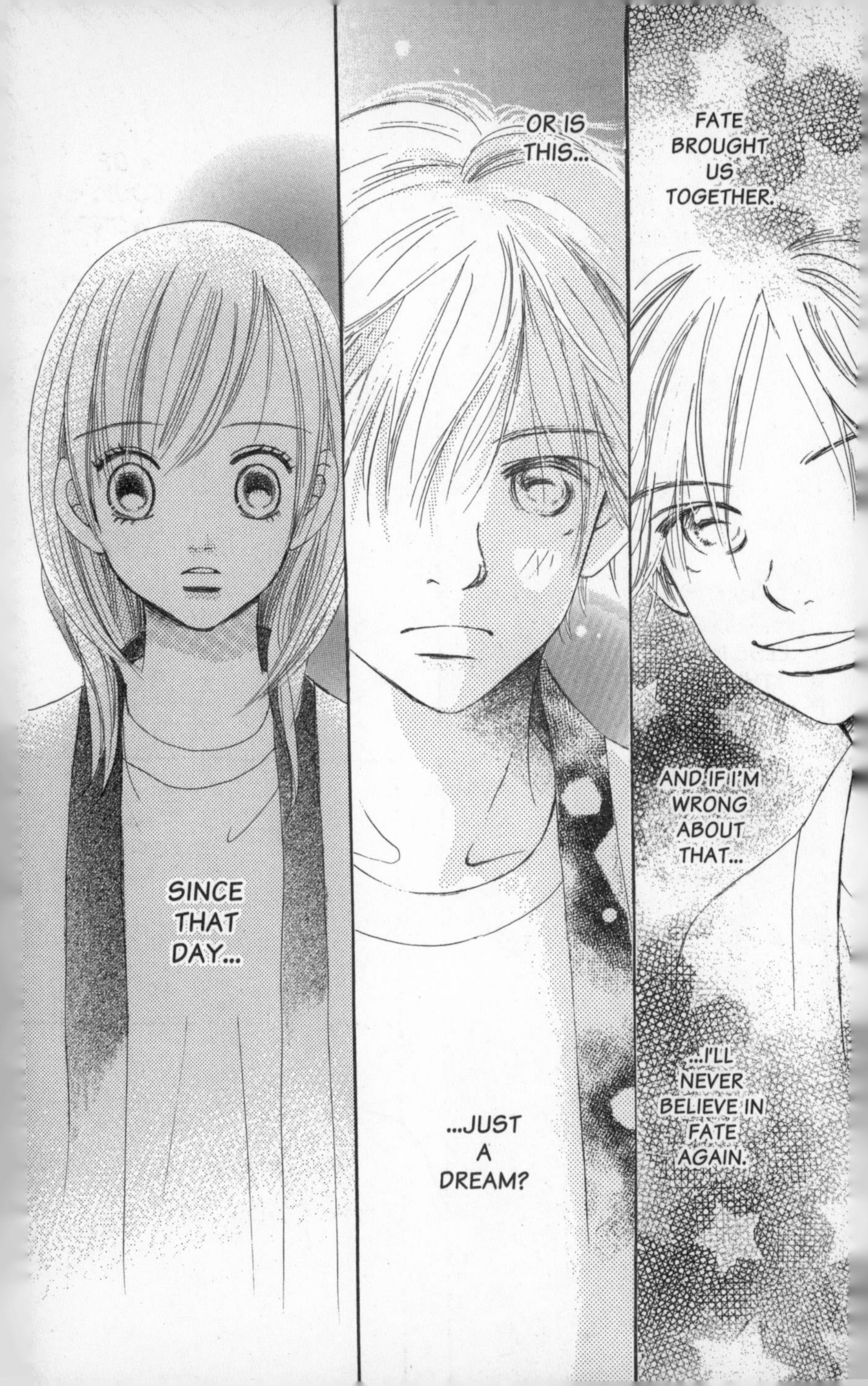
FATE BROUGHT US TOGETHER.
AND IF I'M WRONG ABOUT THAT...
...I'LL NEVER BELIEVE IN FATE AGAIN.
OR IS THIS...
...JUST A DREAM?
SINCE THAT DAY...

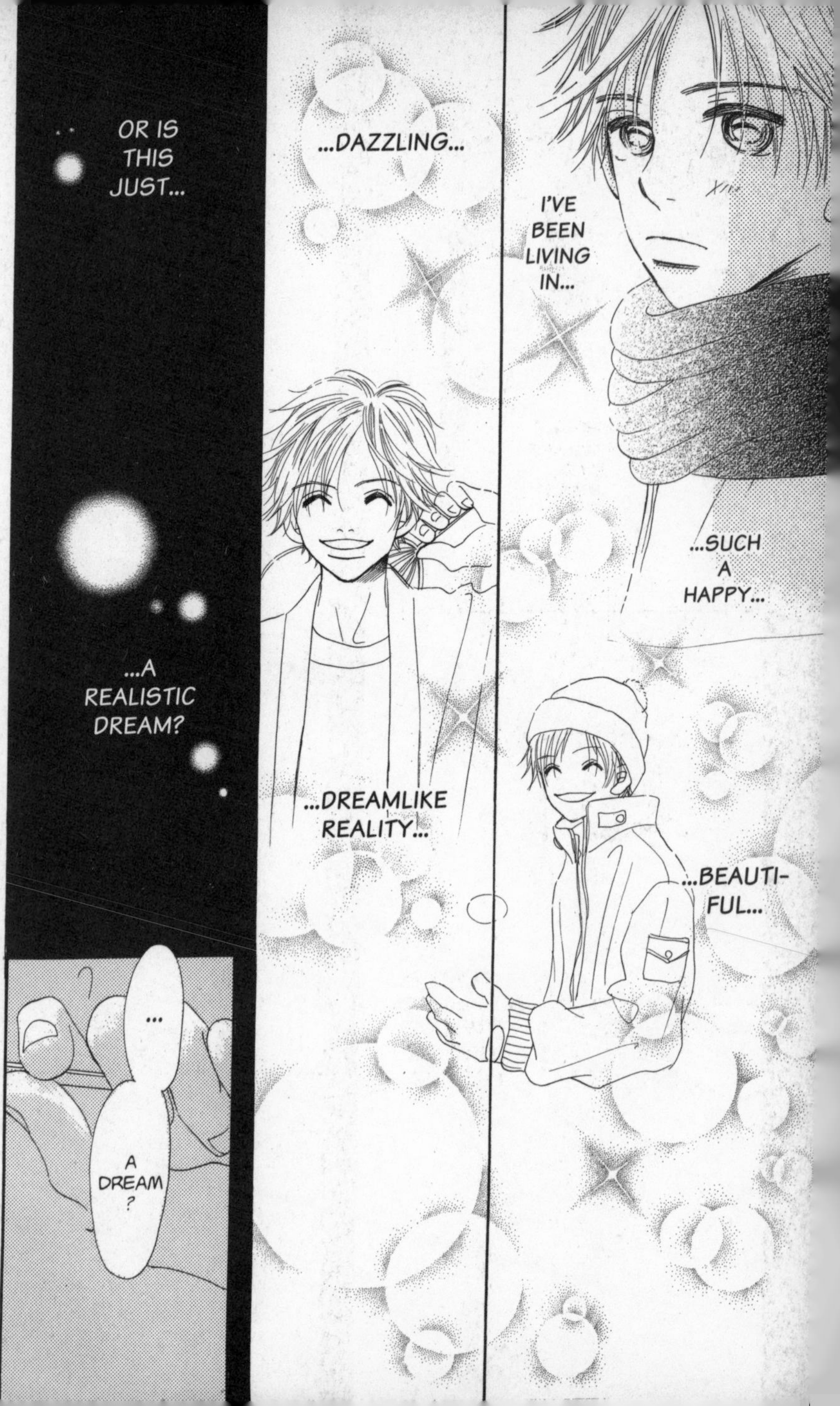
I'VE BEEN LIVING IN...
...SUCH A HAPPY...
...BEAUTI-FUL...
...DAZZLING...
...DREAMLIKE REALITY...
OR IS THIS JUST...
...A REALISTIC DREAM?
...
A DREAM?

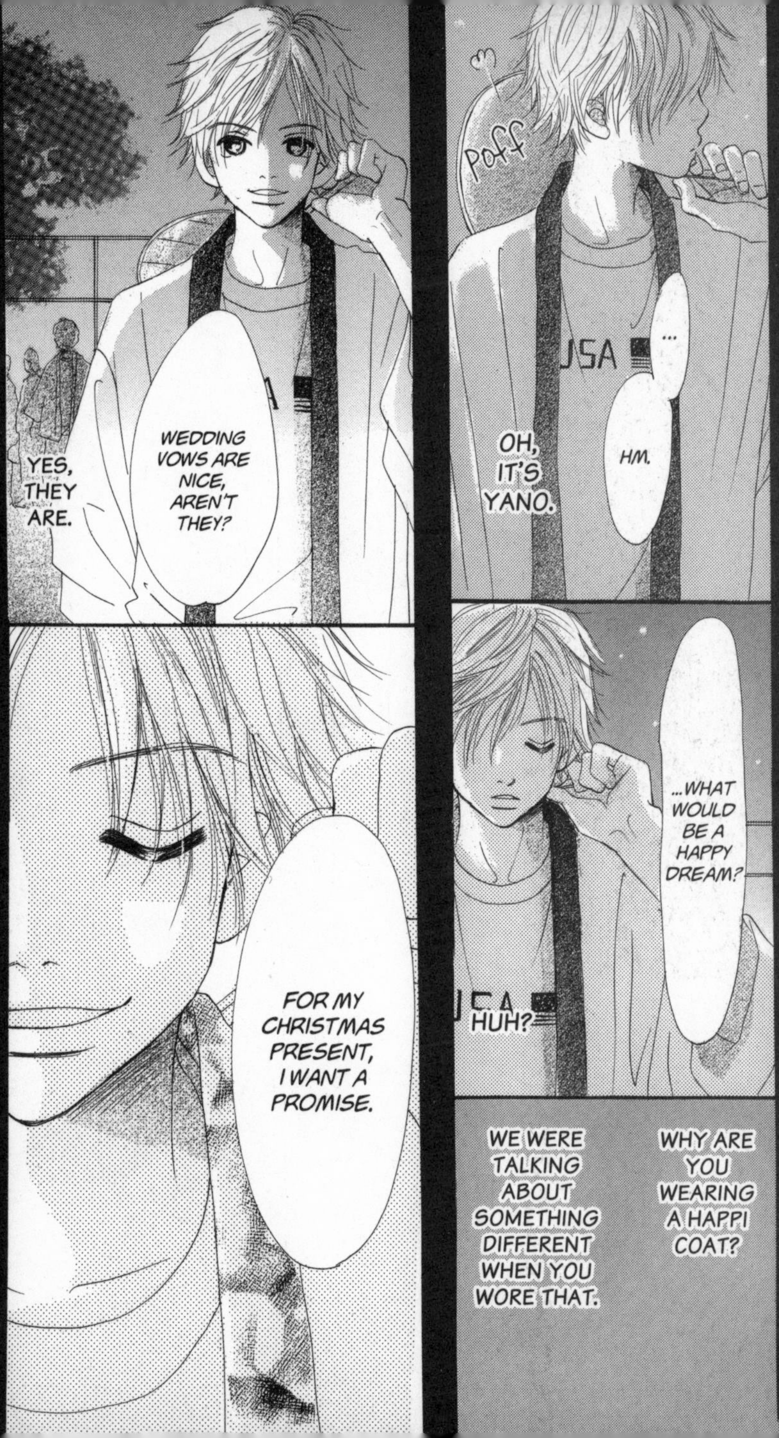
Poff
...
HM.
OH, IT'S YANO.
...WHAT WOULD BE A HAPPY DREAM?
HUH?
WHY ARE YOU WEARING A HAPPI COAT?
WE WERE TALKING ABOUT SOMETHING DIFFERENT WHEN YOU WORE THAT.
WEDDING VOWS ARE NICE, AREN'T THEY?
YES, THEY ARE.
FOR MY CHRISTMAS PRESENT, I WANT A PROMISE.

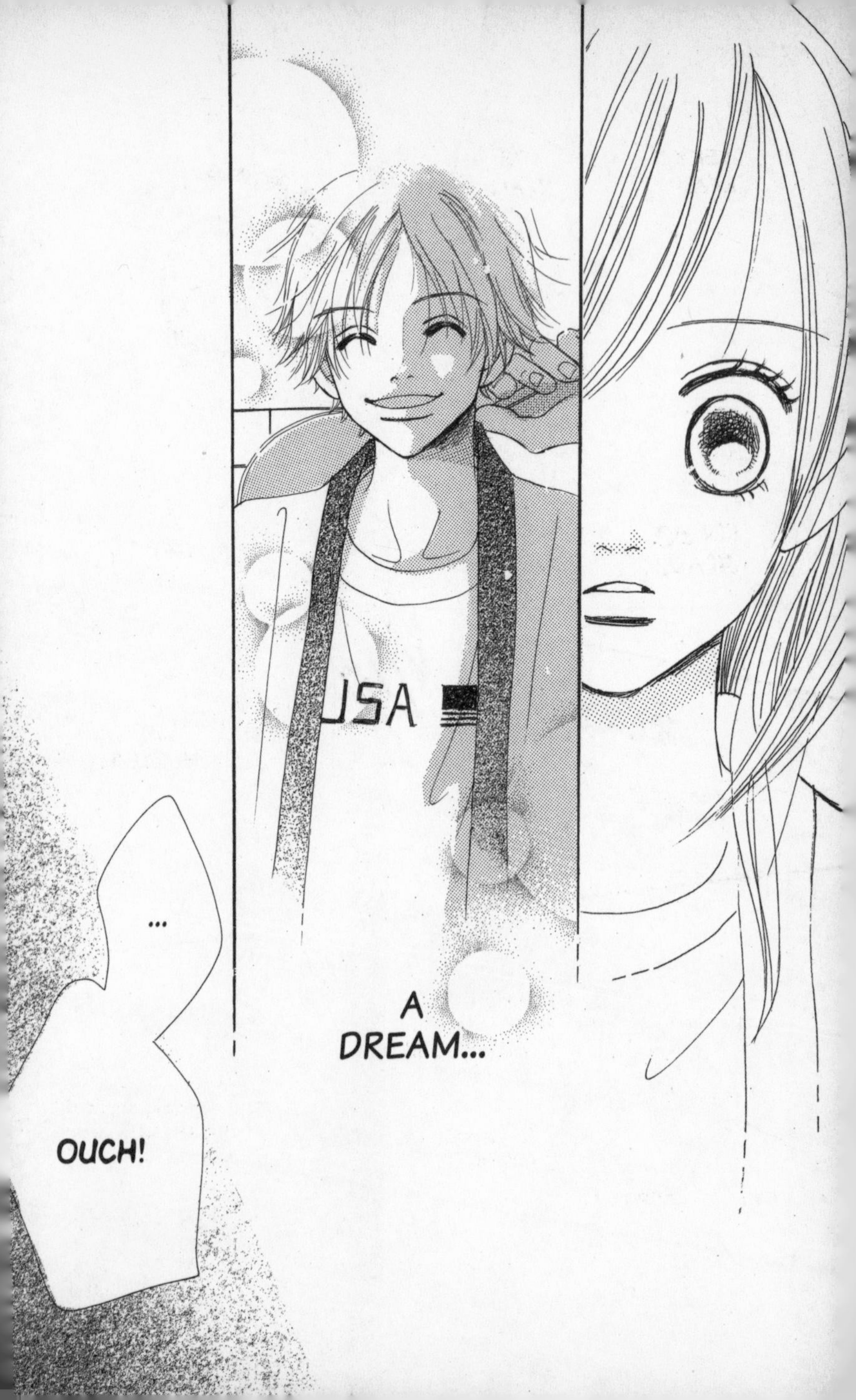
USA
A DREAM...
...
OUCH!

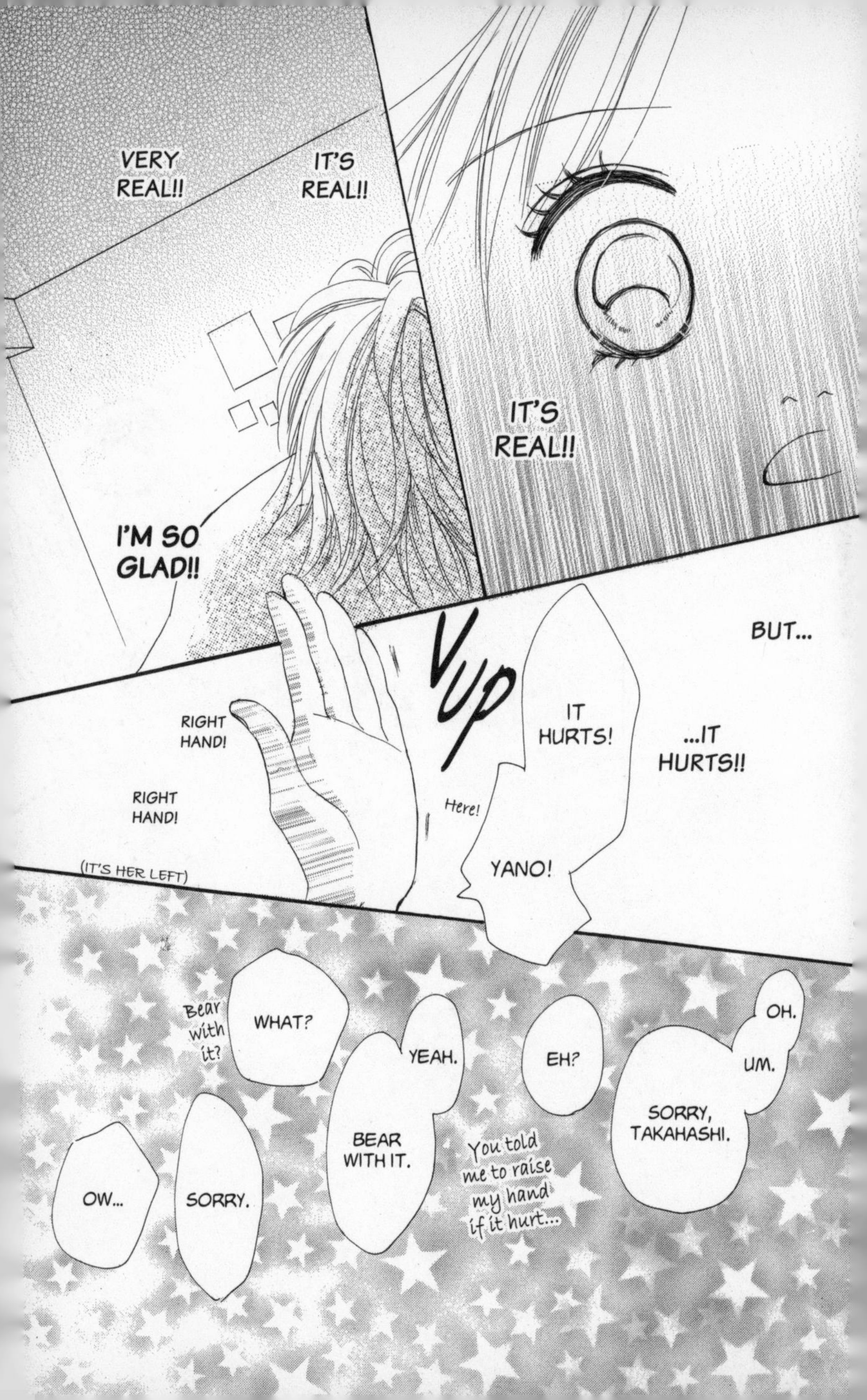
IT'S REAL!!
IT'S REAL!!
VERY REAL!!
I'M SO GLAD!!
BUT...
...IT HURTS!!
IT HURTS!
VUP
Here!
YANO!
RIGHT HAND!
RIGHT HAND!
(IT'S HER LEFT)
OH.
UM.
SORRY, TAKAHASHI.
EH?
You told me to raise my hand if it hurt...
YEAH.
BEAR WITH IT.
WHAT?
Bear with it?
SORRY.
OW...

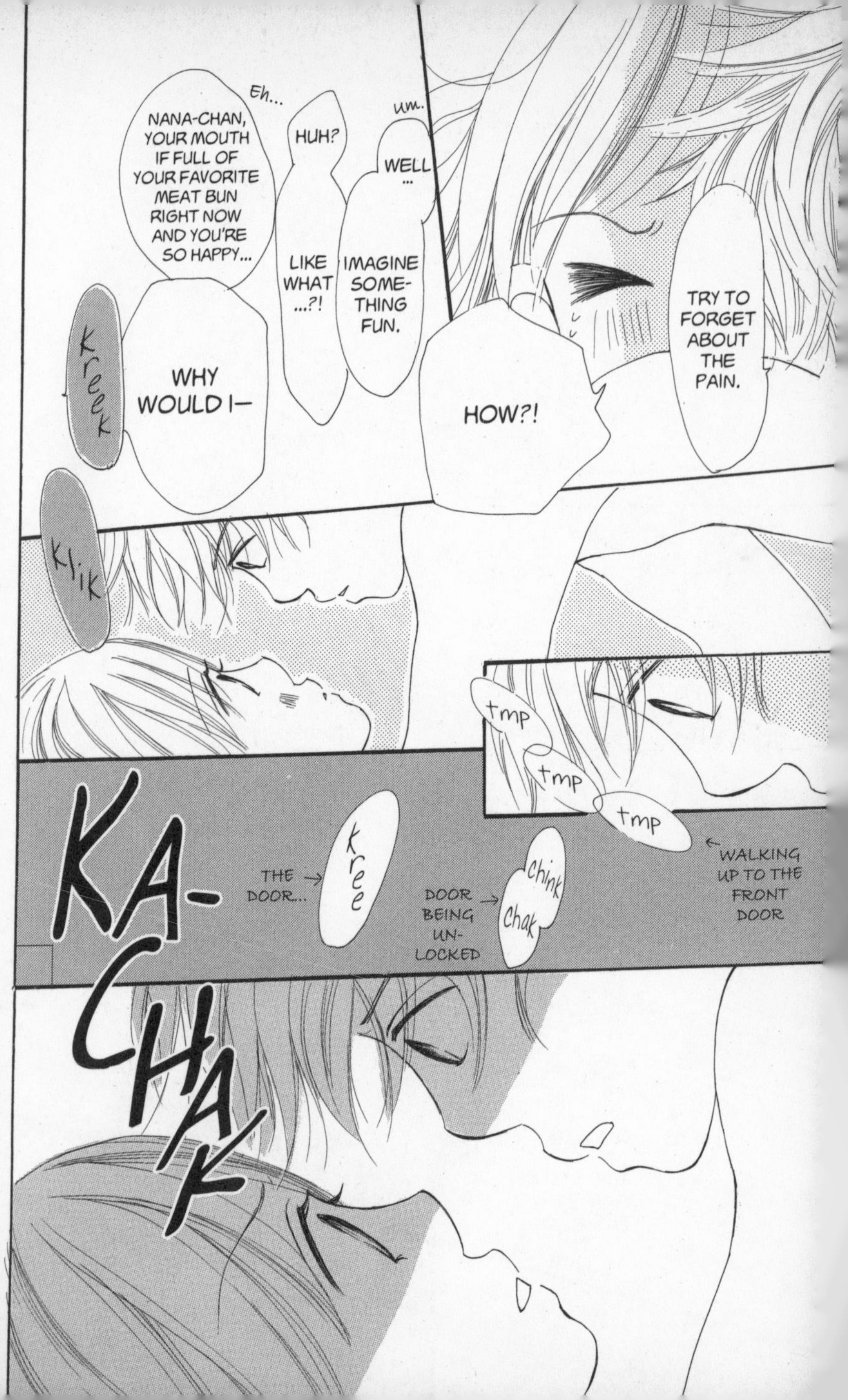
TRY TO FORGET ABOUT THE PAIN.
HOW?!
um..
WELL...
IMAGINE SOME-THING FUN.
Eh...
HUH?
LIKE WHAT ...?!
NANA-CHAN, YOUR MOUTH IF FULL OF YOUR FAVORITE MEAT BUN RIGHT NOW AND YOU'RE SO HAPPY...
WHY WOULD I—
kreek
tmp
tmp
tmp
← WALKING UP TO THE FRONT DOOR
klik
chink
chak
DOOR BEING UN-LOCKED →
kree
THE DOOR... →
KA-CHAK

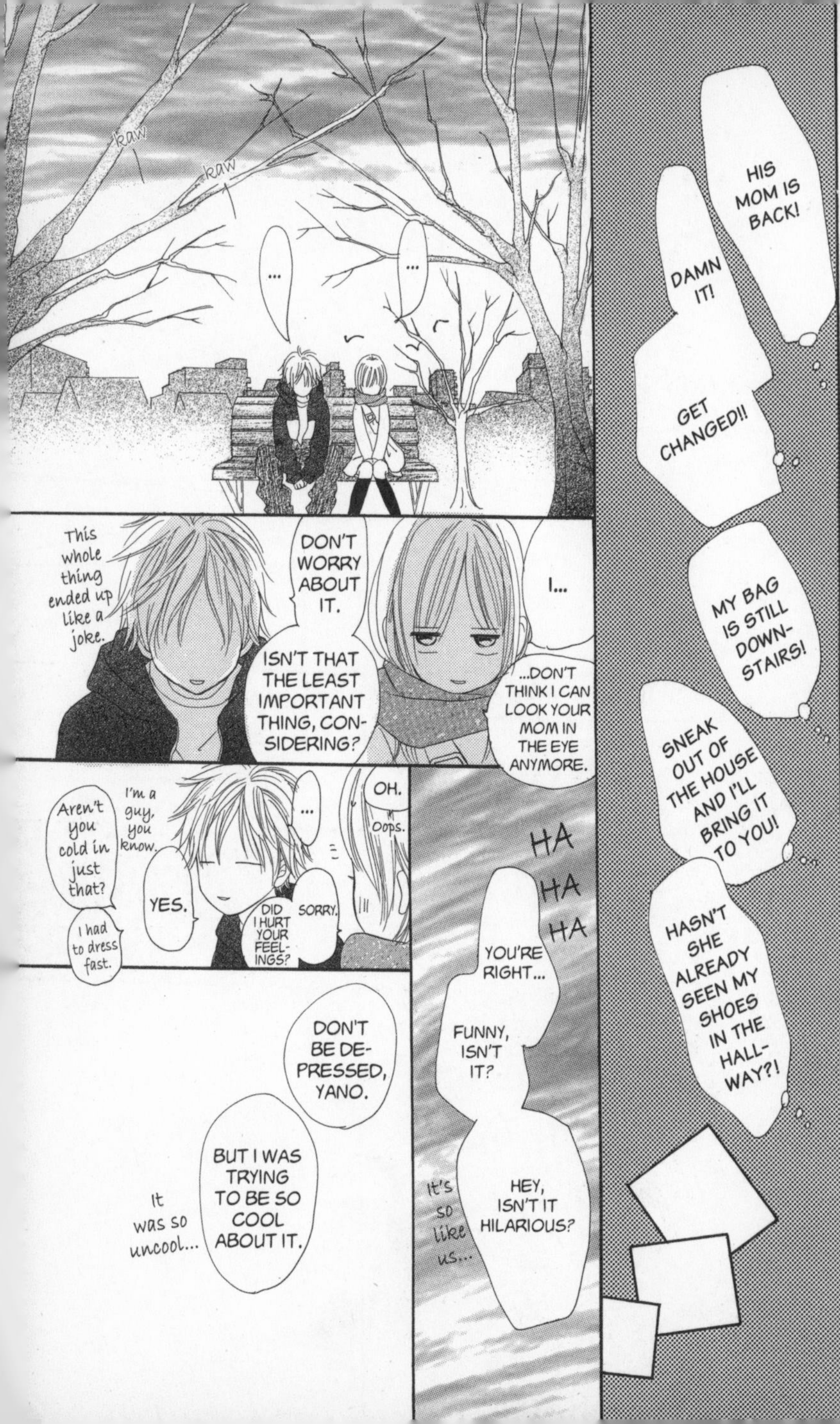
HIS MOM IS BACK!
DAMN IT!
GET CHANGED!!
MY BAG IS STILL DOWN-STAIRS!
SNEAK OUT OF THE HOUSE AND I'LL BRING IT TO YOU!
HASN'T SHE ALREADY SEEN MY SHOES IN THE HALL-WAY?!
raw
raw
...
...
I...
...DON'T THINK I CAN LOOK YOUR MOM IN THE EYE ANYMORE.
DON'T WORRY ABOUT IT.
ISN'T THAT THE LEAST IMPORTANT THING, CON-SIDERING?
This whole thing ended up like a joke.
HA HA HA
YOU'RE RIGHT...
FUNNY, ISN'T IT?
HEY, ISN'T IT HILARIOUS?
It's so like us...
OH.
Oops.
...
SORRY.
DID I HURT YOUR FEEL-INGS?
YES.
I'm a guy, you know.
Aren't you cold in just that?
I had to dress fast.
DON'T BE DE-PRESSED, YANO.
BUT I WAS TRYING TO BE SO COOL ABOUT IT.
It was so uncool...

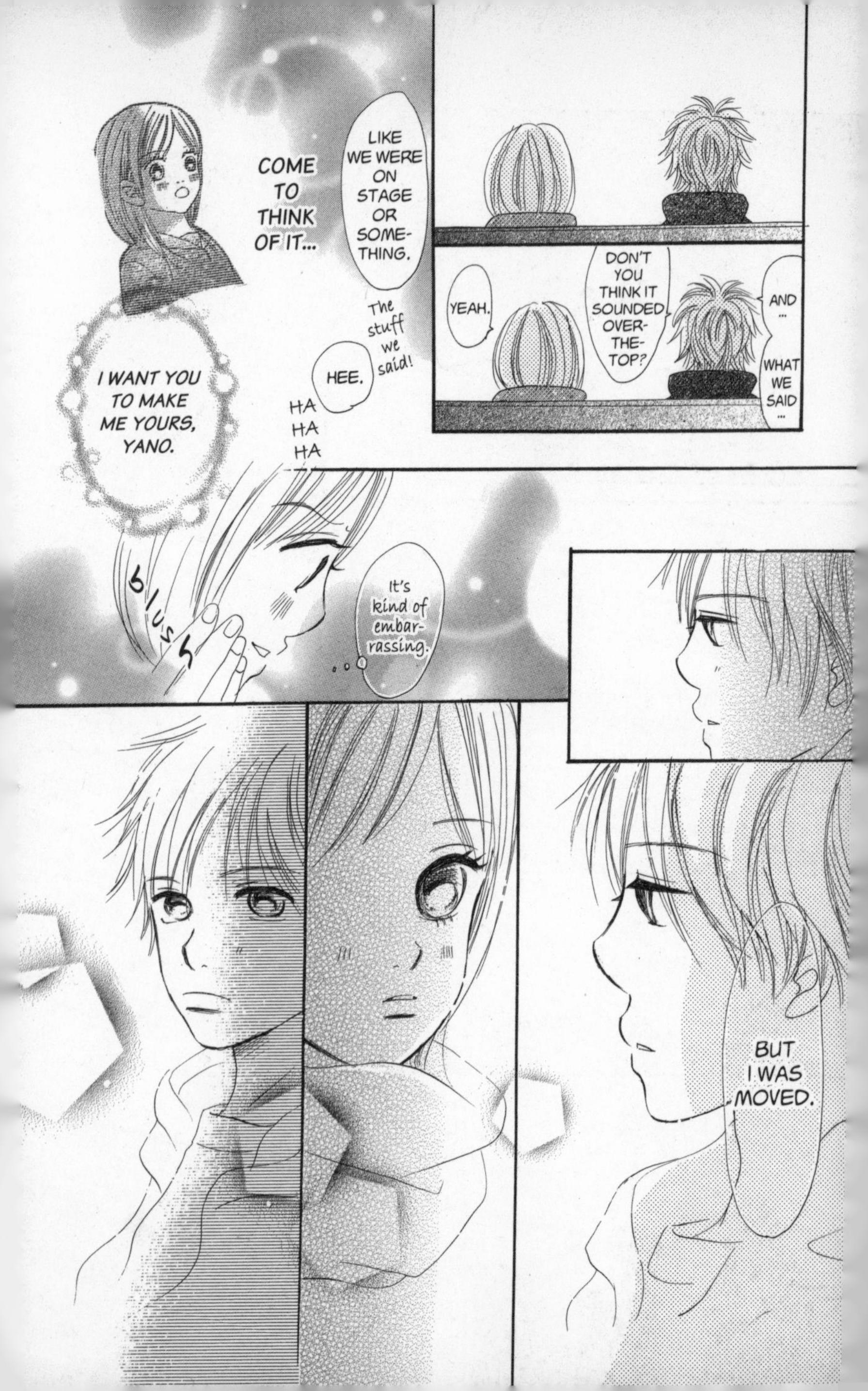
AND ... WHAT WE SAID ...
DON'T YOU THINK IT SOUNDED OVER-THE-TOP?
YEAH.
LIKE WE WERE ON STAGE OR SOME-THING.
COME TO THINK OF IT...
I WANT YOU TO MAKE ME YOURS, YANO.
The stuff we said!
HEE.
HA HA HA
It's kind of embar-rassing.
blush
BUT I WAS MOVED.

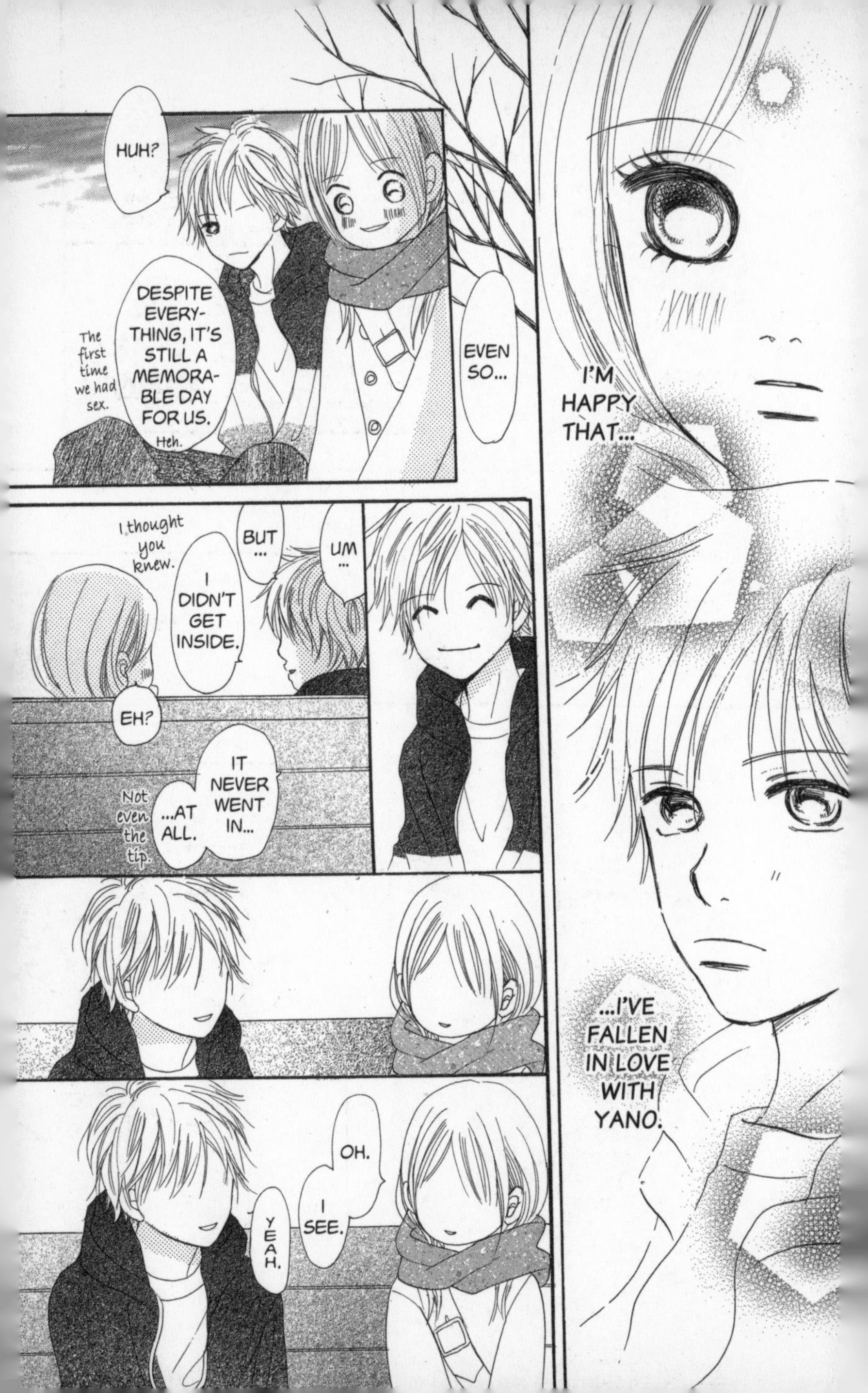
I'M HAPPY THAT...
...I'VE FALLEN IN LOVE WITH YANO.
EVEN SO...
HUH?
DESPITE EVERY-THING, IT'S STILL A MEMORA-BLE DAY FOR US.
Heh.
The first time we had sex.
UM ...
BUT ...
I DIDN'T GET INSIDE.
I thought you knew.
EH?
IT NEVER WENT IN...
...AT ALL.
Not even the tip.
OH.
I SEE.
YEAH.

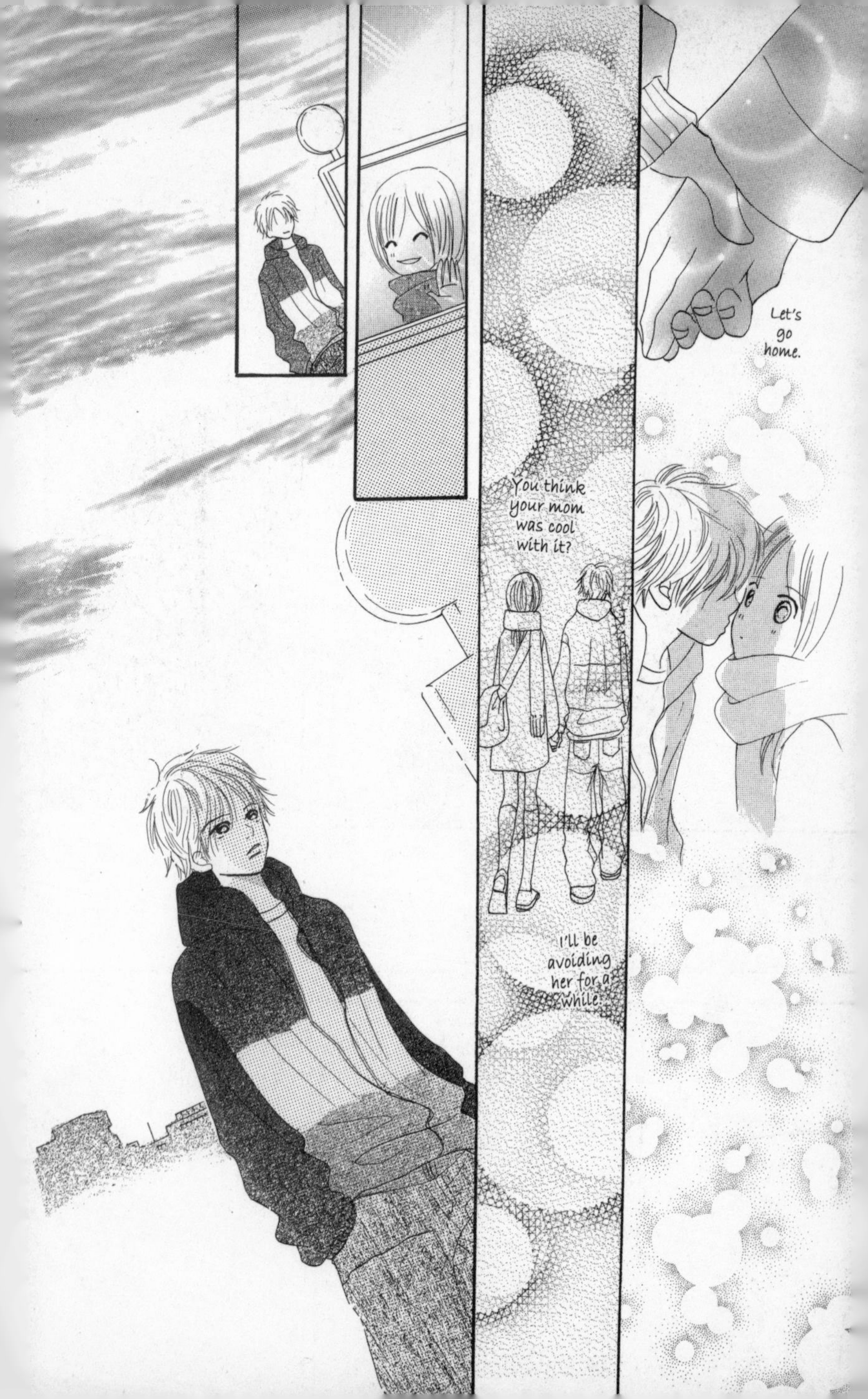
Let's go home.
You think your mom was cool with it?
I'll be avoiding her for a while.

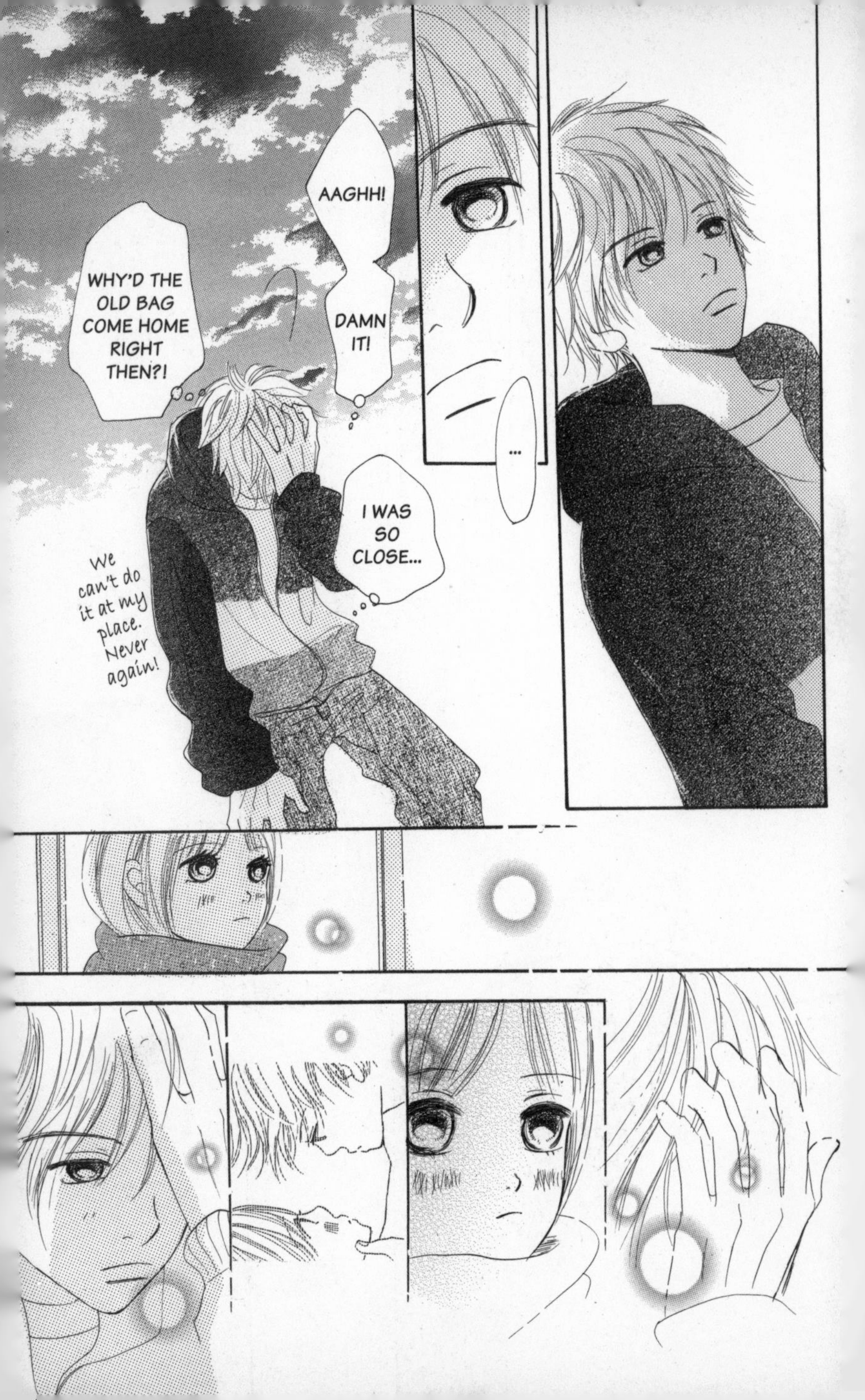
...
AAGHH!
DAMN IT!
WHY'D THE OLD BAG COME HOME RIGHT THEN?!
I WAS SO CLOSE...
We can't do it at my place. Never again!

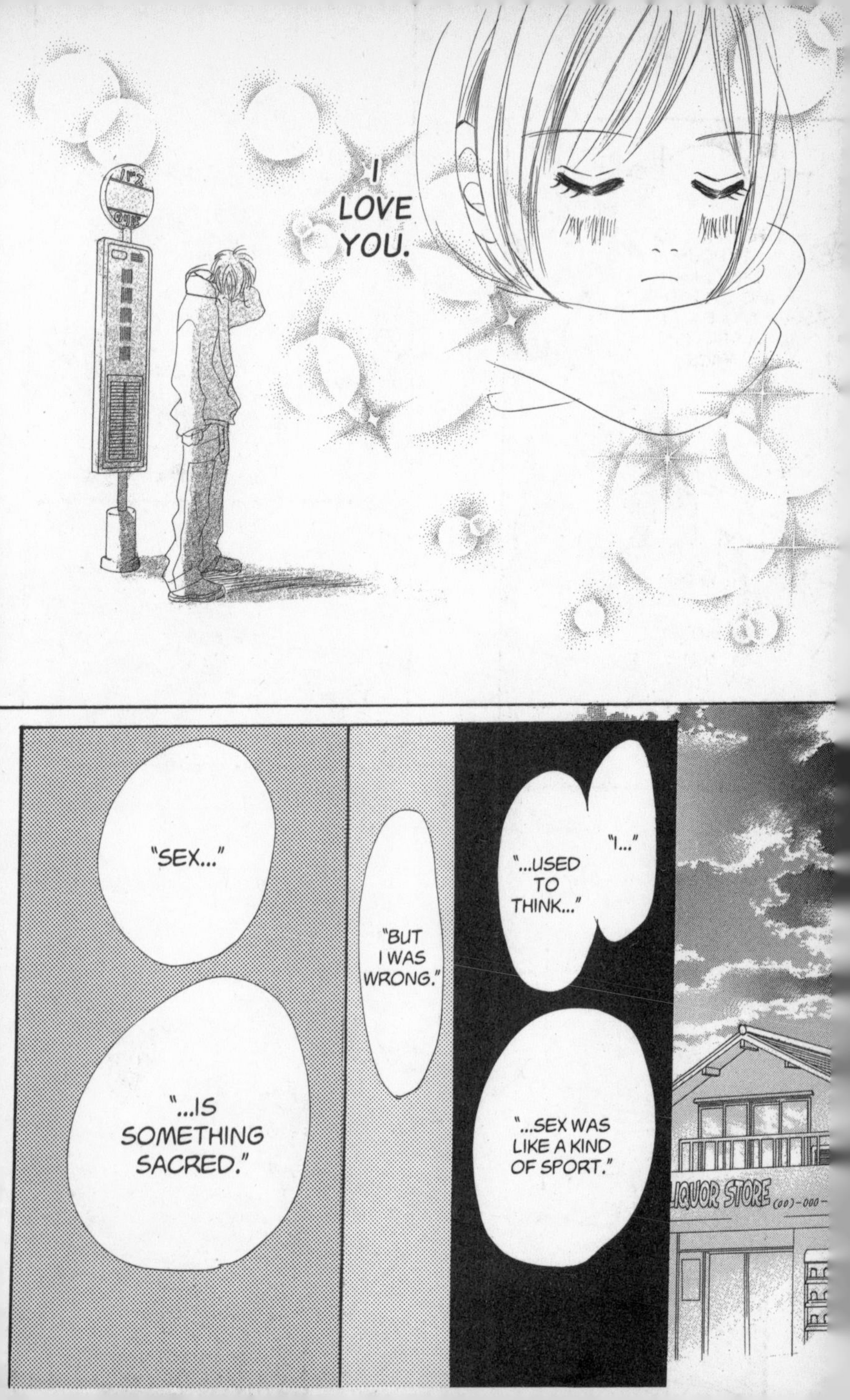
I LOVE YOU.
LIQUOR STORE (00)-000-
"I..."
"...USED TO THINK..."
"...SEX WAS LIKE A KIND OF SPORT."
"BUT I WAS WRONG."
"SEX..."
"...IS SOMETHING SACRED."

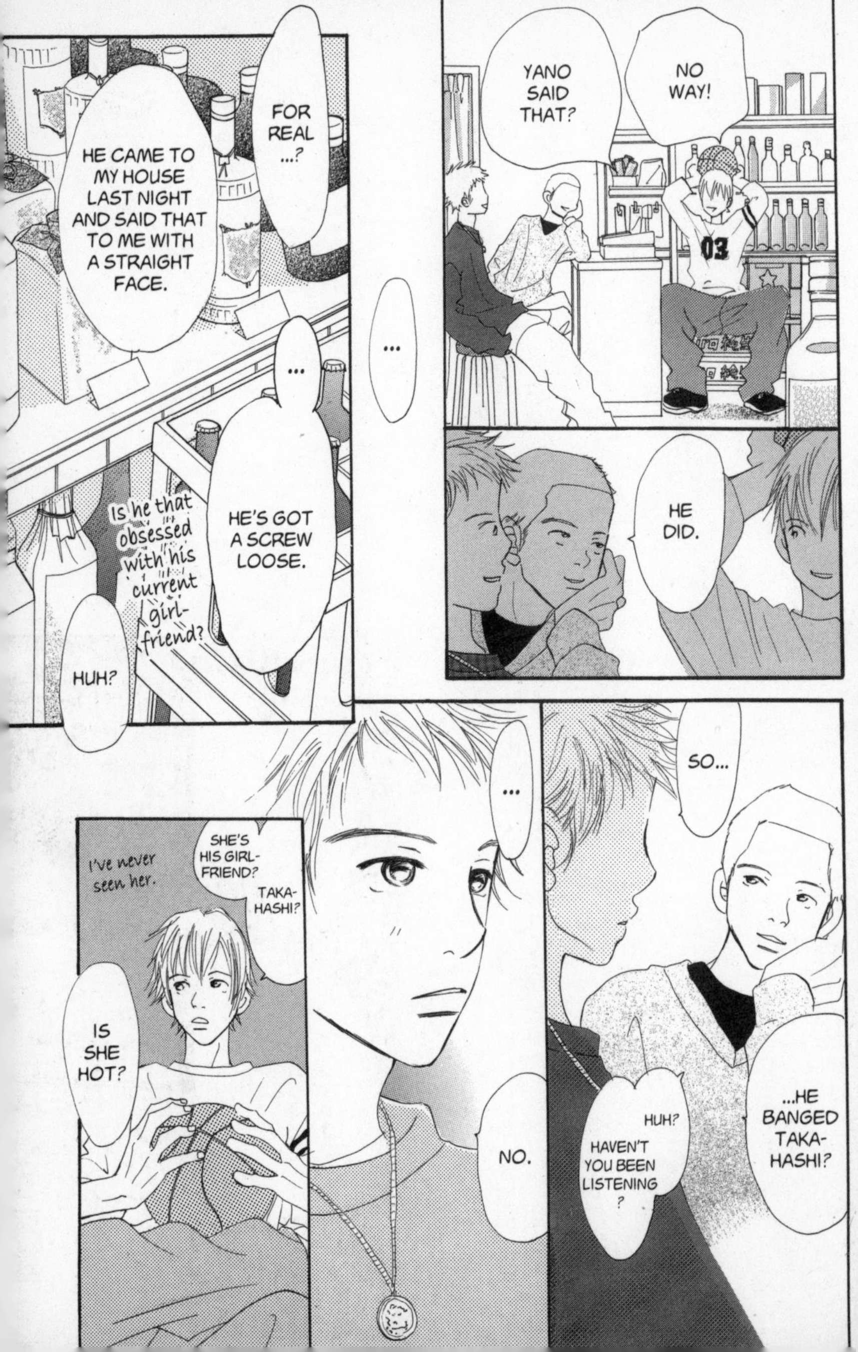
NO WAY!
YANO SAID THAT?
HE DID.
...
FOR REAL ...?
HE CAME TO MY HOUSE LAST NIGHT AND SAID THAT TO ME WITH A STRAIGHT FACE.
...
HE'S GOT A SCREW LOOSE.
Is he that obsessed with his current girl-friend?
HUH?
SO...
...HE BANGED TAKA-HASHI?
HUH? HAVEN'T YOU BEEN LISTENING?
NO.
...
SHE'S HIS GIRL-FRIEND?
TAKA-HASHI?
I've never seen her.
IS SHE HOT?

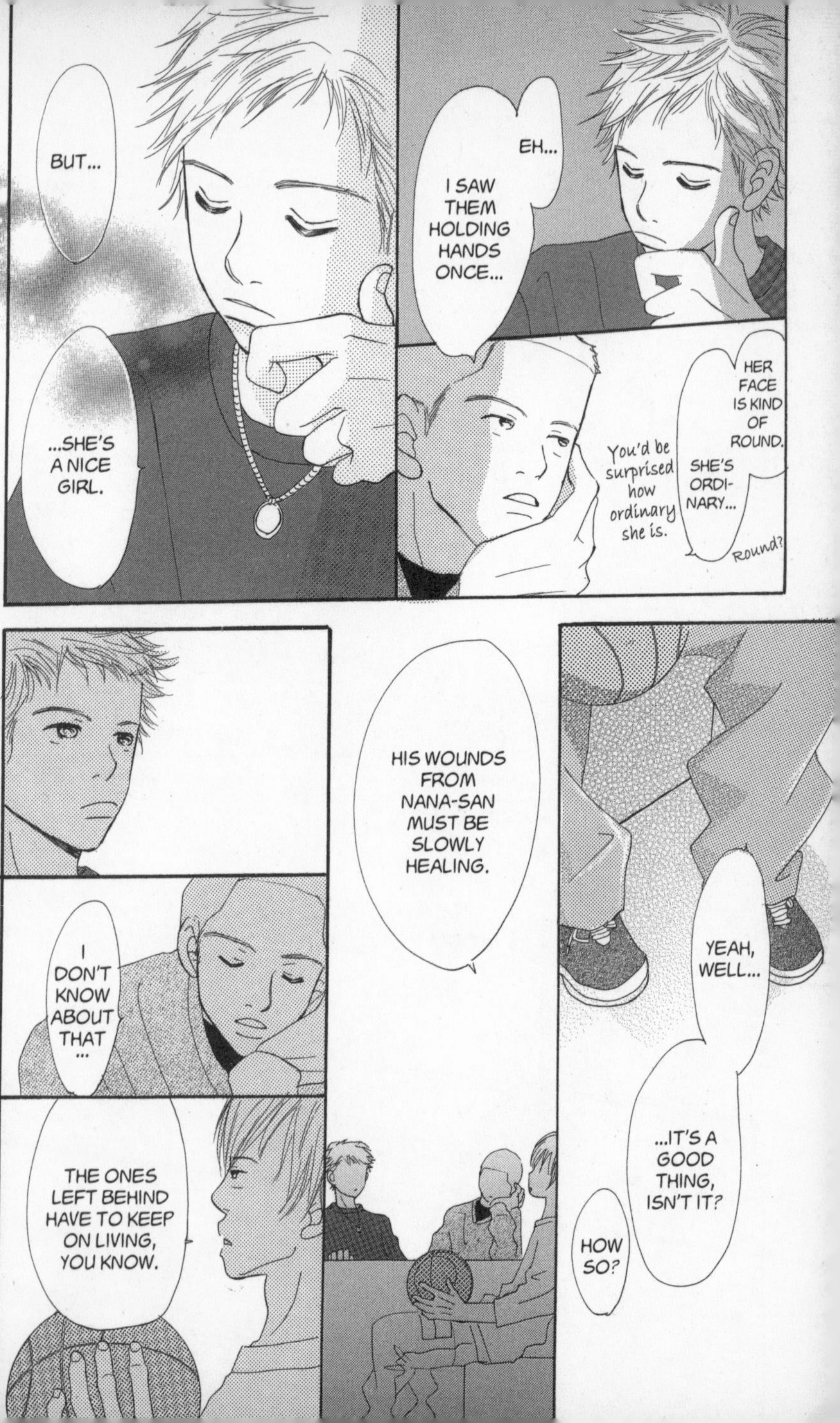
EH...
I SAW THEM HOLDING HANDS ONCE...
HER FACE IS KIND OF ROUND.
SHE'S ORDINARY...
You'd be surprised how ordinary she is.
Round?
BUT...
...SHE'S A NICE GIRL.
YEAH, WELL...
...IT'S A GOOD THING, ISN'T IT?
HOW SO?
HIS WOUNDS FROM NANA-SAN MUST BE SLOWLY HEALING.
I DON'T KNOW ABOUT THAT...
THE ONES LEFT BEHIND HAVE TO KEEP ON LIVING, YOU KNOW.

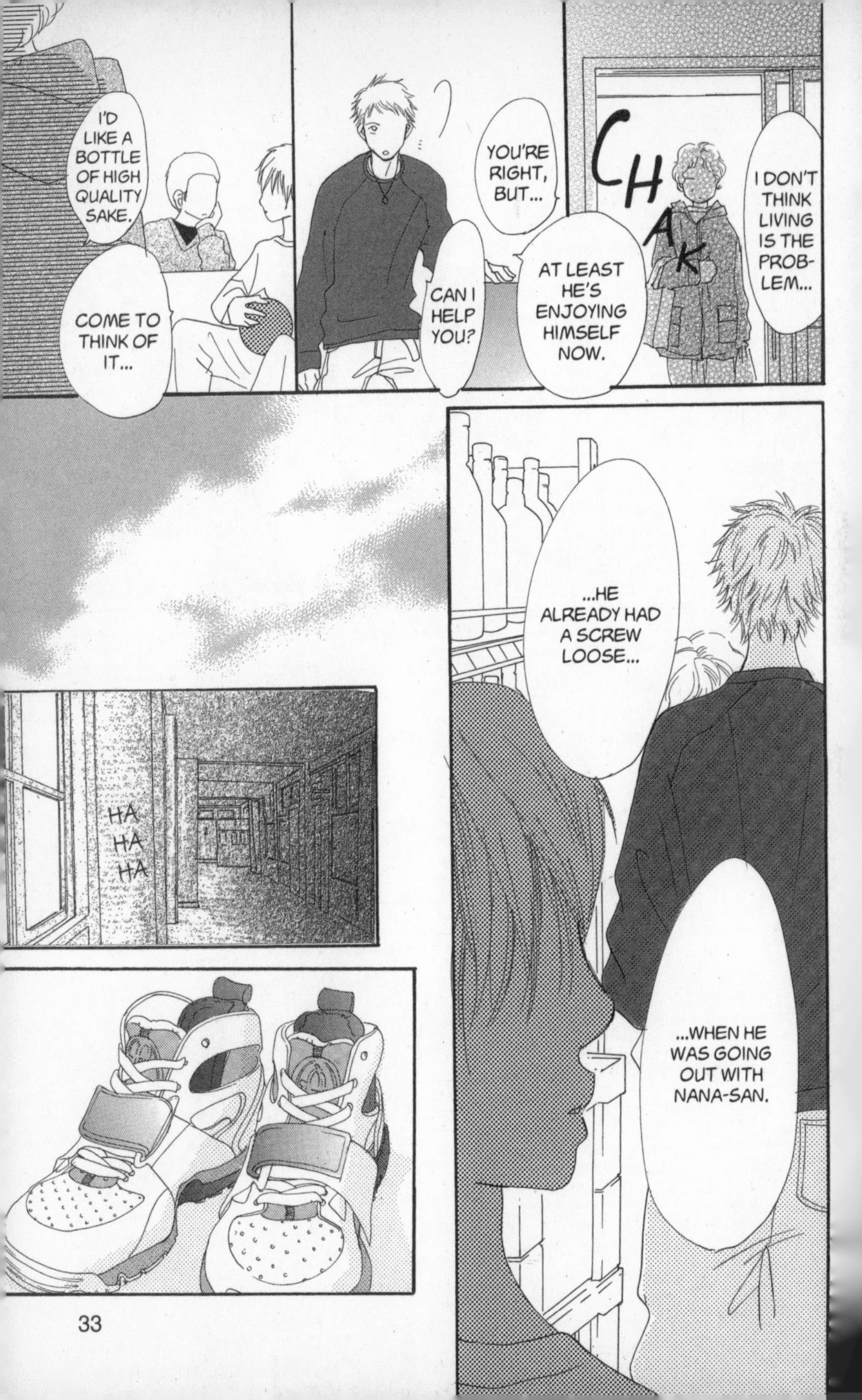
I DON'T THINK LIVING IS THE PROBLEM...
CHAK
AT LEAST HE'S ENJOYING HIMSELF NOW.
YOU'RE RIGHT, BUT...
CAN I HELP YOU?
I'D LIKE A BOTTLE OF HIGH QUALITY SAKE.
COME TO THINK OF IT...
...HE ALREADY HAD A SCREW LOOSE...
...WHEN HE WAS GOING OUT WITH NANA-SAN.
HA HA HA

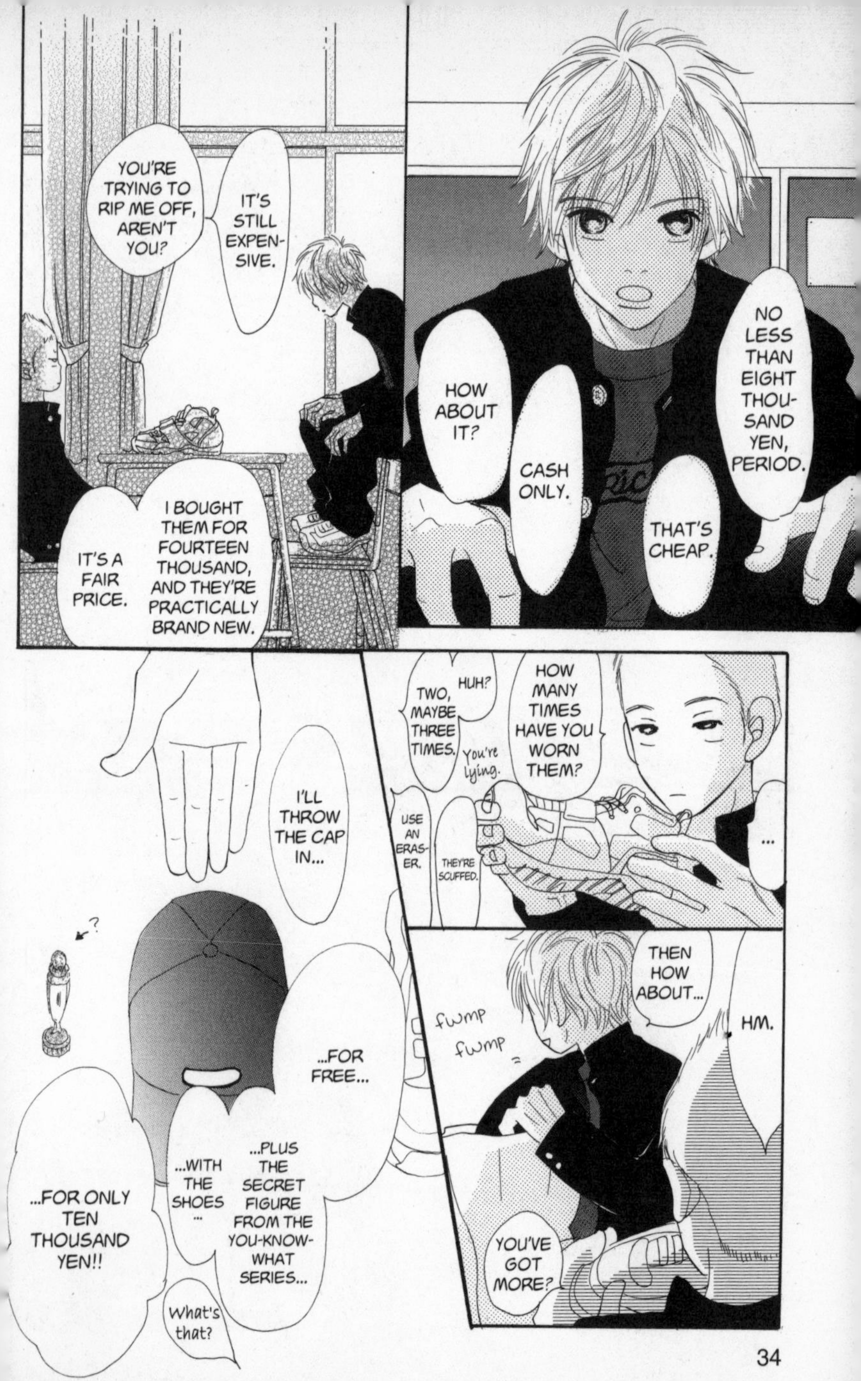
NO LESS THAN EIGHT THOUSAND YEN, PERIOD.
THAT'S CHEAP.
CASH ONLY.
HOW ABOUT IT?
IT'S STILL EXPENSIVE.
YOU'RE TRYING TO RIP ME OFF, AREN'T YOU?
I BOUGHT THEM FOR FOURTEEN THOUSAND, AND THEY'RE PRACTICALLY BRAND NEW.
IT'S A FAIR PRICE.
HOW MANY TIMES HAVE YOU WORN THEM?
HUH?
TWO, MAYBE THREE TIMES.
You're lying.
...
THEY'RE SCUFFED.
USE AN ERASER.
HM.
THEN HOW ABOUT...
fwmp
fwmp
YOU'VE GOT MORE?
I'LL THROW THE CAP IN...
...FOR FREE...
...PLUS THE SECRET FIGURE FROM THE YOU-KNOW-WHAT SERIES...
...WITH THE SHOES...
What's that?
...FOR ONLY TEN THOUSAND YEN!!

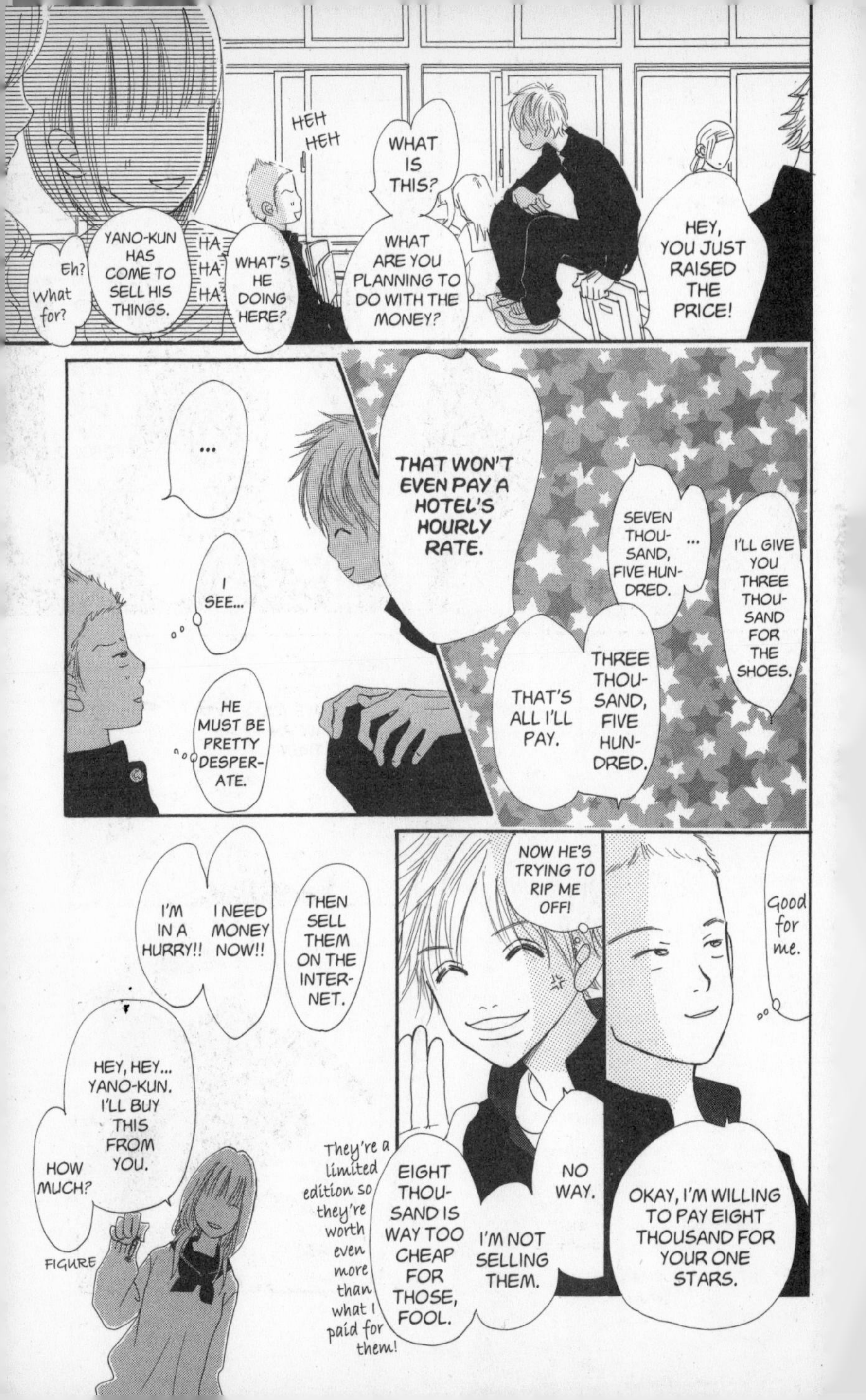
HEY, YOU JUST RAISED THE PRICE!
WHAT IS THIS?
WHAT ARE YOU PLANNING TO DO WITH THE MONEY?
HEH HEH
WHAT'S HE DOING HERE?
HA HA HA
YANO-KUN HAS COME TO SELL HIS THINGS.
Eh? What for?
I'LL GIVE YOU THREE THOUSAND FOR THE SHOES.
SEVEN THOUSAND, FIVE HUNDRED.
...
THREE THOUSAND, FIVE HUNDRED.
THAT'S ALL I'LL PAY.
THAT WON'T EVEN PAY A HOTEL'S HOURLY RATE.
...
I SEE...
HE MUST BE PRETTY DESPERATE.
NOW HE'S TRYING TO RIP ME OFF!
Good for me.
OKAY, I'M WILLING TO PAY EIGHT THOUSAND FOR YOUR ONE STARS.
NO WAY.
I'M NOT SELLING THEM.
EIGHT THOUSAND IS WAY TOO CHEAP FOR THOSE, FOOL.
They're a limited edition so they're worth even more than what I paid for them!
THEN SELL THEM ON THE INTERNET.
I NEED MONEY NOW!!
I'M IN A HURRY!!
HEY, HEY... YANO-KUN. I'LL BUY THIS FROM YOU.
HOW MUCH?
FIGURE

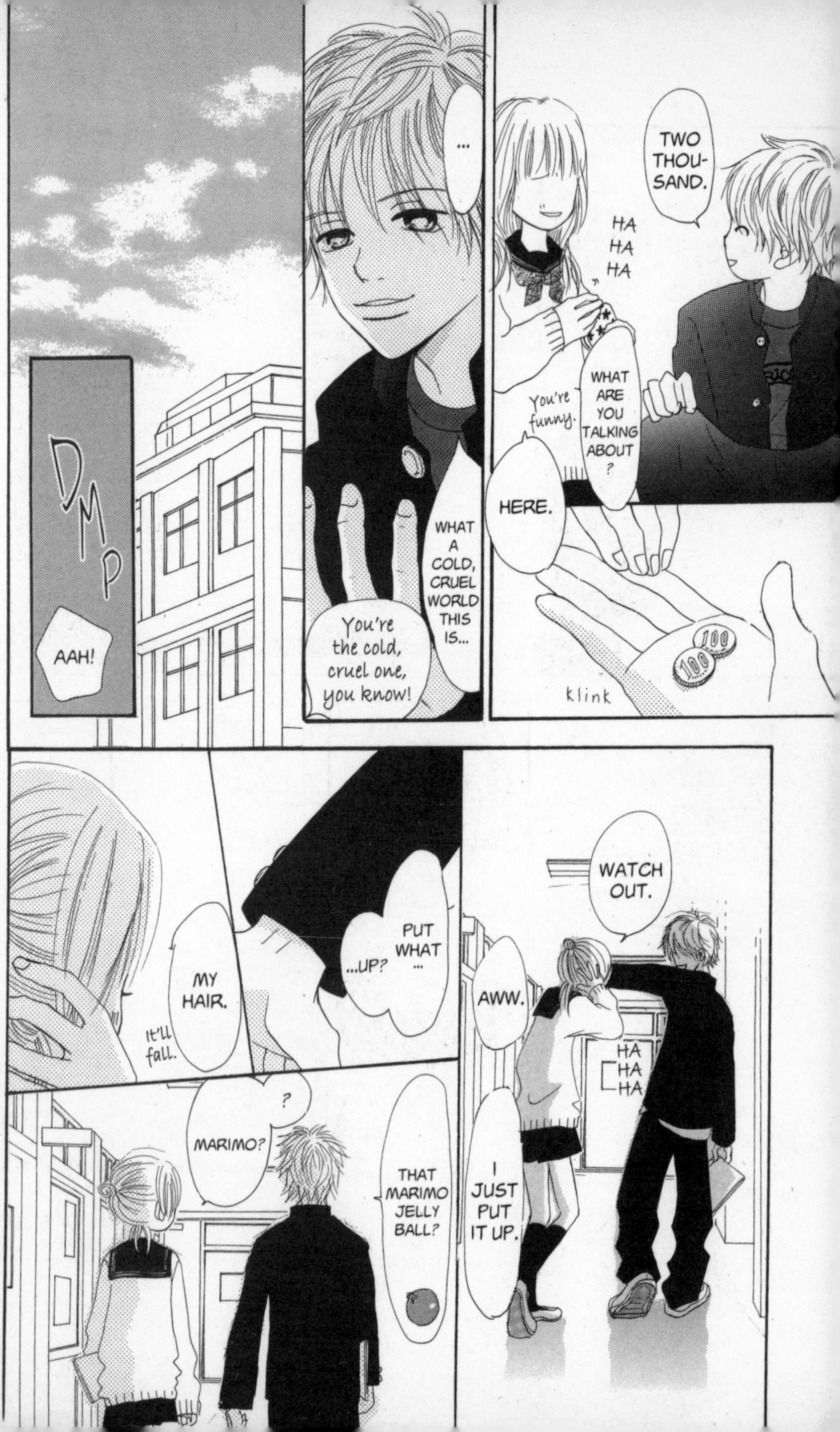
TWO THOUSAND.
HA HA HA
WHAT ARE YOU TALKING ABOUT?
You're funny.
HERE.
klink
...
WHAT A COLD, CRUEL WORLD THIS IS...
You're the cold, cruel one, you know!
DMP
AAH!
WATCH OUT.
AWW.
HA HA HA
I JUST PUT IT UP.
PUT WHAT ...
...UP?
MY HAIR.
It'll fall.
?
MARIMO?
THAT MARIMO JELLY BALL?

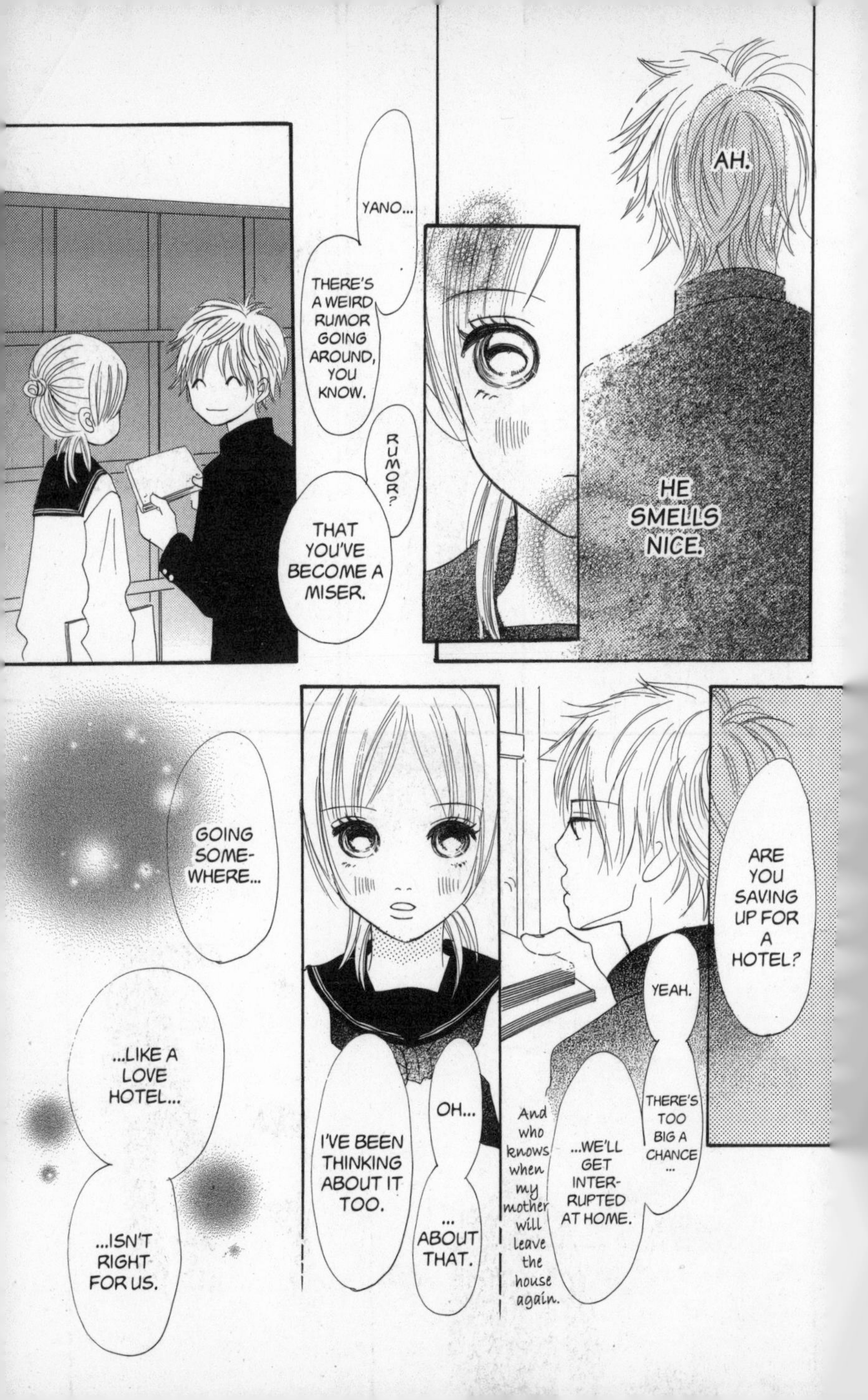
AH.
HE SMELLS NICE.
YANO...
THERE'S A WEIRD RUMOR GOING AROUND, YOU KNOW.
RUMOR?
THAT YOU'VE BECOME A MISER.
ARE YOU SAVING UP FOR A HOTEL?
YEAH.
THERE'S TOO BIG A CHANCE...
...WE'LL GET INTER-RUPTED AT HOME.
And who knows when my mother will leave the house again.
OH...
...ABOUT THAT.
I'VE BEEN THINKING ABOUT IT TOO.
GOING SOME-WHERE...
...LIKE A LOVE HOTEL...
...ISN'T RIGHT FOR US.

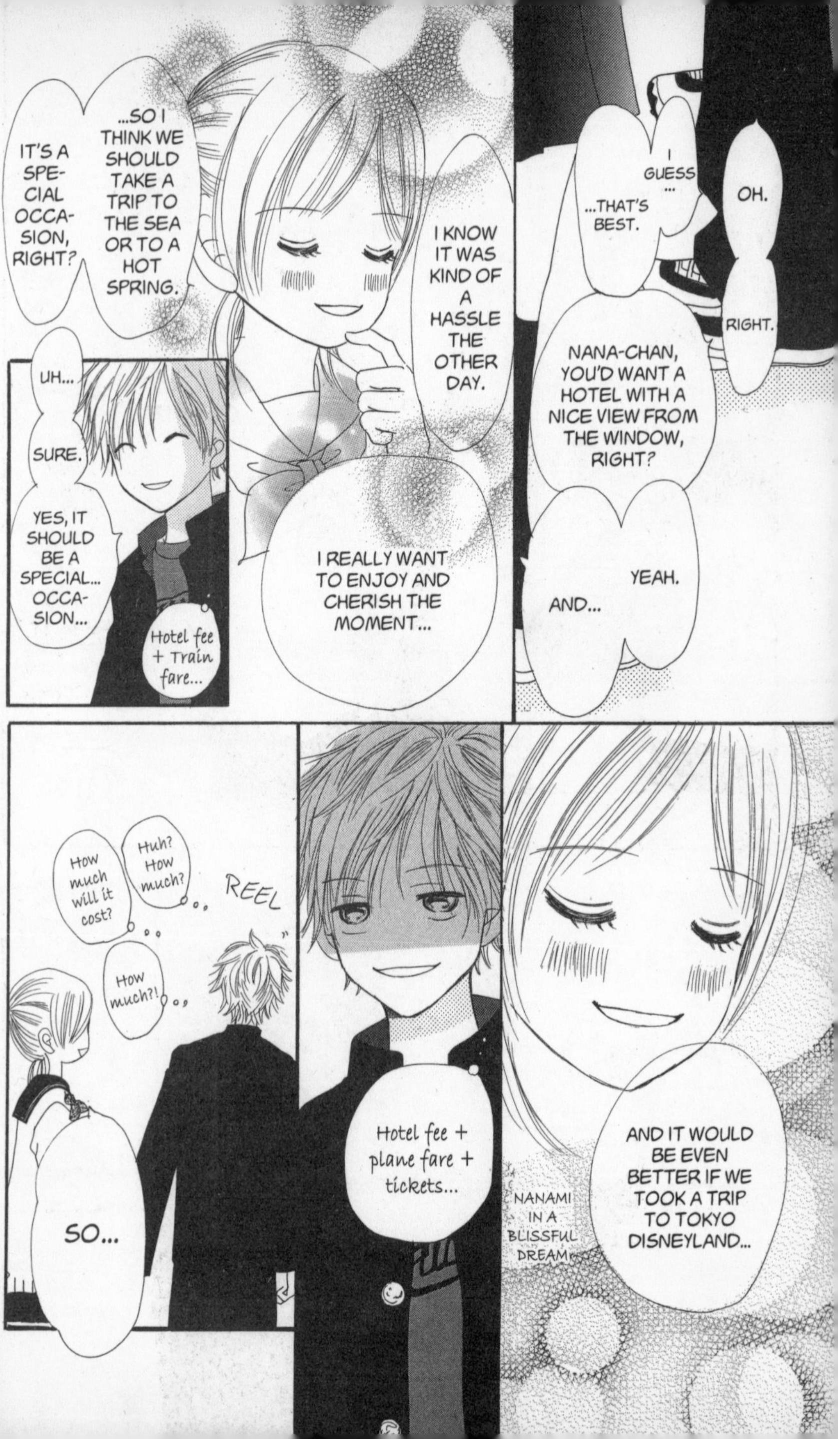
OH.
RIGHT.
I GUESS...
...THAT'S BEST.
NANA-CHAN, YOU'D WANT A HOTEL WITH A NICE VIEW FROM THE WINDOW, RIGHT?
YEAH.
AND...
I KNOW IT WAS KIND OF A HASSLE THE OTHER DAY.
...SO I THINK WE SHOULD TAKE A TRIP TO THE SEA OR TO A HOT SPRING.
IT'S A SPECIAL OCCASION, RIGHT?
I REALLY WANT TO ENJOY AND CHERISH THE MOMENT...
UH...
SURE.
YES, IT SHOULD BE A SPECIAL... OCCASION...
Hotel fee + Train fare...
AND IT WOULD BE EVEN BETTER IF WE TOOK A TRIP TO TOKYO DISNEYLAND...
NANAMI IN A BLISSFUL DREAM
Hotel fee + plane fare + tickets...
REEL
Huh? How much?
How much will it cost?
How much?!
SO...

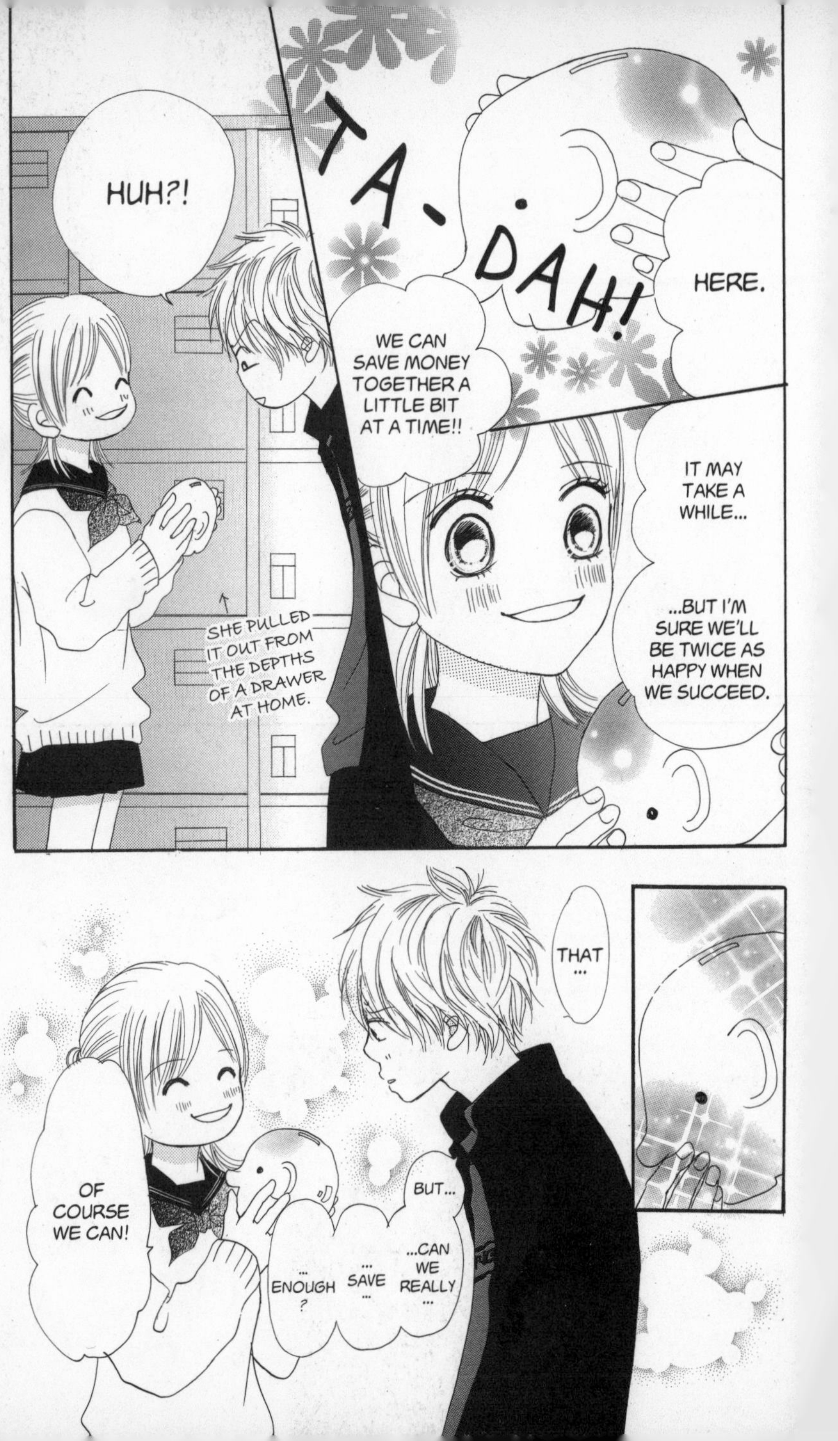
HERE.
TA-DAH!
WE CAN SAVE MONEY TOGETHER A LITTLE BIT AT A TIME!!
IT MAY TAKE A WHILE...
...BUT I'M SURE WE'LL BE TWICE AS HAPPY WHEN WE SUCCEED.
HUH?!
SHE PULLED IT OUT FROM THE DEPTHS OF A DRAWER AT HOME.
THAT...
BUT...
...CAN WE REALLY...
...SAVE...
...ENOUGH?
OF COURSE WE CAN!

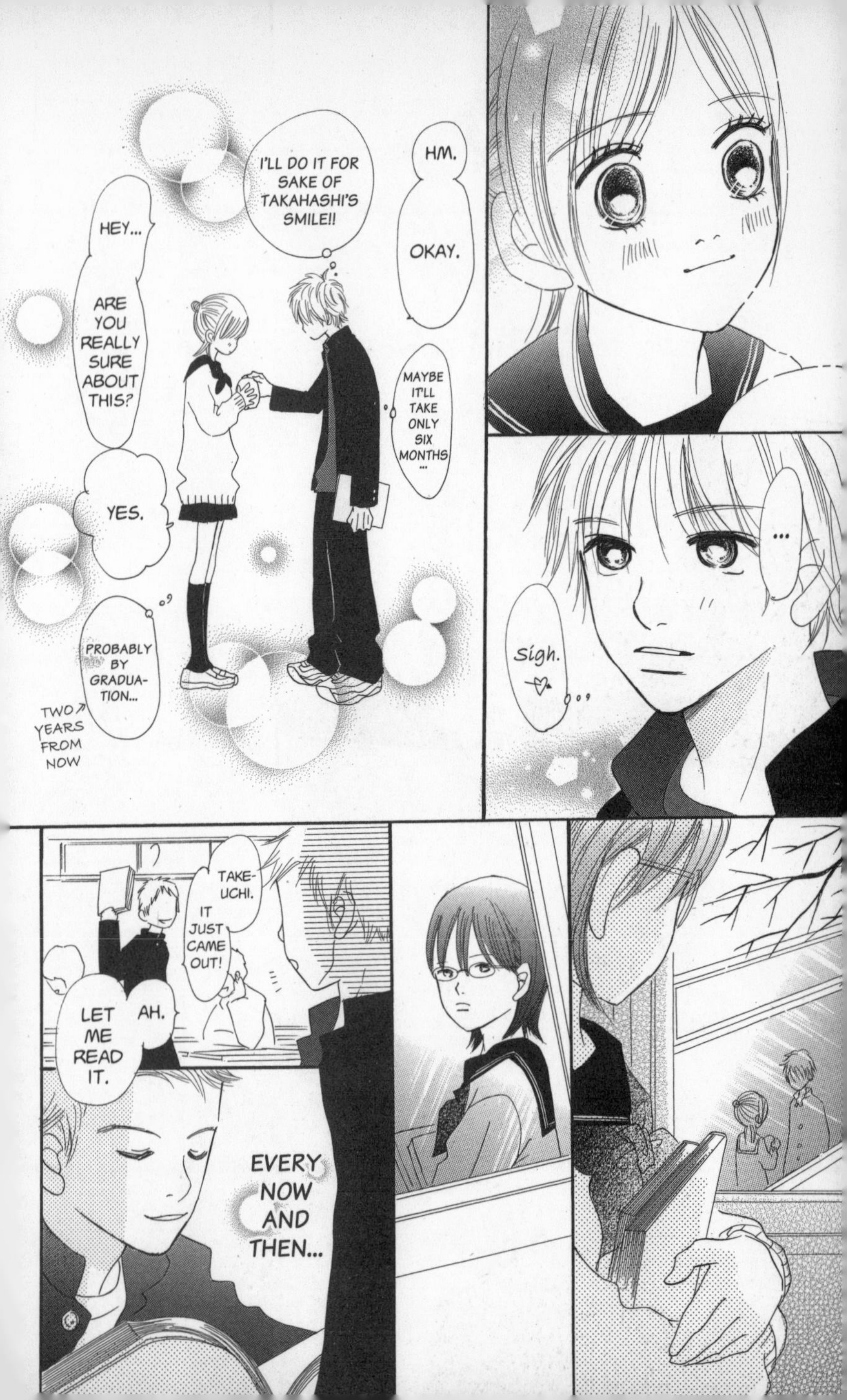
...
Sigh.
HM. OKAY.
I'LL DO IT FOR SAKE OF TAKAHASHI'S SMILE!!
MAYBE IT'LL TAKE ONLY SIX MONTHS...
HEY... ARE YOU REALLY SURE ABOUT THIS?
YES.
PROBABLY BY GRADUATION...
TWO YEARS FROM NOW
TAKE-UCHI.
IT JUST CAME OUT!
AH.
LET ME READ IT.
EVERY NOW AND THEN...

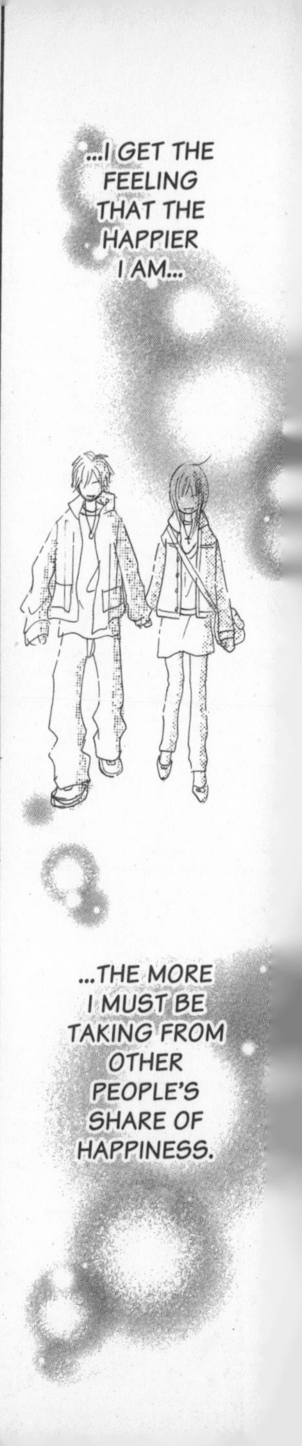
...I GET THE FEELING THAT THE HAPPIER I AM...
...THE MORE I MUST BE TAKING FROM OTHER PEOPLE'S SHARE OF HAPPINESS.
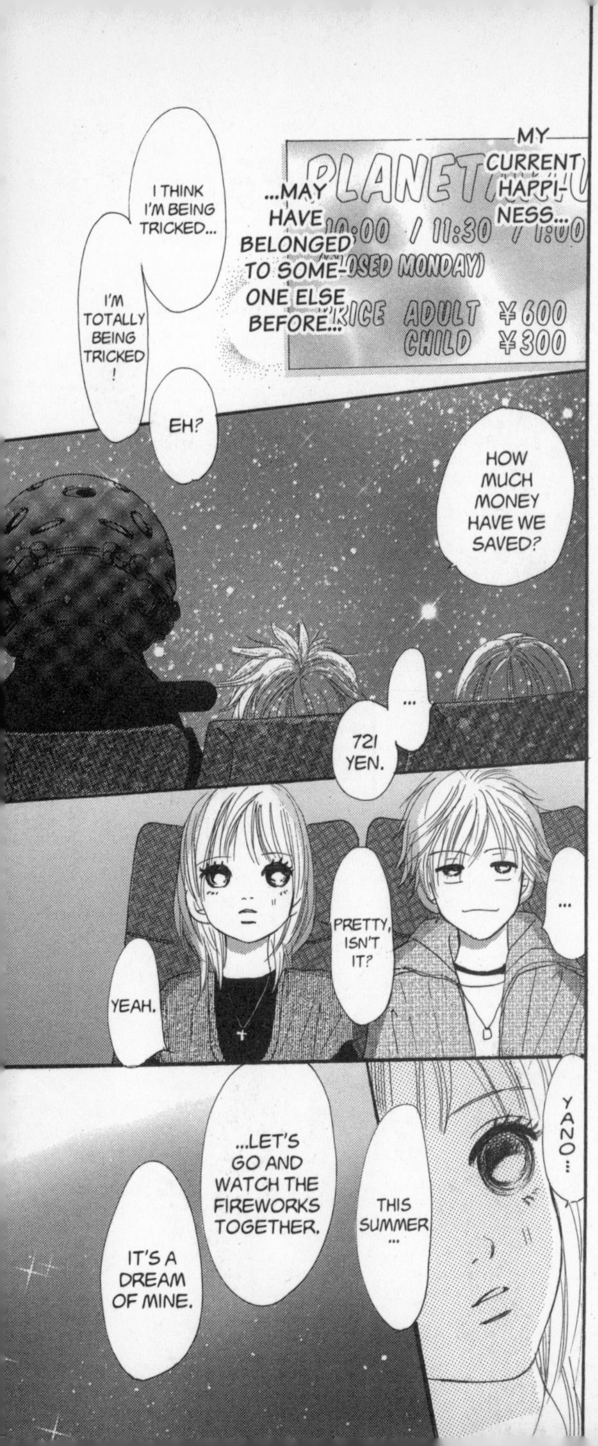
MY CURRENT HAPPINESS...
...MAY HAVE BELONGED TO SOMEONE ELSE BEFORE...
ADULT ¥600
CHILD ¥300
I THINK I'M BEING TRICKED...
I'M TOTALLY BEING TRICKED!
HOW MUCH MONEY HAVE WE SAVED?
EH?
...
721 YEN.
...
PRETTY, ISN'T IT?
YEAH.
YANO...
THIS SUMMER...
...LET'S GO AND WATCH THE FIREWORKS TOGETHER.
IT'S A DREAM OF MINE.

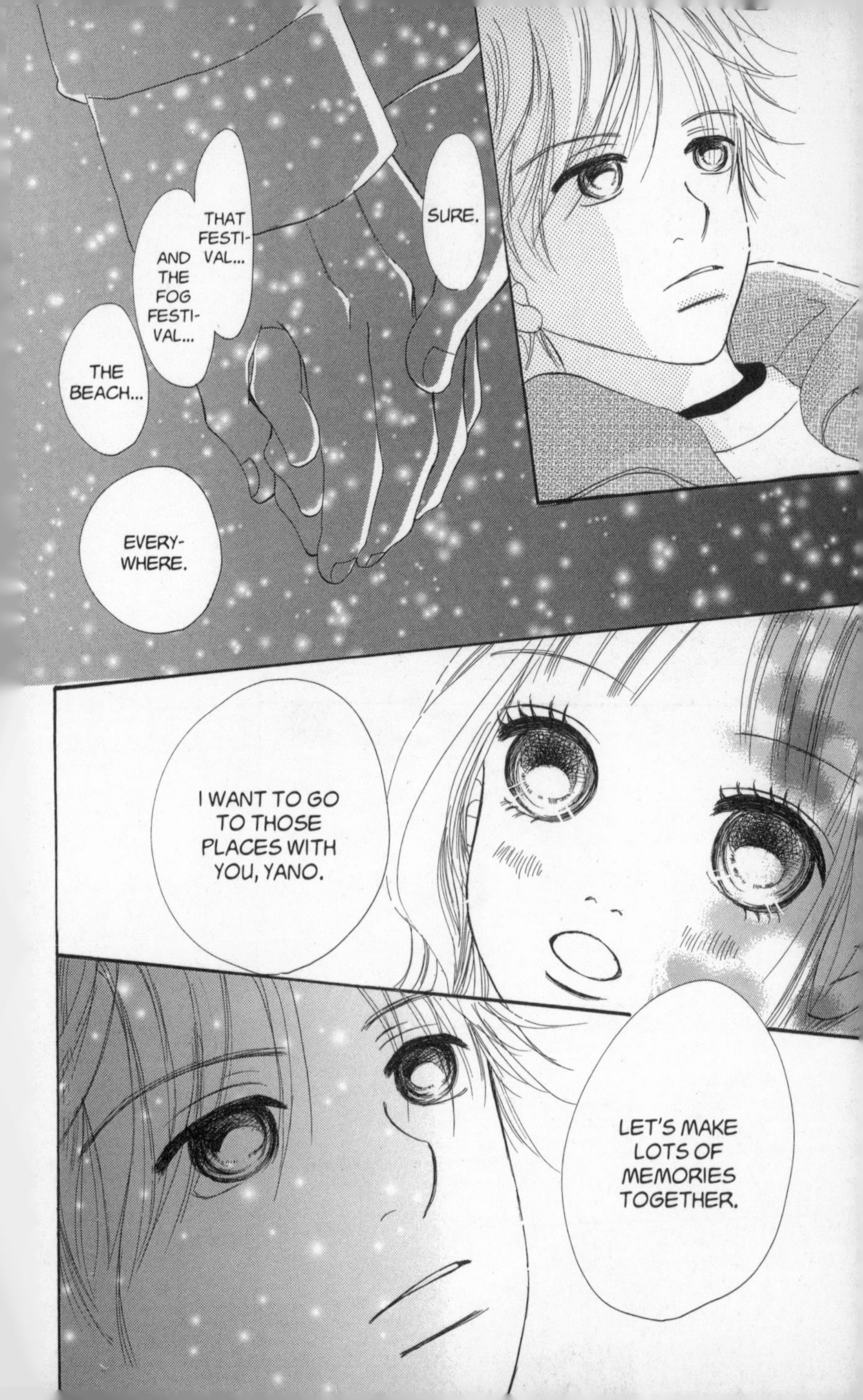
SURE.
THAT FESTIVAL...
AND THE FOG FESTIVAL...
THE BEACH...
EVERYWHERE.
I WANT TO GO TO THOSE PLACES WITH YOU, YANO.
LET'S MAKE LOTS OF MEMORIES TOGETHER.

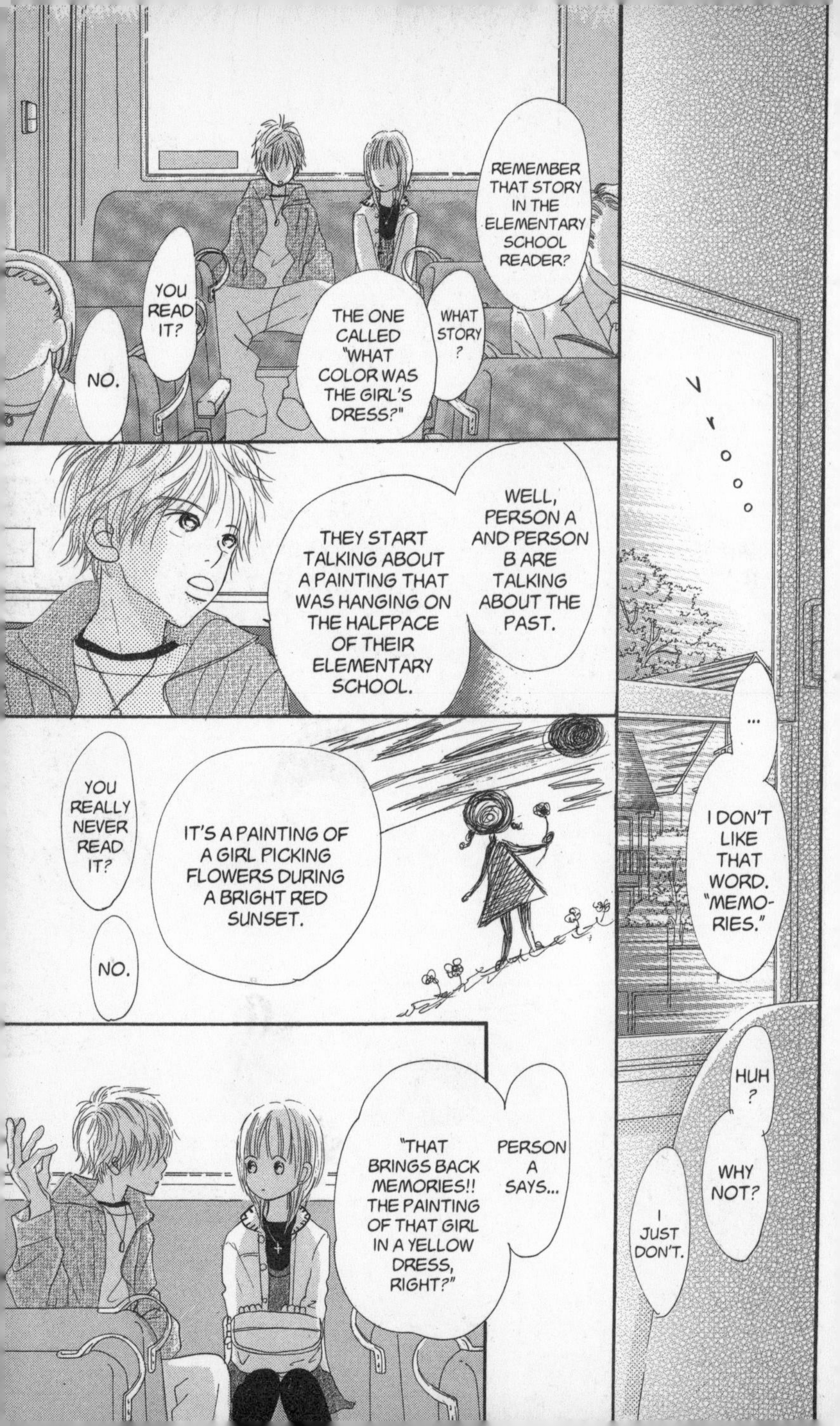

Vrooo
...
I DON'T LIKE THAT WORD. "MEMORIES."
HUH?
WHY NOT?
I JUST DON'T.
REMEMBER THAT STORY IN THE ELEMENTARY SCHOOL READER?
WHAT STORY?
THE ONE CALLED "WHAT COLOR WAS THE GIRL'S DRESS?"
YOU READ IT?
NO.
WELL, PERSON A AND PERSON B ARE TALKING ABOUT THE PAST.
THEY START TALKING ABOUT A PAINTING THAT WAS HANGING ON THE HALFPACE OF THEIR ELEMENTARY SCHOOL.
IT'S A PAINTING OF A GIRL PICKING FLOWERS DURING A BRIGHT RED SUNSET.
YOU REALLY NEVER READ IT?
NO.
PERSON A SAYS...
"THAT BRINGS BACK MEMORIES!! THE PAINTING OF THAT GIRL IN A YELLOW DRESS, RIGHT?"

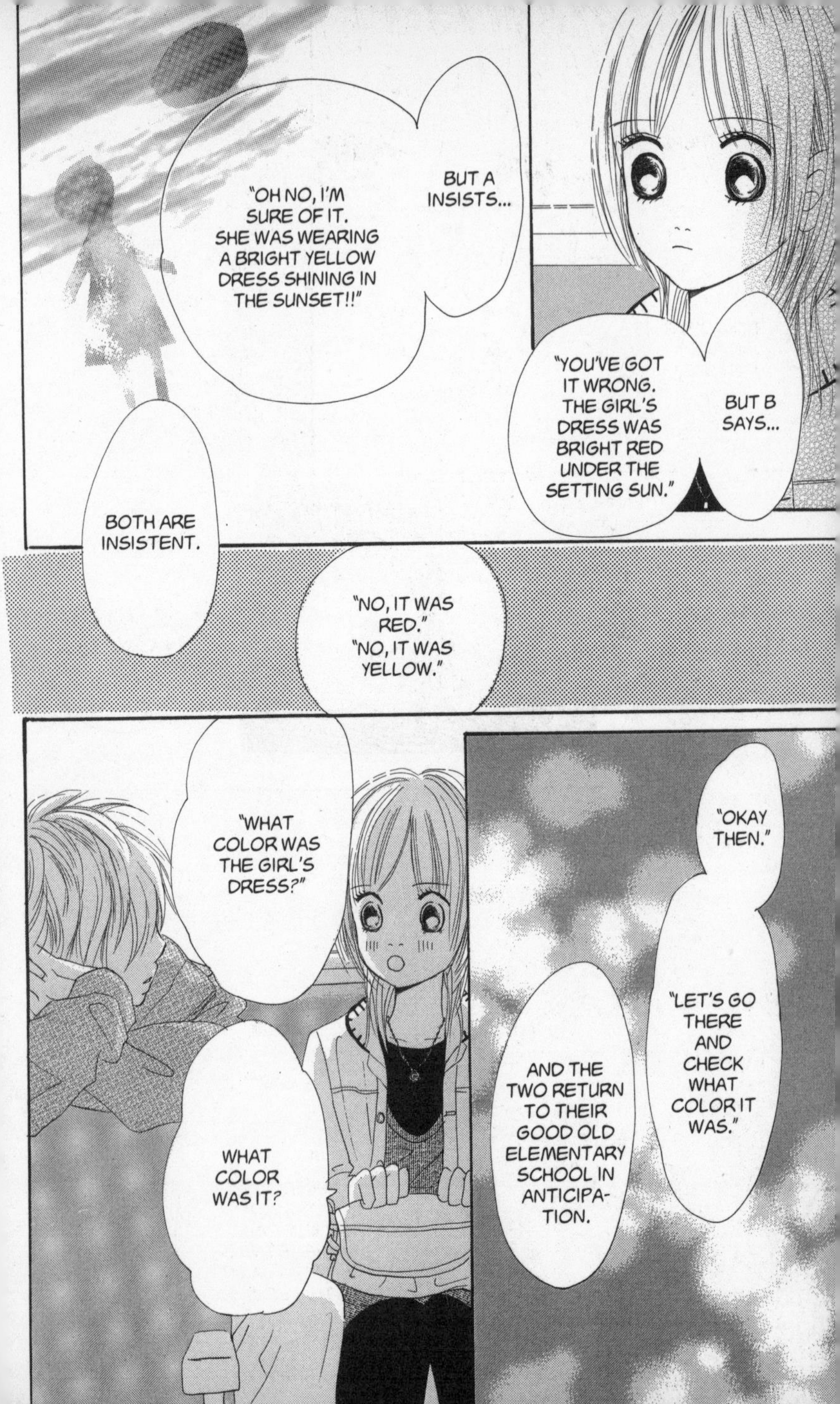
BUT B SAYS...
"YOU'VE GOT IT WRONG. THE GIRL'S DRESS WAS BRIGHT RED UNDER THE SETTING SUN."
BUT A INSISTS...
"OH NO, I'M SURE OF IT. SHE WAS WEARING A BRIGHT YELLOW DRESS SHINING IN THE SUNSET!!"
BOTH ARE INSISTENT.
"NO, IT WAS RED." "NO, IT WAS YELLOW."
"OKAY THEN."
"LET'S GO THERE AND CHECK WHAT COLOR IT WAS."
AND THE TWO RETURN TO THEIR GOOD OLD ELEMENTARY SCHOOL IN ANTICIPA-TION.
"WHAT COLOR WAS THE GIRL'S DRESS?"
WHAT COLOR WAS IT?

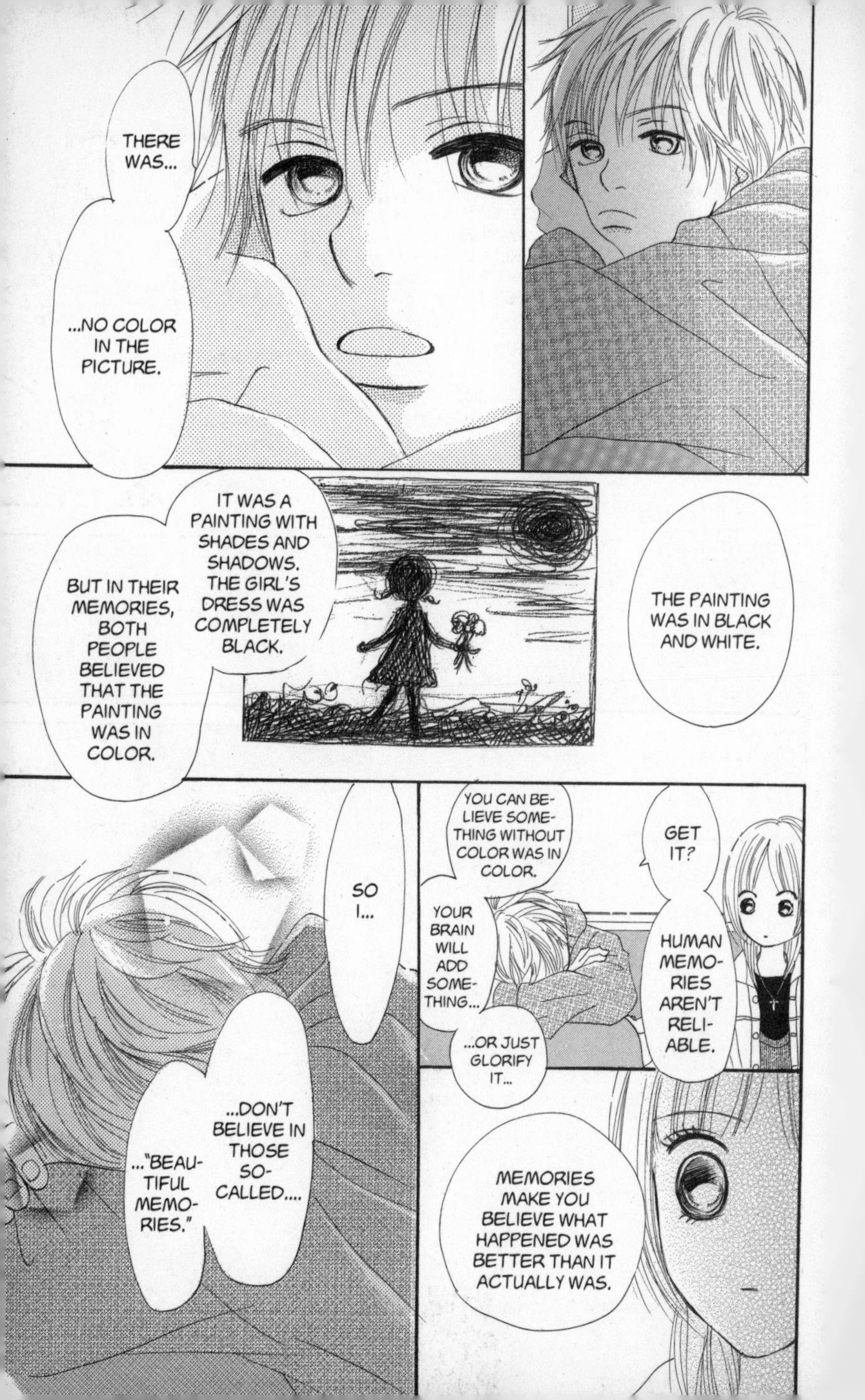

THERE WAS...
...NO COLOR IN THE PICTURE.
THE PAINTING WAS IN BLACK AND WHITE.
IT WAS A PAINTING WITH SHADES AND SHADOWS. THE GIRL'S DRESS WAS COMPLETELY BLACK.
BUT IN THEIR MEMORIES, BOTH PEOPLE BELIEVED THAT THE PAINTING WAS IN COLOR.
GET IT?
HUMAN MEMORIES AREN'T RELIABLE.
YOU CAN BELIEVE SOMETHING WITHOUT COLOR WAS IN COLOR.
YOUR BRAIN WILL ADD SOMETHING...
...OR JUST GLORIFY IT...
MEMORIES MAKE YOU BELIEVE WHAT HAPPENED WAS BETTER THAN IT ACTUALLY WAS.
SO I...
...DON'T BELIEVE IN THOSE SO-CALLED....
..."BEAUTIFUL MEMORIES."

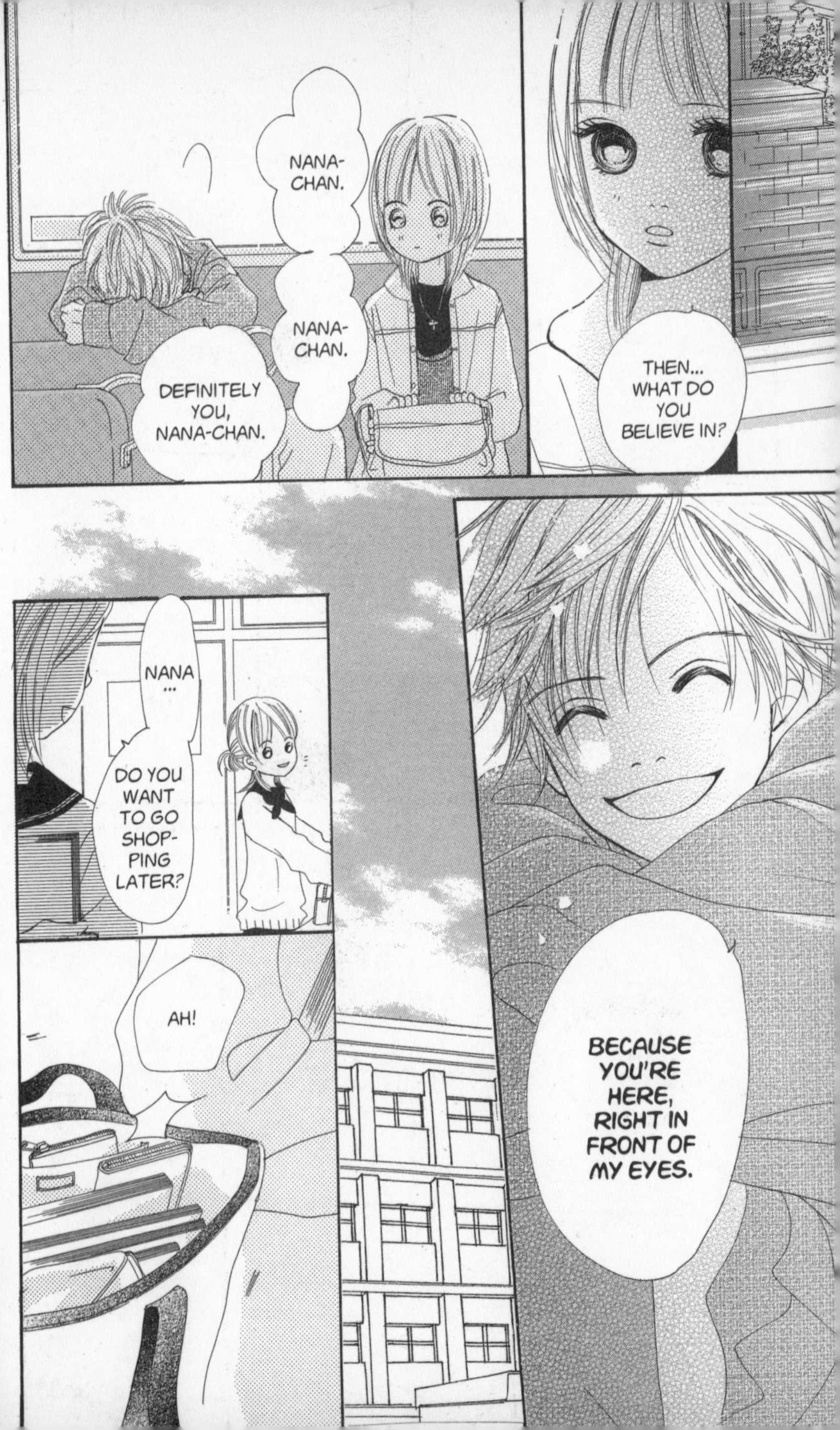
THEN... WHAT DO YOU BELIEVE IN?
NANA-CHAN.
NANA-CHAN.
DEFINITELY YOU, NANA-CHAN.
BECAUSE YOU'RE HERE, RIGHT IN FRONT OF MY EYES.
NANA...
DO YOU WANT TO GO SHOP-PING LATER?
AH!

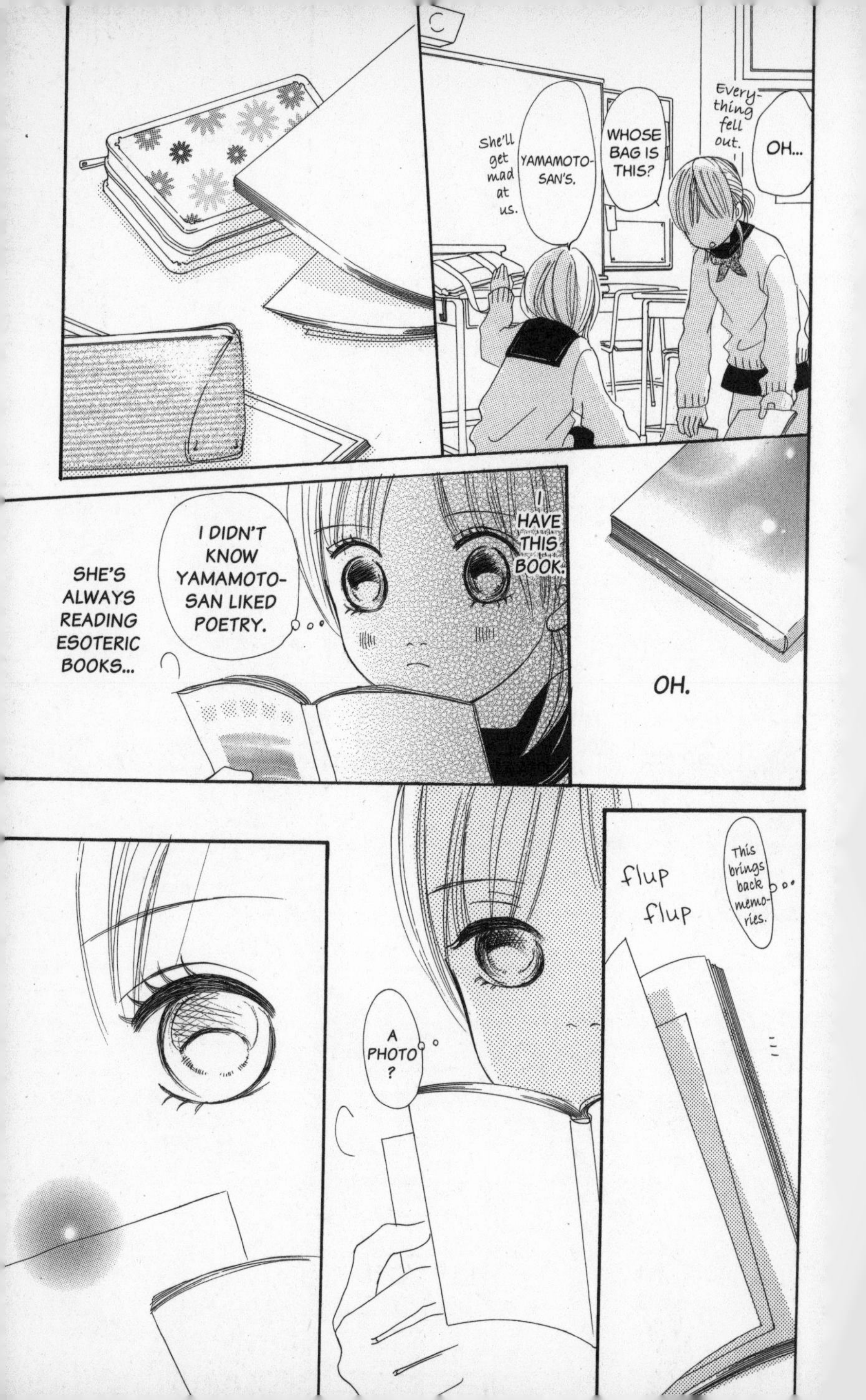
Everything fell out.
OH...
WHOSE BAG IS THIS?
YAMAMOTO-SAN'S.
She'll get mad at us.
OH.
I HAVE THIS BOOK.
I DIDN'T KNOW YAMAMOTO-SAN LIKED POETRY.
SHE'S ALWAYS READING ESOTERIC BOOKS...
This brings back memories.
flup flup
A PHOTO?

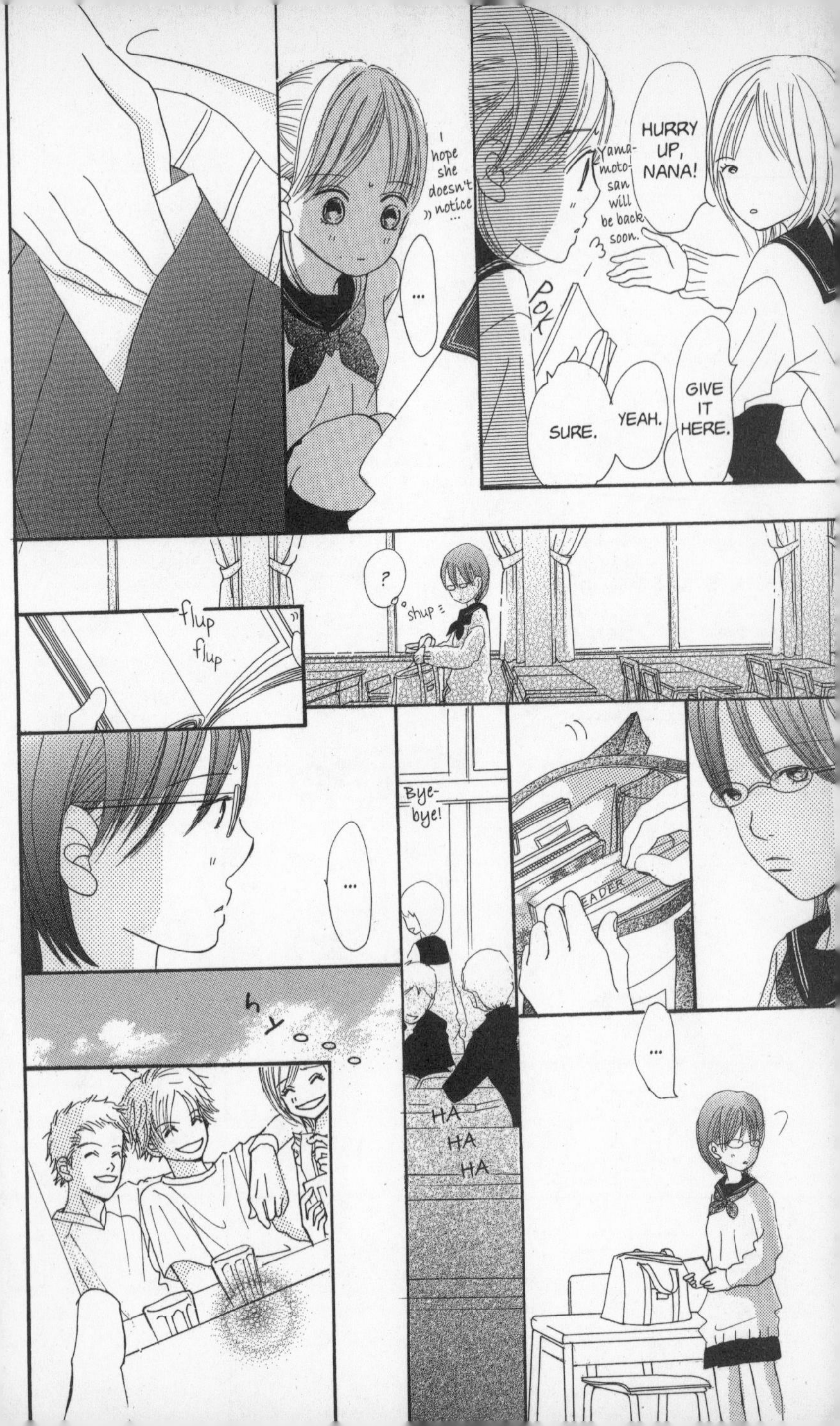
HURRY UP, NANA!
Yamamoto-san will be back soon.
POK
GIVE IT HERE.
YEAH.
SURE.
I hope she doesn't notice...
...
?
shup
flup
flup
...
Bye-bye!
HA HA HA
...

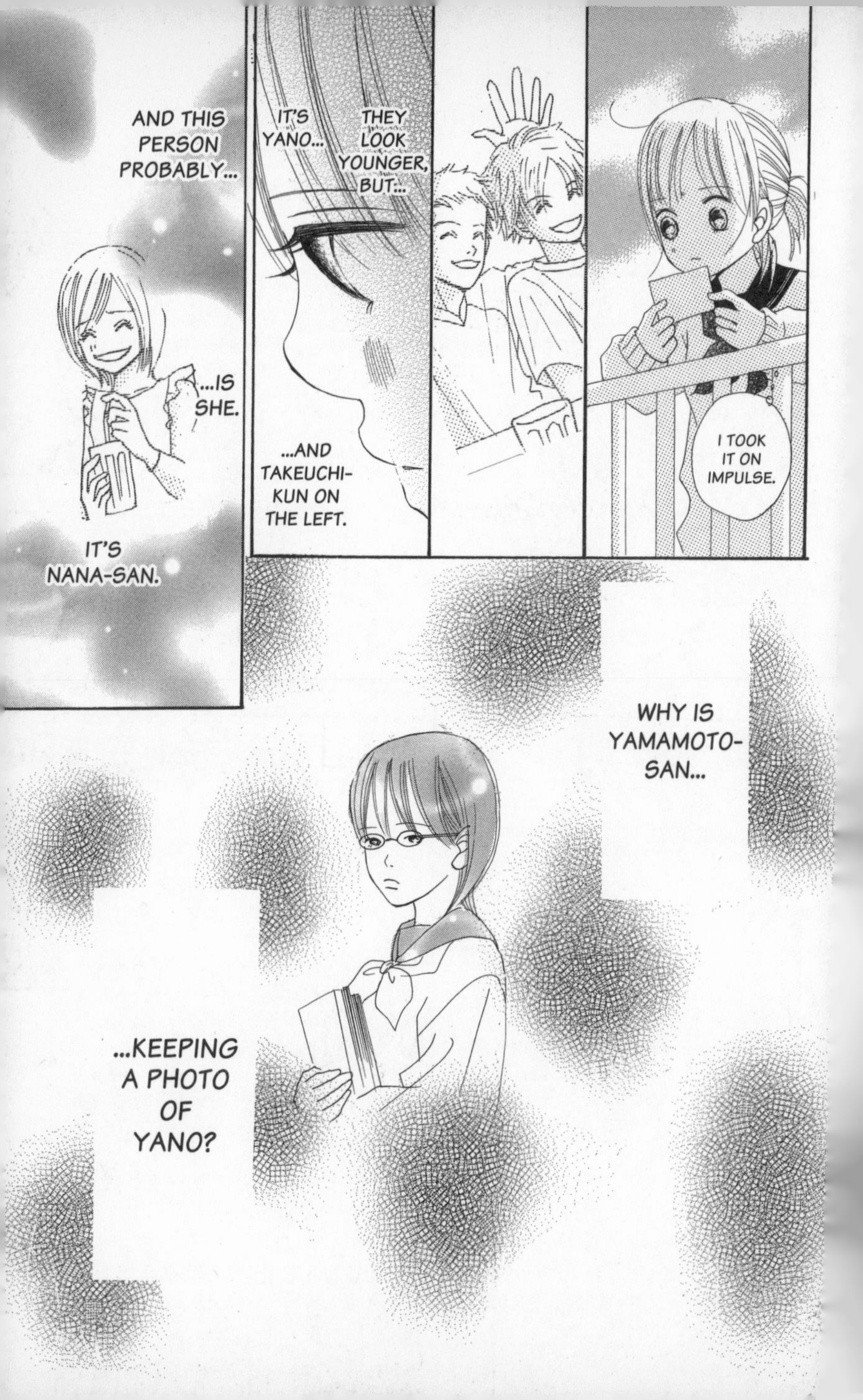
I TOOK IT ON IMPULSE.
THEY LOOK YOUNGER, BUT...
IT'S YANO...
...AND TAKEUCHI-KUN ON THE LEFT.
AND THIS PERSON PROBABLY...
...IS SHE.
IT'S NANA-SAN.
WHY IS YAMAMOTO-SAN...
...KEEPING A PHOTO OF YANO?

Chapter 14

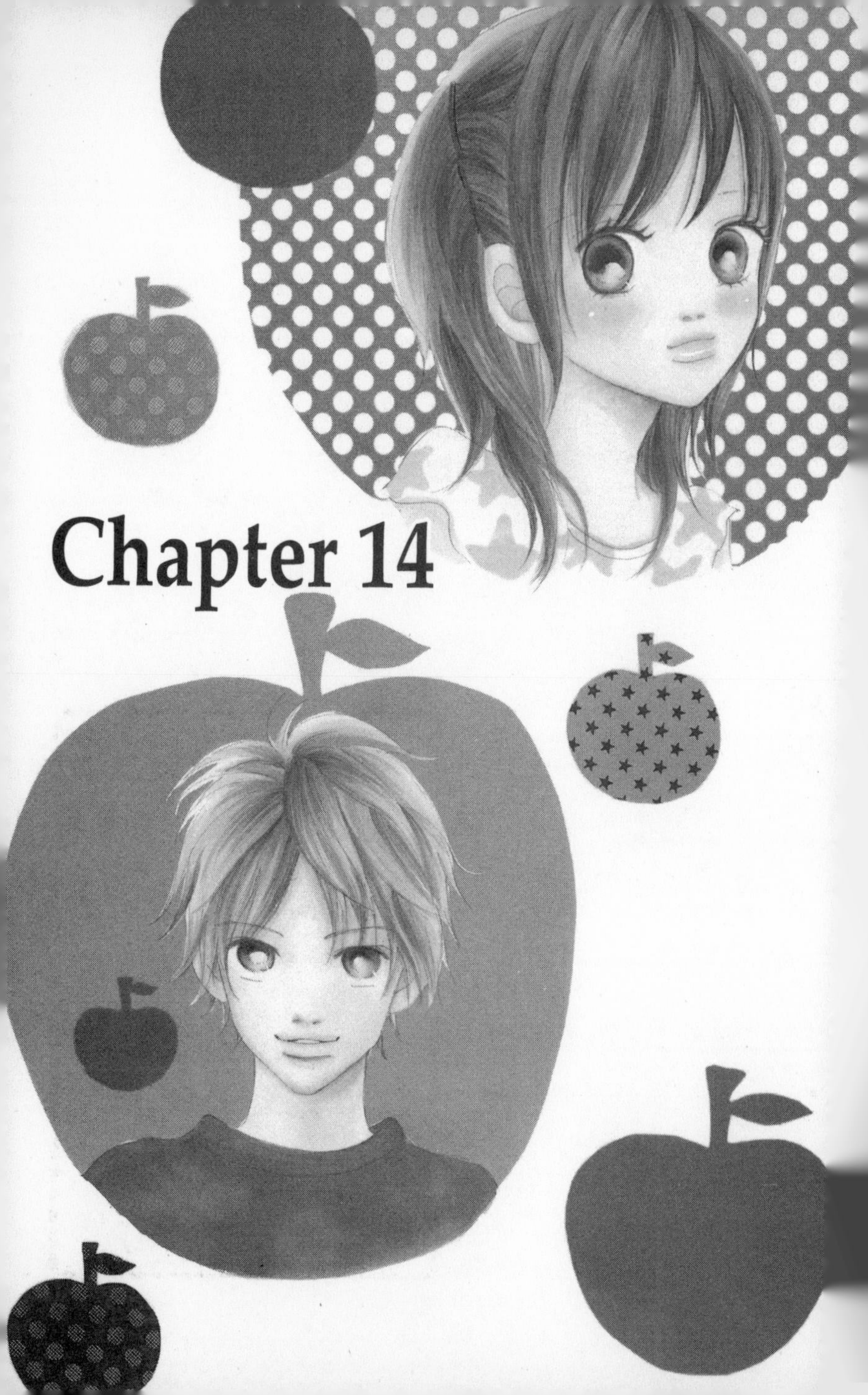

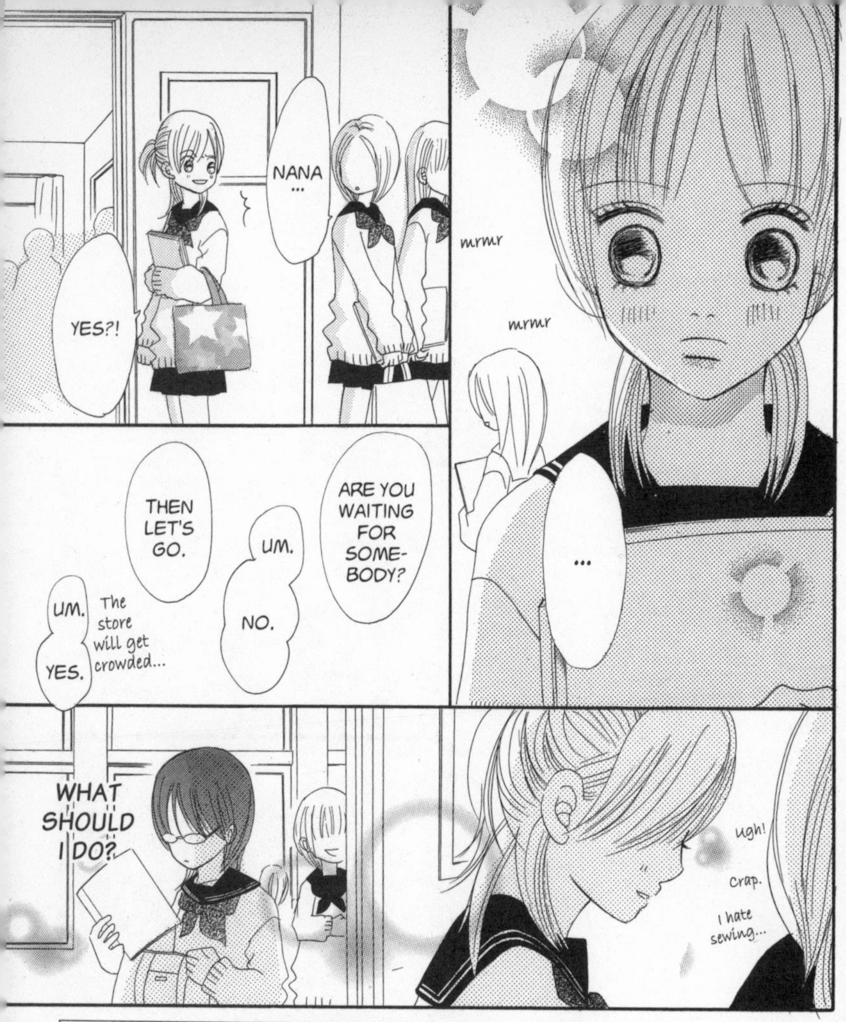
mrmr
mrmr
...
NANA ...
YES?!
ARE YOU WAITING FOR SOMEBODY?
UM.
NO.
THEN LET'S GO.
UM.
The store will get crowded...
YES.
ugh!
Crap.
I hate sewing...
WHAT SHOULD I DO?
Hm?

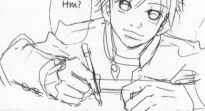

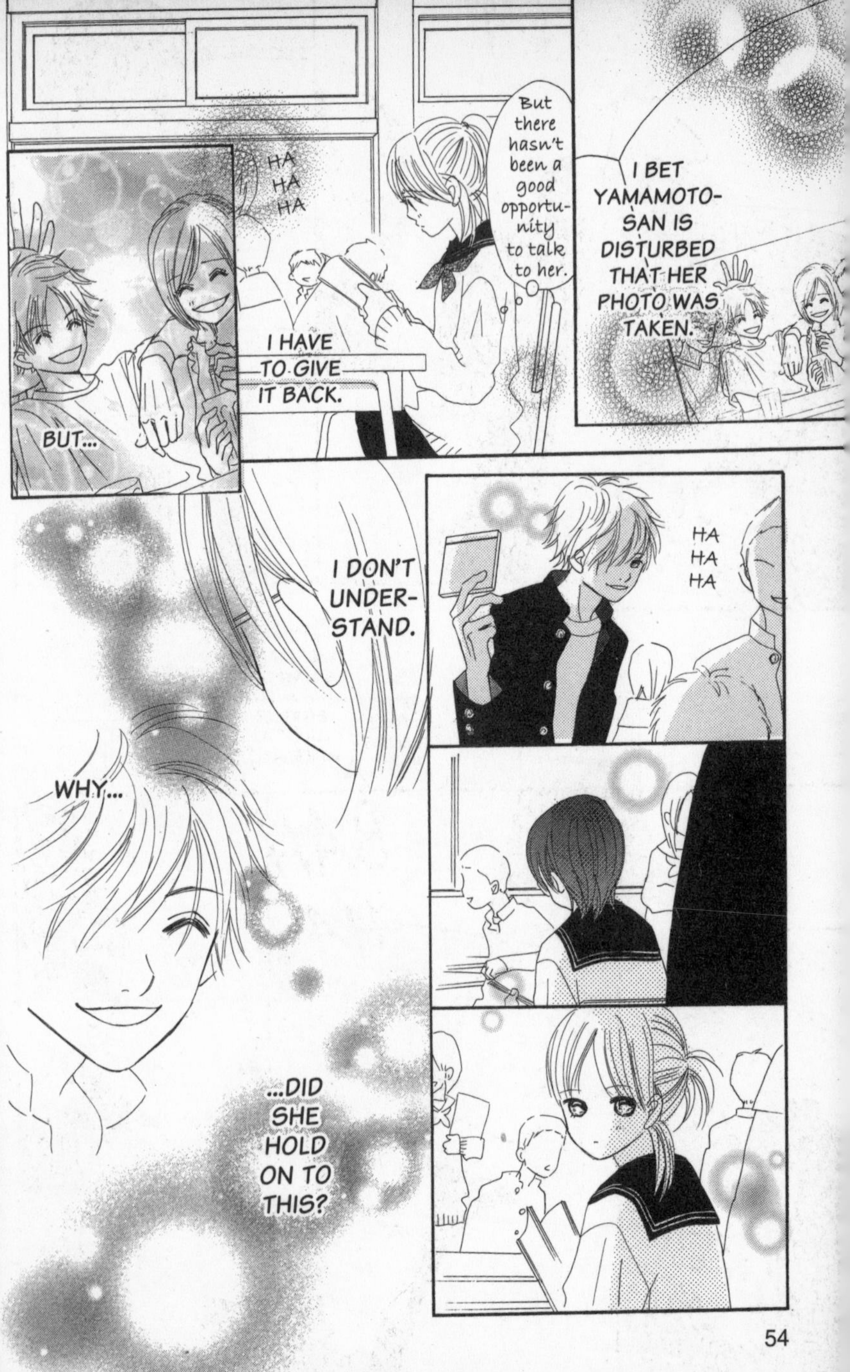
I BET YAMAMOTO-SAN IS DISTURBED THAT HER PHOTO WAS TAKEN.
But there hasn't been a good opportunity to talk to her.
HA HA HA
I HAVE TO GIVE IT BACK.
BUT...
HA HA HA
I DON'T UNDERSTAND.
WHY...
...DID SHE HOLD ON TO THIS?

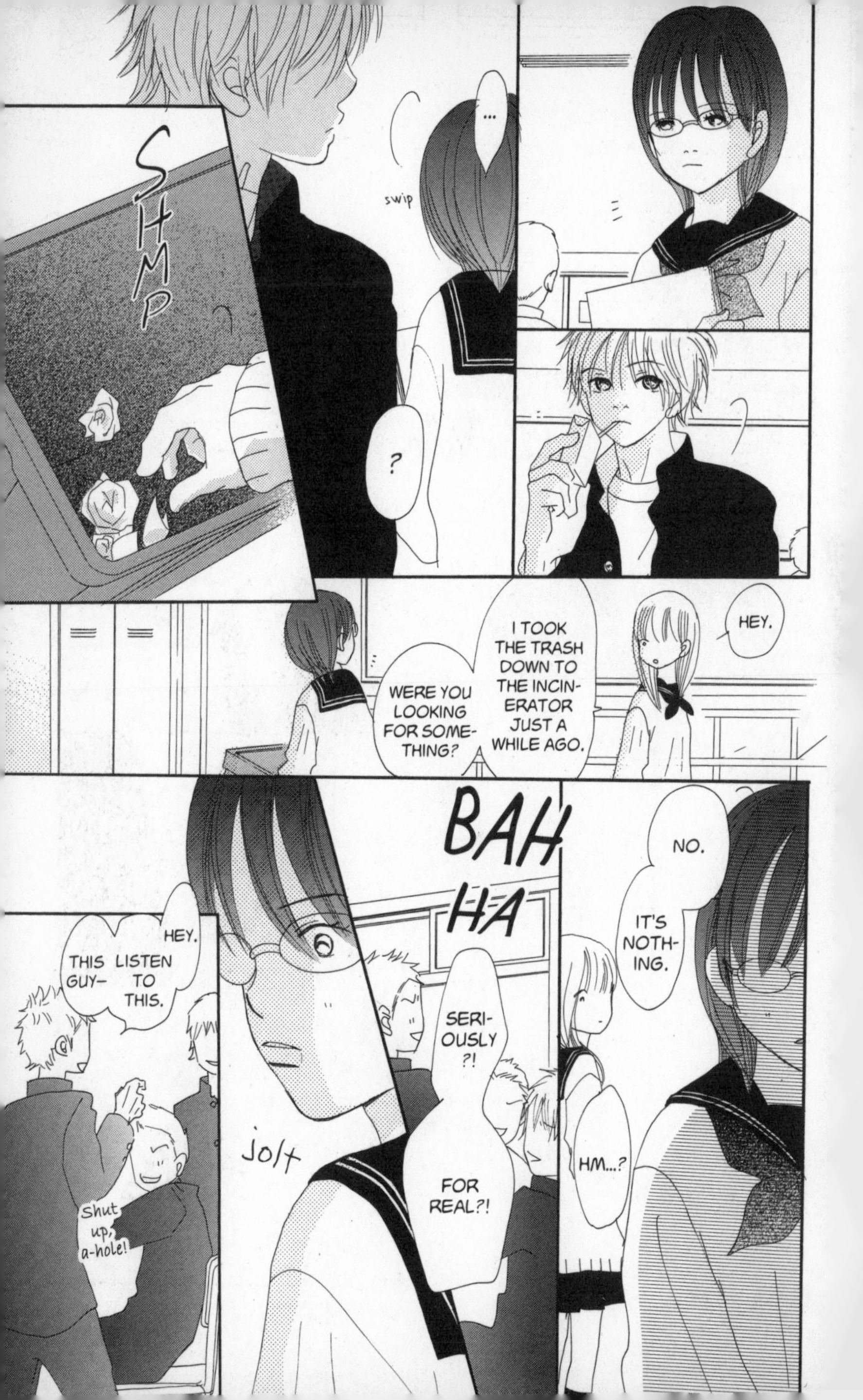
...
swip
?
SHMP
HEY.
I TOOK THE TRASH DOWN TO THE INCINERATOR JUST A WHILE AGO.
WERE YOU LOOKING FOR SOMETHING?
NO.
IT'S NOTHING.
HM...?
BAH HA
SERIOUSLY?!
FOR REAL?!
jolt
HEY.
LISTEN TO THIS.
THIS GUY—
Shut up, a-hole!

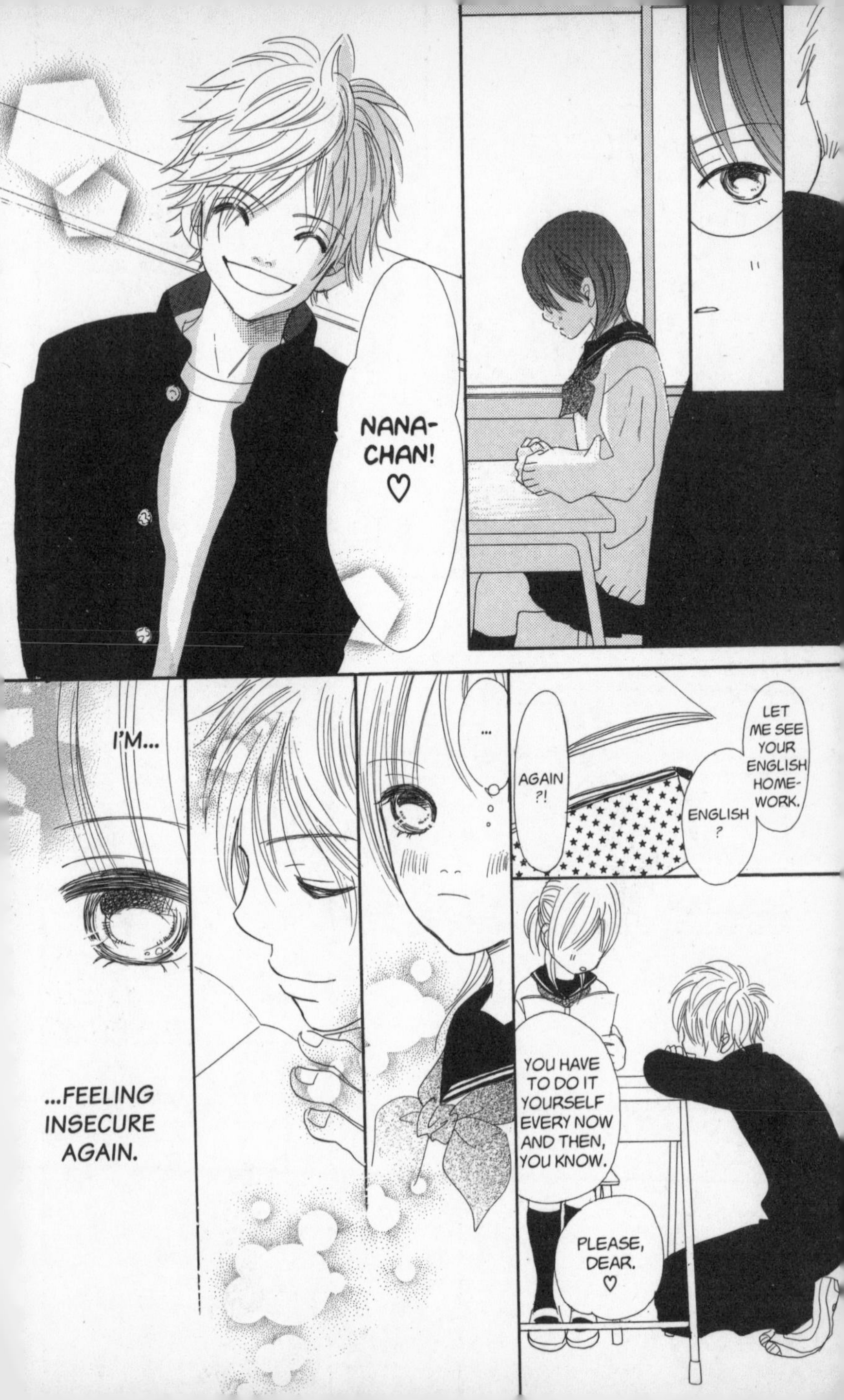
NANA-CHAN! ♡
LET ME SEE YOUR ENGLISH HOMEWORK.
ENGLISH?
AGAIN?!
YOU HAVE TO DO IT YOURSELF EVERY NOW AND THEN, YOU KNOW.
PLEASE, DEAR. ♡
...
I'M...
...FEELING INSECURE AGAIN.

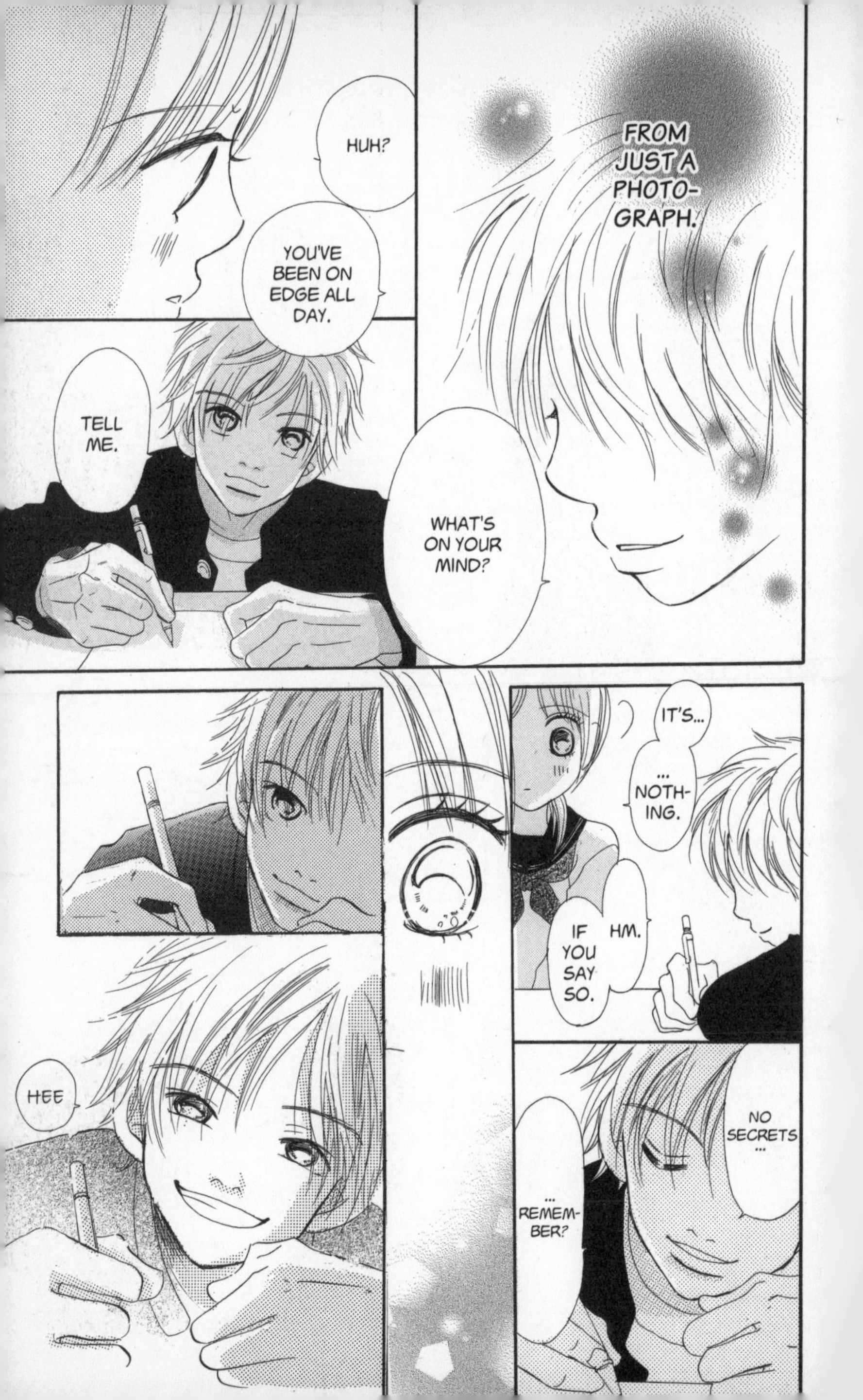

FROM JUST A PHOTO-GRAPH.
HUH?
YOU'VE BEEN ON EDGE ALL DAY.
TELL ME.
WHAT'S ON YOUR MIND?
IT'S...
...NOTH-ING.
HM.
IF YOU SAY SO.
NO SECRETS...
...REMEM-BER?
HEE

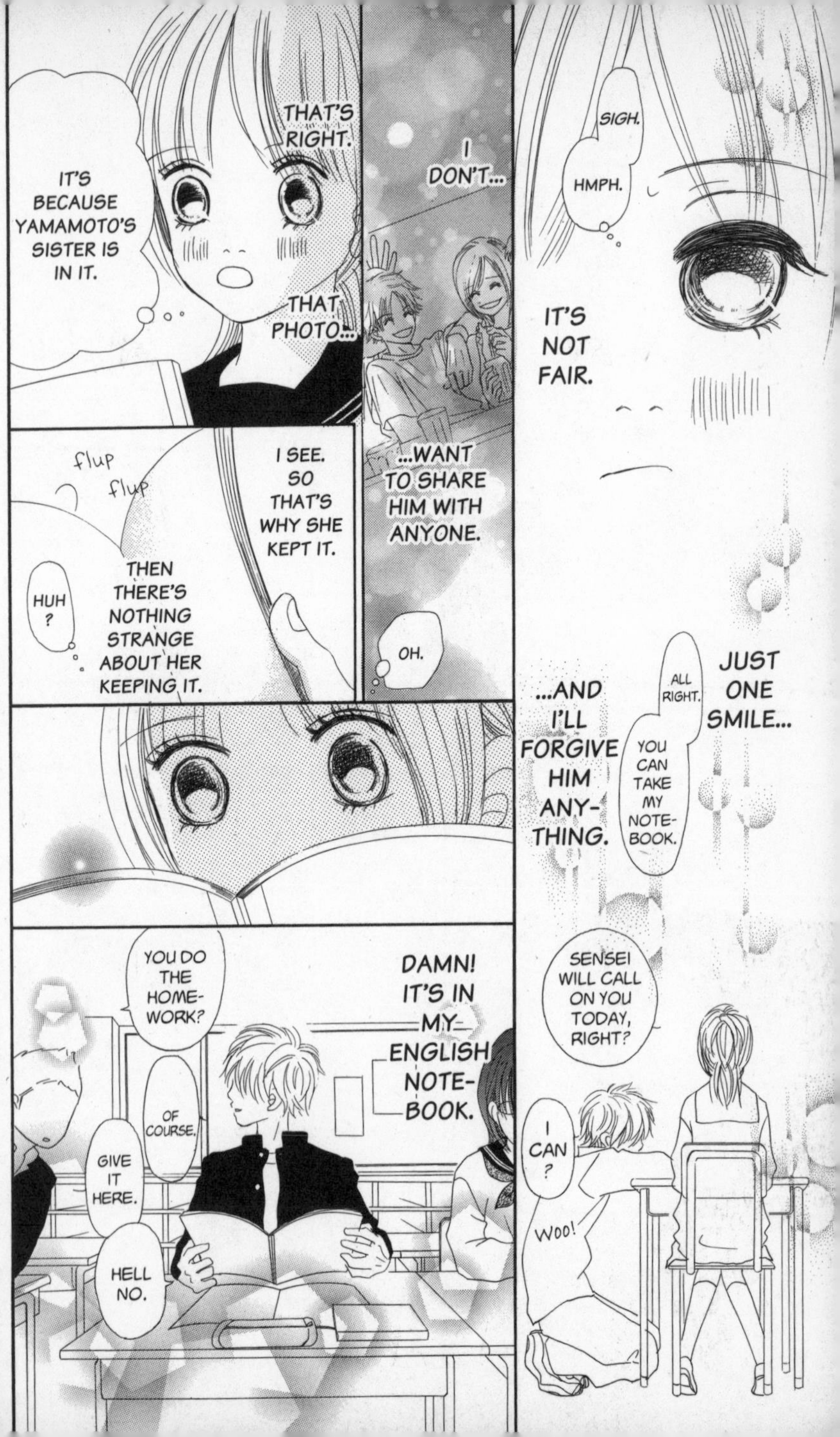
THAT'S RIGHT.
IT'S BECAUSE YAMAMOTO'S SISTER IS IN IT.
THAT PHOTO...
flup flup
I SEE. SO THAT'S WHY SHE KEPT IT.
THEN THERE'S NOTHING STRANGE ABOUT HER KEEPING IT.
HUH?
I DON'T...
...WANT TO SHARE HIM WITH ANYONE.
OH.
YOU DO THE HOMEWORK?
OF COURSE.
GIVE IT HERE.
HELL NO.
DAMN! IT'S IN MY ENGLISH NOTEBOOK.
SIGH.
HMPH.
IT'S JUST NOT FAIR.
JUST ONE SMILE...
...AND I'LL FORGIVE HIM ANYTHING.
ALL RIGHT.
YOU CAN TAKE MY NOTEBOOK.
SENSEI WILL CALL ON YOU TODAY, RIGHT?
I CAN?
Woo!

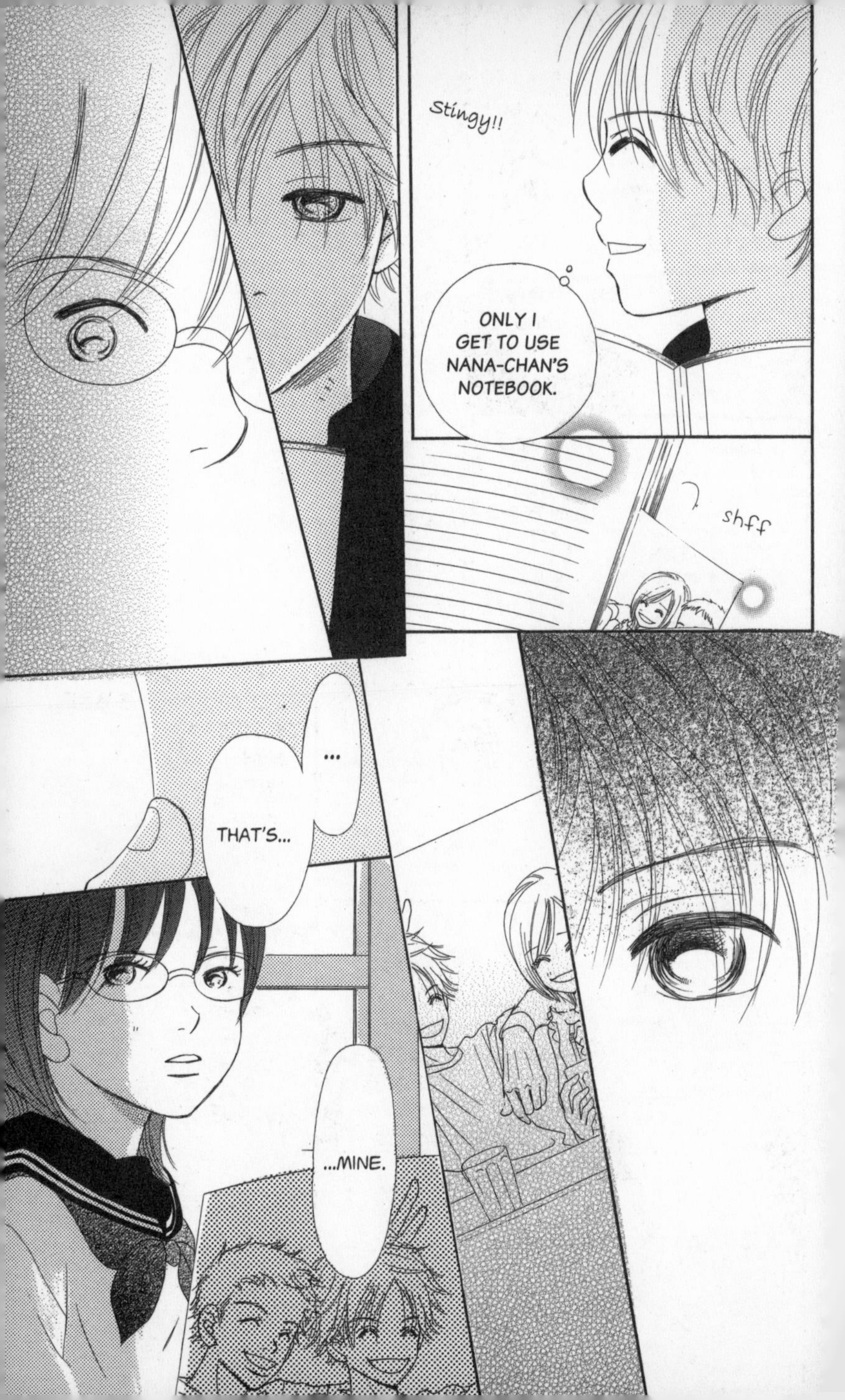
Stingy!!
ONLY I GET TO USE NANA-CHAN'S NOTEBOOK.
shff
...
THAT'S...
...MINE.

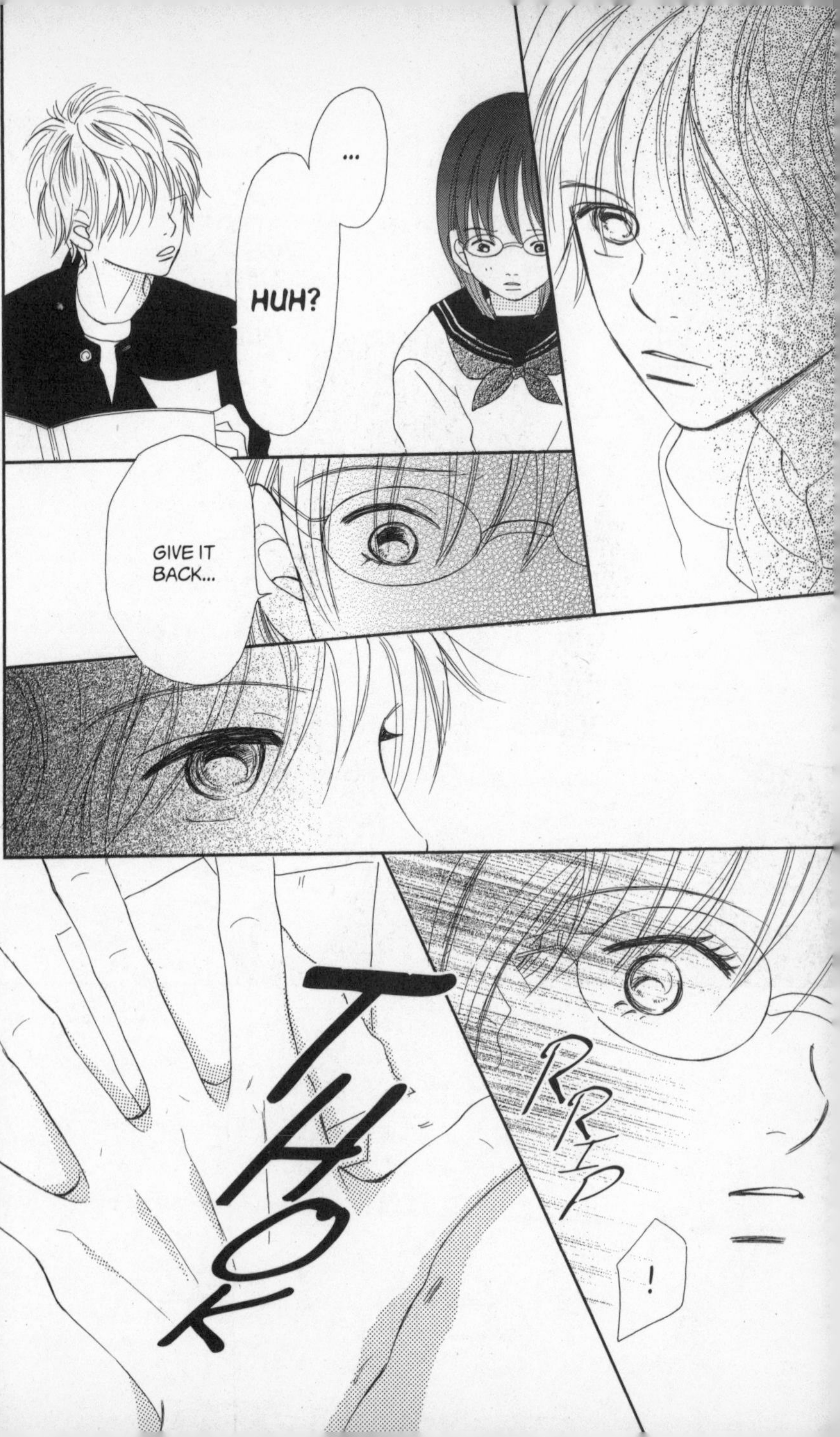
... HUH?
GIVE IT BACK...
RRIP
!
THOK

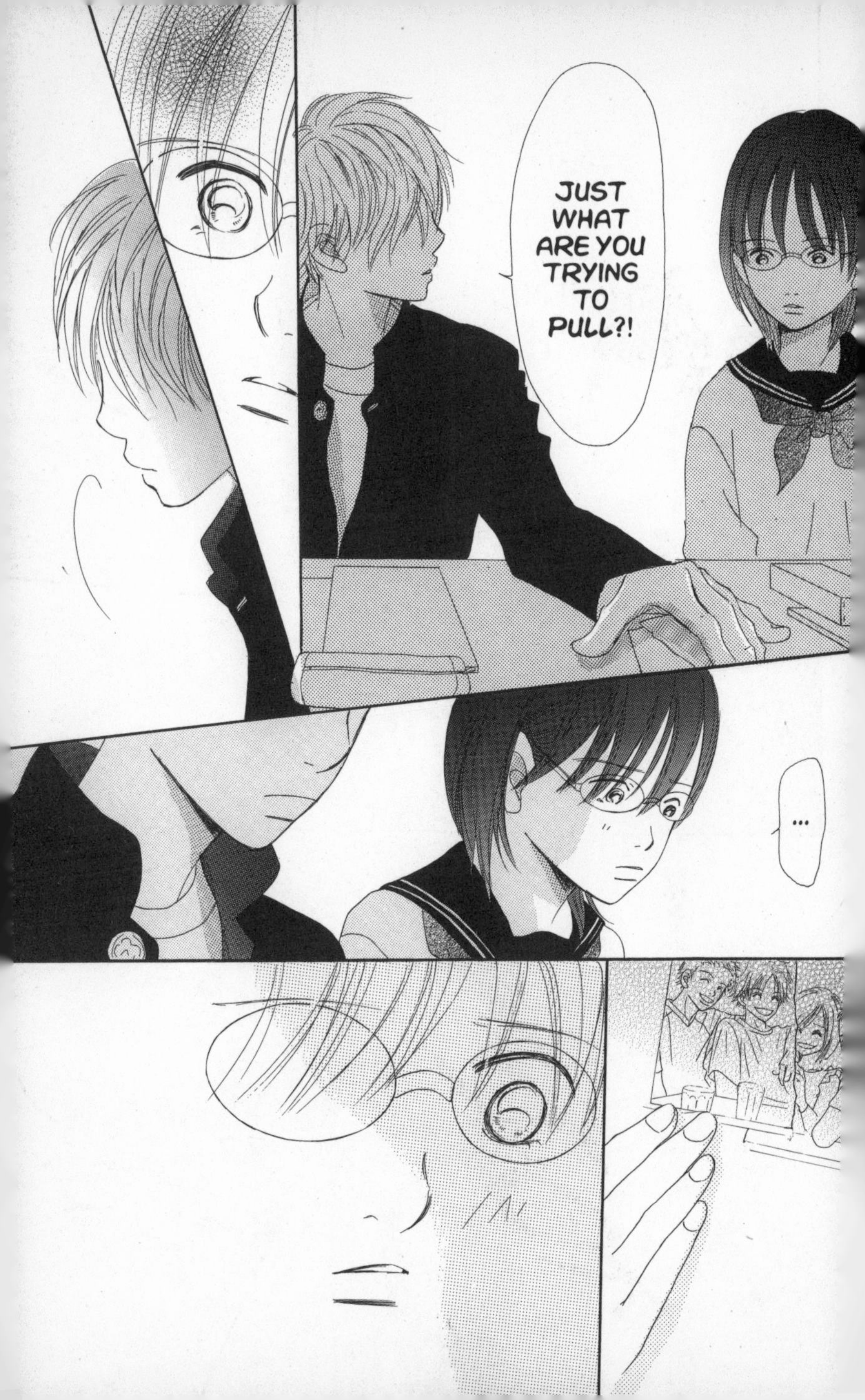
JUST WHAT ARE YOU TRYING TO PULL?!
...

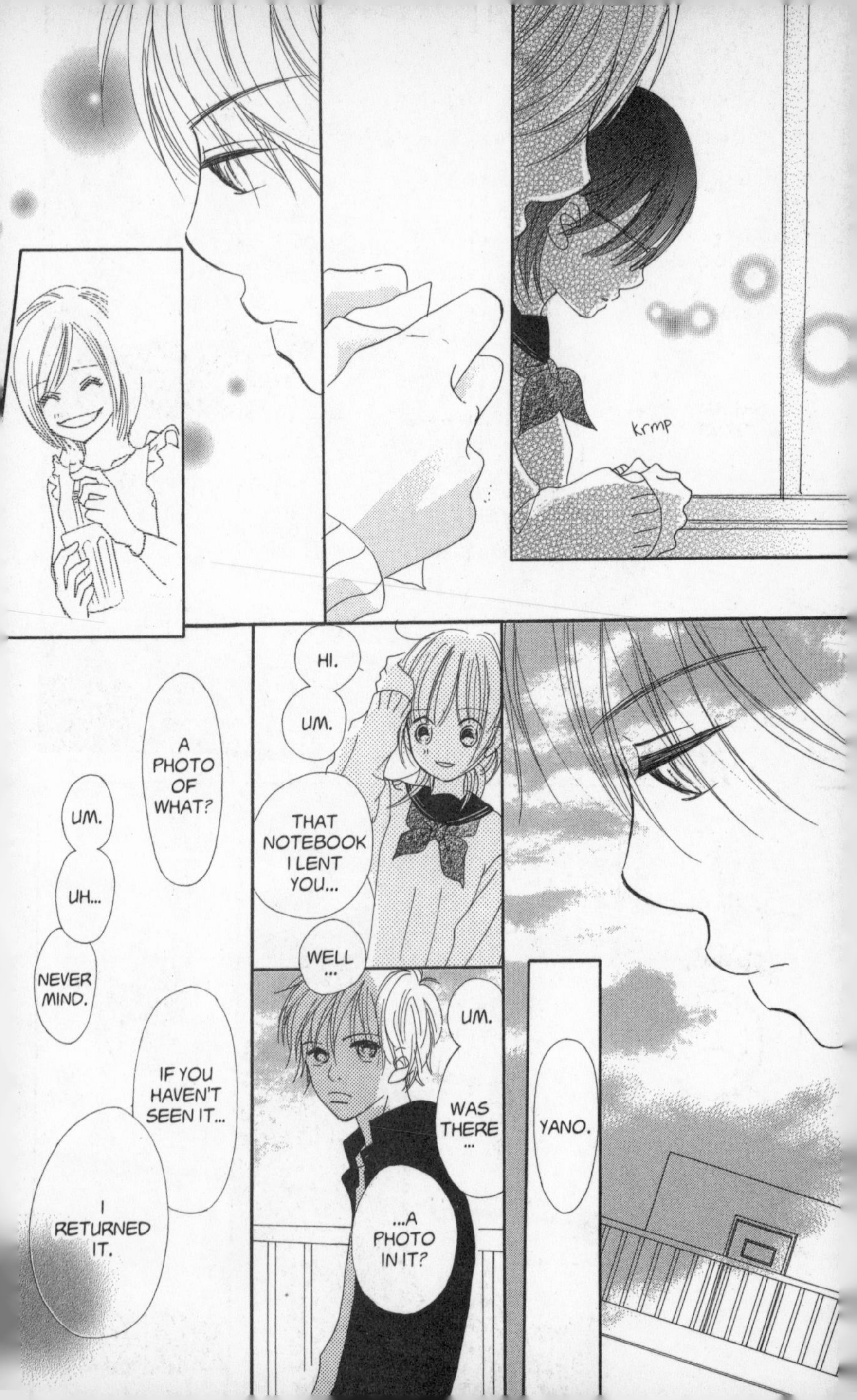
krmp
YANO.
HI.
UM.
THAT NOTEBOOK I LENT YOU...
WELL...
UM.
WAS THERE...
...A PHOTO IN IT?
A PHOTO OF WHAT?
UM.
UH...
NEVER MIND.
IF YOU HAVEN'T SEEN IT...
I RETURNED IT.

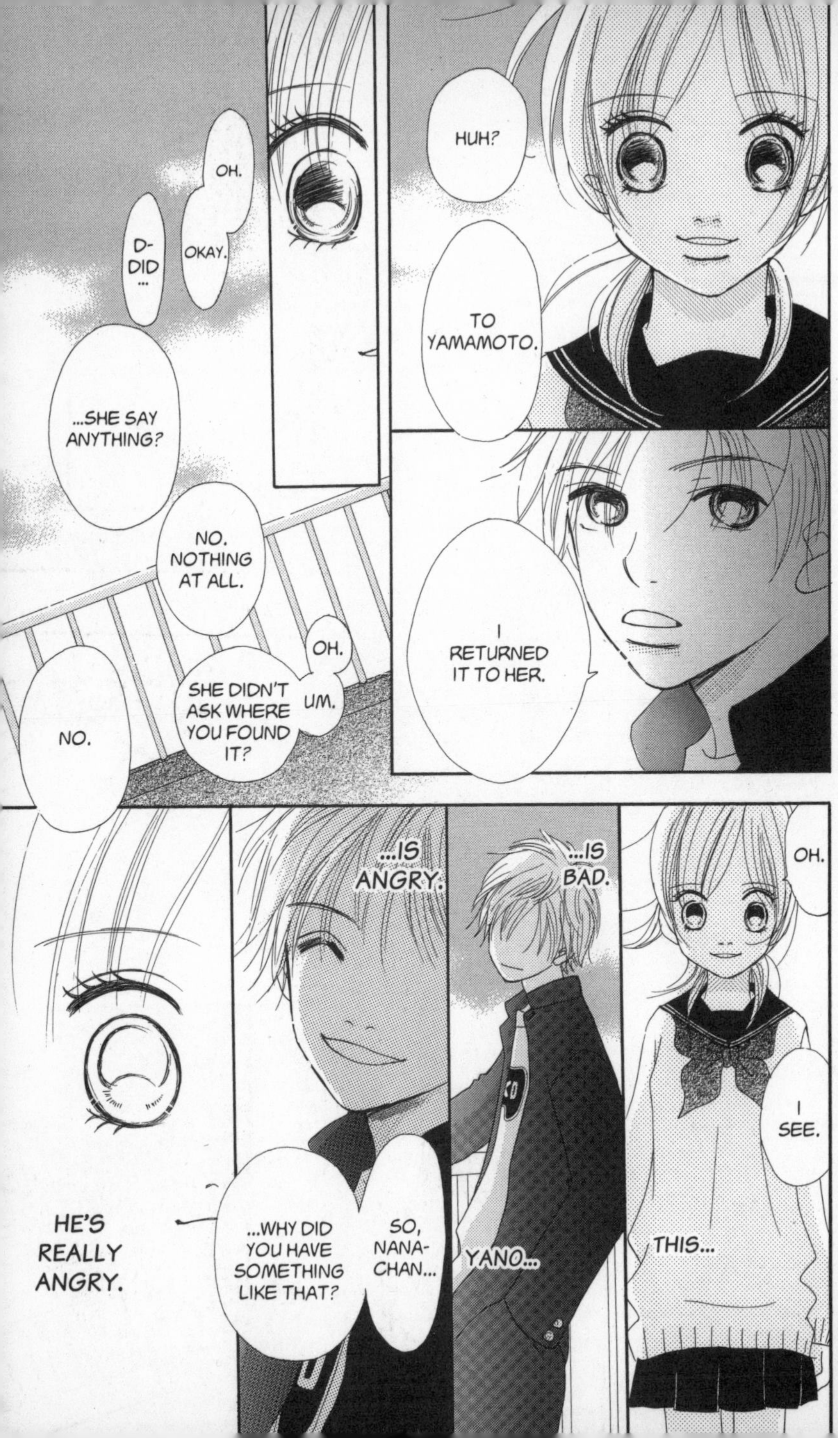
HUH?
TO YAMAMOTO.
I RETURNED IT TO HER.
OH.
OKAY.
D-DID...
...SHE SAY ANYTHING?
NO. NOTHING AT ALL.
OH.
UM.
SHE DIDN'T ASK WHERE YOU FOUND IT?
NO.
OH.
I SEE.
THIS...
...IS BAD.
YANO...
...IS ANGRY.
SO, NANA-CHAN...
...WHY DID YOU HAVE SOMETHING LIKE THAT?
HE'S REALLY ANGRY.

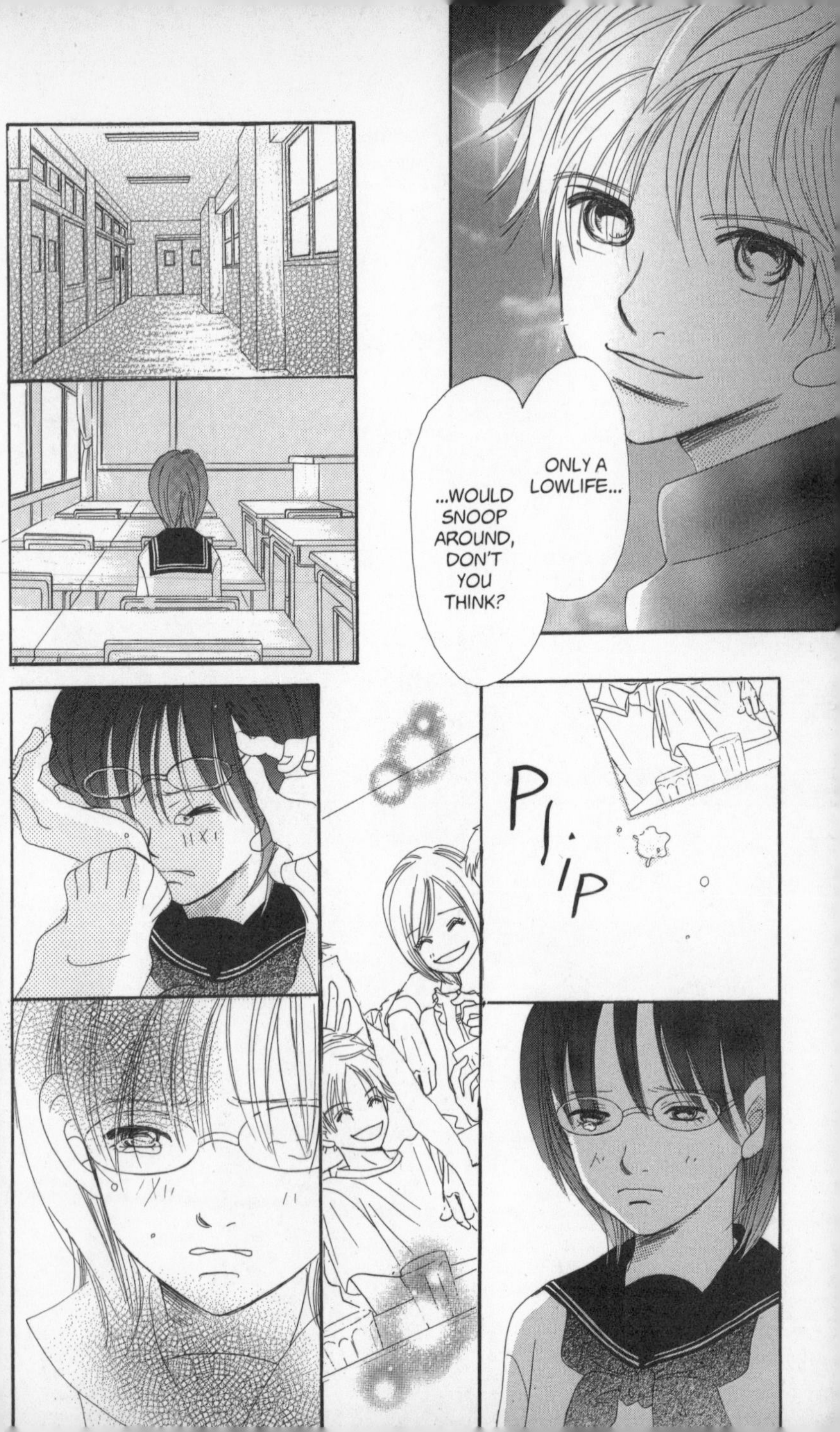
ONLY A LOWLIFE...
...WOULD SNOOP AROUND, DON'T YOU THINK?
PLIP

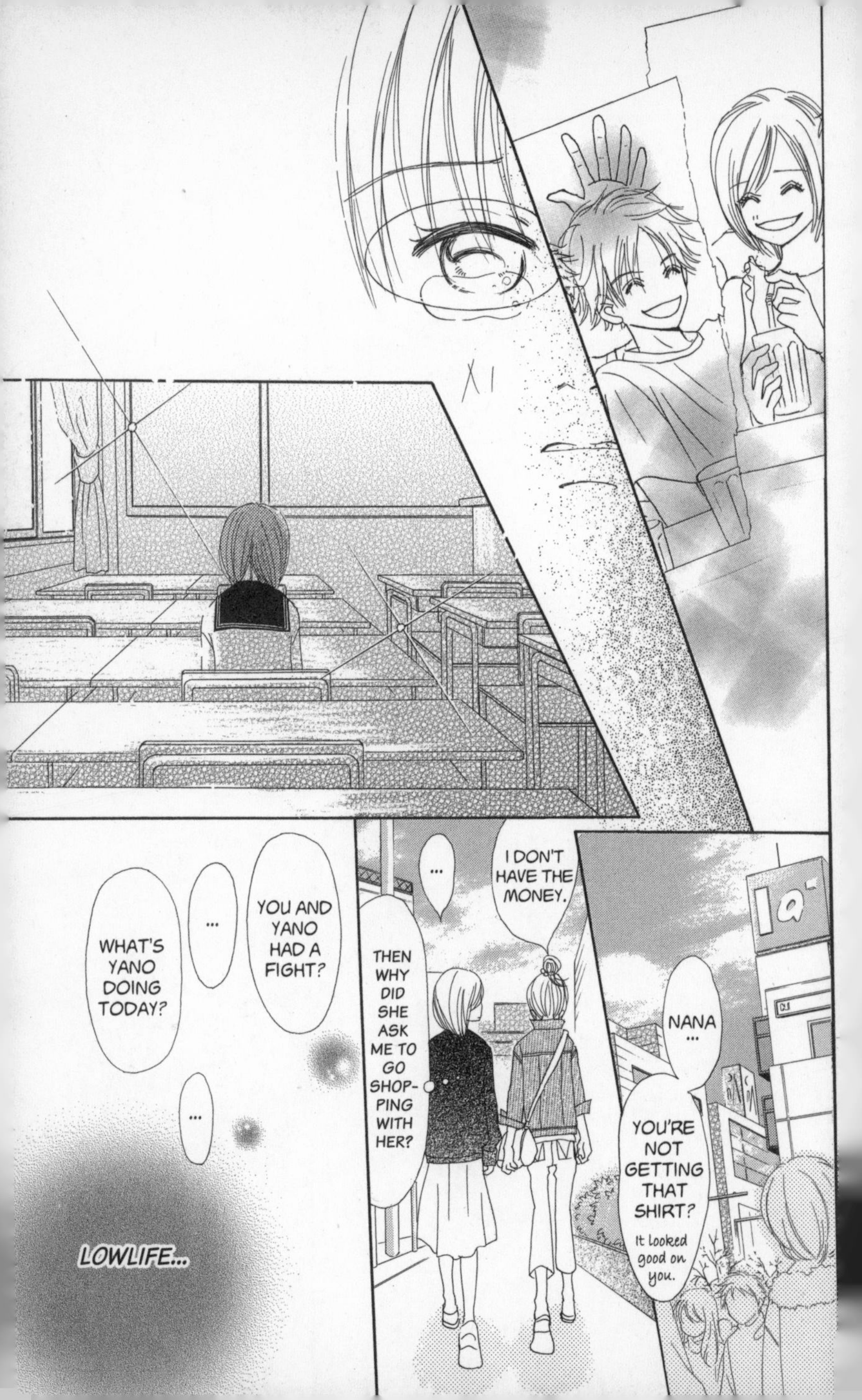
NANA ...
YOU'RE NOT GETTING THAT SHIRT?
It looked good on you.
I DON'T HAVE THE MONEY.
...
THEN WHY DID SHE ASK ME TO GO SHOP-PING WITH HER?
YOU AND YANO HAD A FIGHT?
...
WHAT'S YANO DOING TODAY?
...
LOWLIFE...

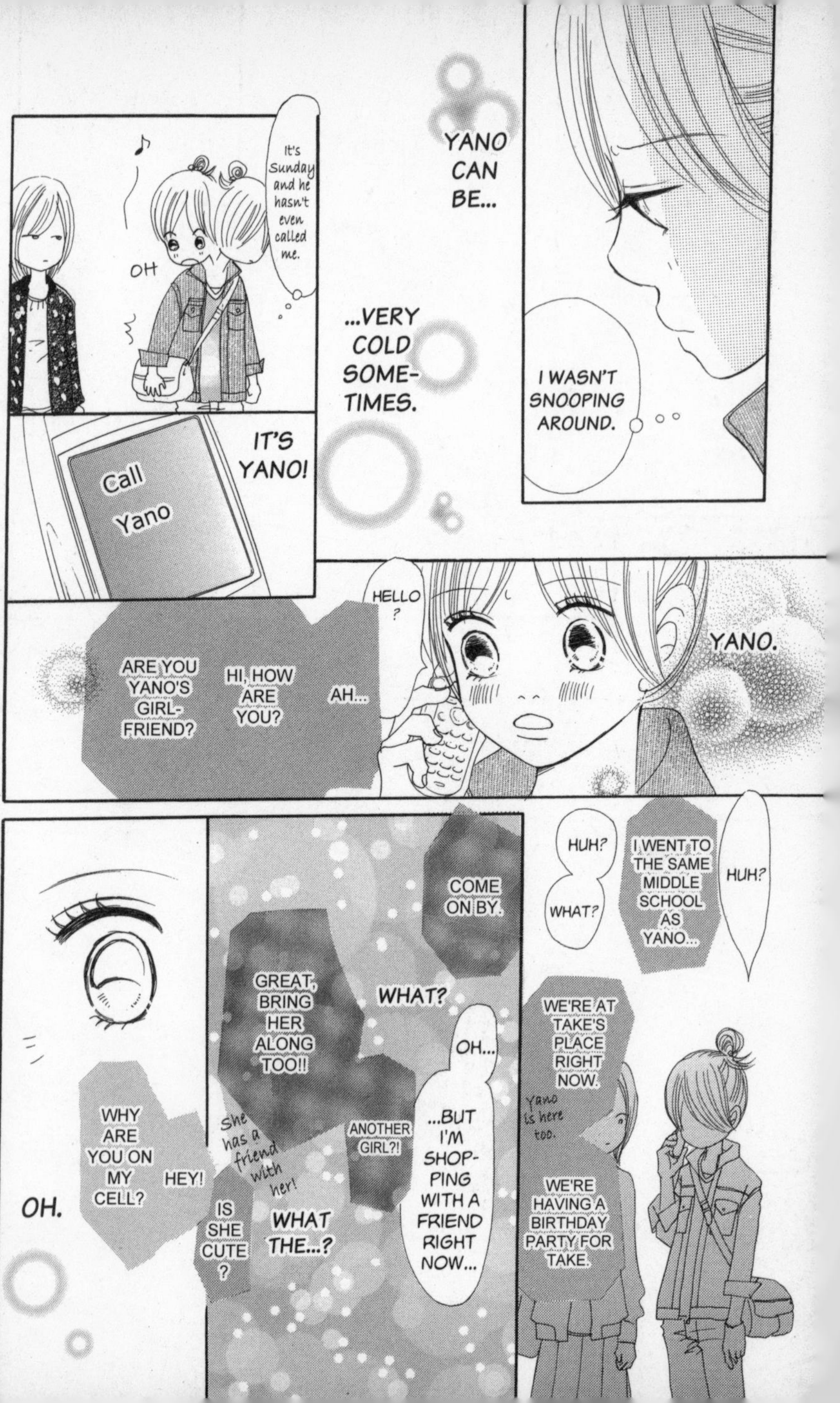
YANO CAN BE...
...VERY COLD SOMETIMES.
I WASN'T SNOOPING AROUND.
It's Sunday and he hasn't even called me.
OH
Call Yano
IT'S YANO!
YANO.
HELLO?
AH...
HI, HOW ARE YOU?
ARE YOU YANO'S GIRLFRIEND?
HUH?
I WENT TO THE SAME MIDDLE SCHOOL AS YANO...
HUH?
WHAT?
WE'RE AT TAKE'S PLACE RIGHT NOW.
Yano is here too.
WE'RE HAVING A BIRTHDAY PARTY FOR TAKE.
COME ON BY.
WHAT?
OH...
GREAT, BRING HER ALONG TOO!!
...BUT I'M SHOPPING WITH A FRIEND RIGHT NOW...
ANOTHER GIRL?!
She has a friend with her!
WHAT THE...?
IS SHE CUTE?
HEY!
WHY ARE YOU ON MY CELL?
OH.

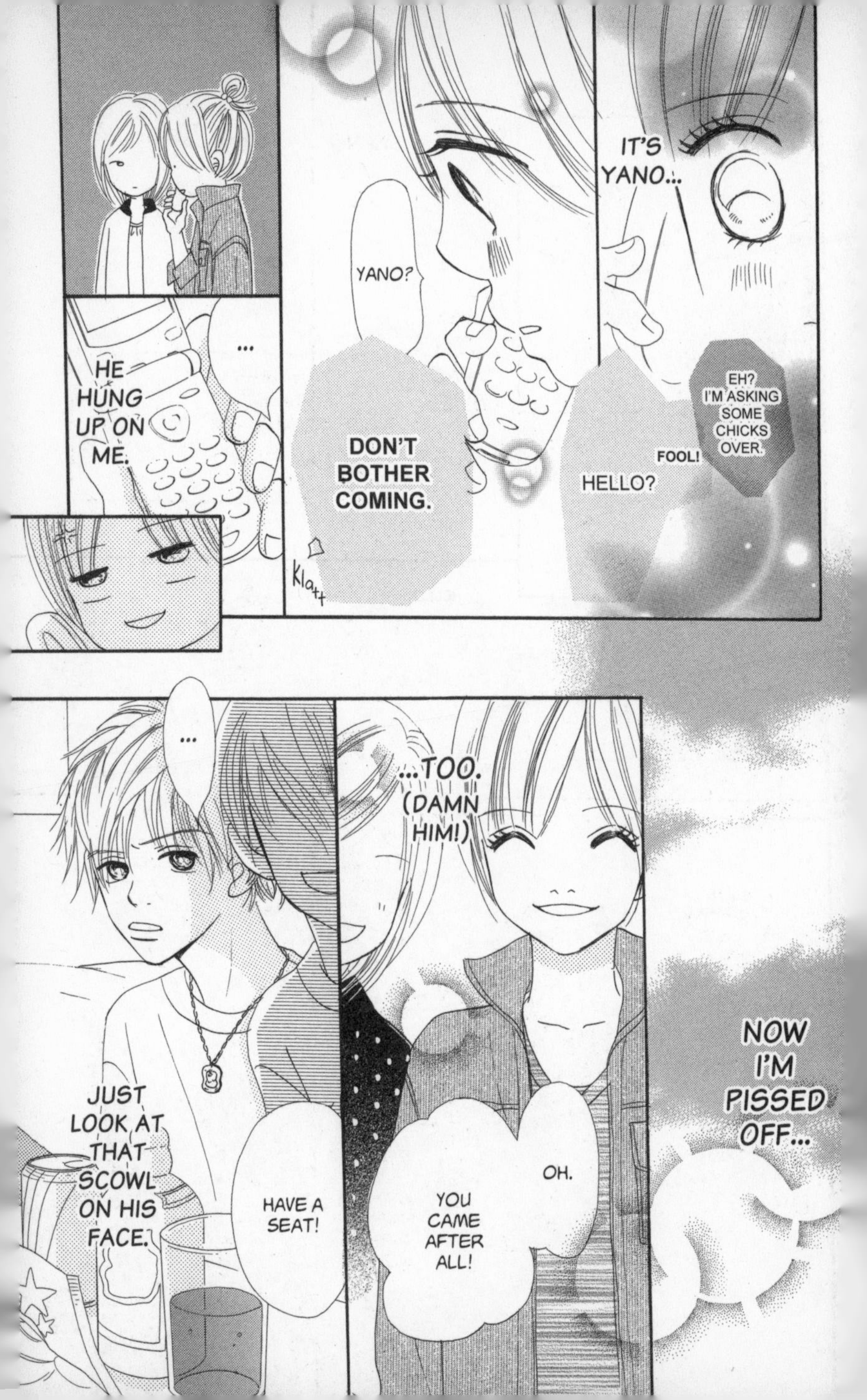
IT'S YANO...
EH? I'M ASKING SOME CHICKS OVER.
FOOL!
HELLO?
YANO?
DON'T BOTHER COMING.
Klatt
...
HE HUNG UP ON ME.
NOW I'M PISSED OFF...
...TOO. (DAMN HIM!)
OH.
YOU CAME AFTER ALL!
...
HAVE A SEAT!
JUST LOOK AT THAT SCOWL ON HIS FACE.

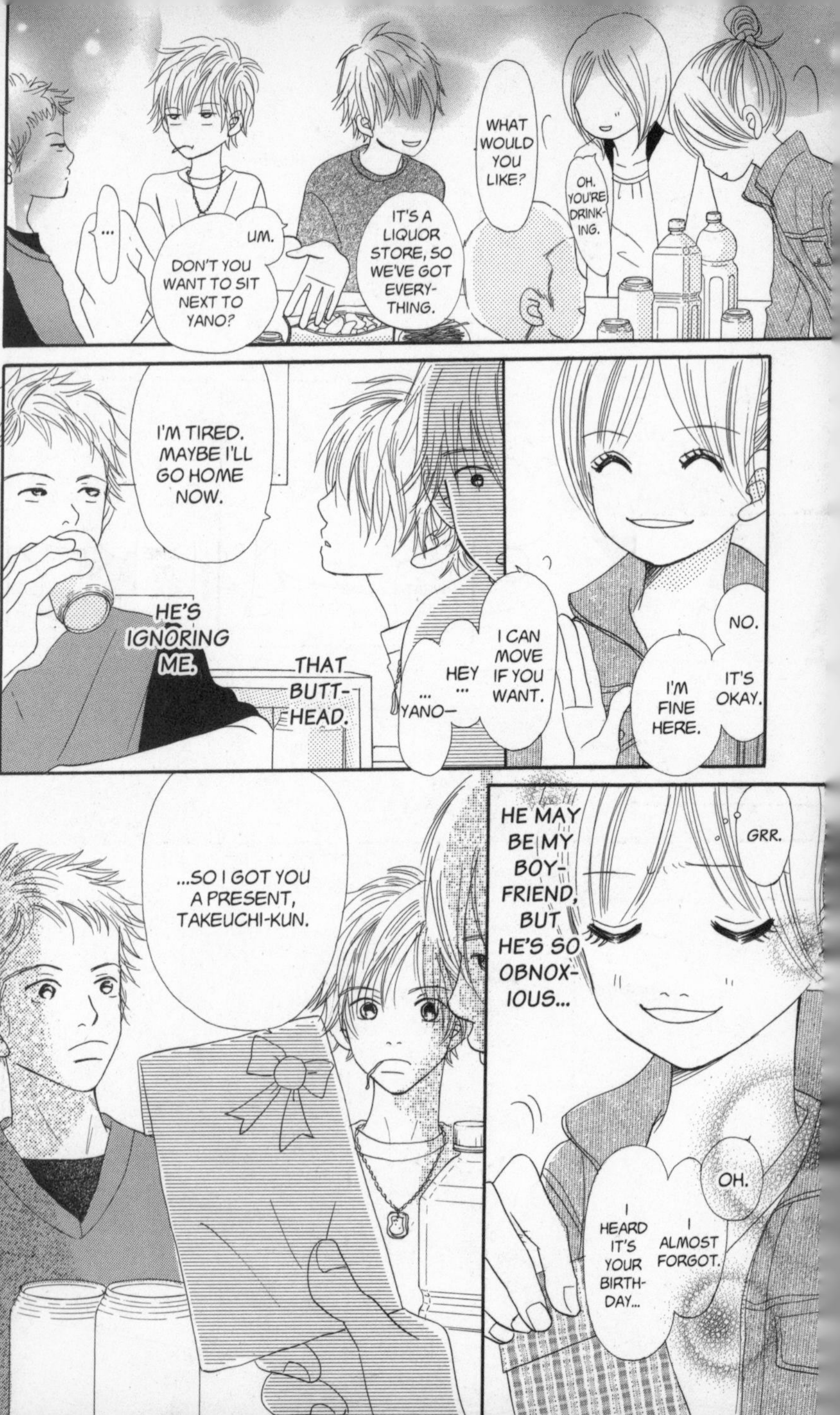
WHAT WOULD YOU LIKE?
OH. YOU'RE DRINKING.
IT'S A LIQUOR STORE, SO WE'VE GOT EVERYTHING.
UM. DON'T YOU WANT TO SIT NEXT TO YANO?
...
NO.
IT'S OKAY. I'M FINE HERE.
I CAN MOVE IF YOU WANT.
HEY ... ... YANO—
I'M TIRED. MAYBE I'LL GO HOME NOW.
HE'S IGNORING ME.
THAT BUTT-HEAD.
GRR.
HE MAY BE MY BOYFRIEND, BUT HE'S SO OBNOXIOUS...
OH. I ALMOST FORGOT.
I HEARD IT'S YOUR BIRTHDAY...
...SO I GOT YOU A PRESENT, TAKEUCHI-KUN.

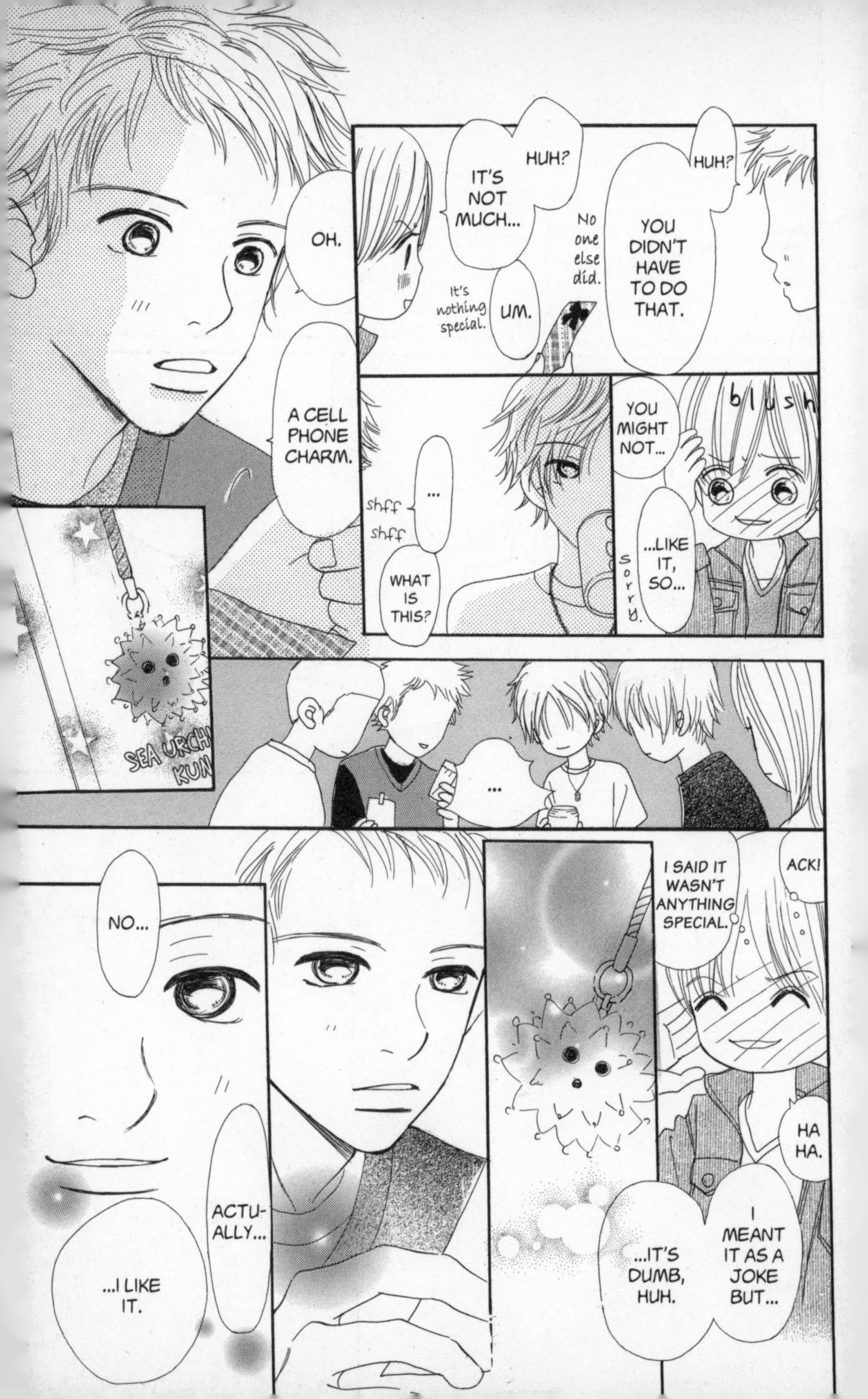
HUH?
YOU DIDN'T HAVE TO DO THAT.
No one else did.
HUH?
IT'S NOT MUCH...
UM.
It's nothing special.
blush
YOU MIGHT NOT...
...LIKE IT, SO...
sorry.
...
shff
shff
WHAT IS THIS?
OH.
A CELL PHONE CHARM.
SEA URCHIN KUN
...
ACK!
I SAID IT WASN'T ANYTHING SPECIAL.
HA HA.
I MEANT IT AS A JOKE BUT...
...IT'S DUMB, HUH.
NO...
ACTU-ALLY...
...I LIKE IT.

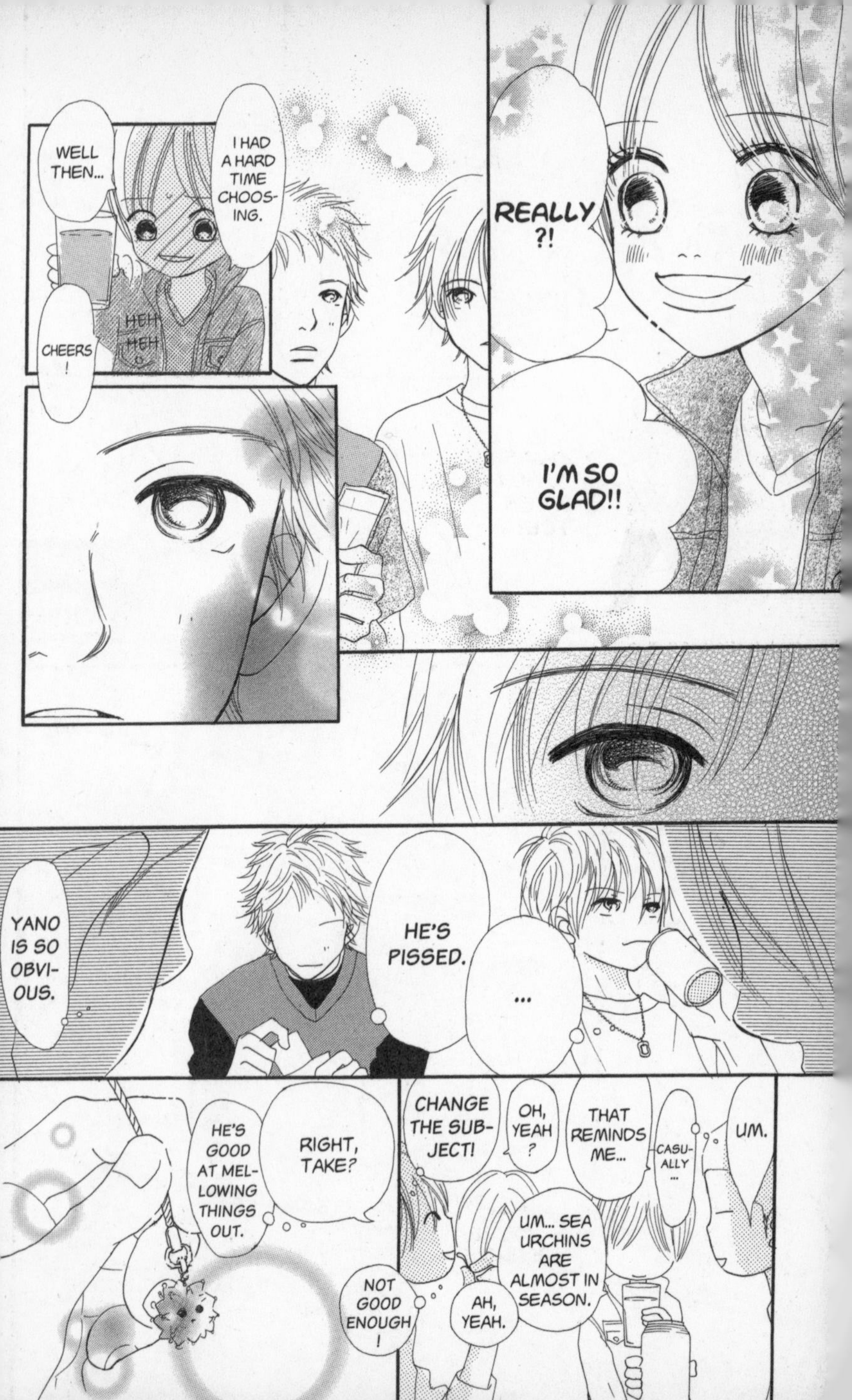
REALLY ?!
I'M SO GLAD!!
I HAD A HARD TIME CHOOS-ING.
WELL THEN...
HEH HEH
CHEERS !
...
HE'S PISSED.
YANO IS SO OBVI-OUS.
UM.
CASU-ALLY ...
THAT REMINDS ME...
OH, YEAH ?
CHANGE THE SUB-JECT!
UM... SEA URCHINS ARE ALMOST IN SEASON.
AH, YEAH.
NOT GOOD ENOUGH !
RIGHT, TAKE?
HE'S GOOD AT MEL-LOWING THINGS OUT.

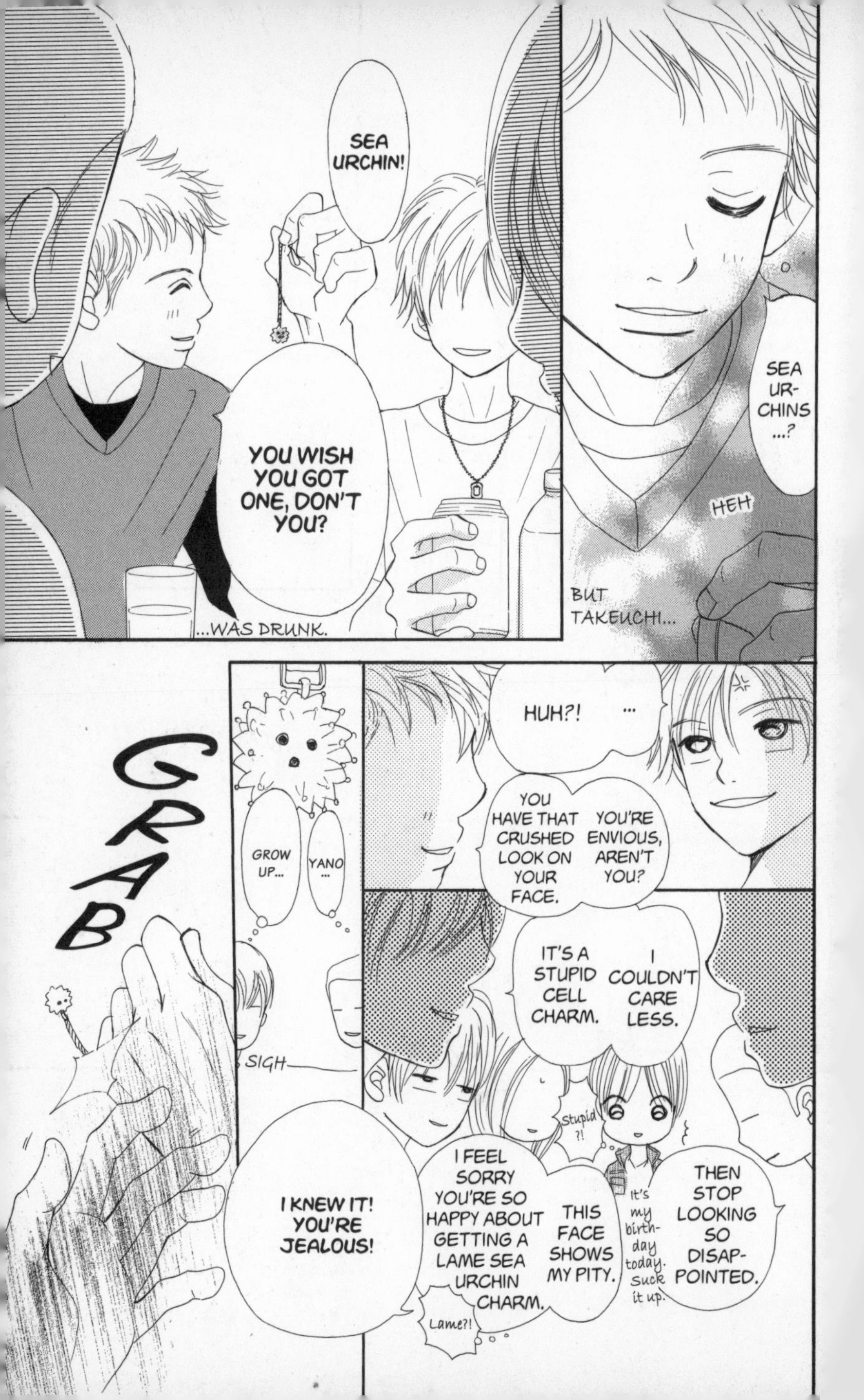
SEA URCHINS ...?
HEH
BUT TAKEUCHI...
SEA URCHIN!
YOU WISH YOU GOT ONE, DON'T YOU?
...WAS DRUNK.
HUH?! ...
YOU'RE ENVIOUS, AREN'T YOU?
YOU HAVE THAT CRUSHED LOOK ON YOUR FACE.
I COULDN'T CARE LESS.
IT'S A STUPID CELL CHARM.
Stupid?!
THEN STOP LOOKING SO DISAPPOINTED.
It's my birthday today. Suck it up.
THIS FACE SHOWS MY PITY.
I FEEL SORRY YOU'RE SO HAPPY ABOUT GETTING A LAME SEA URCHIN CHARM.
Lame?!
I KNEW IT! YOU'RE JEALOUS!
YANO ...
GROW UP...
SIGH
GRAB

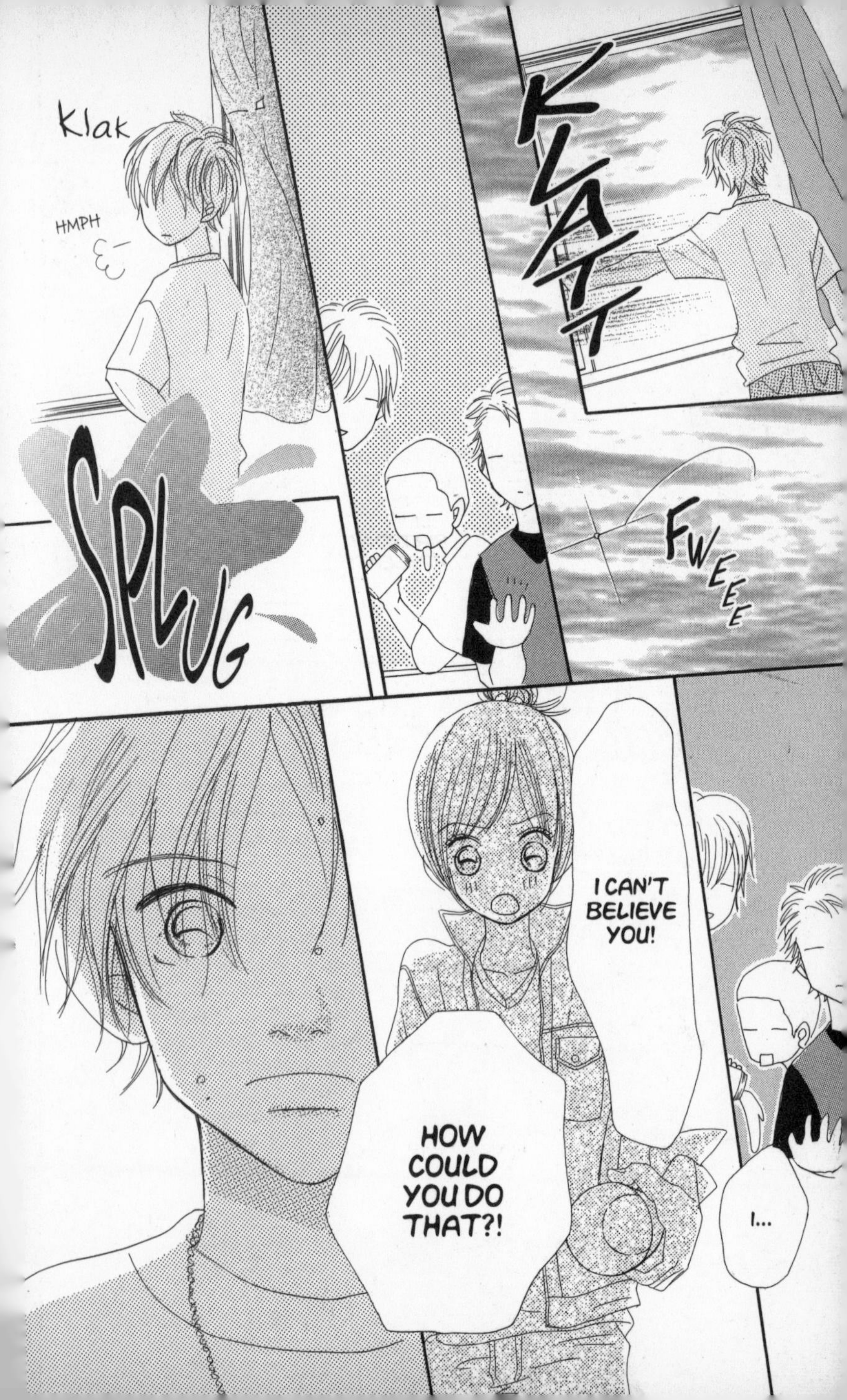
KLATT
FWEEE
Klak
HMPH
SPLUG
I CAN'T BELIEVE YOU!
HOW COULD YOU DO THAT?!
I...

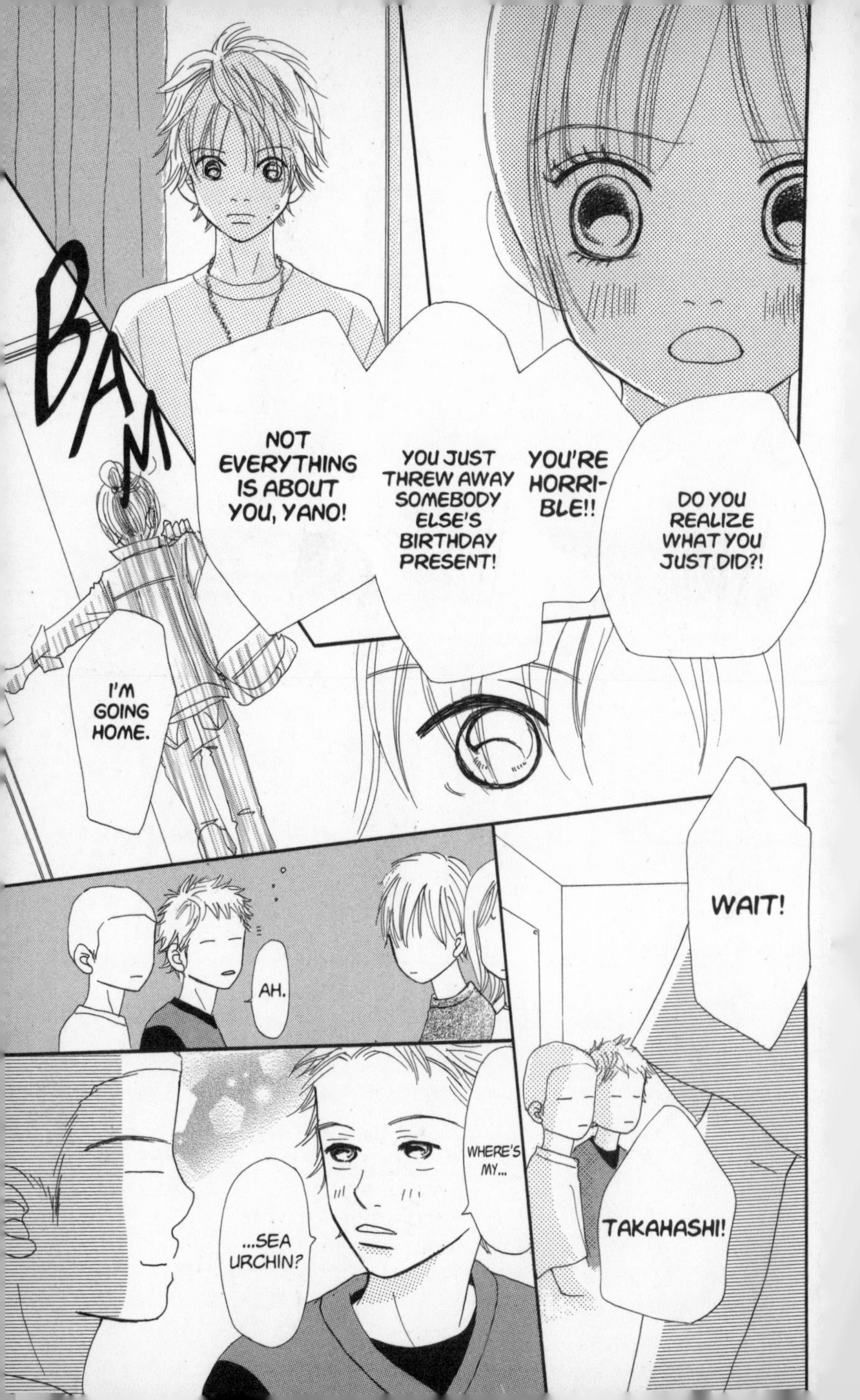
DO YOU REALIZE WHAT YOU JUST DID?!
YOU'RE HORRIBLE!!
YOU JUST THREW AWAY SOMEBODY ELSE'S BIRTHDAY PRESENT!
NOT EVERYTHING IS ABOUT YOU, YANO!
BAM
I'M GOING HOME.
WAIT!
AH.
TAKAHASHI!
WHERE'S MY...
...SEA URCHIN?

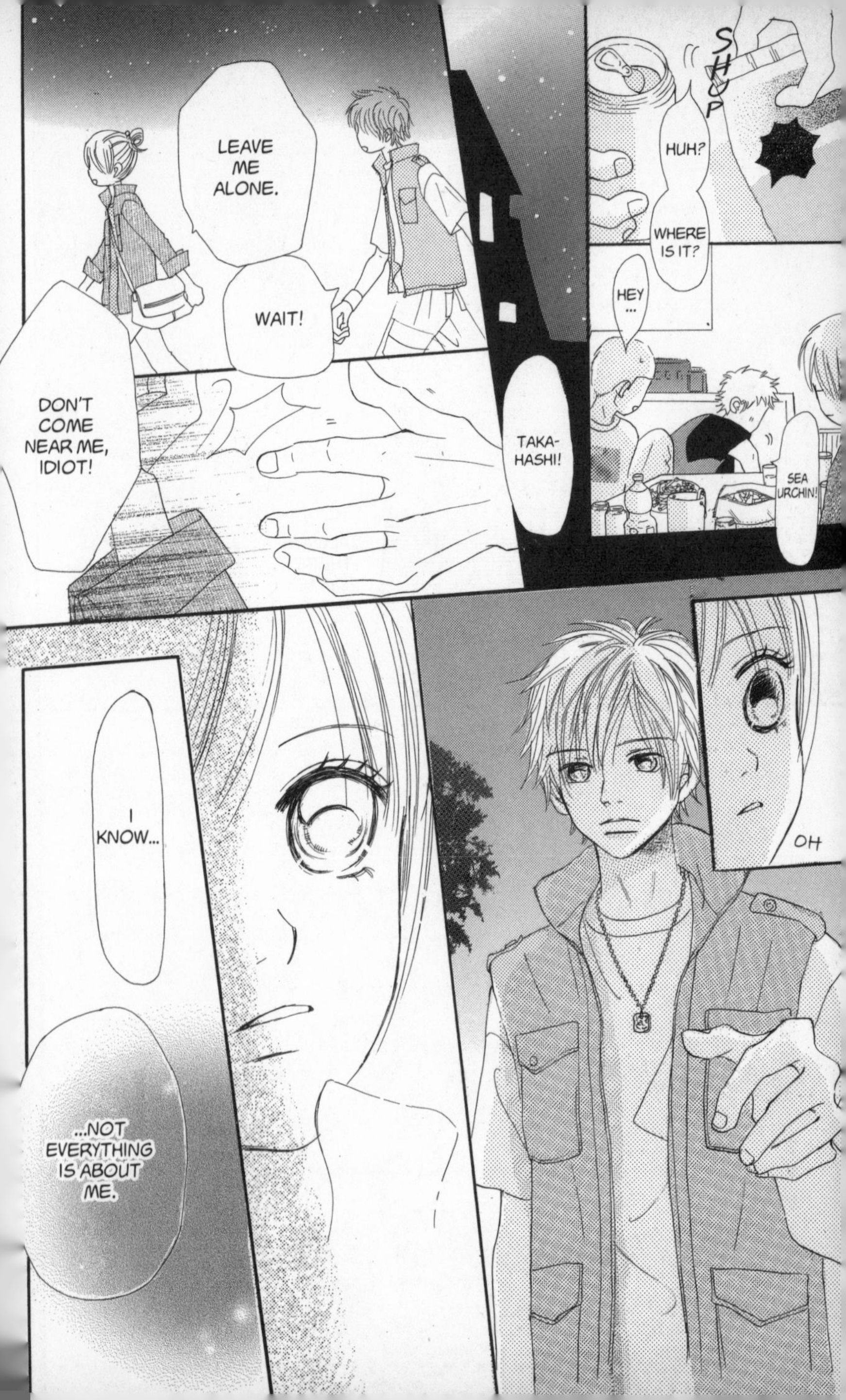
SHUP
HUH?
WHERE IS IT?
HEY ...
SEA URCHIN!
TAKA-HASHI!
LEAVE ME ALONE.
WAIT!
DON'T COME NEAR ME, IDIOT!
OH
I KNOW...
...NOT EVERYTHING IS ABOUT ME.

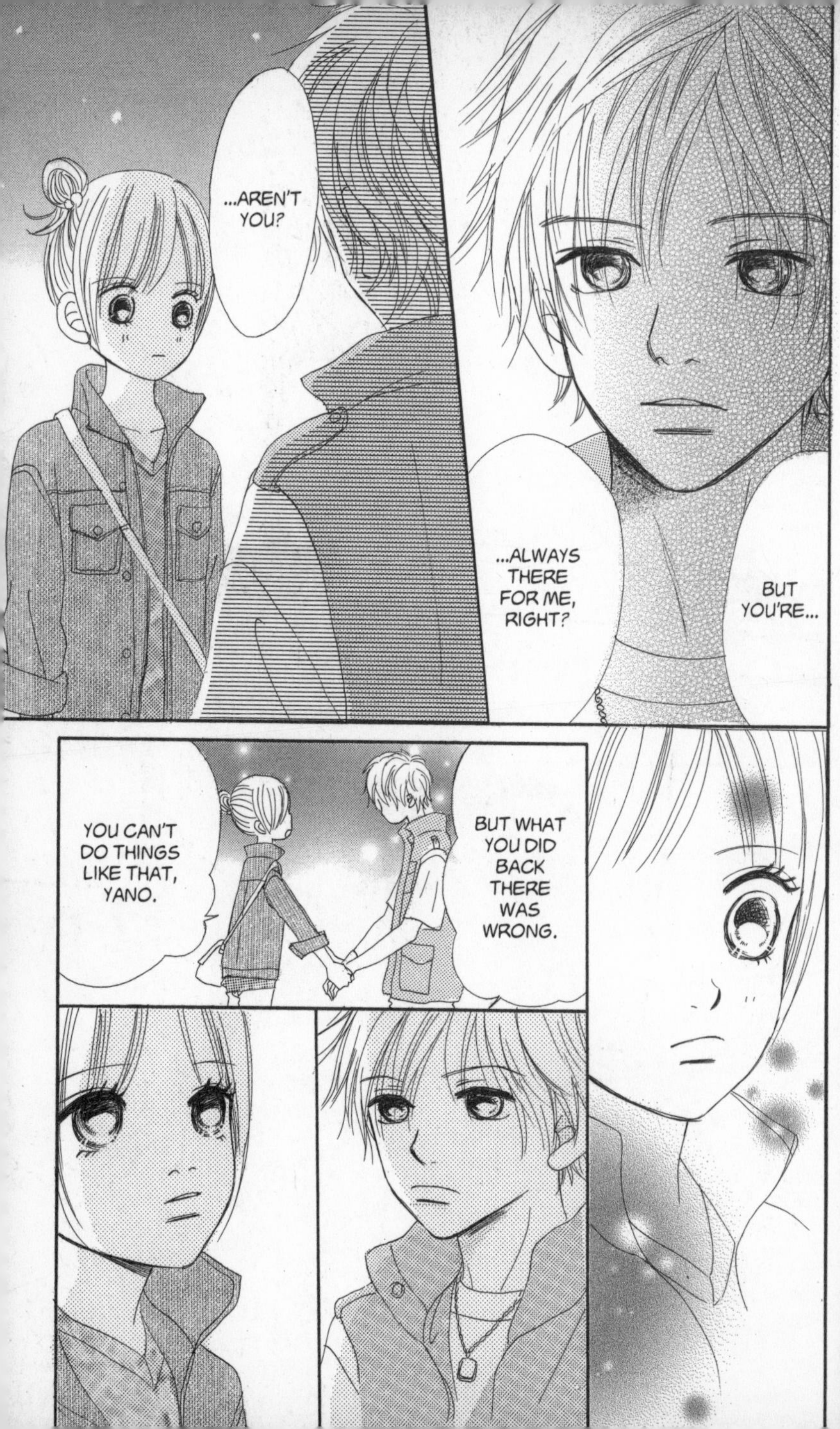
BUT YOU'RE...
...ALWAYS THERE FOR ME, RIGHT?
...AREN'T YOU?
BUT WHAT YOU DID BACK THERE WAS WRONG.
YOU CAN'T DO THINGS LIKE THAT, YANO.

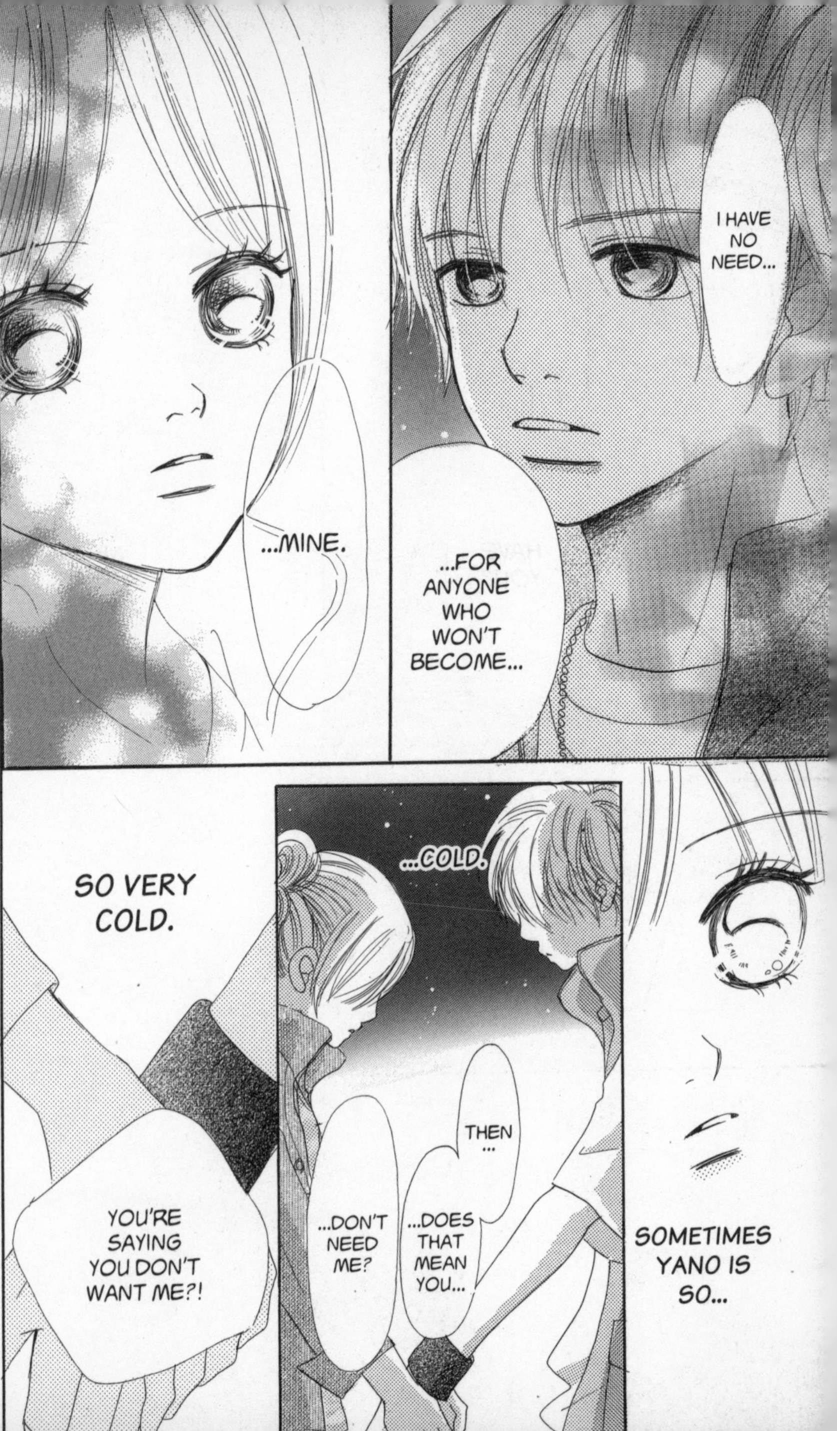
I HAVE NO NEED...
...FOR ANYONE WHO WON'T BECOME...
...MINE.
SOMETIMES YANO IS SO...
...COLD.
THEN...
...DOES THAT MEAN YOU...
...DON'T NEED ME?
SO VERY COLD.
YOU'RE SAYING YOU DON'T WANT ME?!

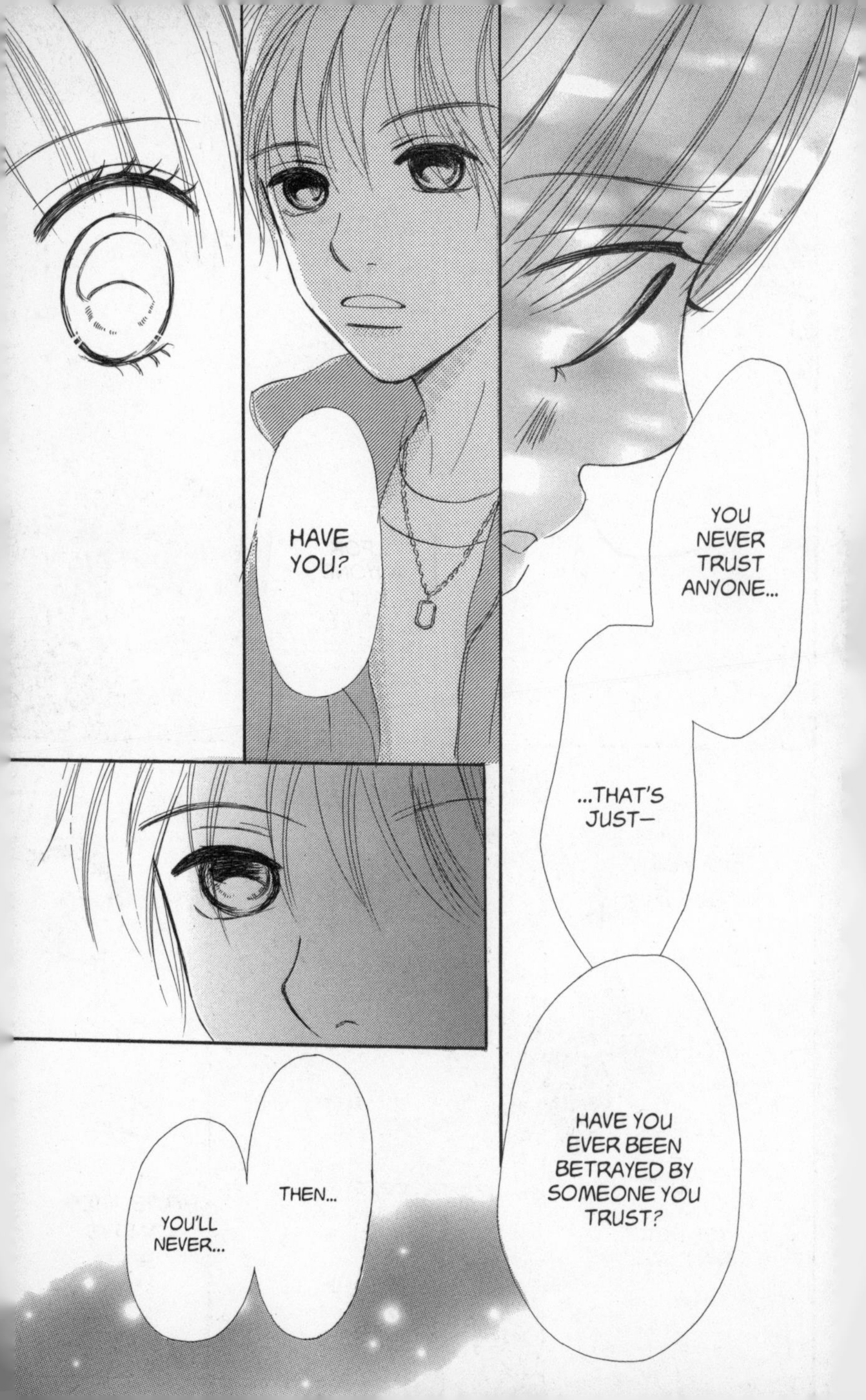

YOU NEVER TRUST ANYONE...
...THAT'S JUST—
HAVE YOU EVER BEEN BETRAYED BY SOMEONE YOU TRUST?
HAVE YOU?
THEN...
YOU'LL NEVER...

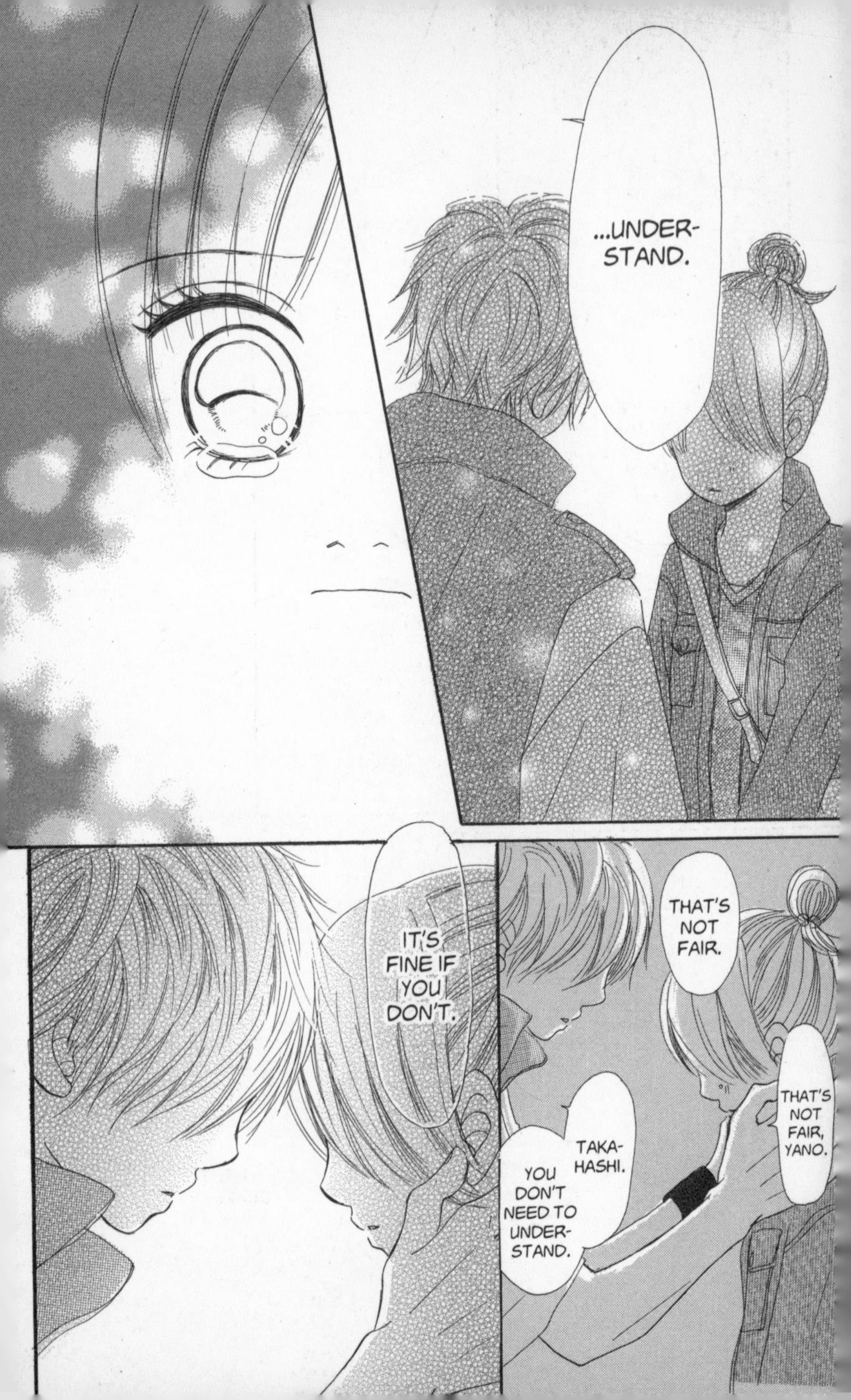
...UNDER-
STAND.
THAT'S NOT FAIR.
THAT'S NOT FAIR, YANO.
TAKA-
HASHI.
YOU DON'T NEED TO UNDER-
STAND.
IT'S FINE IF YOU DON'T.

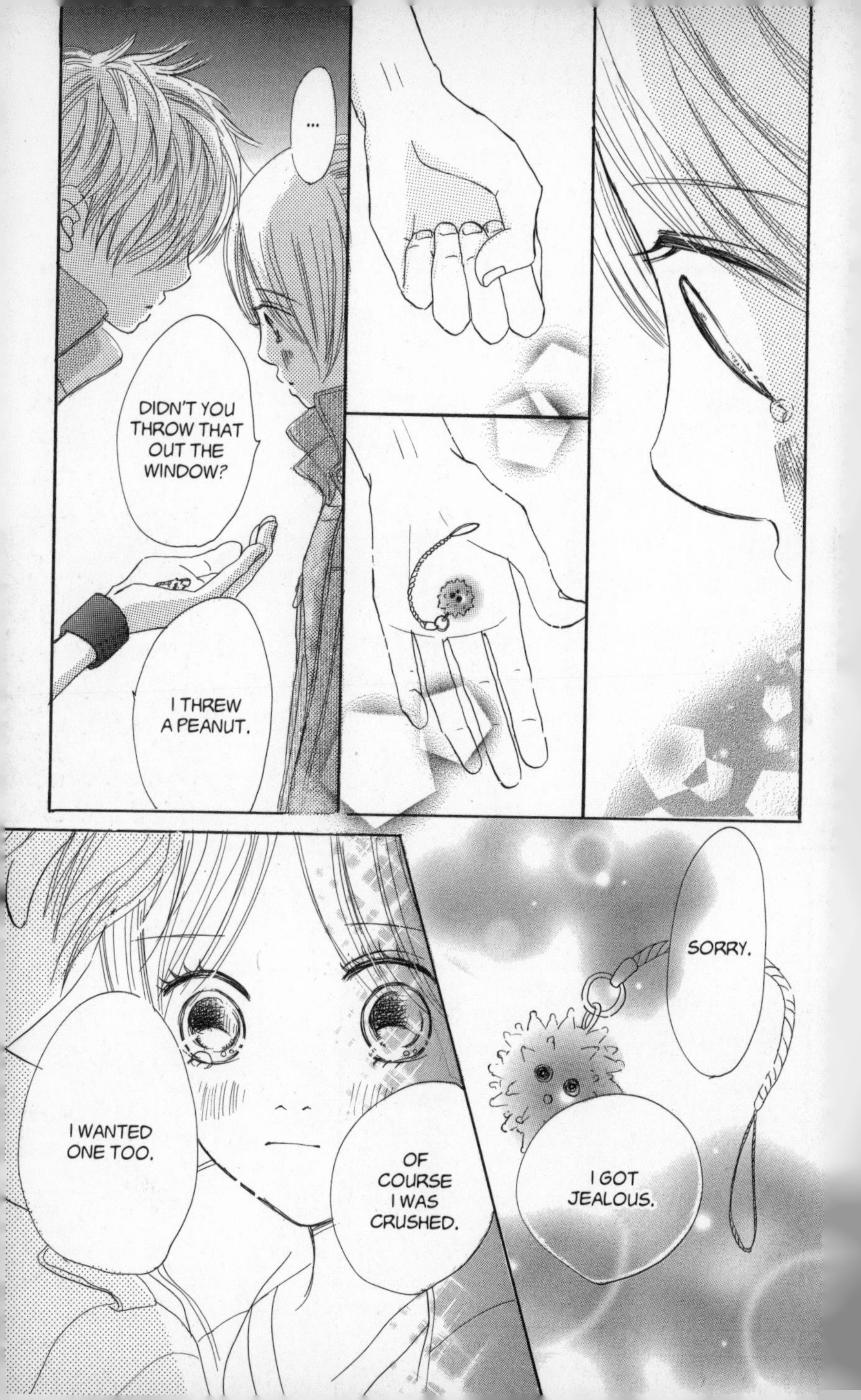
...
DIDN'T YOU THROW THAT OUT THE WINDOW?
I THREW A PEANUT.
SORRY.
I GOT JEALOUS.
OF COURSE I WAS CRUSHED.
I WANTED ONE TOO.

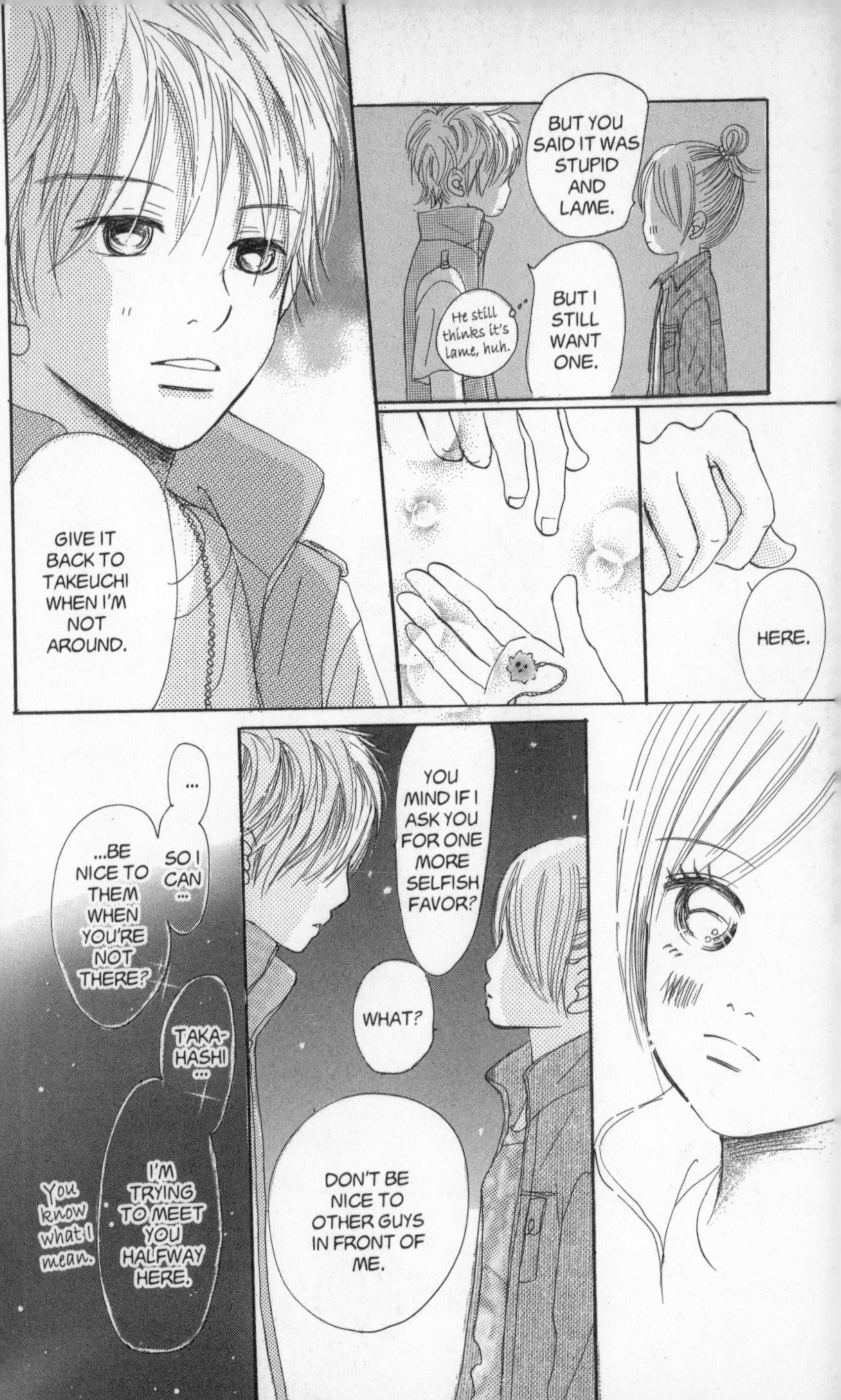
BUT YOU SAID IT WAS STUPID AND LAME.
BUT I STILL WANT ONE.
He still thinks it's lame, huh.
HERE.
GIVE IT BACK TO TAKEUCHI WHEN I'M NOT AROUND.
YOU MIND IF I ASK YOU FOR ONE MORE SELFISH FAVOR?
WHAT?
DON'T BE NICE TO OTHER GUYS IN FRONT OF ME.
...
SO I CAN...
...BE NICE TO THEM WHEN YOU'RE NOT THERE?
TAKA-HASHI...
I'M TRYING TO MEET YOU HALFWAY HERE.
You know what I mean.

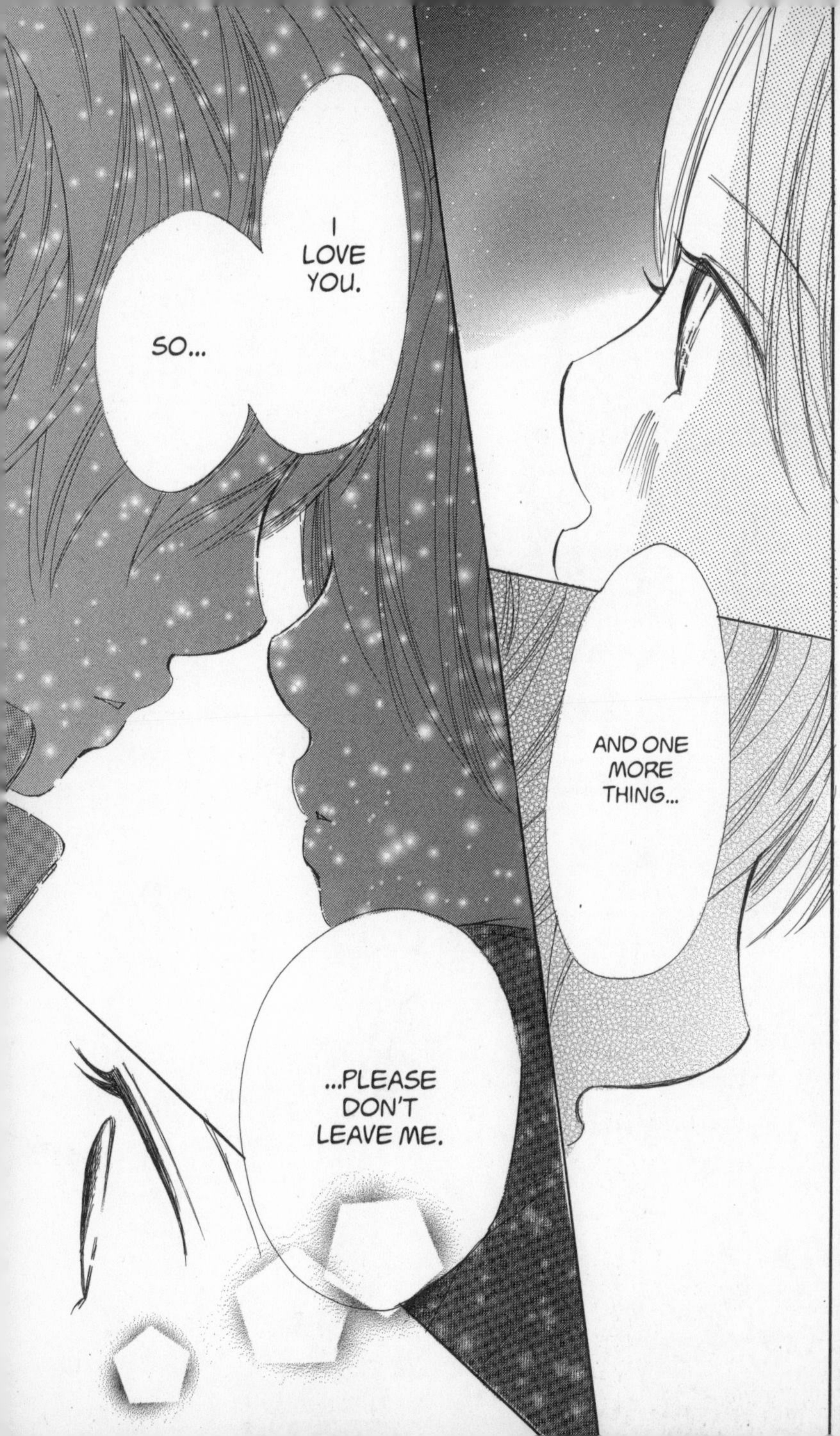
AND ONE MORE THING...
I LOVE YOU.
SO...
...PLEASE DON'T LEAVE ME.

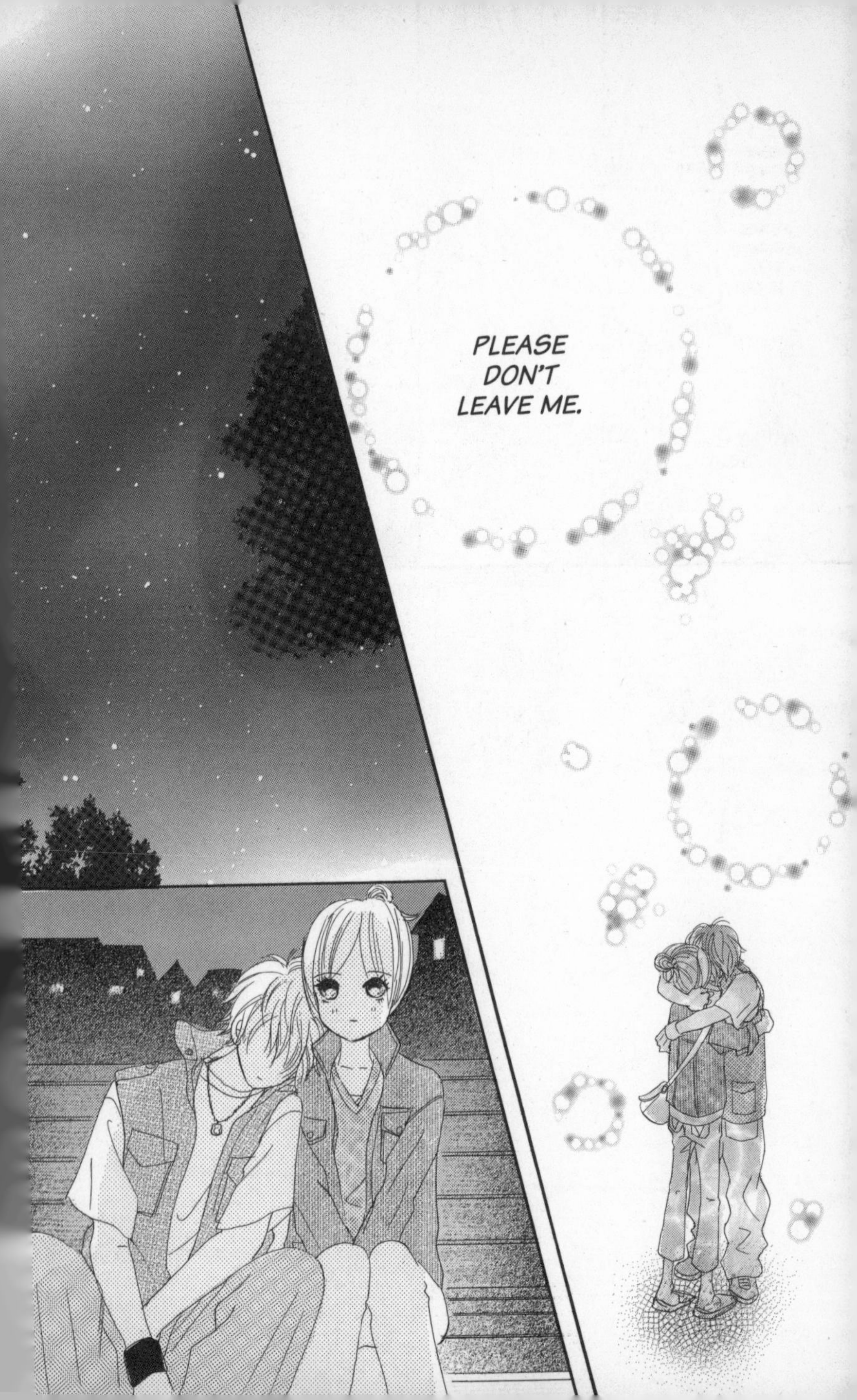
PLEASE DON'T LEAVE ME.

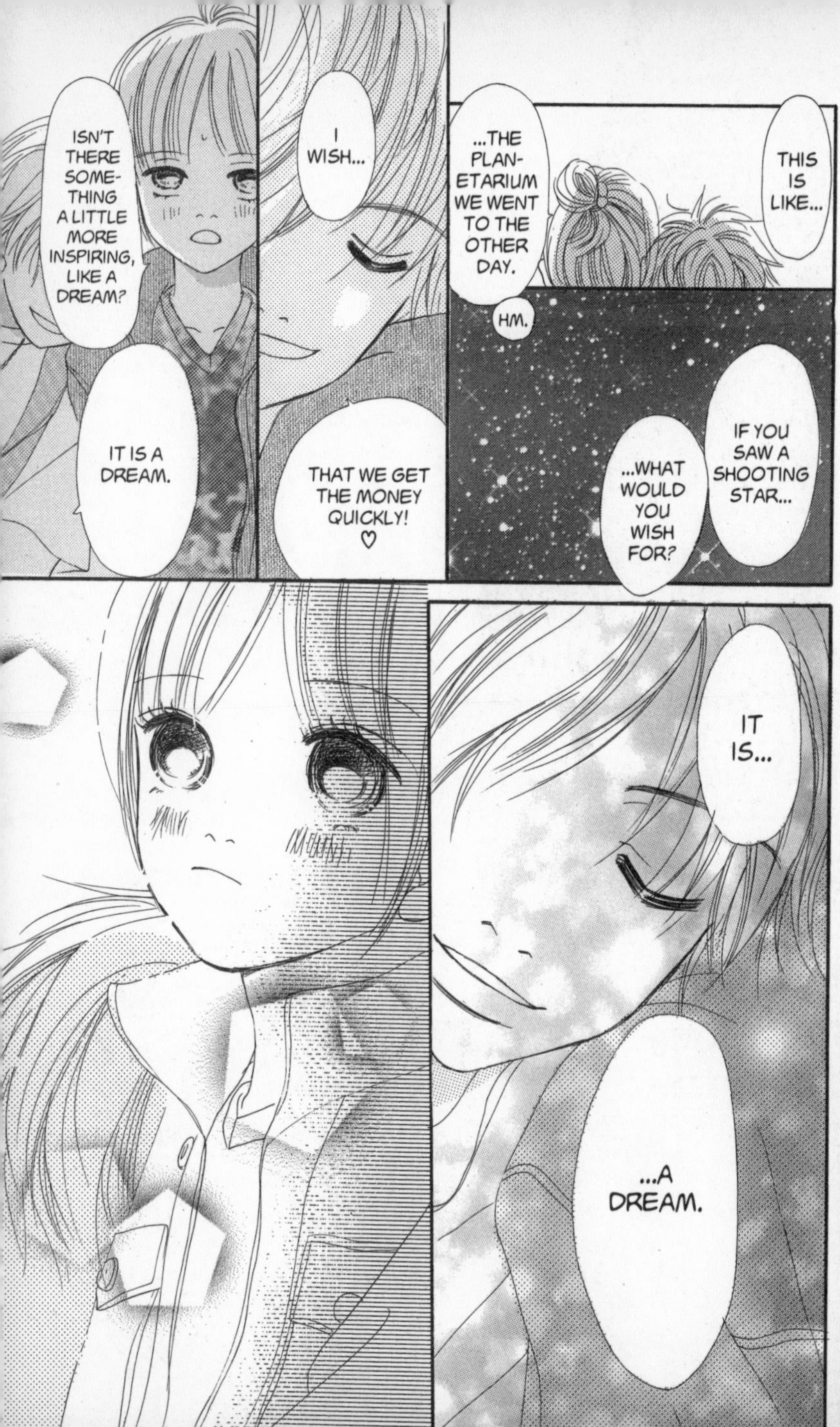
THIS IS LIKE...
...THE PLANETARIUM WE WENT TO THE OTHER DAY.
HM.
IF YOU SAW A SHOOTING STAR...
...WHAT WOULD YOU WISH FOR?
I WISH...
THAT WE GET THE MONEY QUICKLY! ♡
ISN'T THERE SOMETHING A LITTLE MORE INSPIRING, LIKE A DREAM?
IT IS A DREAM.
IT IS...
...A DREAM.

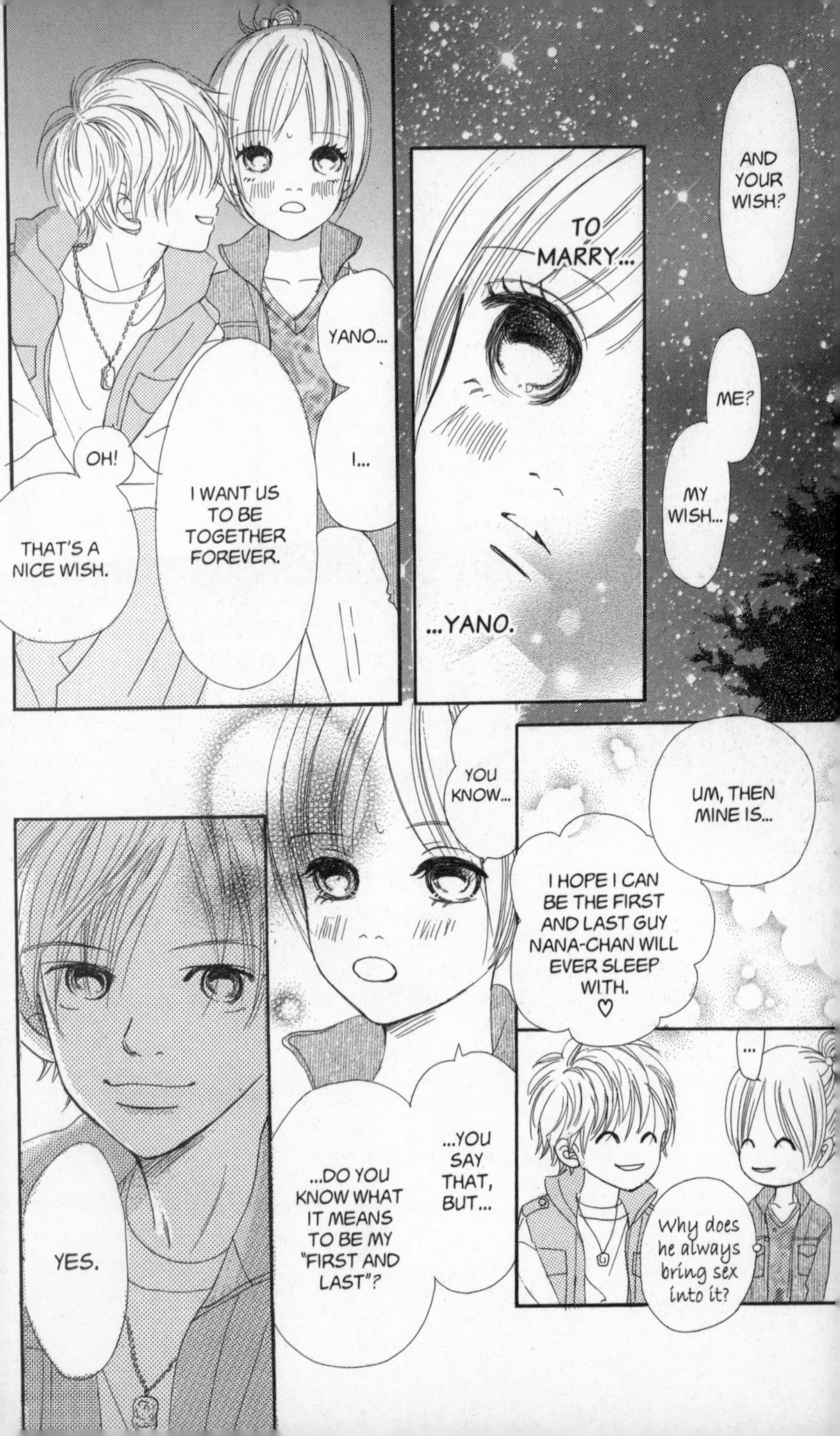
AND YOUR WISH?
ME?
MY WISH...
TO MARRY...
...YANO.
YANO...
I...
I WANT US TO BE TOGETHER FOREVER.
OH!
THAT'S A NICE WISH.
UM, THEN MINE IS...
I HOPE I CAN BE THE FIRST AND LAST GUY NANA-CHAN WILL EVER SLEEP WITH. ♡
...
Why does he always bring sex into it?
YOU KNOW...
...YOU SAY THAT, BUT...
...DO YOU KNOW WHAT IT MEANS TO BE MY "FIRST AND LAST"?
YES.

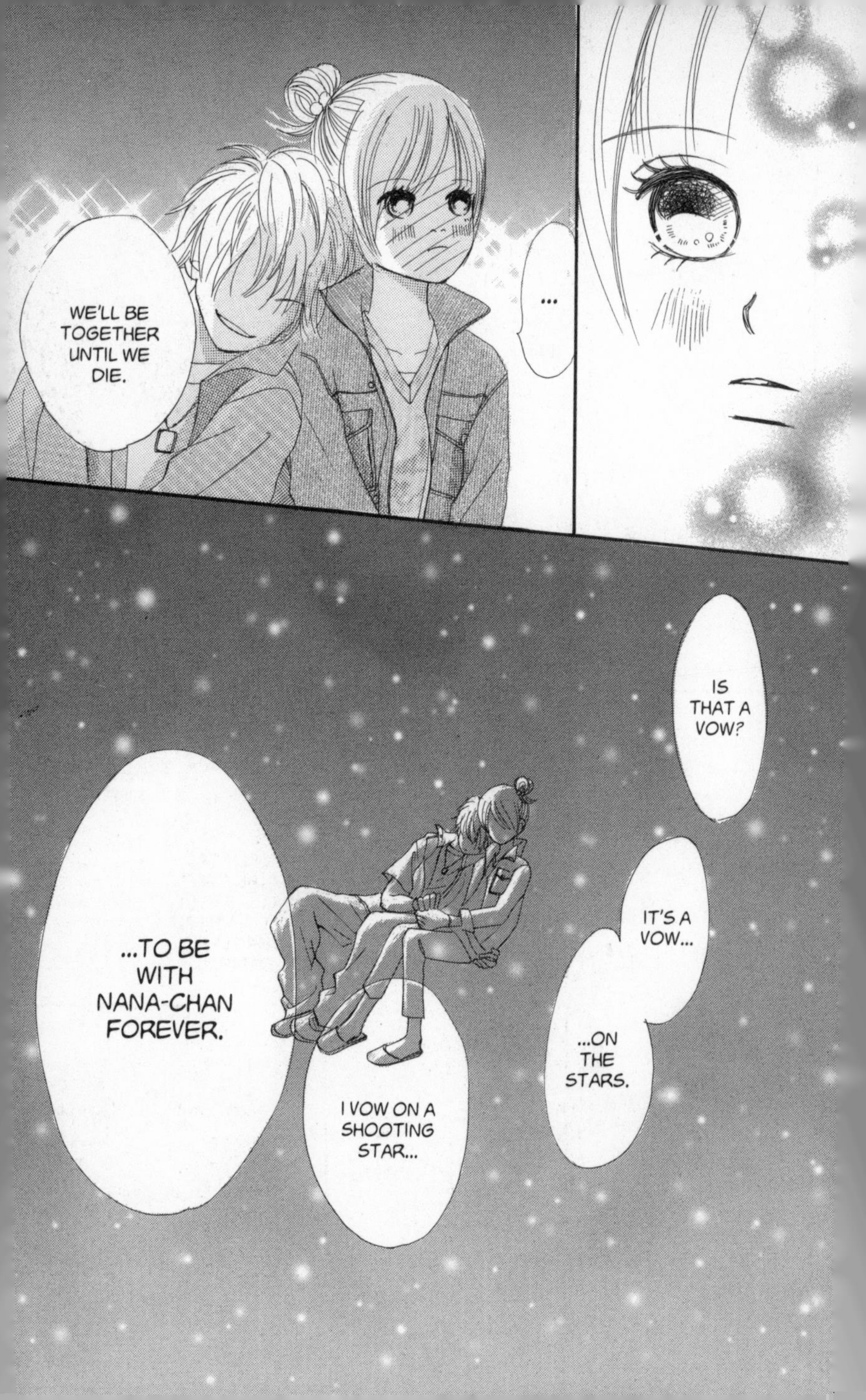
...
WE'LL BE TOGETHER UNTIL WE DIE.
IS THAT A VOW?
IT'S A VOW...
...ON THE STARS.
I VOW ON A SHOOTING STAR...
...TO BE WITH NANA-CHAN FOREVER.

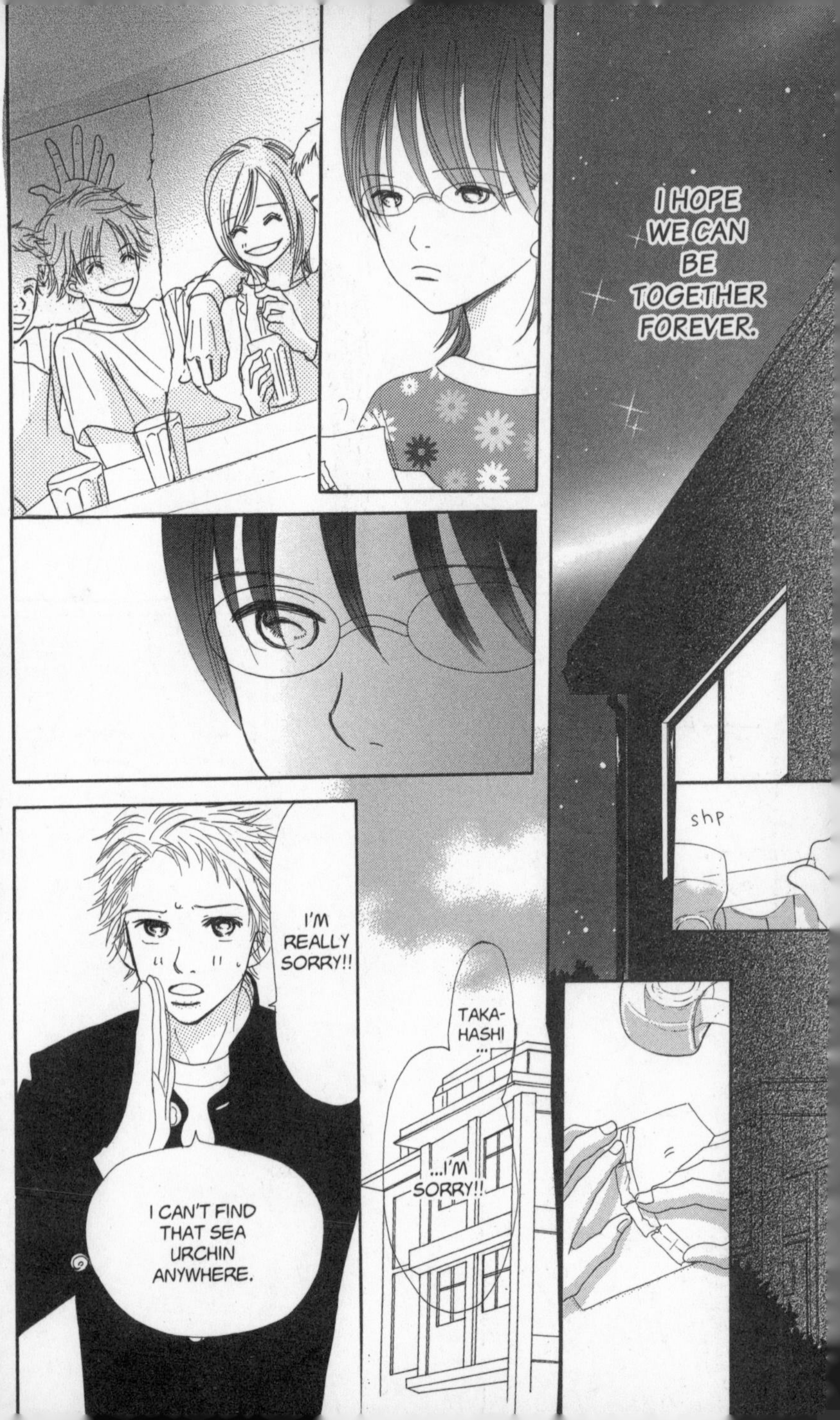
I HOPE WE CAN BE TOGETHER FOREVER.
shp
TAKA-HASHI...
...I'M SORRY!!
I'M REALLY SORRY!!
I CAN'T FIND THAT SEA URCHIN ANYWHERE.

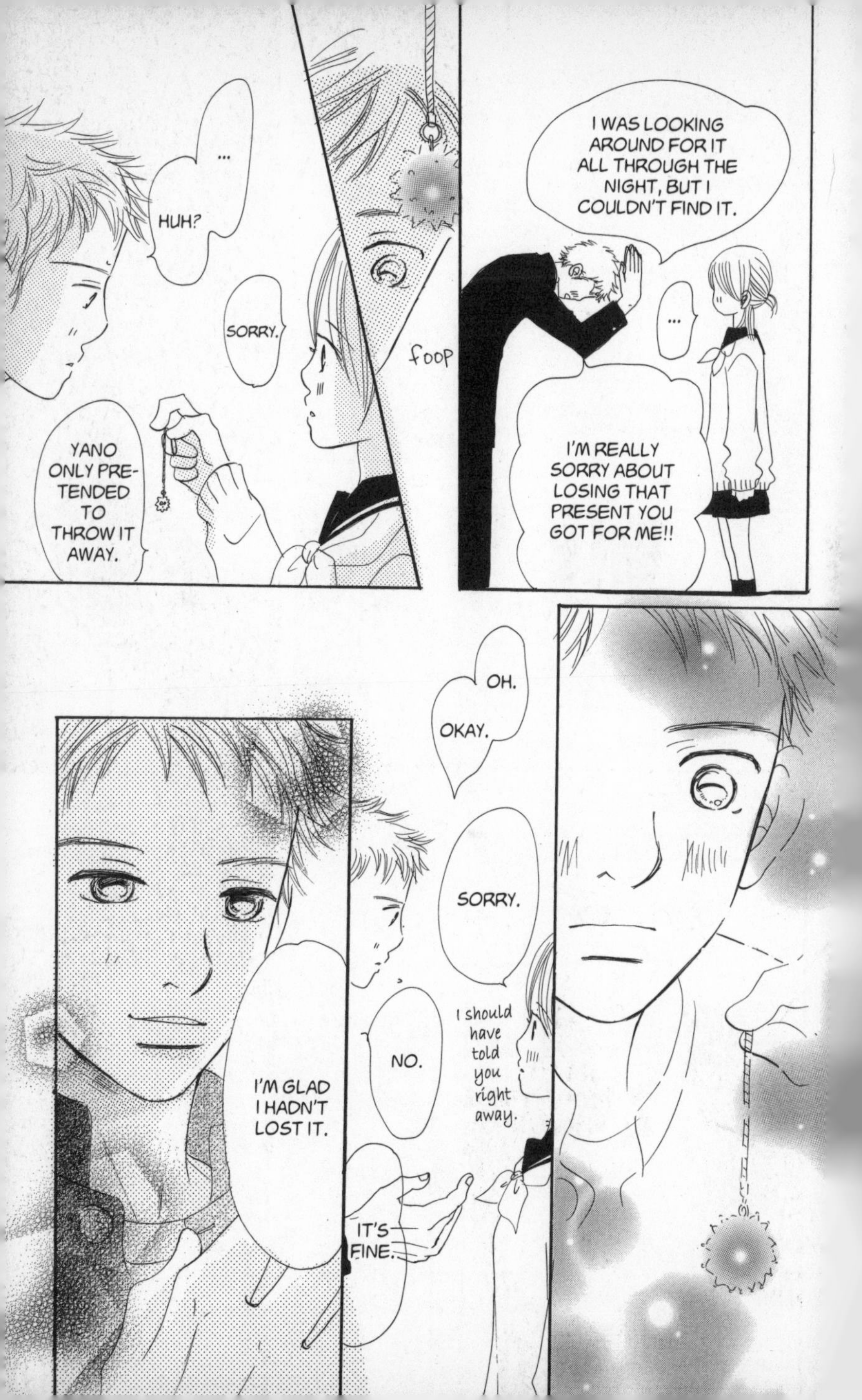
I WAS LOOKING AROUND FOR IT ALL THROUGH THE NIGHT, BUT I COULDN'T FIND IT.
...
I'M REALLY SORRY ABOUT LOSING THAT PRESENT YOU GOT FOR ME!!
foop
...
HUH?
SORRY.
YANO ONLY PRE-TENDED TO THROW IT AWAY.
OH.
OKAY.
SORRY.
I should have told you right away.
NO.
IT'S FINE.
I'M GLAD I HADN'T LOST IT.

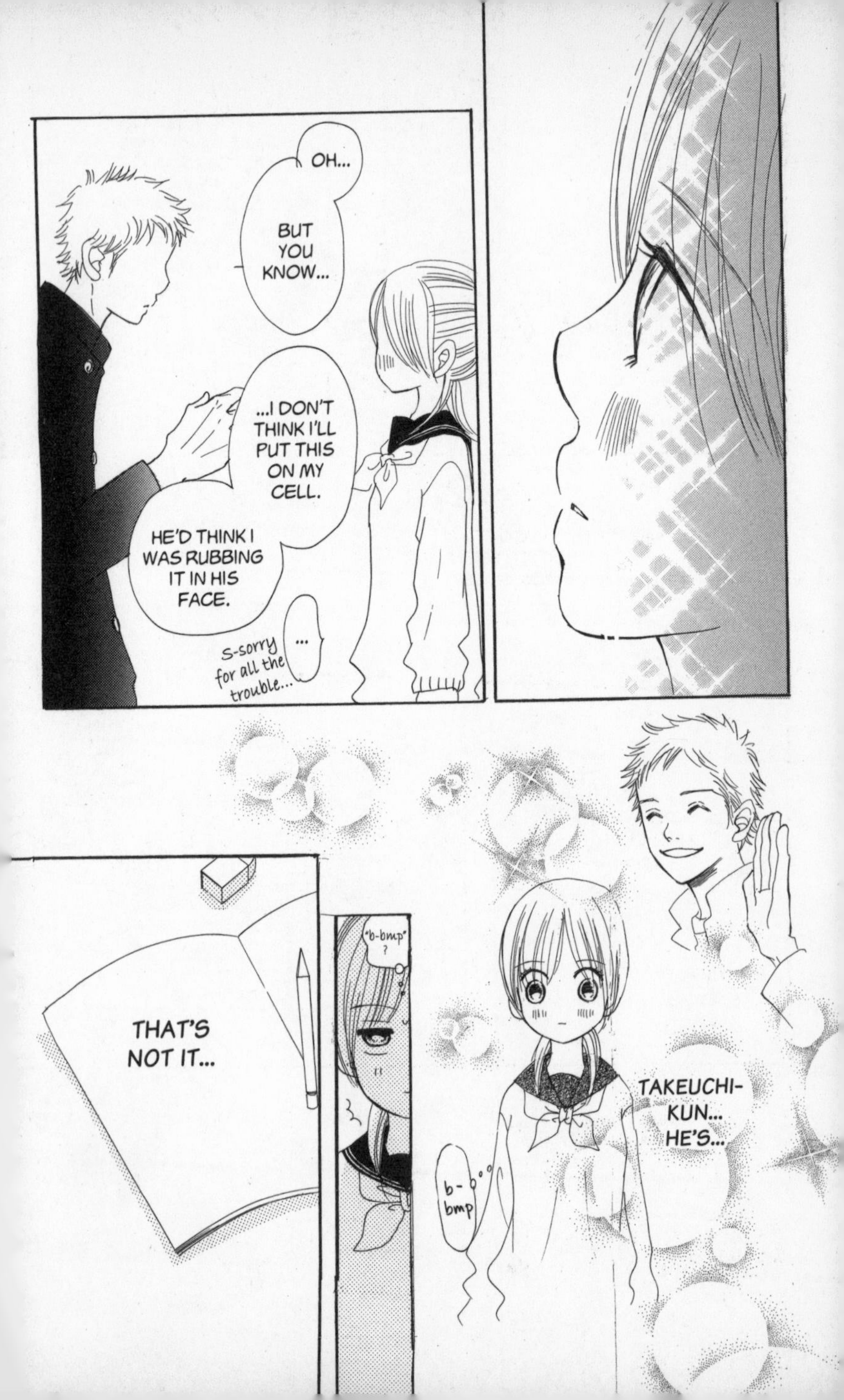
OH...
BUT YOU KNOW...
...I DON'T THINK I'LL PUT THIS ON MY CELL.
HE'D THINK I WAS RUBBING IT IN HIS FACE.
...
S-sorry for all the trouble...
TAKEUCHI-KUN... HE'S...
b-bmp
"b-bmp"?
THAT'S NOT IT...

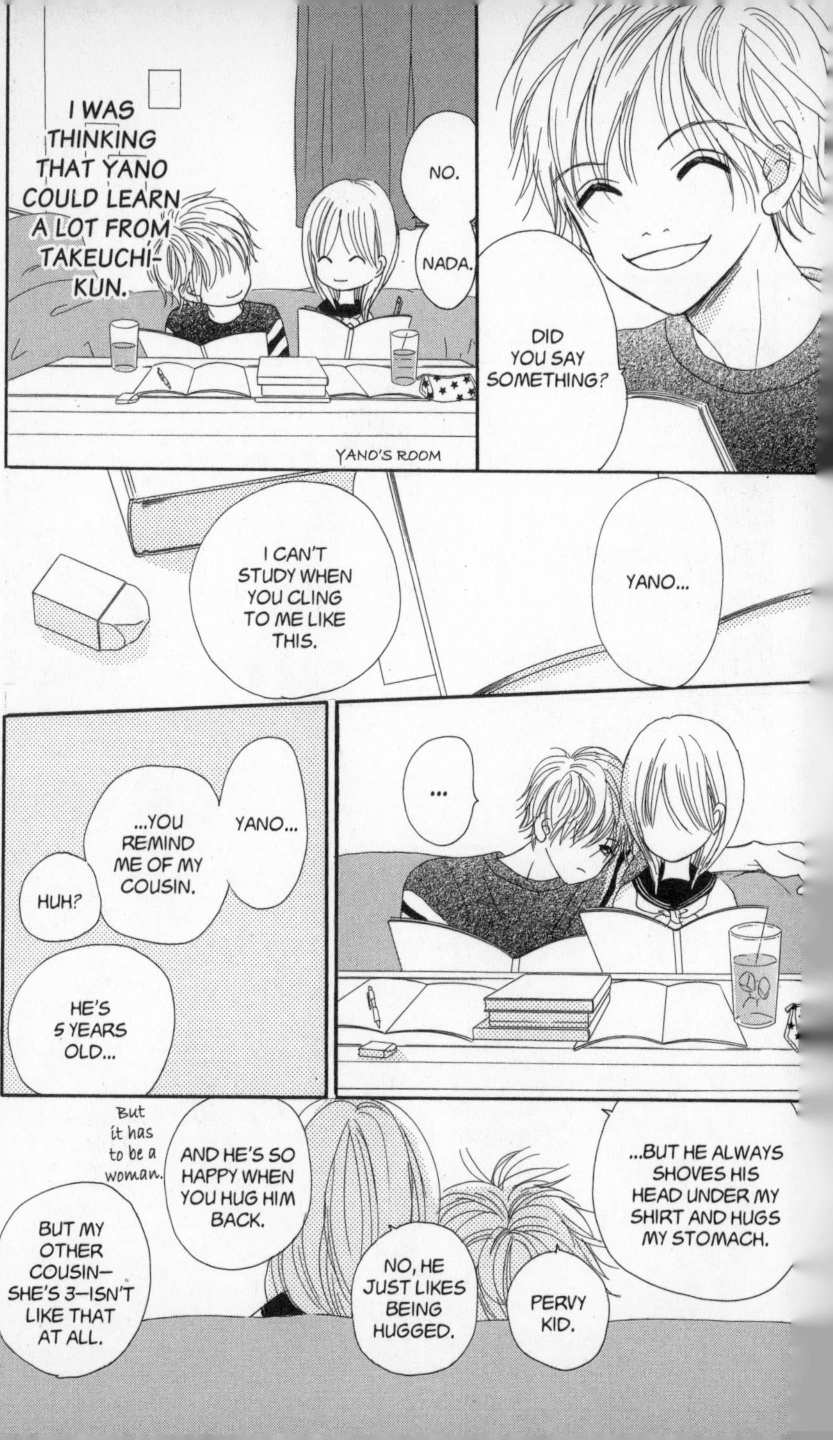
DID YOU SAY SOMETHING?
NO.
NADA.
I WAS THINKING THAT YANO COULD LEARN A LOT FROM TAKEUCHI-KUN.
YANO'S ROOM
YANO...
I CAN'T STUDY WHEN YOU CLING TO ME LIKE THIS.
...
YANO...
...YOU REMIND ME OF MY COUSIN.
HUH?
HE'S 5 YEARS OLD...
...BUT HE ALWAYS SHOVES HIS HEAD UNDER MY SHIRT AND HUGS MY STOMACH.
PERVY KID.
NO, HE JUST LIKES BEING HUGGED.
AND HE'S SO HAPPY WHEN YOU HUG HIM BACK.
But it has to be a woman.
BUT MY OTHER COUSIN—SHE'S 3—ISN'T LIKE THAT AT ALL.

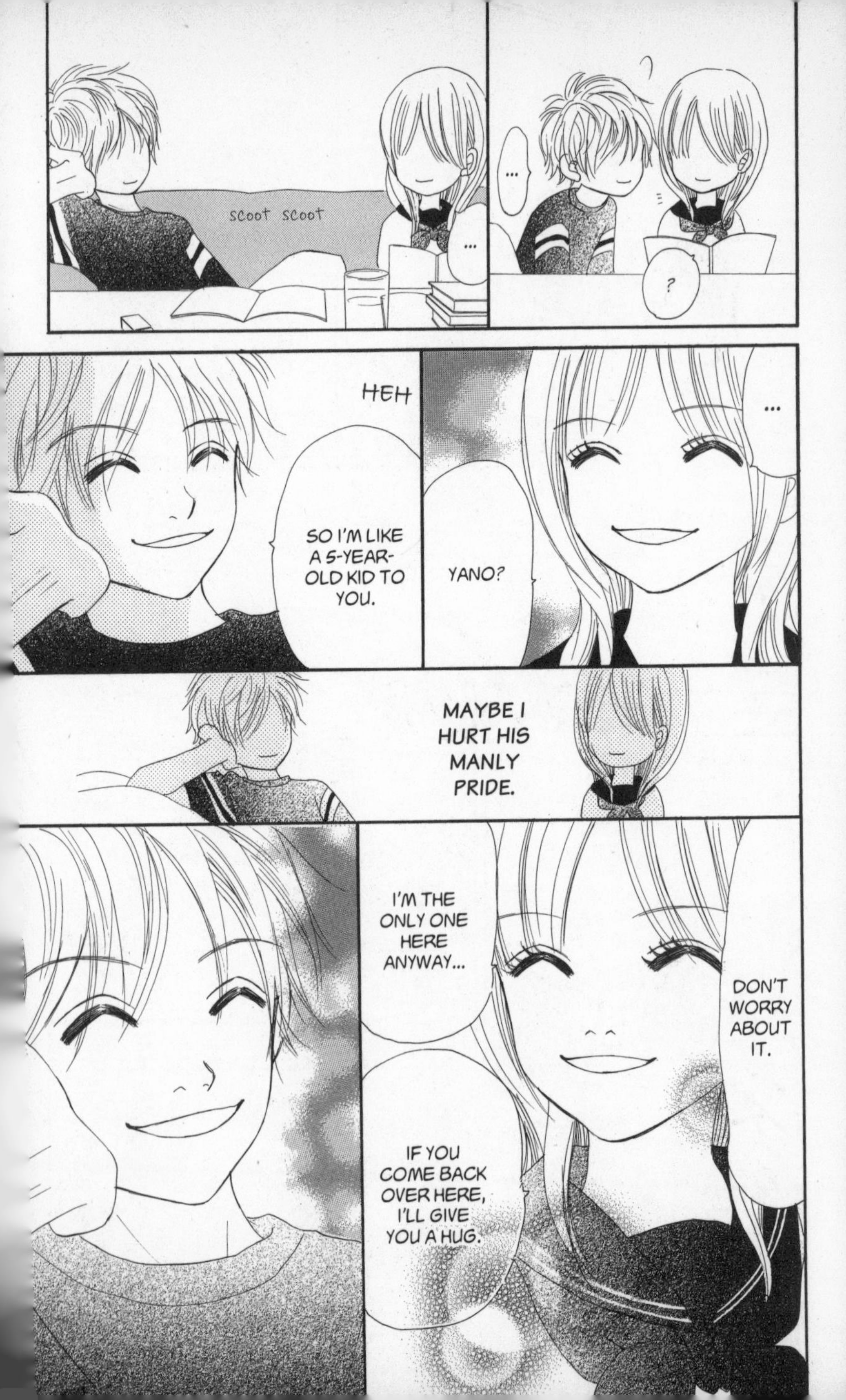
...
?
scoot scoot
...
...
YANO?
HEH
SO I'M LIKE A 5-YEAR-OLD KID TO YOU.
MAYBE I HURT HIS MANLY PRIDE.
DON'T WORRY ABOUT IT.
I'M THE ONLY ONE HERE ANYWAY...
IF YOU COME BACK OVER HERE, I'LL GIVE YOU A HUG.

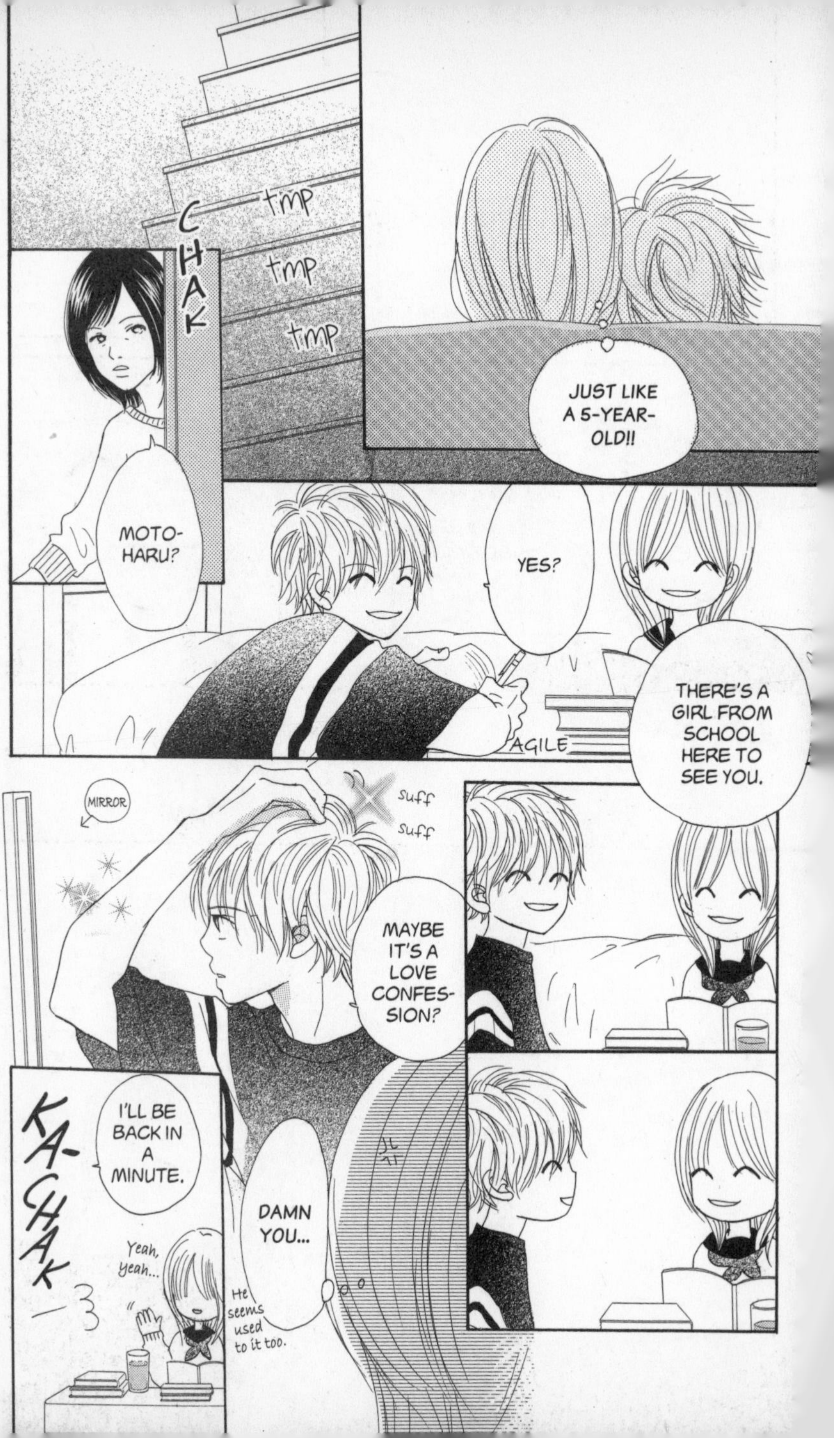
JUST LIKE A 5-YEAR-OLD!!
tmp
tmp
tmp
CHAK
MOTO-HARU?
YES?
AGILE
THERE'S A GIRL FROM SCHOOL HERE TO SEE YOU.
MAYBE IT'S A LOVE CONFES-SION?
suff
suff
MIRROR
DAMN YOU...
He seems used to it too.
I'LL BE BACK IN A MINUTE.
KA-CHAK
Yeah, yeah...

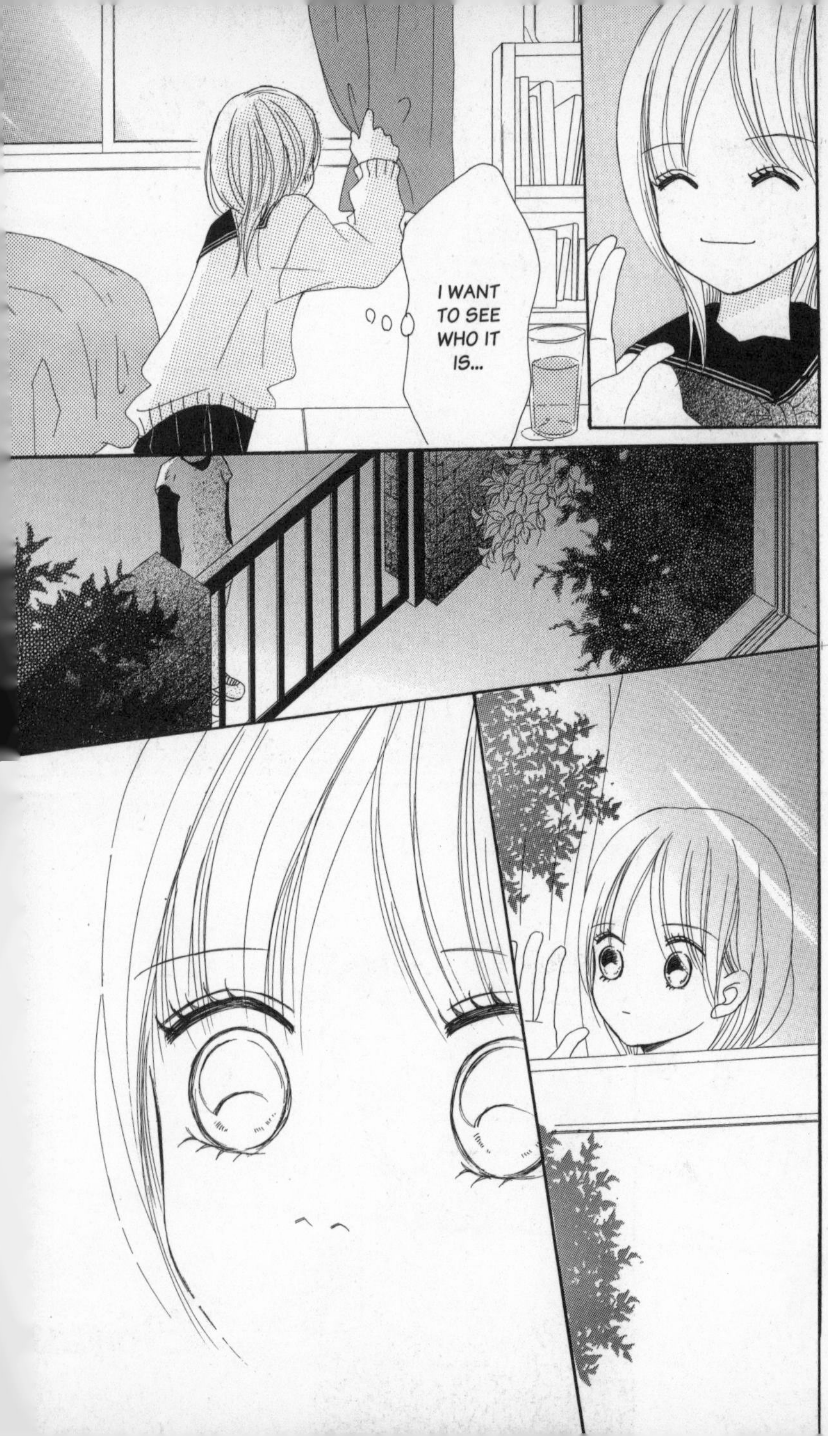
I WANT TO SEE WHO IT IS...

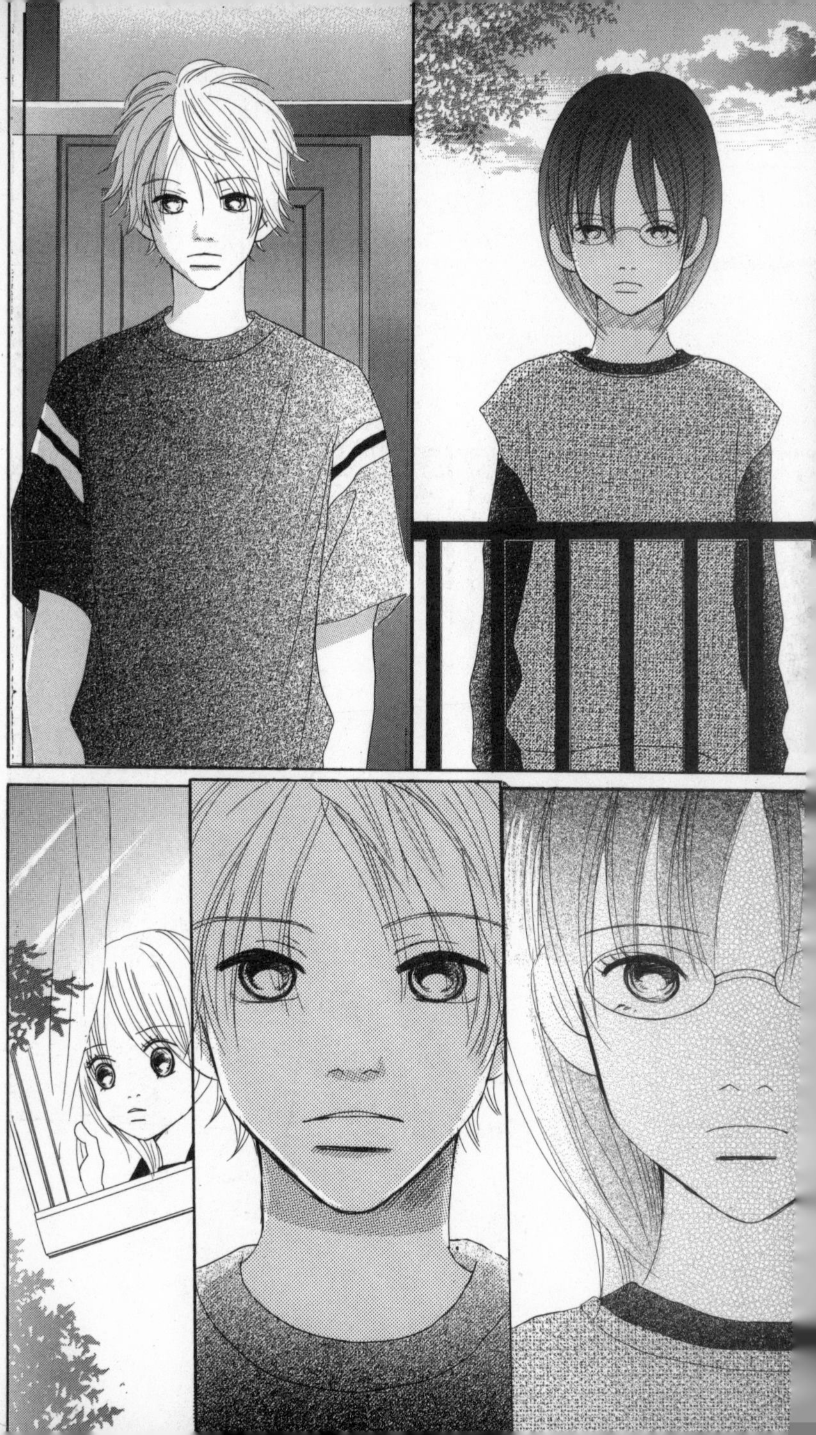

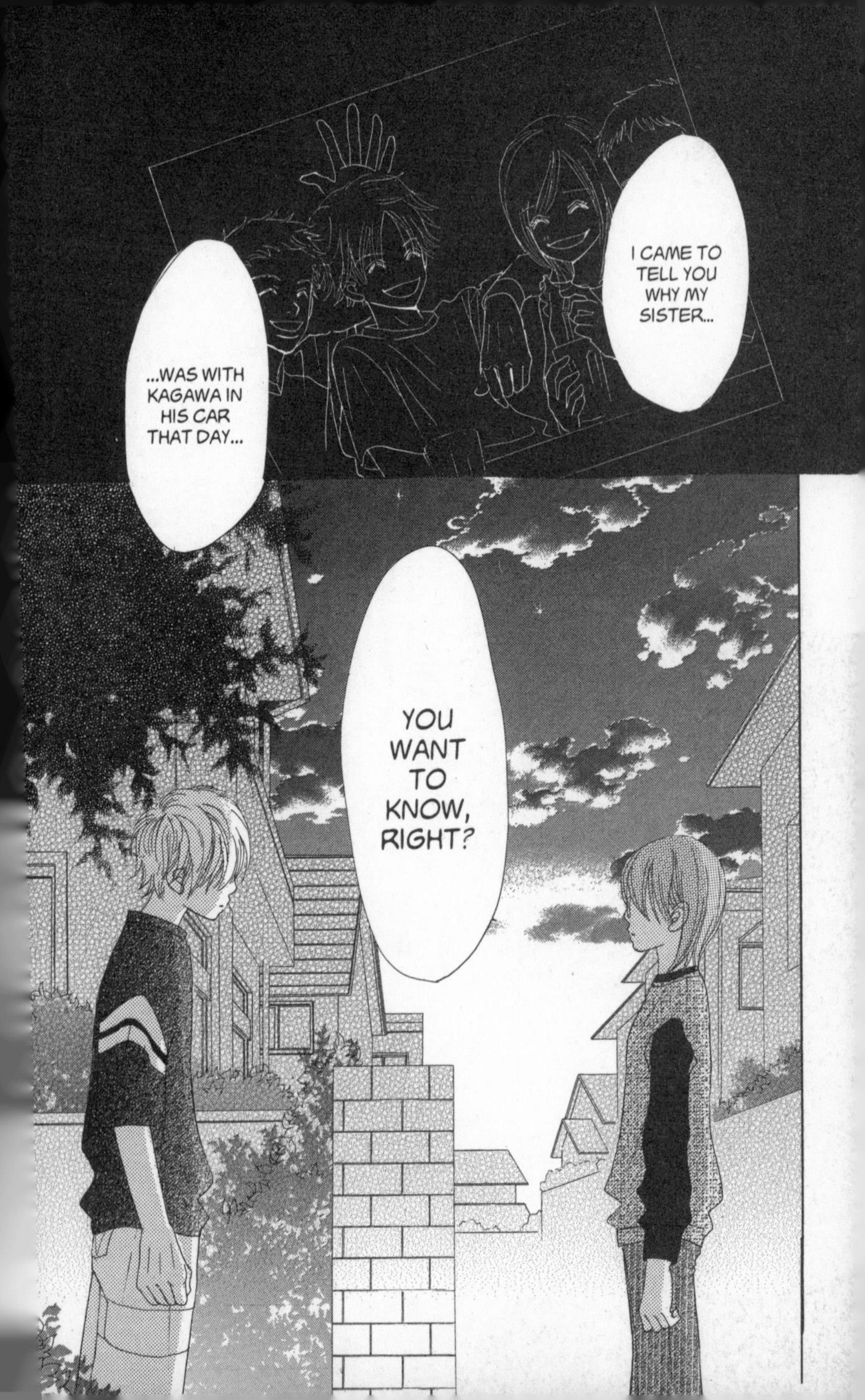
I CAME TO TELL YOU WHY MY SISTER...
...WAS WITH KAGAWA IN HIS CAR THAT DAY...
YOU WANT TO KNOW, RIGHT?

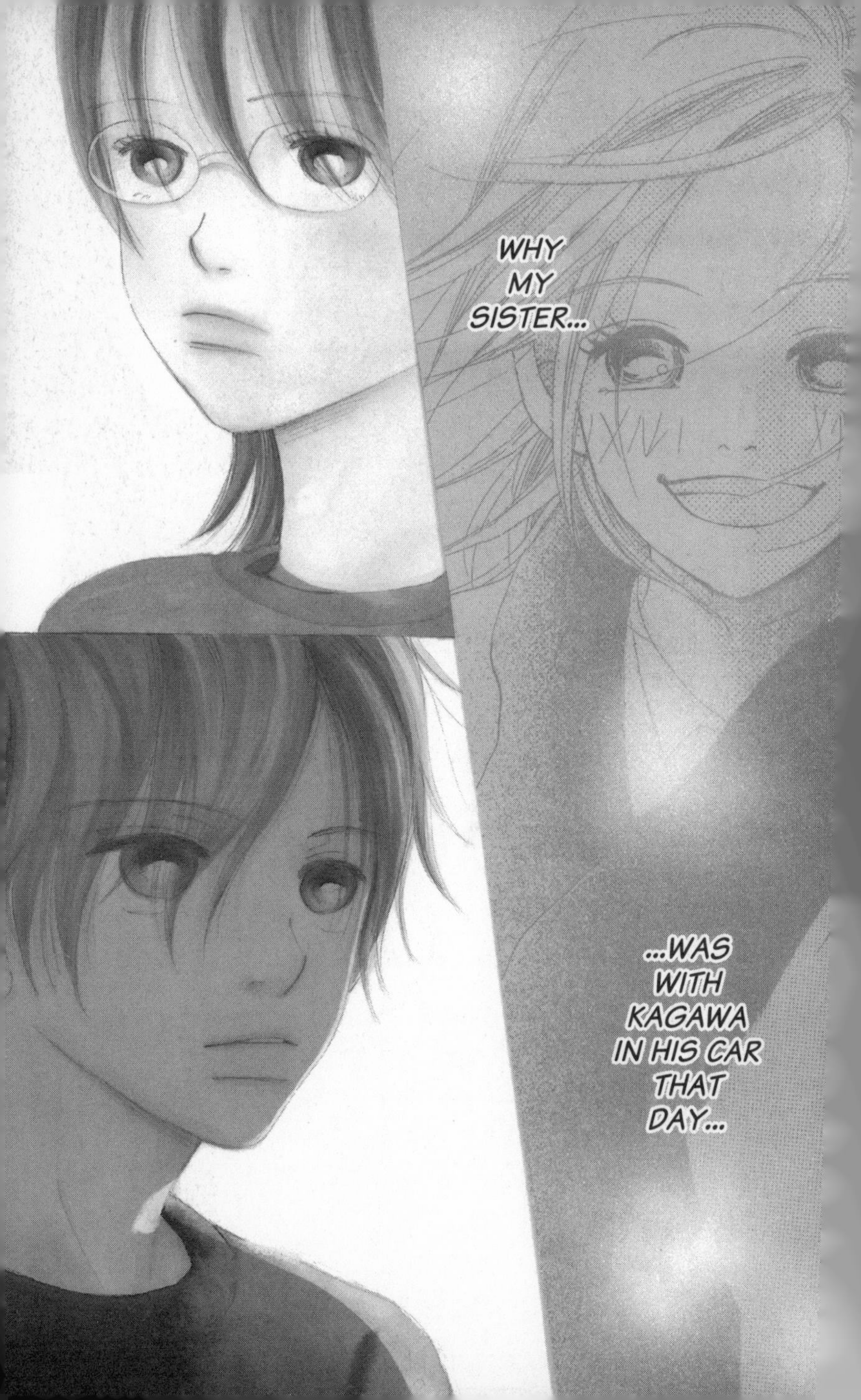
WHY MY SISTER...
...WAS WITH KAGAWA IN HIS CAR THAT DAY...

Chapter 15

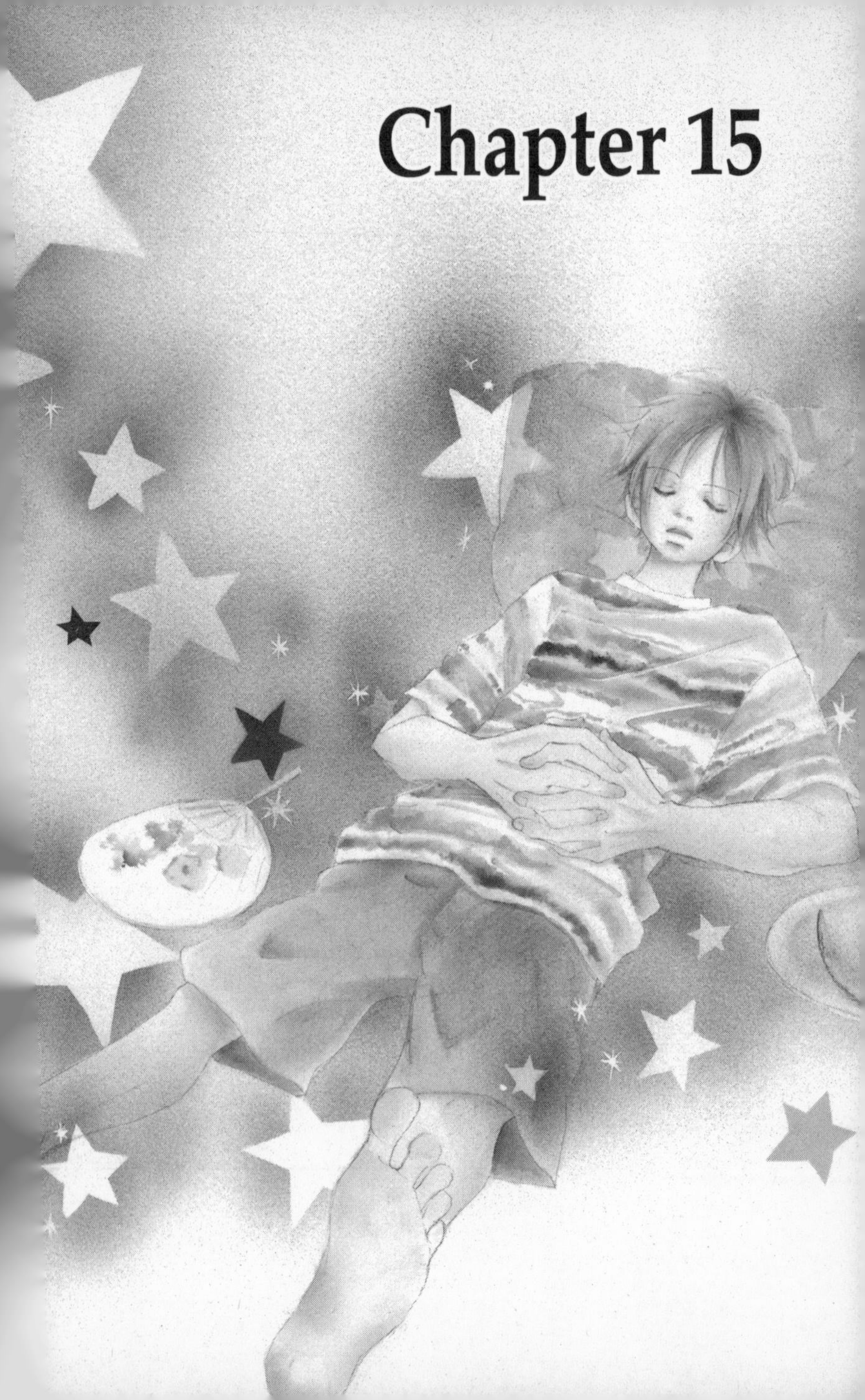

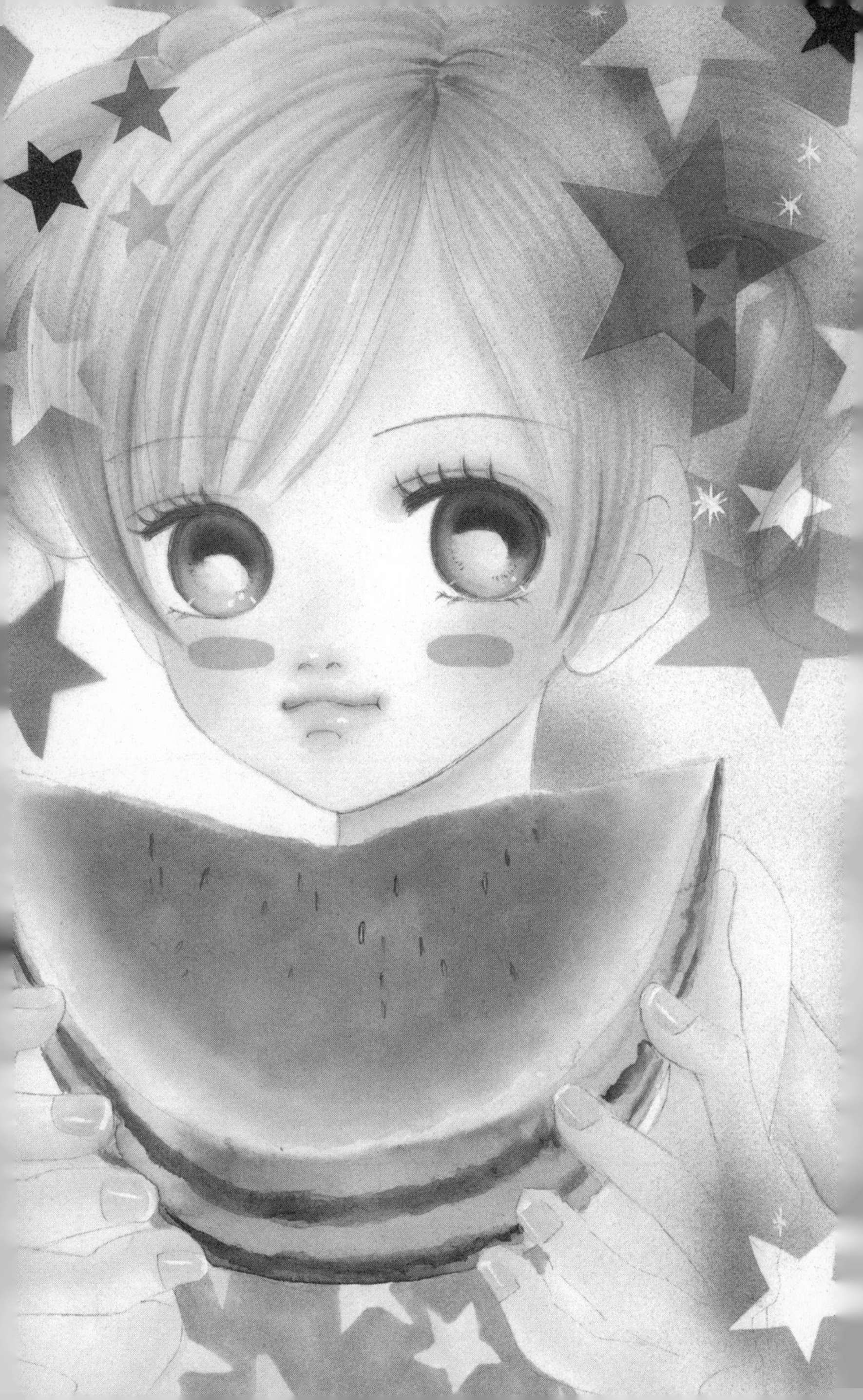

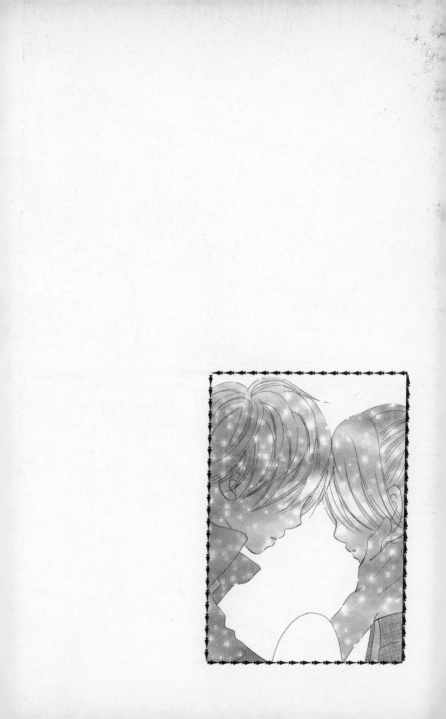

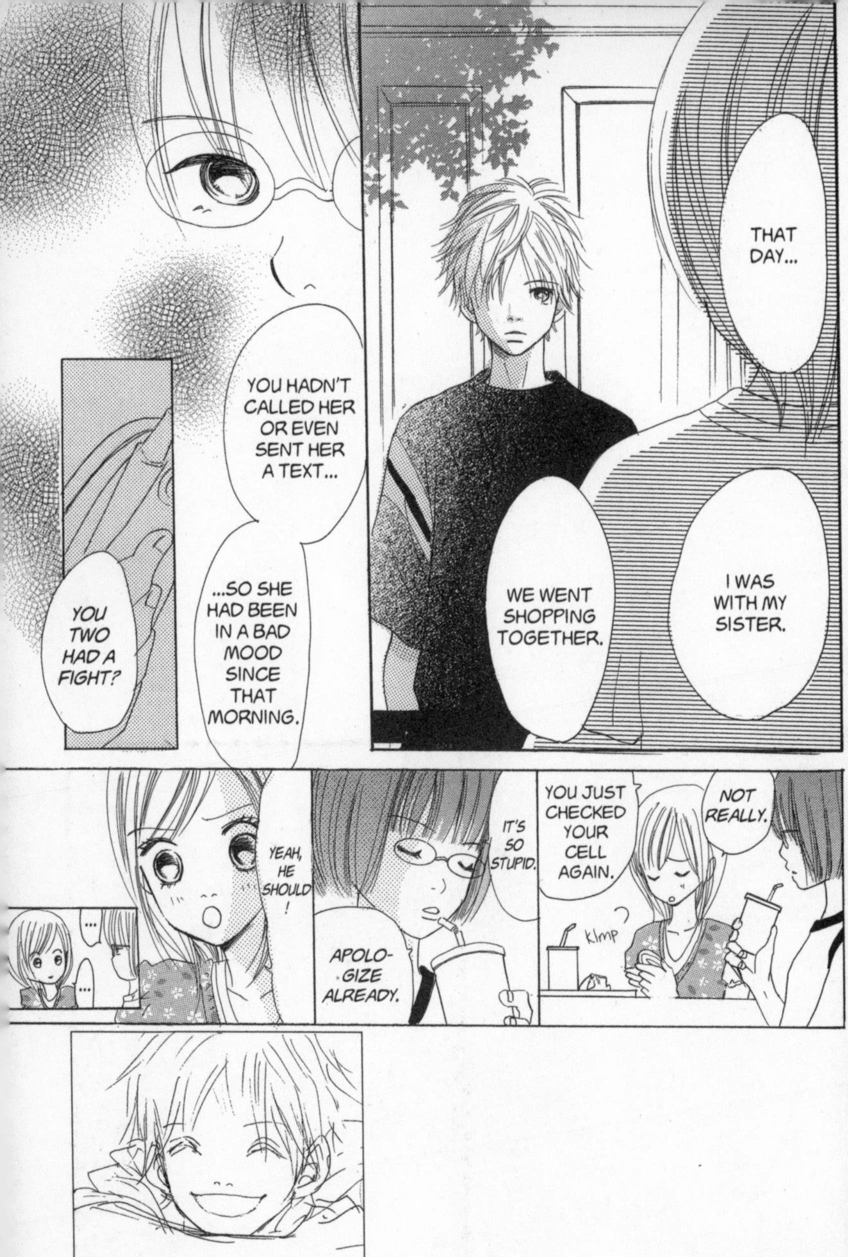
THAT DAY...
I WAS WITH MY SISTER.
WE WENT SHOPPING TOGETHER.
YOU HADN'T CALLED HER OR EVEN SENT HER A TEXT...
...SO SHE HAD BEEN IN A BAD MOOD SINCE THAT MORNING.
YOU TWO HAD A FIGHT?
NOT REALLY.
YOU JUST CHECKED YOUR CELL AGAIN.
klmp
IT'S SO STUPID.
APOLOGIZE ALREADY.
YEAH, HE SHOULD!
...
...

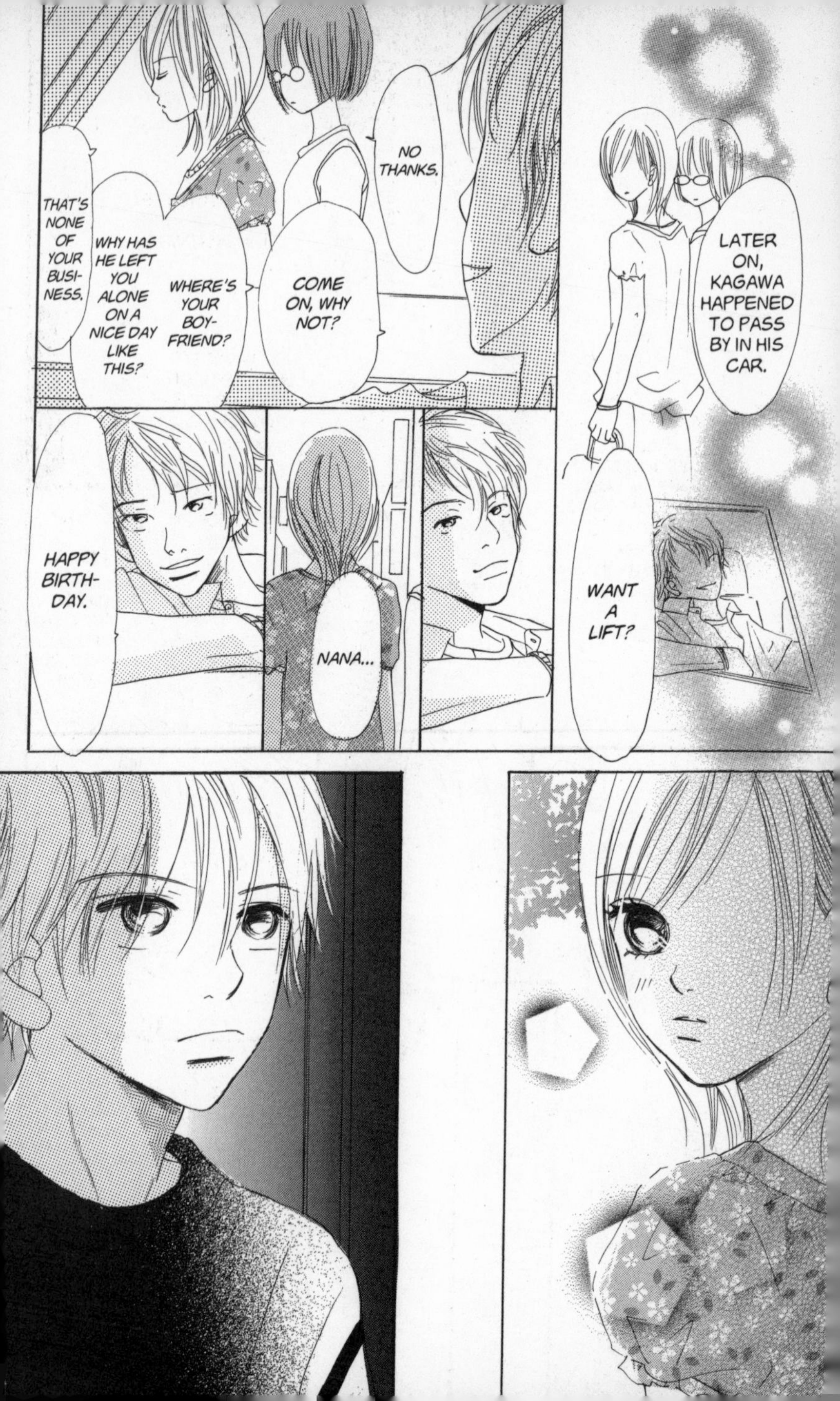
LATER ON, KAGAWA HAPPENED TO PASS BY IN HIS CAR.
WANT A LIFT?
NO THANKS.
COME ON, WHY NOT?
WHERE'S YOUR BOY-FRIEND?
WHY HAS HE LEFT YOU ALONE ON A NICE DAY LIKE THIS?
THAT'S NONE OF YOUR BUSI-NESS.
NANA...
HAPPY BIRTH-DAY.

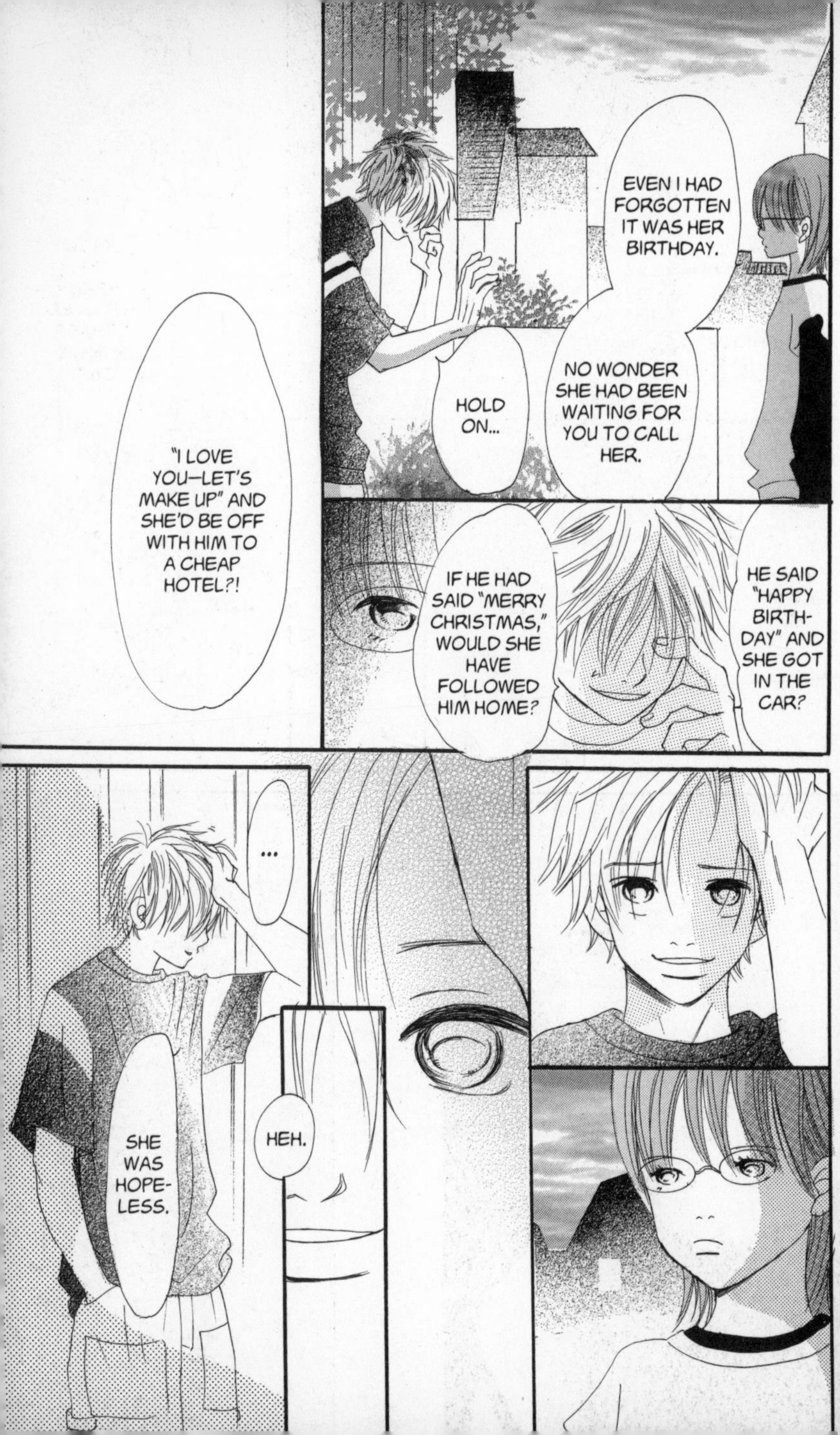
EVEN I HAD FORGOTTEN IT WAS HER BIRTHDAY.
NO WONDER SHE HAD BEEN WAITING FOR YOU TO CALL HER.
HOLD ON...
HE SAID "HAPPY BIRTH-DAY" AND SHE GOT IN THE CAR?
IF HE HAD SAID "MERRY CHRISTMAS," WOULD SHE HAVE FOLLOWED HIM HOME?
"I LOVE YOU—LET'S MAKE UP" AND SHE'D BE OFF WITH HIM TO A CHEAP HOTEL?!
HEH.
...
SHE WAS HOPE-LESS.

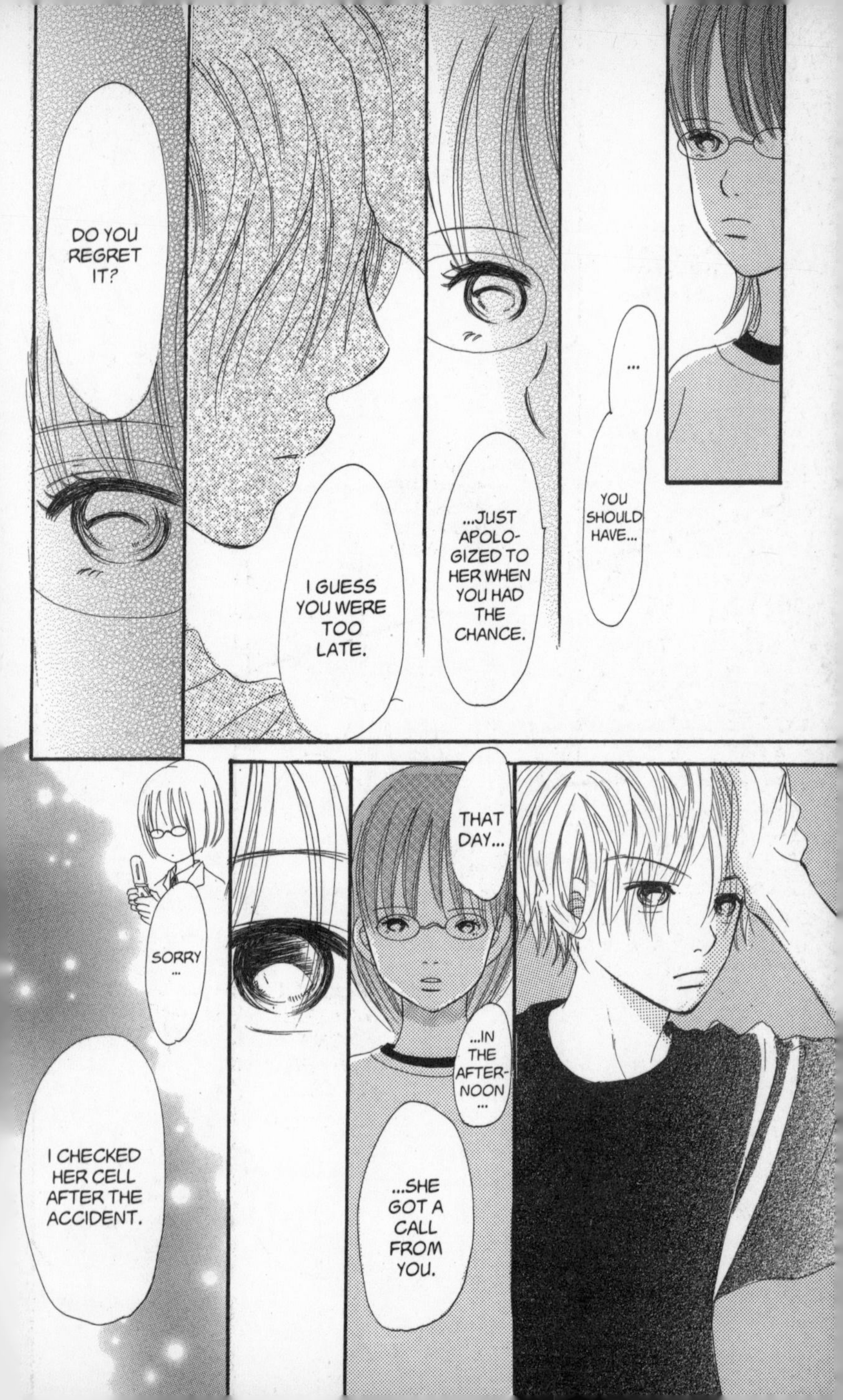
...
YOU SHOULD HAVE...
...JUST APOLOGIZED TO HER WHEN YOU HAD THE CHANCE.
I GUESS YOU WERE TOO LATE.
DO YOU REGRET IT?
THAT DAY...
...IN THE AFTERNOON...
...SHE GOT A CALL FROM YOU.
SORRY...
I CHECKED HER CELL AFTER THE ACCIDENT.

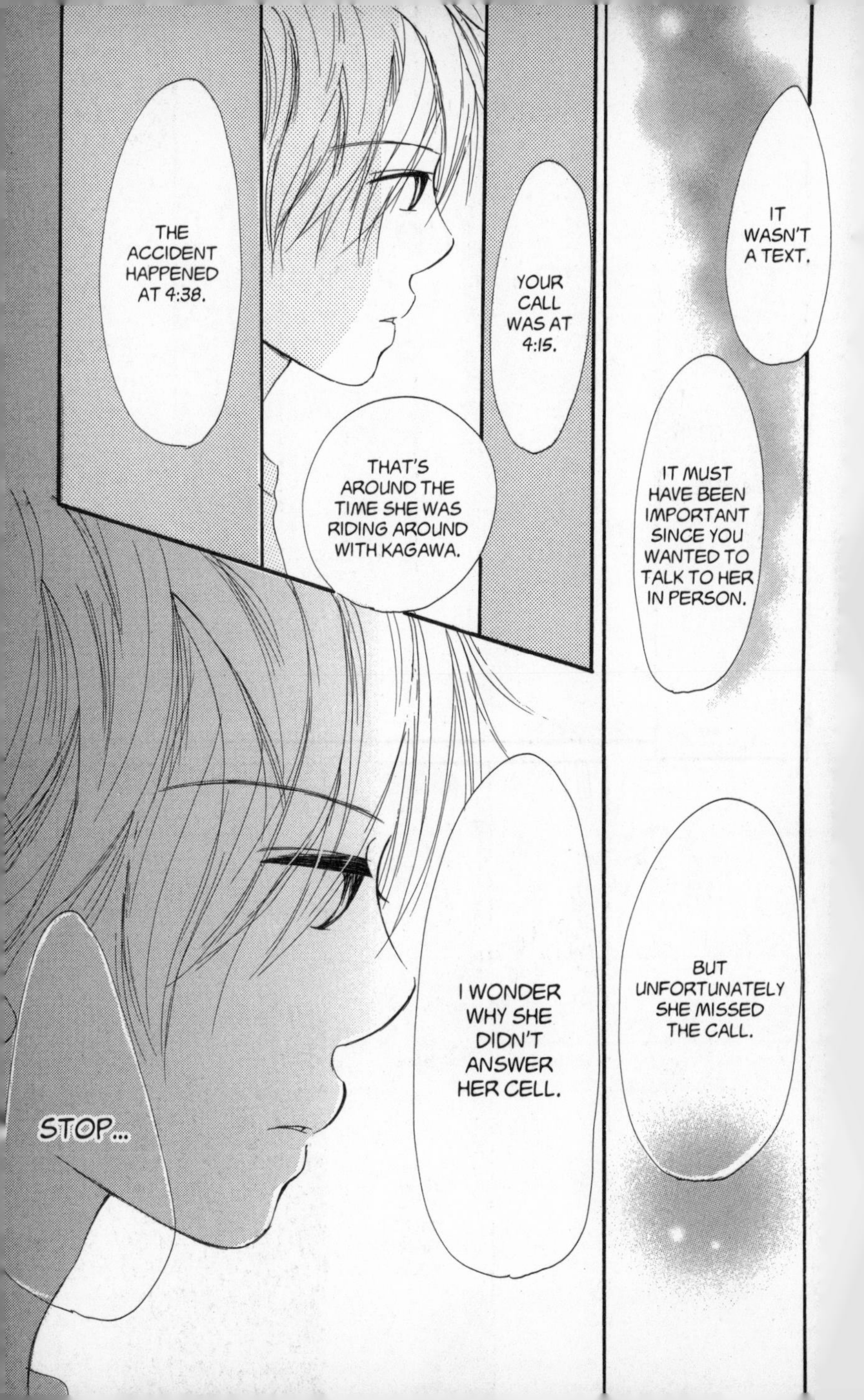
IT WASN'T A TEXT.
IT MUST HAVE BEEN IMPORTANT SINCE YOU WANTED TO TALK TO HER IN PERSON.
BUT UNFORTUNATELY SHE MISSED THE CALL.
YOUR CALL WAS AT 4:15.
THAT'S AROUND THE TIME SHE WAS RIDING AROUND WITH KAGAWA.
THE ACCIDENT HAPPENED AT 4:38.
I WONDER WHY SHE DIDN'T ANSWER HER CELL.
STOP...

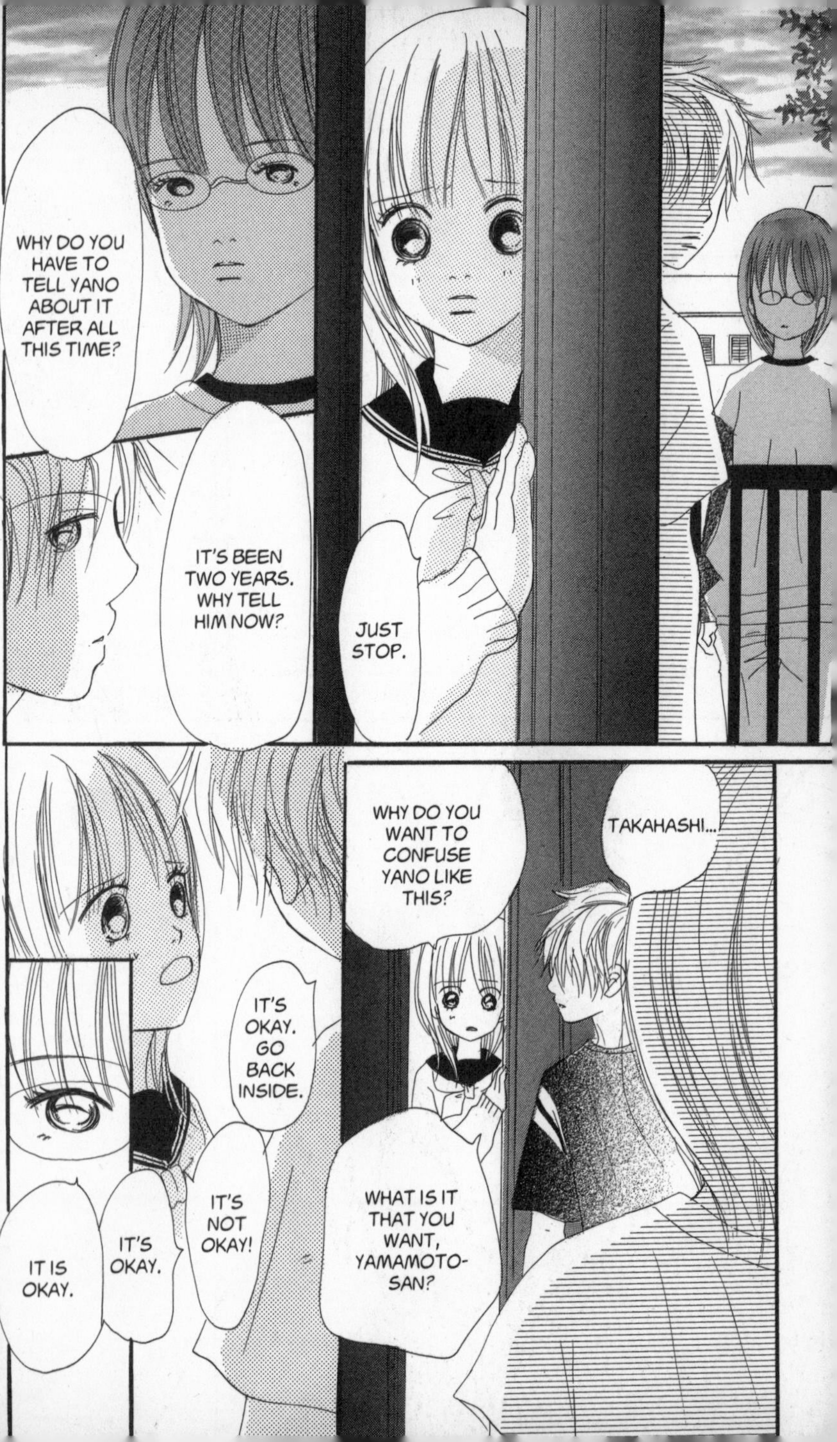
JUST STOP.
WHY DO YOU HAVE TO TELL YANO ABOUT IT AFTER ALL THIS TIME?
IT'S BEEN TWO YEARS. WHY TELL HIM NOW?
TAKAHASHI...
WHY DO YOU WANT TO CONFUSE YANO LIKE THIS?
WHAT IS IT THAT YOU WANT, YAMAMOTO-SAN?
IT'S OKAY. GO BACK INSIDE.
IT'S NOT OKAY!
IT'S OKAY.
IT IS OKAY.

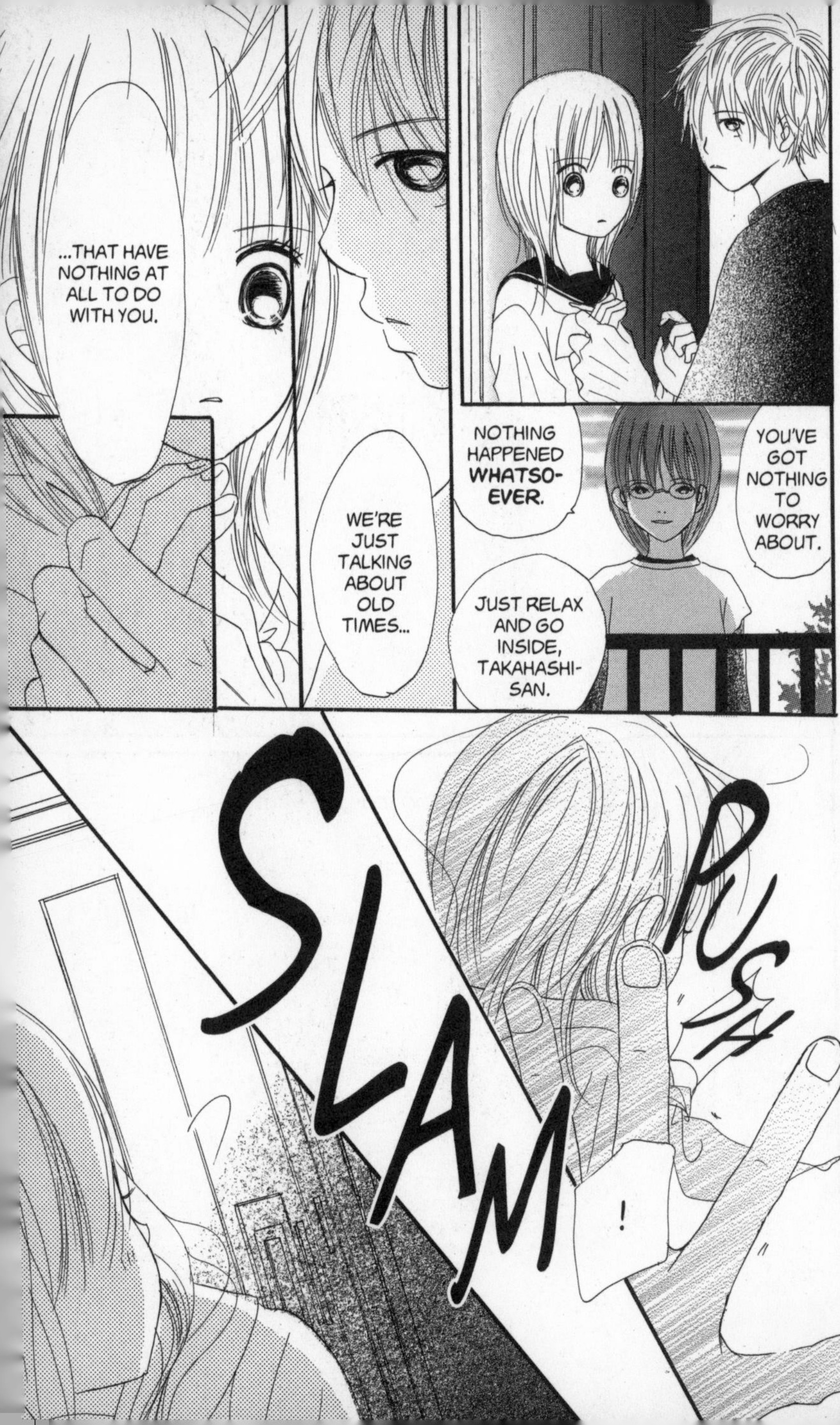
YOU'VE GOT NOTHING TO WORRY ABOUT.
NOTHING HAPPENED WHATSO-EVER.
JUST RELAX AND GO INSIDE, TAKAHASHI-SAN.
WE'RE JUST TALKING ABOUT OLD TIMES...
...THAT HAVE NOTHING AT ALL TO DO WITH YOU.
PUSH
SLAM
!

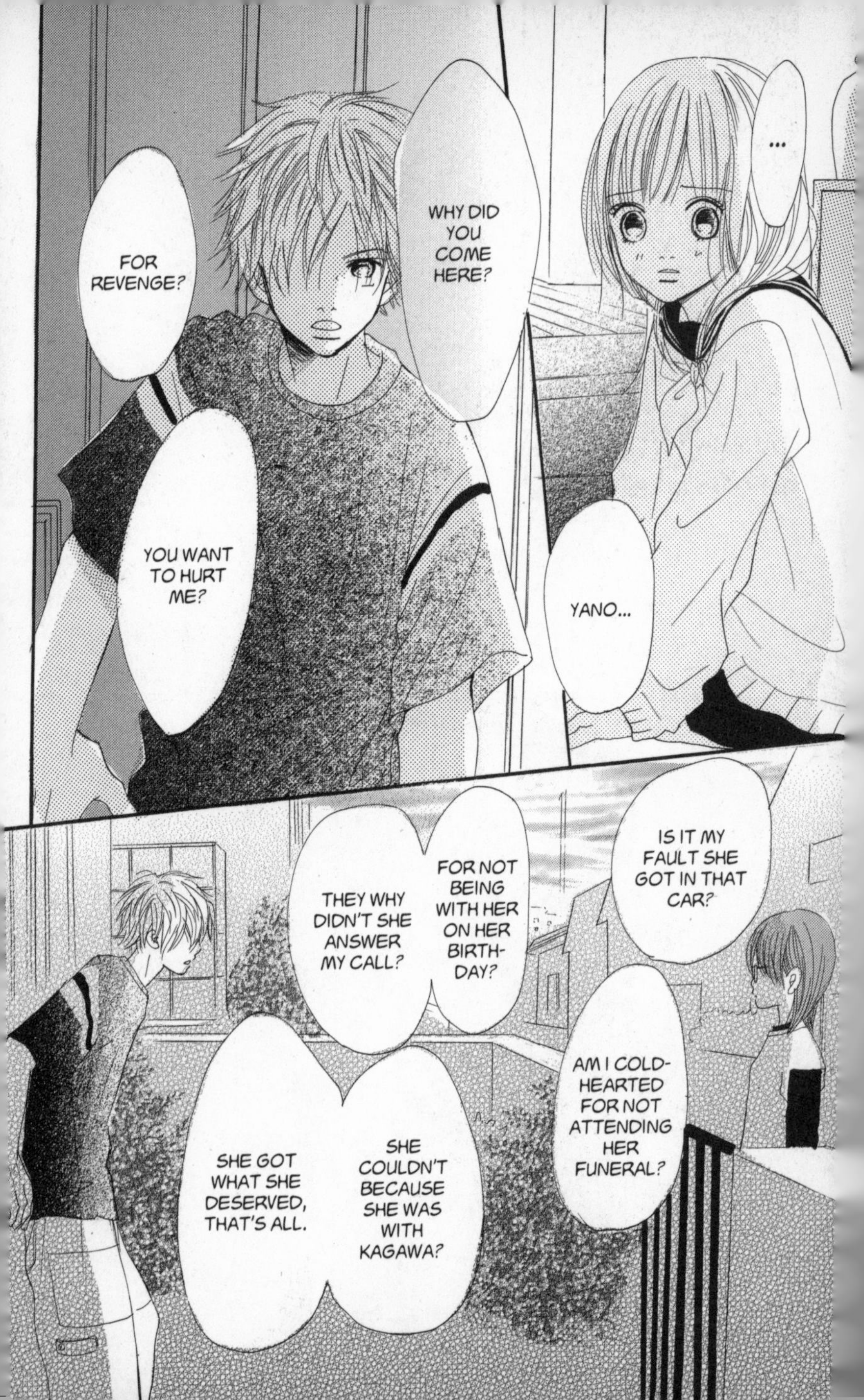
...
YANO...
WHY DID YOU COME HERE?
FOR REVENGE?
YOU WANT TO HURT ME?
IS IT MY FAULT SHE GOT IN THAT CAR?
FOR NOT BEING WITH HER ON HER BIRTH-DAY?
THEY WHY DIDN'T SHE ANSWER MY CALL?
AM I COLD-HEARTED FOR NOT ATTENDING HER FUNERAL?
SHE COULDN'T BECAUSE SHE WAS WITH KAGAWA?
SHE GOT WHAT SHE DESERVED, THAT'S ALL.

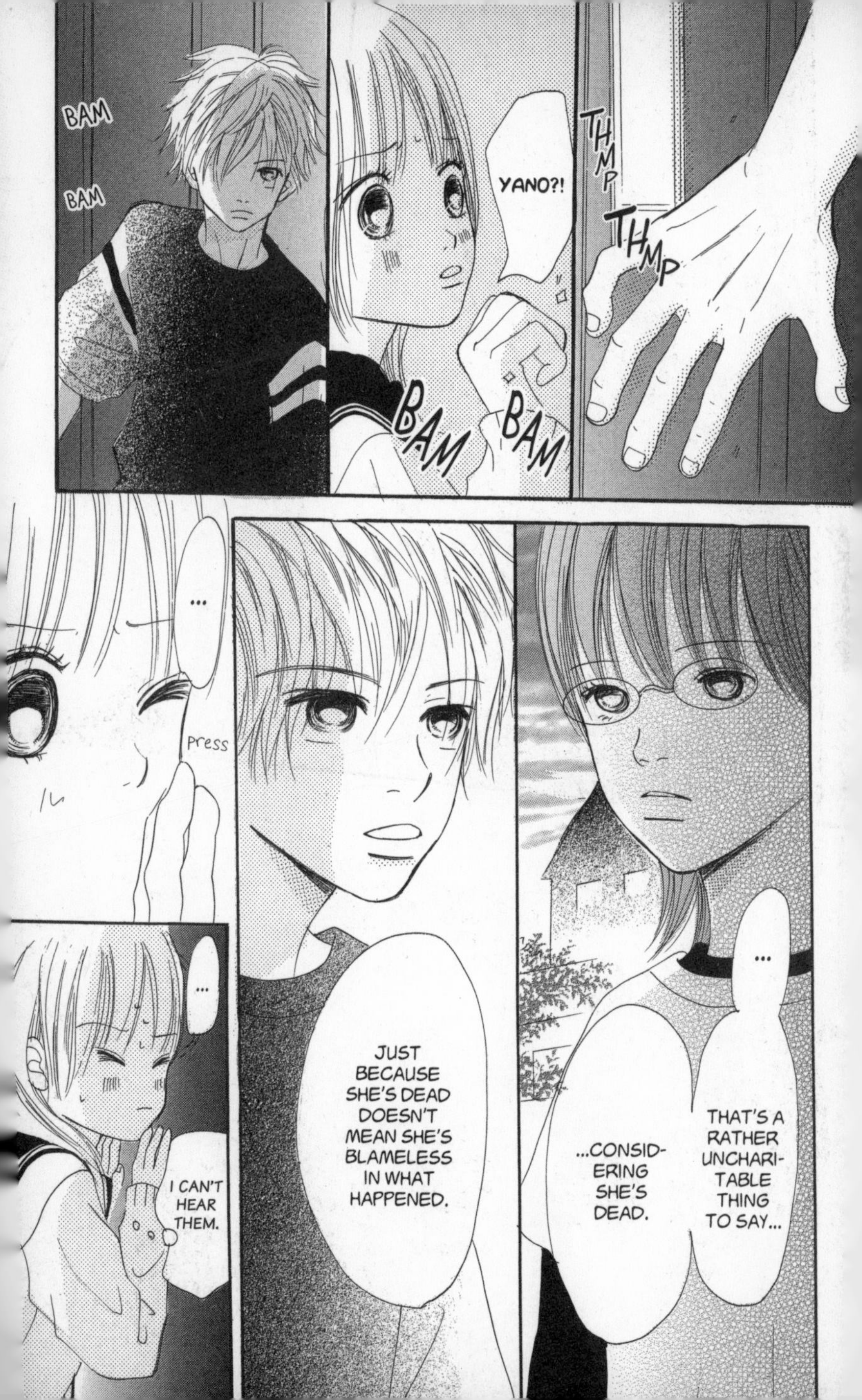
THMP
THMP
YANO?!
BAM
BAM
BAM
BAM
...
THAT'S A RATHER UNCHARI-TABLE THING TO SAY...
...CONSID-ERING SHE'S DEAD.
JUST BECAUSE SHE'S DEAD DOESN'T MEAN SHE'S BLAMELESS IN WHAT HAPPENED.
...
press
...
I CAN'T HEAR THEM.

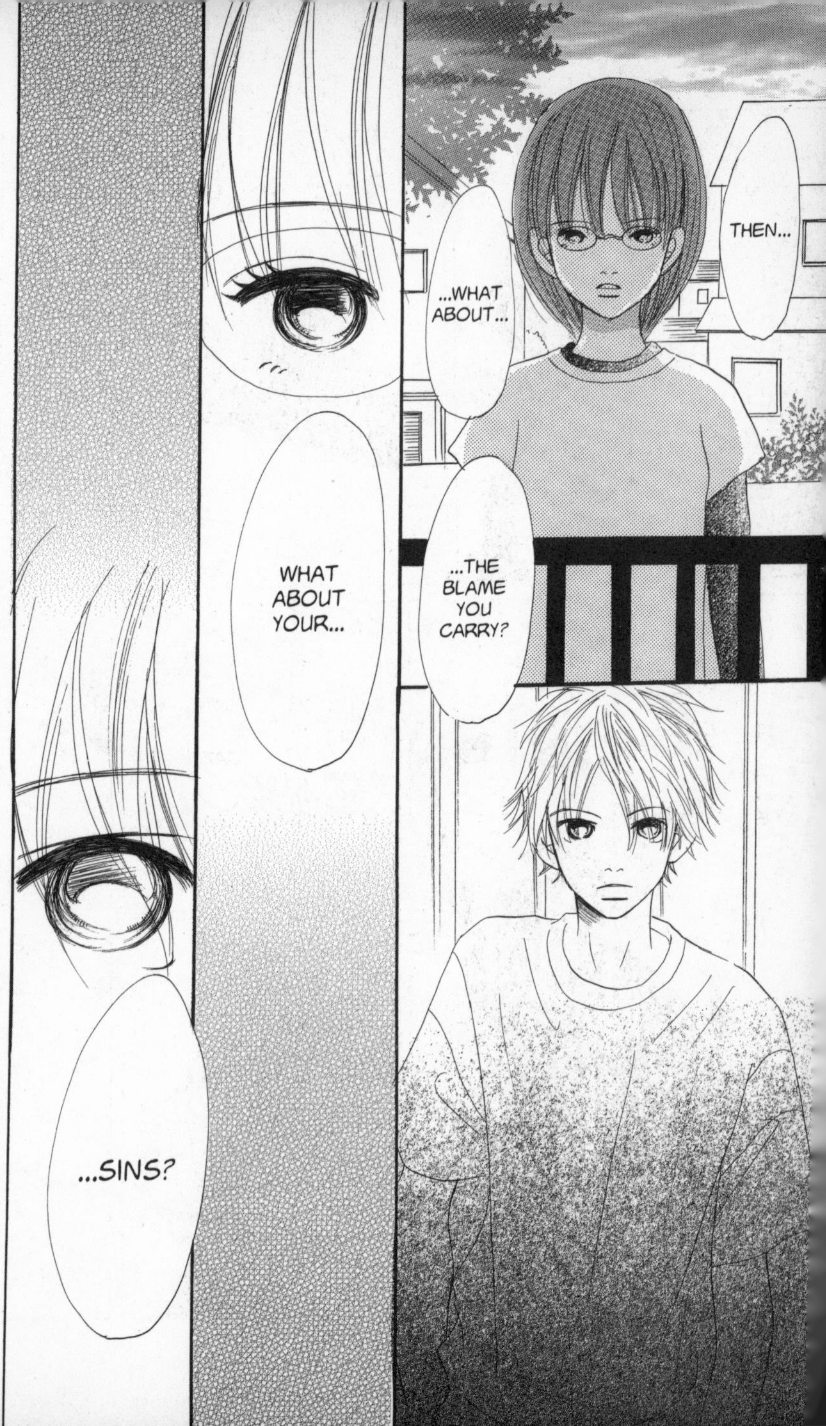
THEN...
...WHAT ABOUT...
...THE BLAME YOU CARRY?
WHAT ABOUT YOUR...
...SINS?

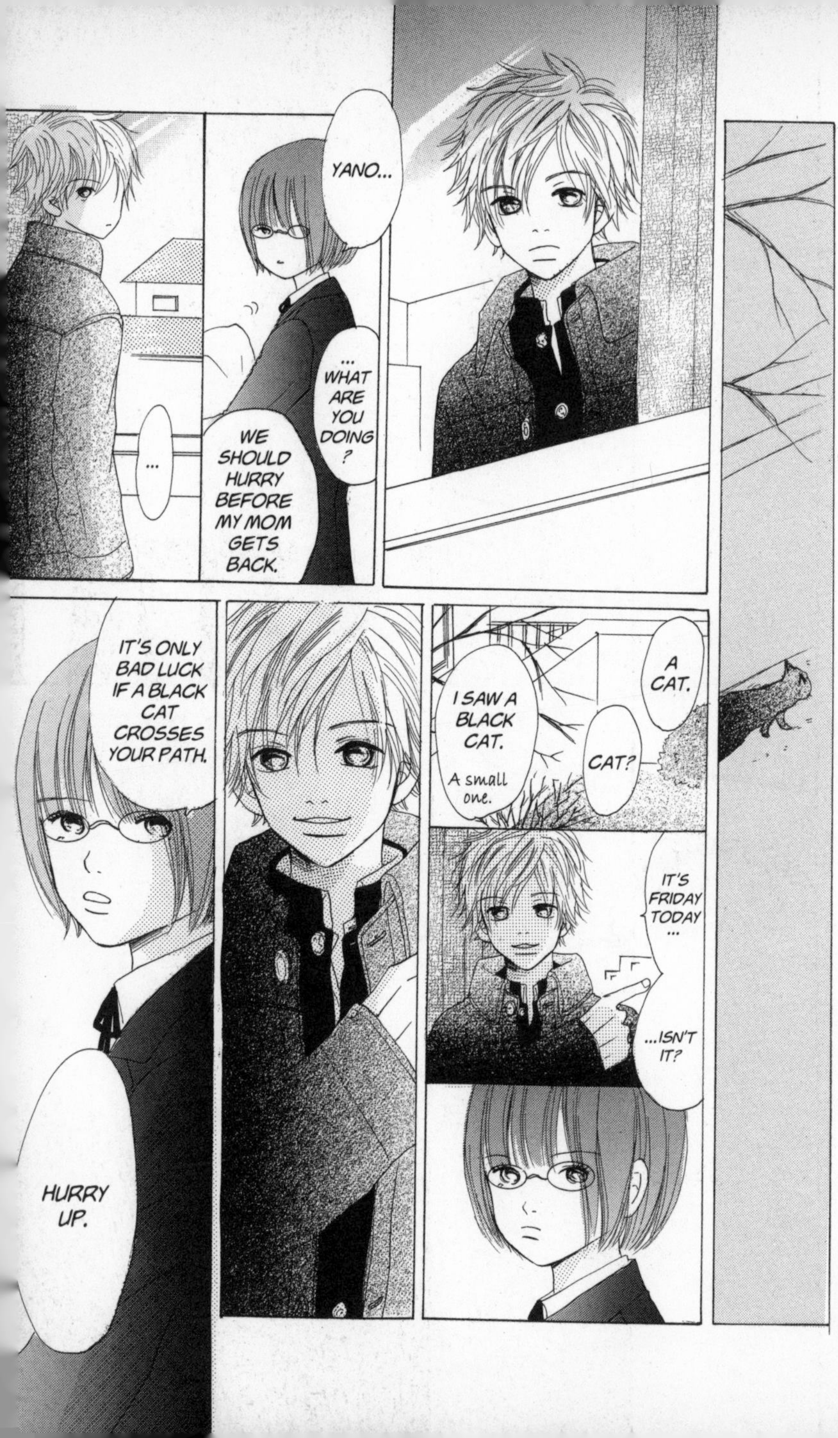
YANO...
...WHAT ARE YOU DOING?
WE SHOULD HURRY BEFORE MY MOM GETS BACK.
...
A CAT.
CAT?
I SAW A BLACK CAT.
A small one.
IT'S FRIDAY TODAY...
...ISN'T IT?
IT'S ONLY BAD LUCK IF A BLACK CAT CROSSES YOUR PATH.
HURRY UP.

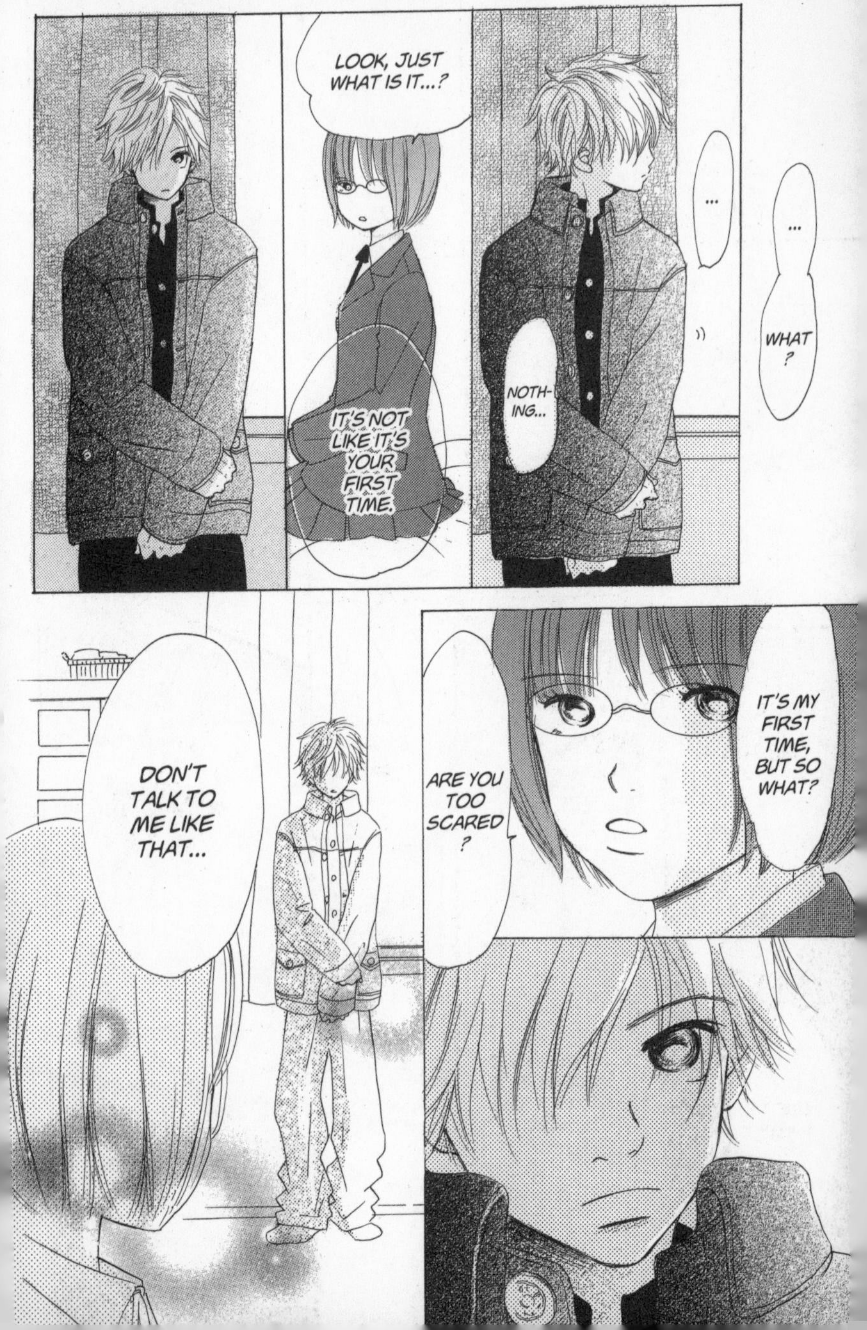
...
WHAT?
...
NOTHING...
LOOK, JUST WHAT IS IT...?
IT'S NOT LIKE IT'S YOUR FIRST TIME.
IT'S MY FIRST TIME, BUT SO WHAT?
ARE YOU TOO SCARED?
DON'T TALK TO ME LIKE THAT...

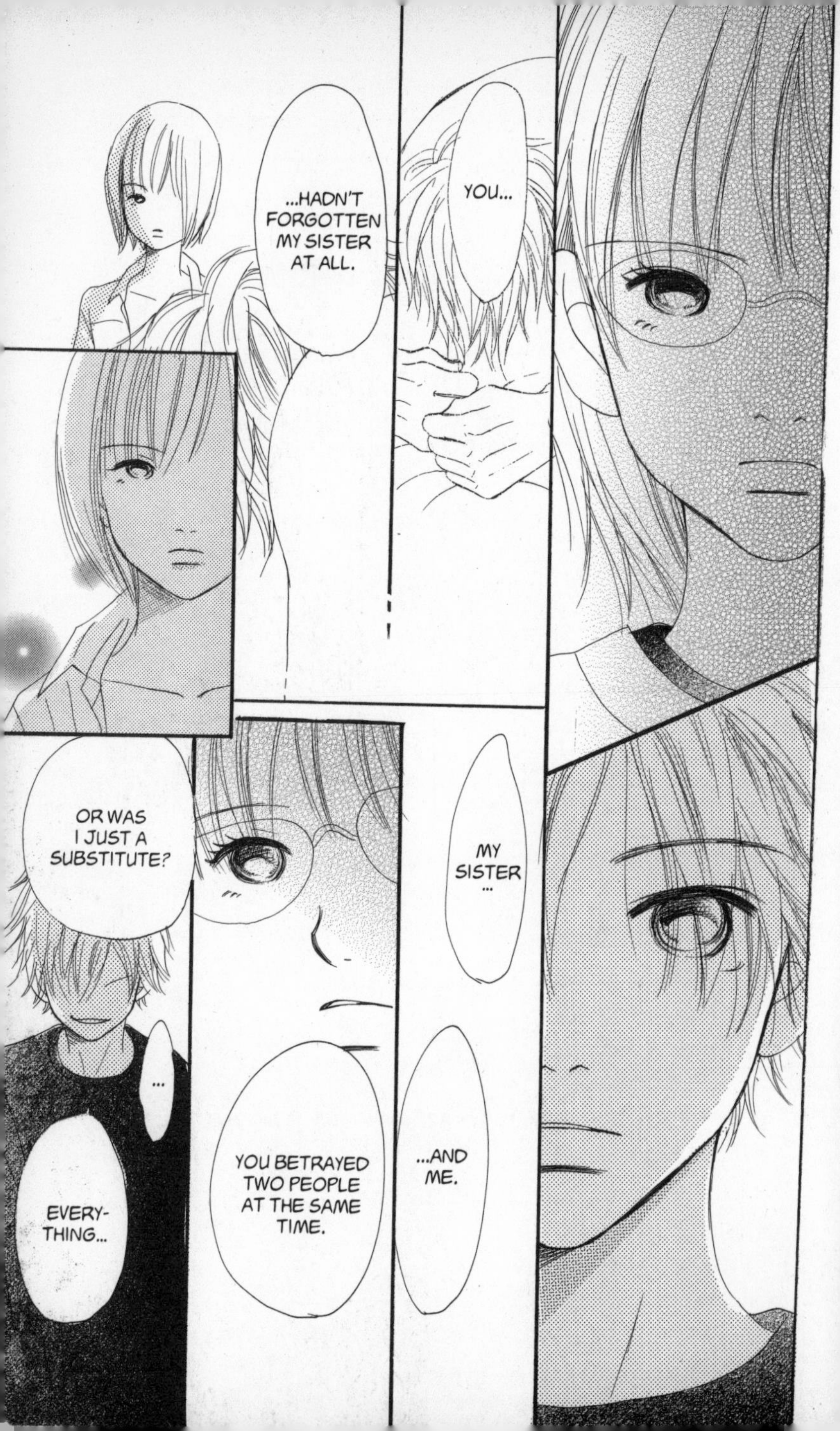
YOU...
...HADN'T FORGOTTEN MY SISTER AT ALL.
MY SISTER ...
...AND ME.
YOU BETRAYED TWO PEOPLE AT THE SAME TIME.
OR WAS I JUST A SUBSTITUTE?
...
EVERY-THING...

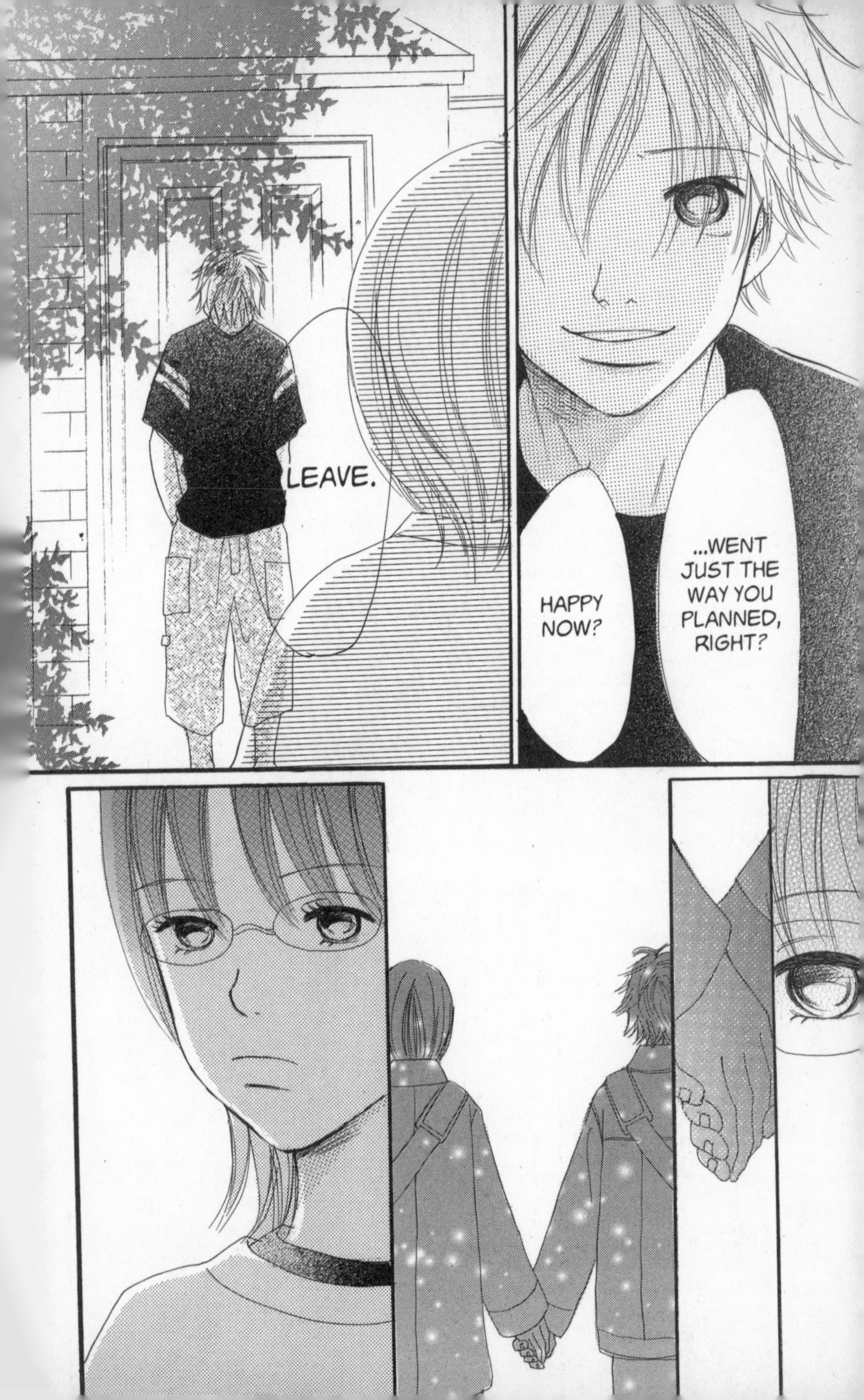
...WENT JUST THE WAY YOU PLANNED, RIGHT?
HAPPY NOW?
LEAVE.

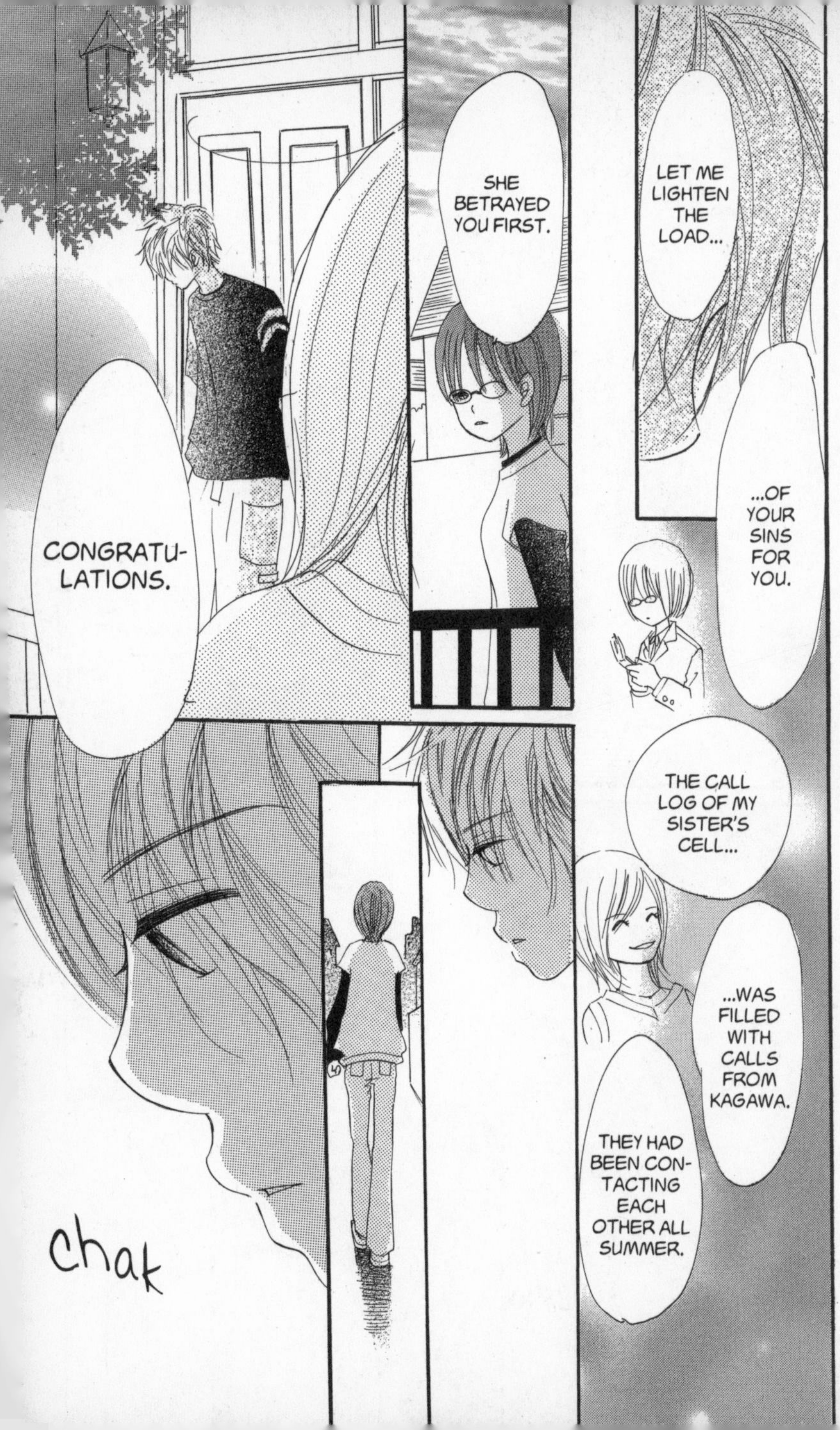
LET ME LIGHTEN THE LOAD...
...OF YOUR SINS FOR YOU.
SHE BETRAYED YOU FIRST.
CONGRATULATIONS.
THE CALL LOG OF MY SISTER'S CELL...
...WAS FILLED WITH CALLS FROM KAGAWA.
THEY HAD BEEN CONTACTING EACH OTHER ALL SUMMER.
Chak

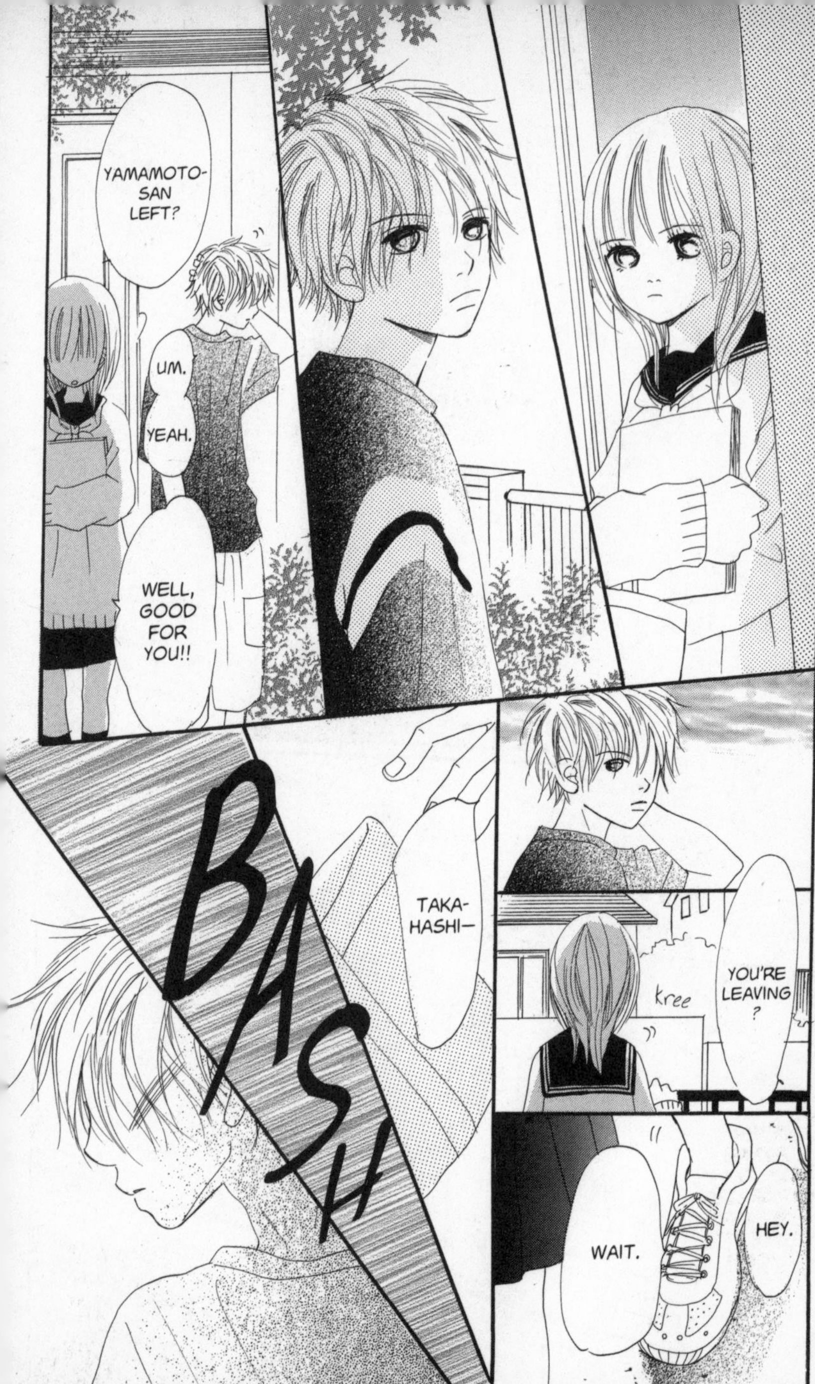
YAMAMOTO-SAN LEFT?
UM.
YEAH.
WELL, GOOD FOR YOU!!
YOU'RE LEAVING?
kree
HEY.
WAIT.
TAKA-HASHI—
BASH

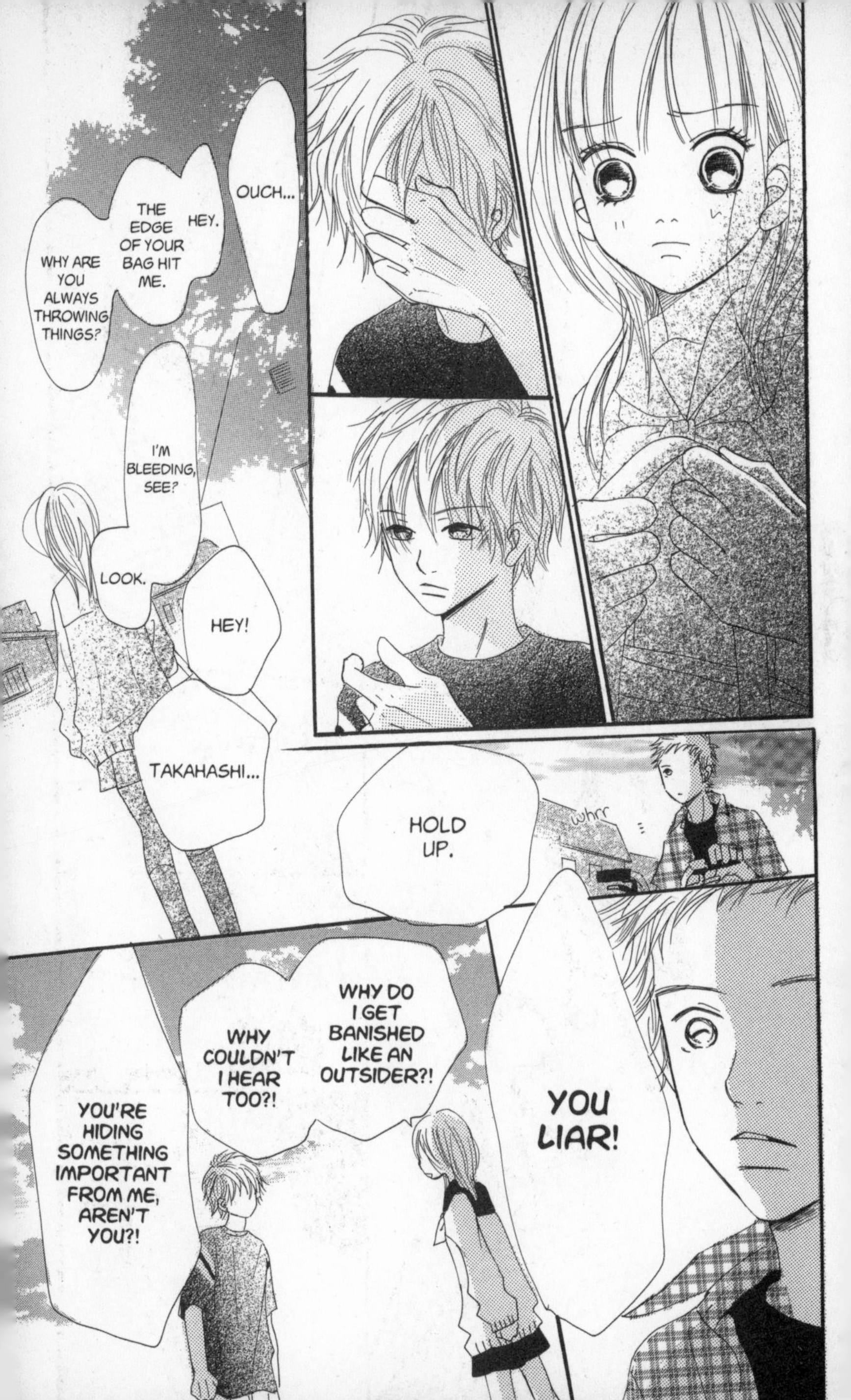
OUCH...
HEY.
THE EDGE OF YOUR BAG HIT ME.
WHY ARE YOU ALWAYS THROWING THINGS?
I'M BLEEDING, SEE?
LOOK.
HEY!
TAKAHASHI...
whrr
HOLD UP.
YOU LIAR!
WHY DO I GET BANISHED LIKE AN OUTSIDER?!
WHY COULDN'T I HEAR TOO?!
YOU'RE HIDING SOMETHING IMPORTANT FROM ME, AREN'T YOU?!

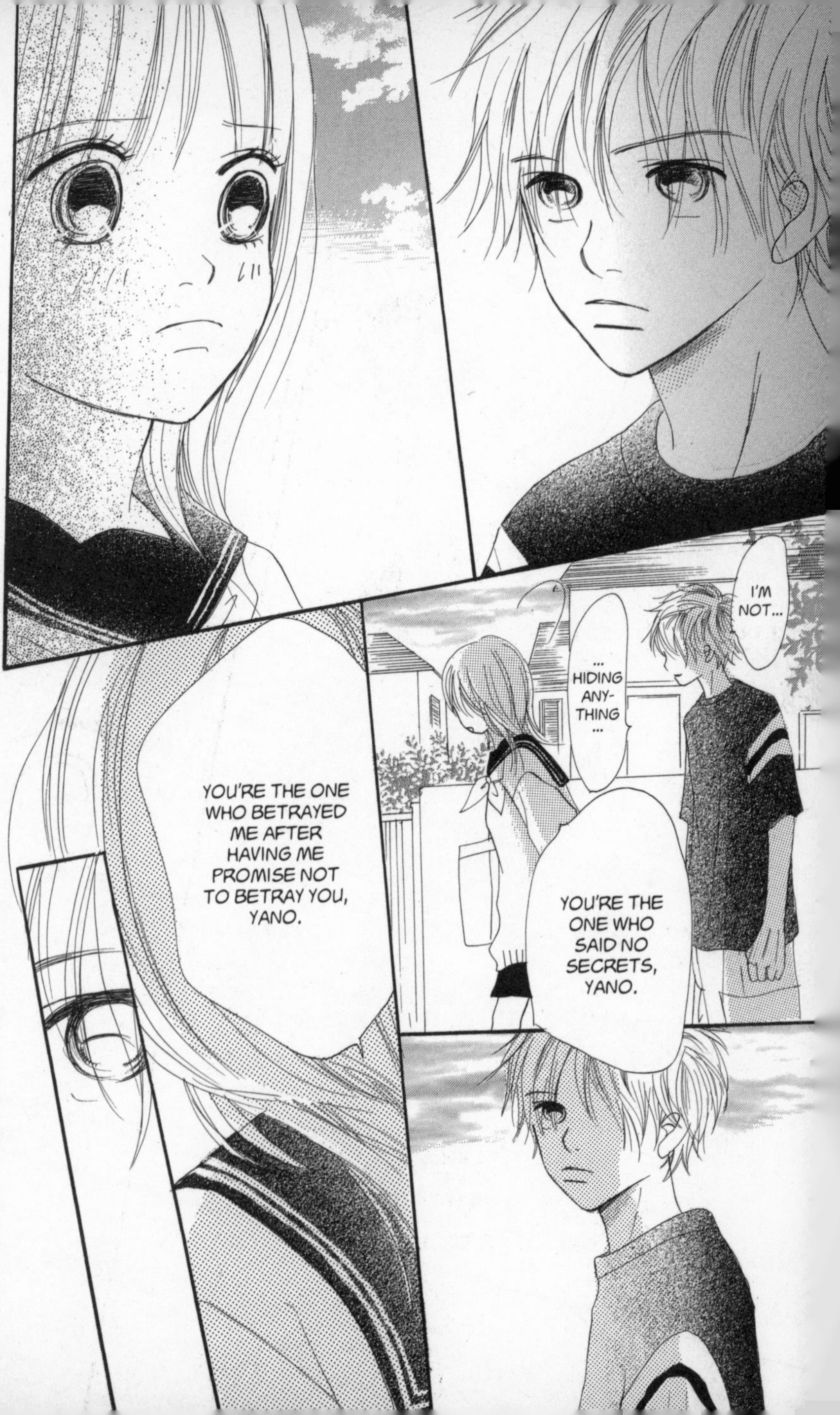
I'M NOT...
... HIDING ANY-THING ...
YOU'RE THE ONE WHO SAID NO SECRETS, YANO.
YOU'RE THE ONE WHO BETRAYED ME AFTER HAVING ME PROMISE NOT TO BETRAY YOU, YANO.

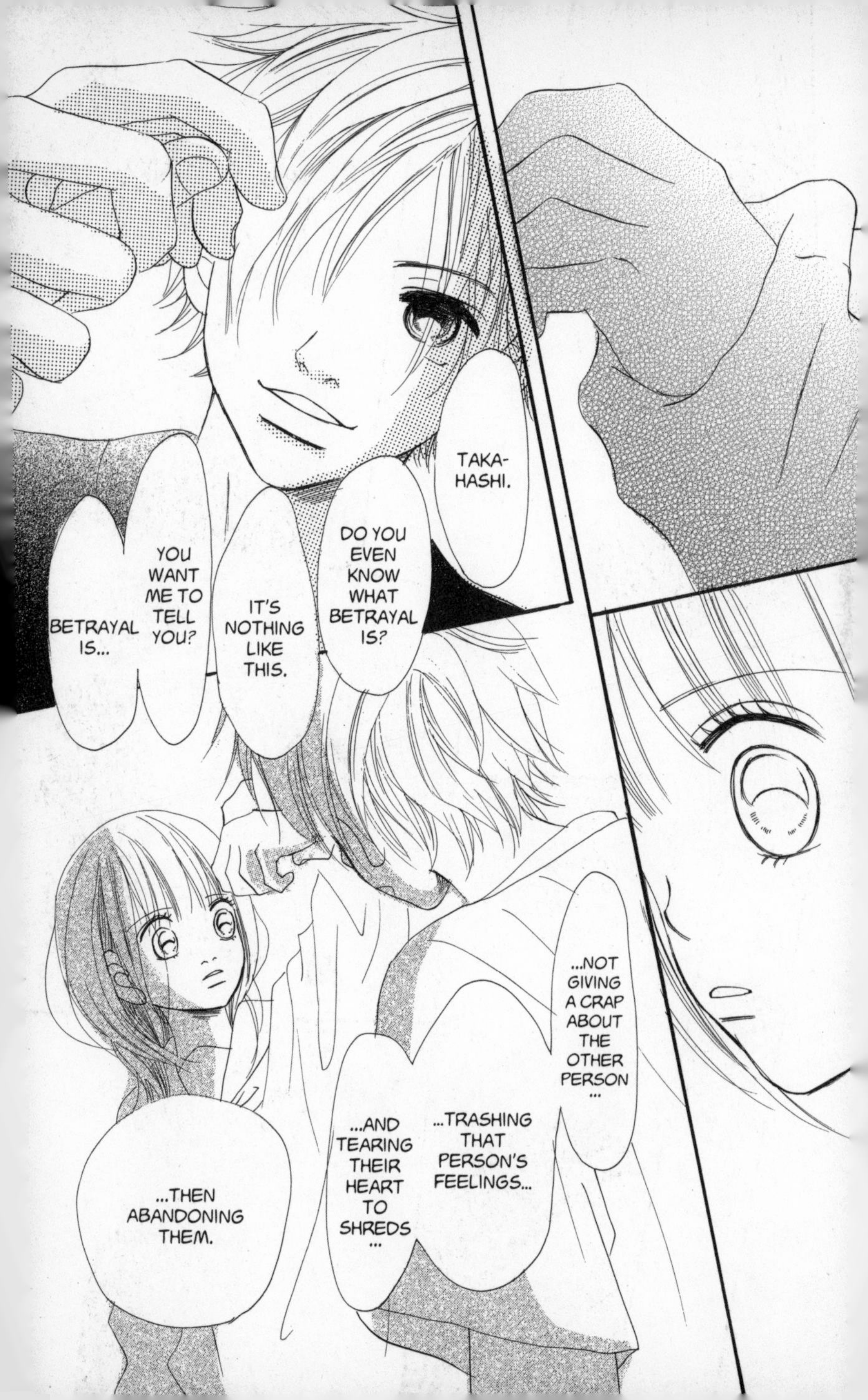
TAKA-HASHI.
DO YOU EVEN KNOW WHAT BETRAYAL IS?
IT'S NOTHING LIKE THIS.
YOU WANT ME TO TELL YOU?
BETRAYAL IS...
...NOT GIVING A CRAP ABOUT THE OTHER PERSON...
...TRASHING THAT PERSON'S FEELINGS...
...AND TEARING THEIR HEART TO SHREDS...
...THEN ABANDONING THEM.

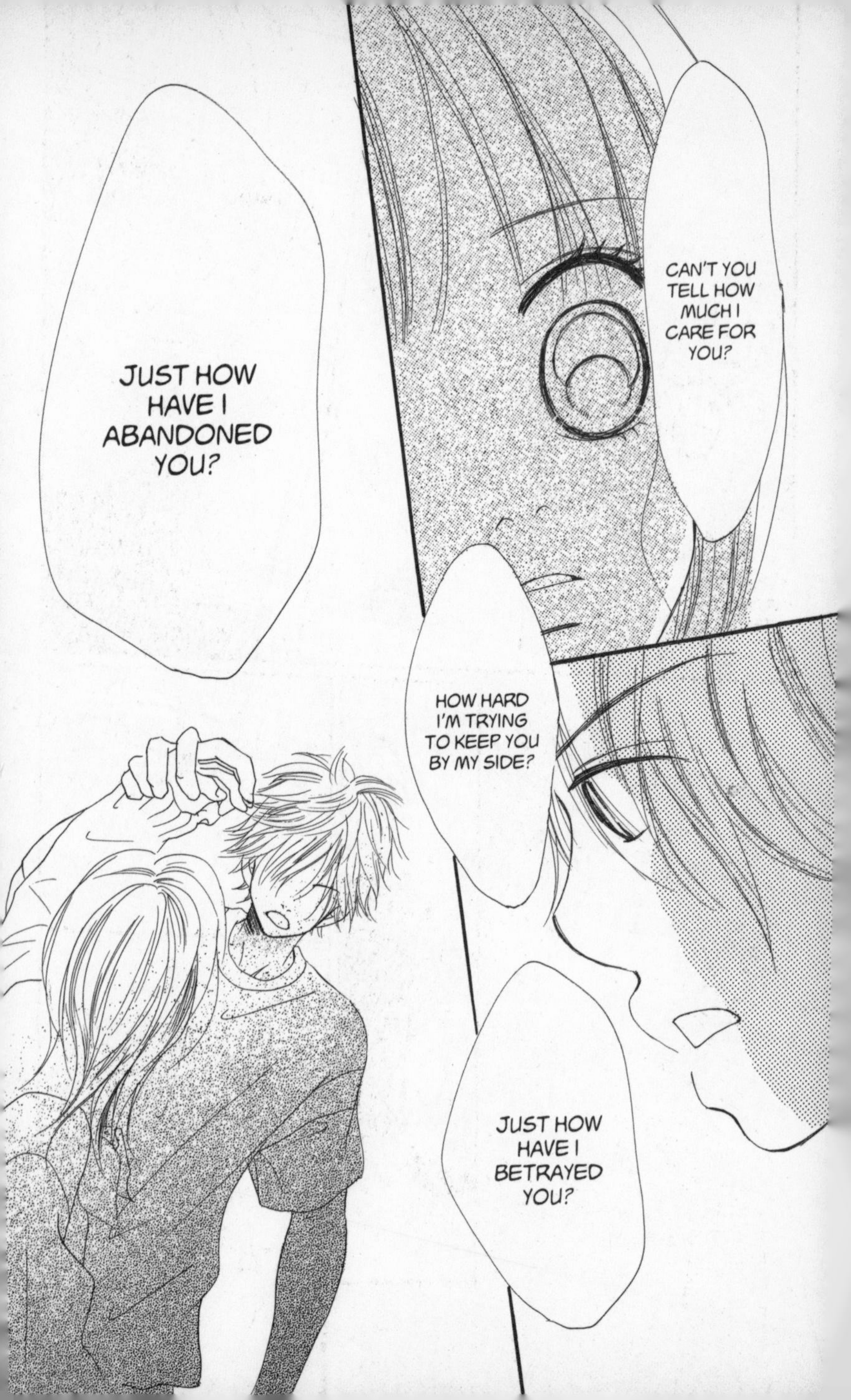
CAN'T YOU TELL HOW MUCH I CARE FOR YOU?
HOW HARD I'M TRYING TO KEEP YOU BY MY SIDE?
JUST HOW HAVE I BETRAYED YOU?
JUST HOW HAVE I ABANDONED YOU?

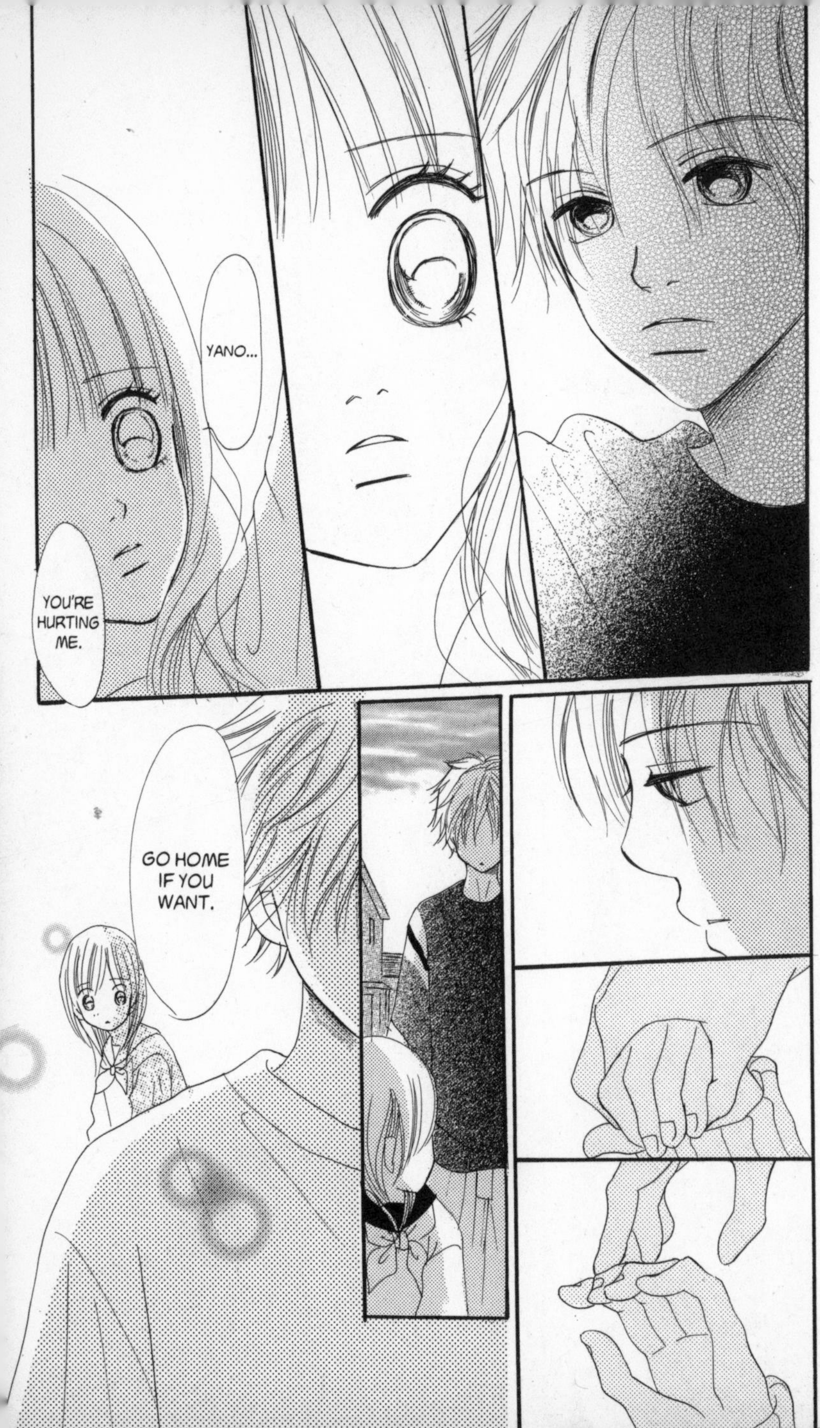
YANO...
YOU'RE HURTING ME.
GO HOME IF YOU WANT.

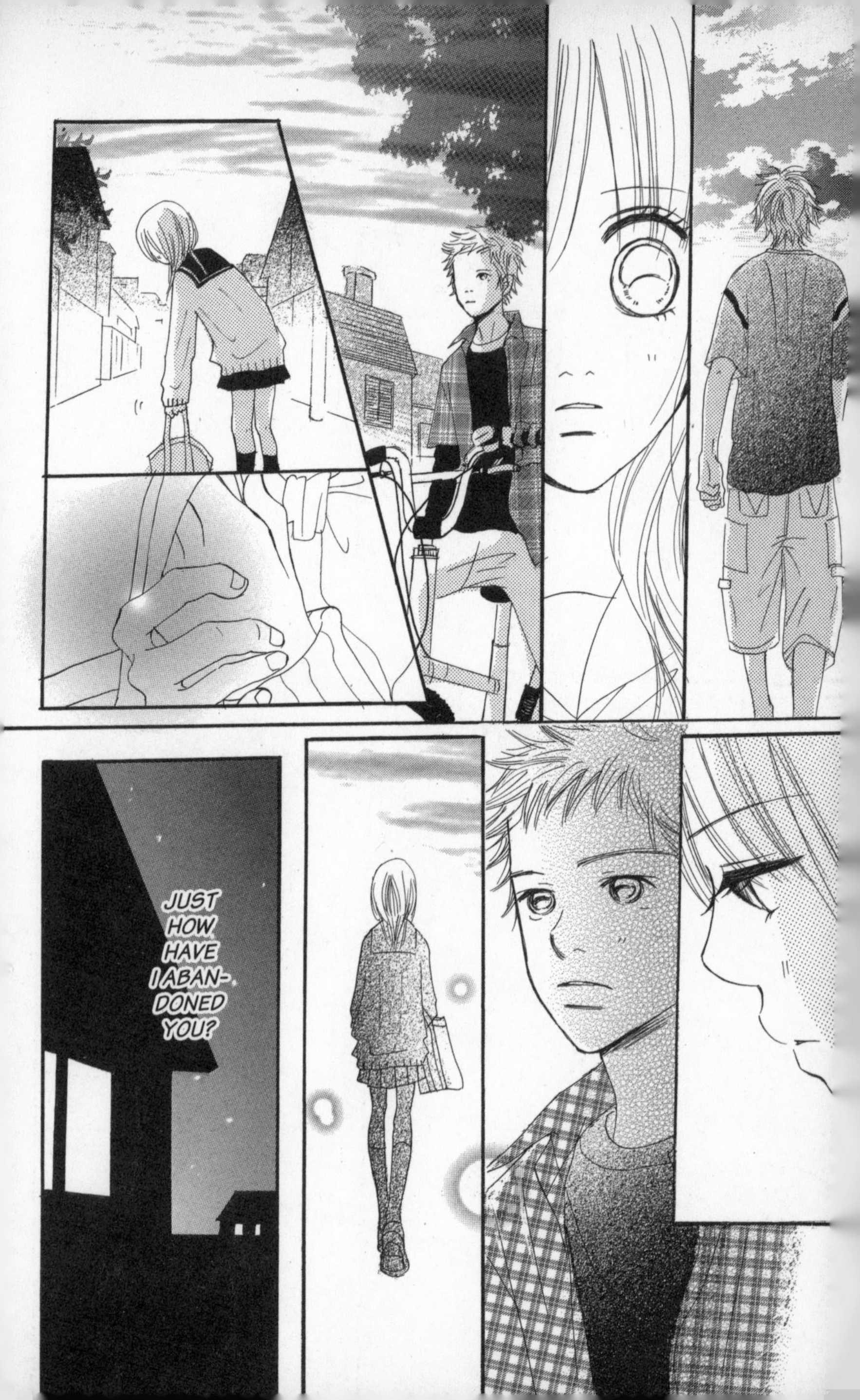
JUST HOW HAVE I ABAN- DONED YOU?

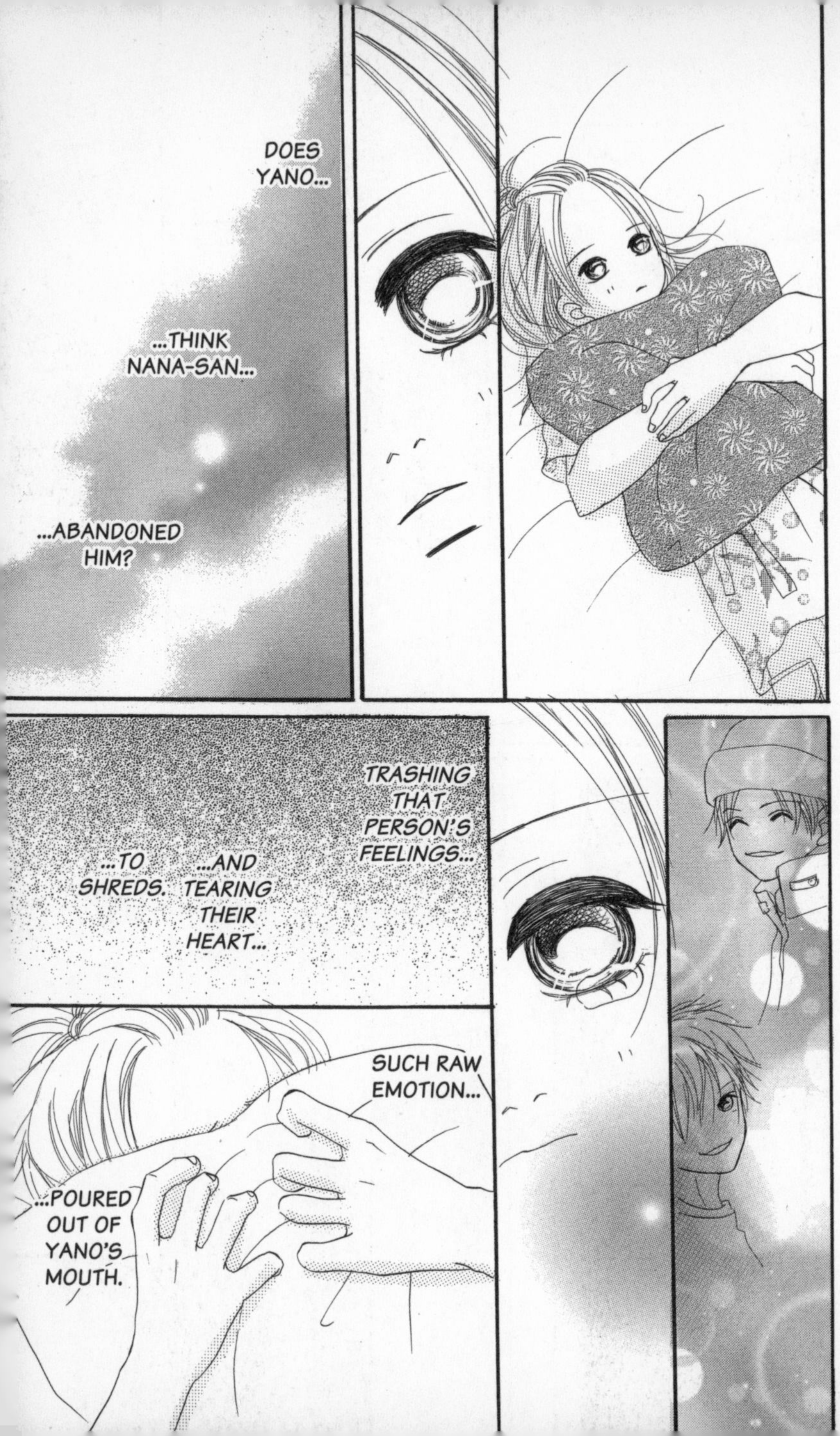
DOES YANO...
...THINK NANA-SAN...
...ABANDONED HIM?
TRASHING THAT PERSON'S FEELINGS...
...AND TEARING THEIR HEART...
...TO SHREDS.
SUCH RAW EMOTION...
...POURED OUT OF YANO'S MOUTH.

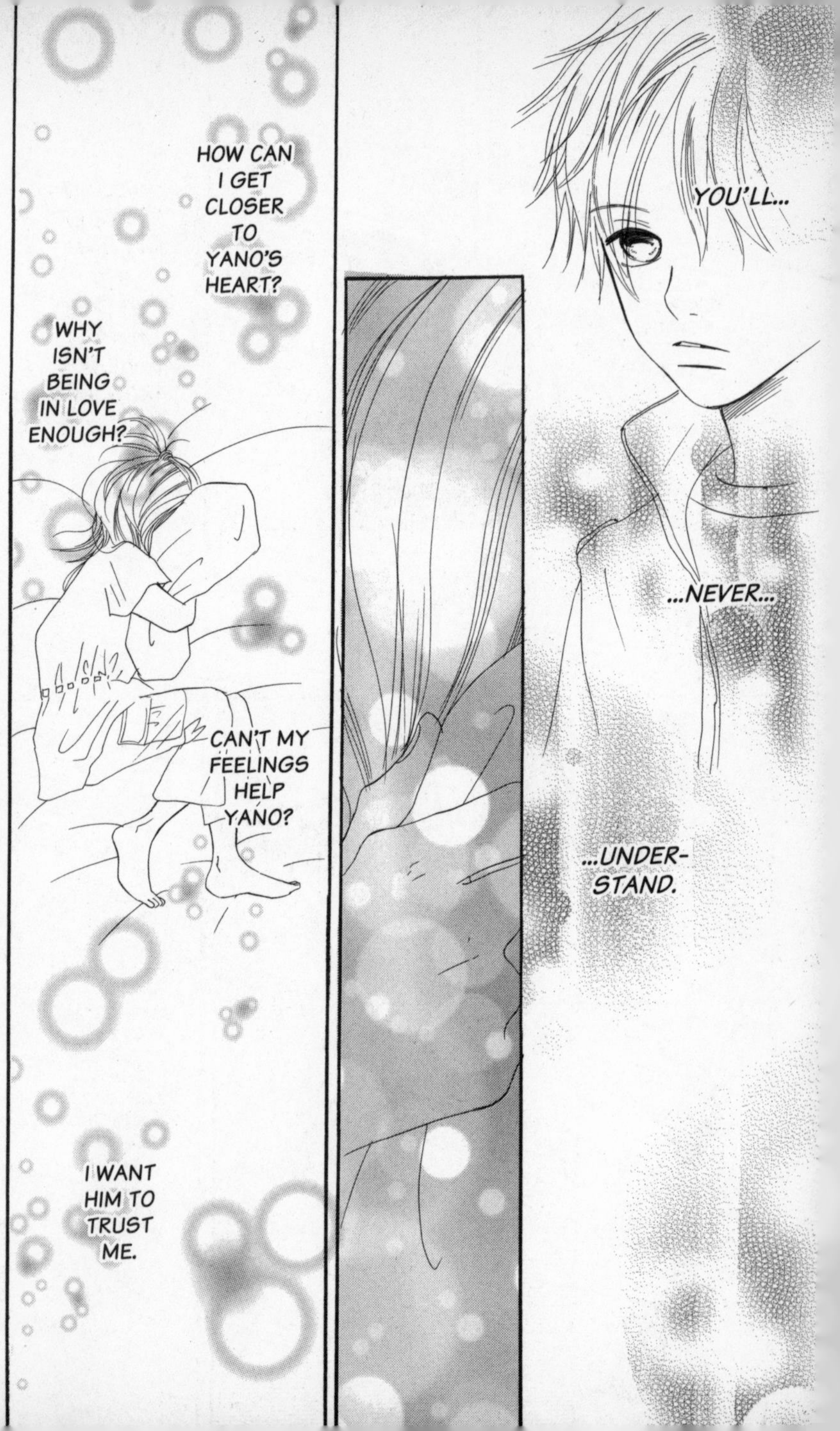
YOU'LL...
...NEVER...
...UNDER-STAND.
HOW CAN I GET CLOSER TO YANO'S HEART?
WHY ISN'T BEING IN LOVE ENOUGH?
CAN'T MY FEELINGS HELP YANO?
I WANT HIM TO TRUST ME.

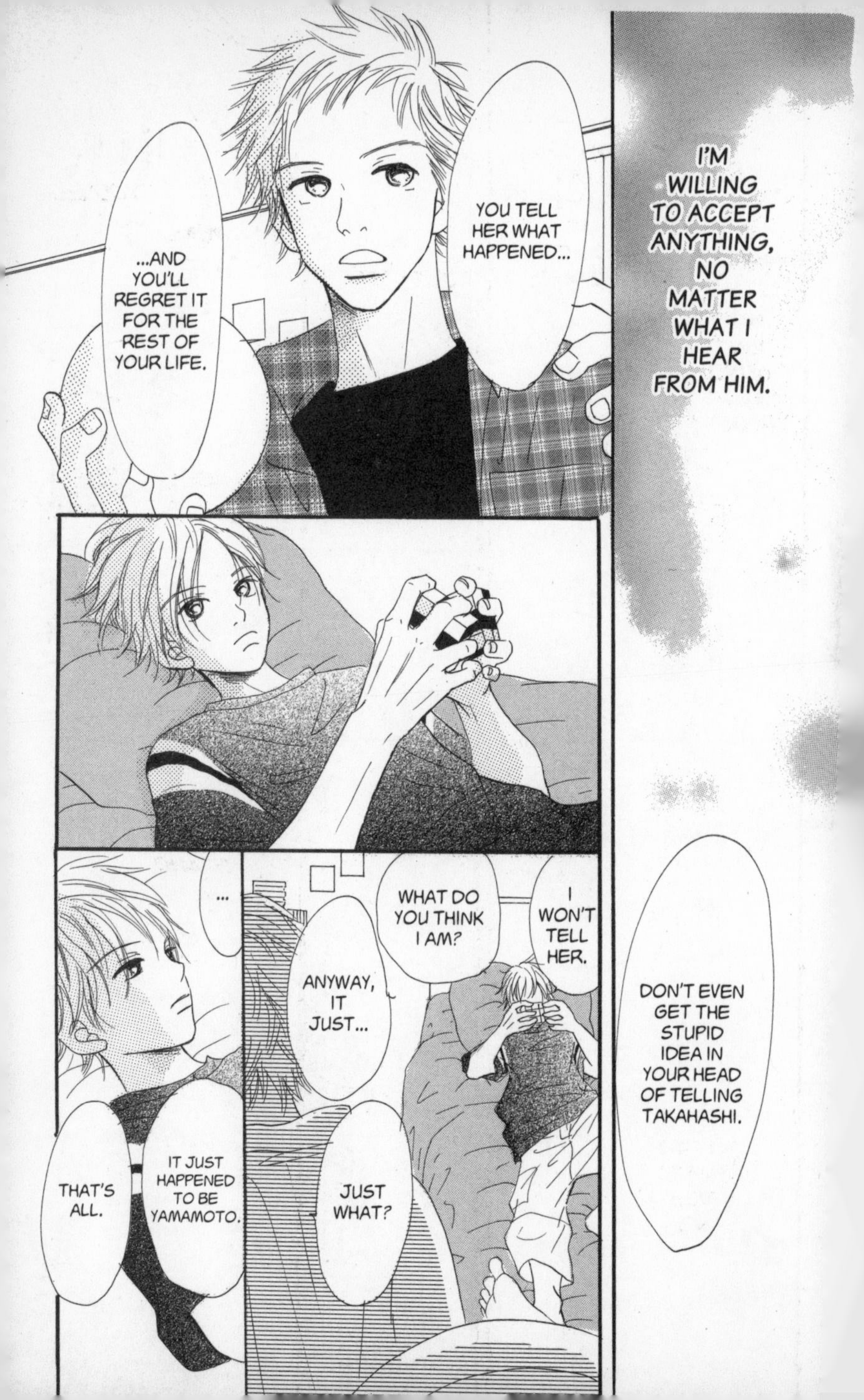
I'M WILLING TO ACCEPT ANYTHING, NO MATTER WHAT I HEAR FROM HIM.
YOU TELL HER WHAT HAPPENED...
...AND YOU'LL REGRET IT FOR THE REST OF YOUR LIFE.
DON'T EVEN GET THE STUPID IDEA IN YOUR HEAD OF TELLING TAKAHASHI.
I WON'T TELL HER.
WHAT DO YOU THINK I AM?
ANYWAY, IT JUST...
JUST WHAT?
...
IT JUST HAPPENED TO BE YAMAMOTO.
THAT'S ALL.

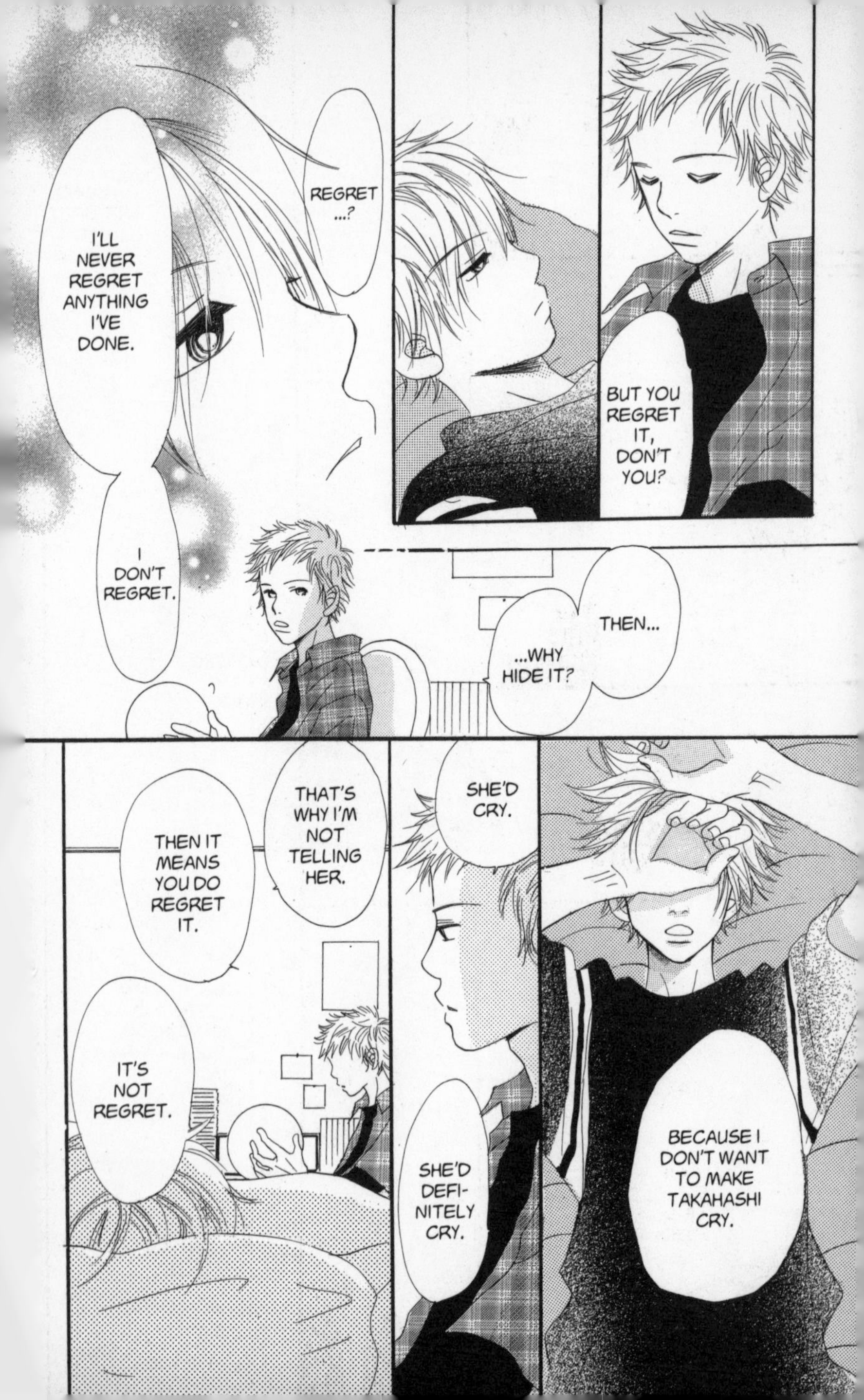
BUT YOU REGRET IT, DON'T YOU?
REGRET ...?
THEN...
...WHY HIDE IT?
I'LL NEVER REGRET ANYTHING I'VE DONE.
I DON'T REGRET.
BECAUSE I DON'T WANT TO MAKE TAKAHASHI CRY.
SHE'D CRY.
SHE'D DEFI-NITELY CRY.
THAT'S WHY I'M NOT TELLING HER.
THEN IT MEANS YOU DO REGRET IT.
IT'S NOT REGRET.

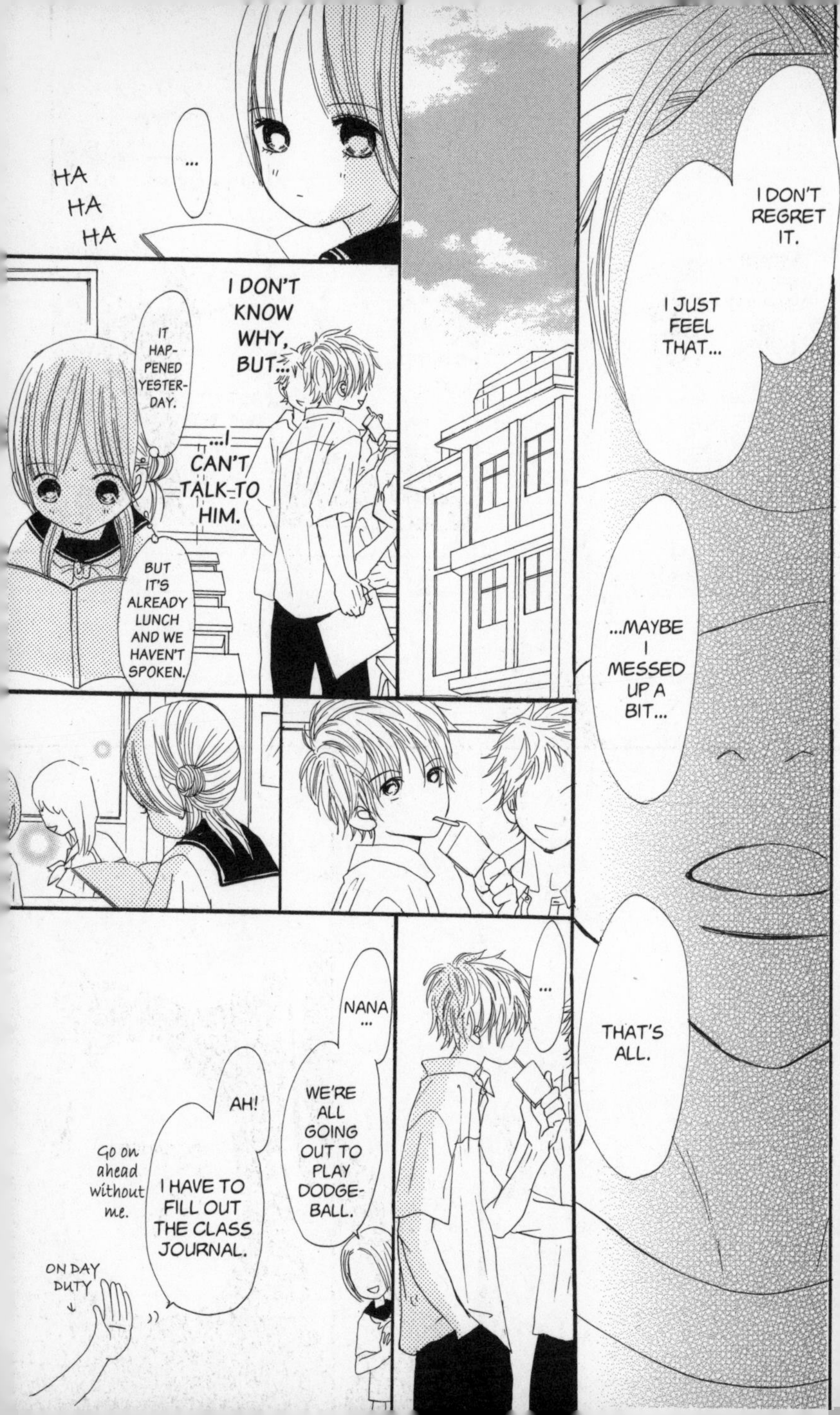
I DON'T REGRET IT.
I JUST FEEL THAT...
...MAYBE I MESSED UP A BIT...
THAT'S ALL.
...
HA HA HA
I DON'T KNOW WHY, BUT...
...I CAN'T TALK TO HIM.
IT HAP-PENED YESTER-DAY.
BUT IT'S ALREADY LUNCH AND WE HAVEN'T SPOKEN.
...
NANA ...
WE'RE ALL GOING OUT TO PLAY DODGE-BALL.
AH!
I HAVE TO FILL OUT THE CLASS JOURNAL.
Go on ahead without me.
ON DAY DUTY

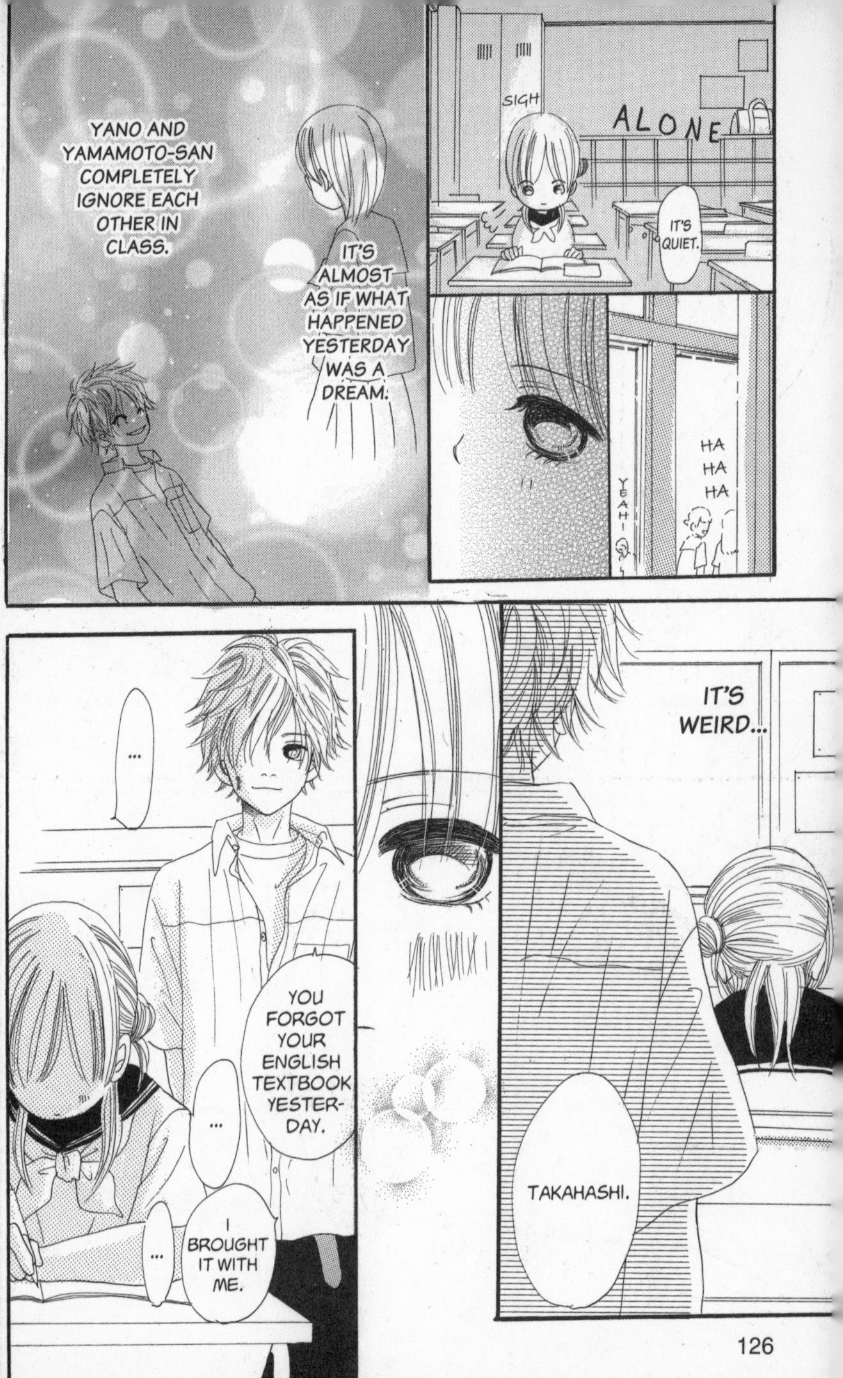
SIGH
ALONE
IT'S QUIET.
HA HA HA
YEAH!
YANO AND YAMAMOTO-SAN COMPLETELY IGNORE EACH OTHER IN CLASS.
IT'S ALMOST AS IF WHAT HAPPENED YESTERDAY WAS A DREAM.
IT'S WEIRD...
TAKAHASHI.
...
YOU FORGOT YOUR ENGLISH TEXTBOOK YESTER-DAY.
...
I BROUGHT IT WITH ME.
...

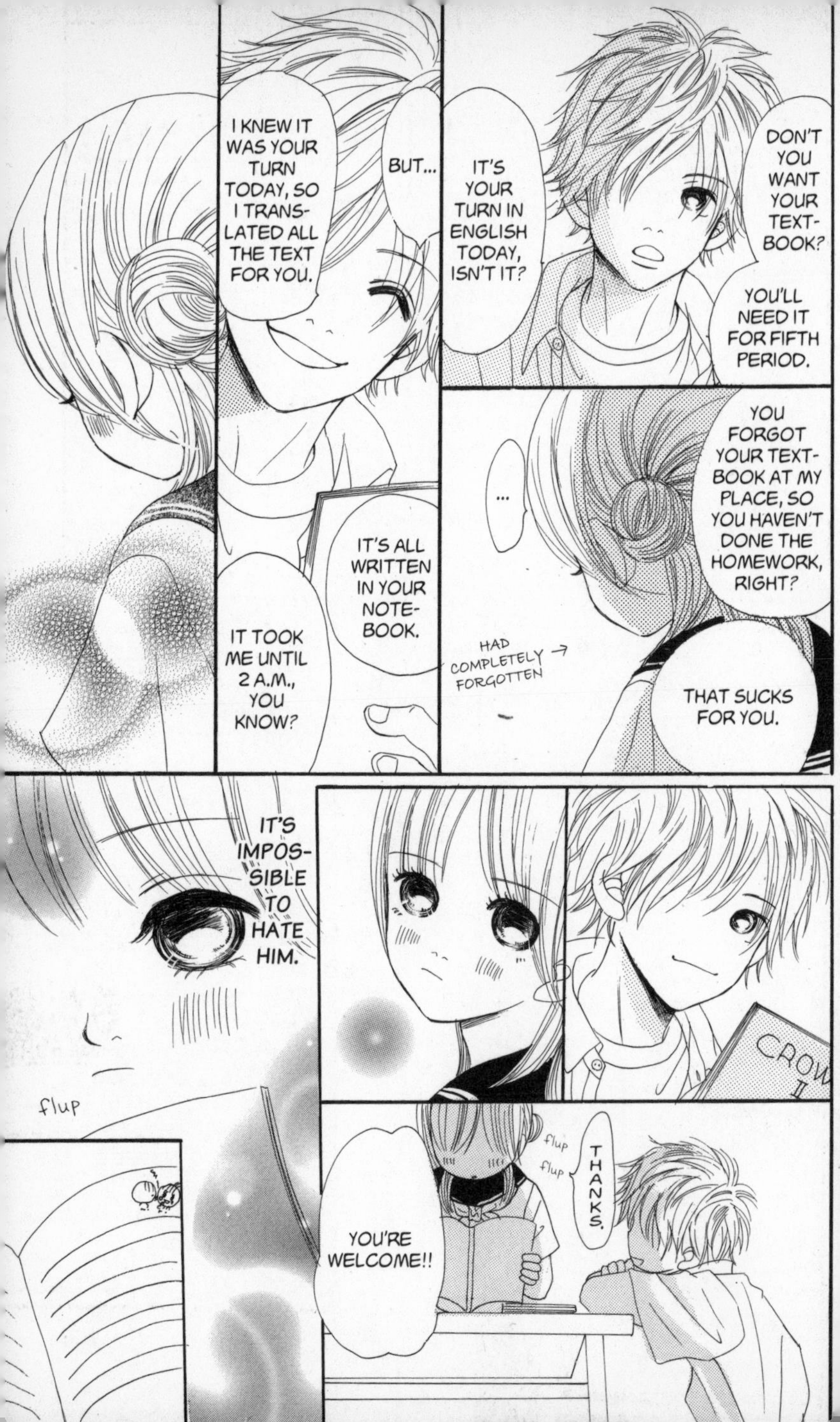
DON'T YOU WANT YOUR TEXT-BOOK?
YOU'LL NEED IT FOR FIFTH PERIOD.
IT'S YOUR TURN IN ENGLISH TODAY, ISN'T IT?
YOU FORGOT YOUR TEXT-BOOK AT MY PLACE, SO YOU HAVEN'T DONE THE HOMEWORK, RIGHT?
...
HAD COMPLETELY FORGOTTEN
THAT SUCKS FOR YOU.
BUT...
I KNEW IT WAS YOUR TURN TODAY, SO I TRANS-LATED ALL THE TEXT FOR YOU.
IT'S ALL WRITTEN IN YOUR NOTE-BOOK.
IT TOOK ME UNTIL 2 A.M., YOU KNOW?
CROW II
IT'S IMPOS-SIBLE TO HATE HIM.
THANKS.
flup
flup
YOU'RE WELCOME!!
flup

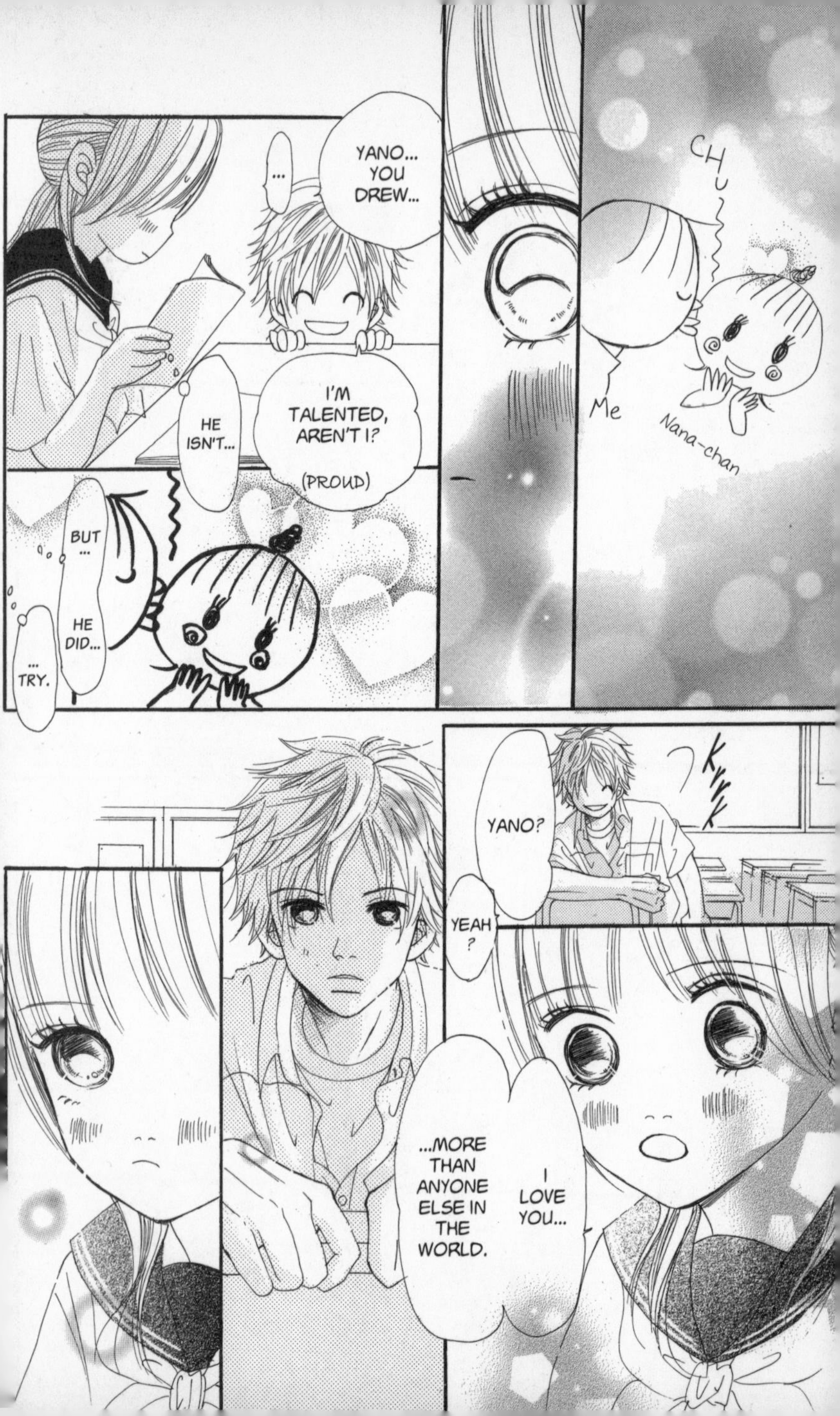
CHU
Me
Nana-chan
YANO... YOU DREW...
...
I'M TALENTED, AREN'T I?
(PROUD)
HE ISN'T...
BUT ...
HE DID...
... TRY.
YANO?
YEAH?
I LOVE YOU...
...MORE THAN ANYONE ELSE IN THE WORLD.

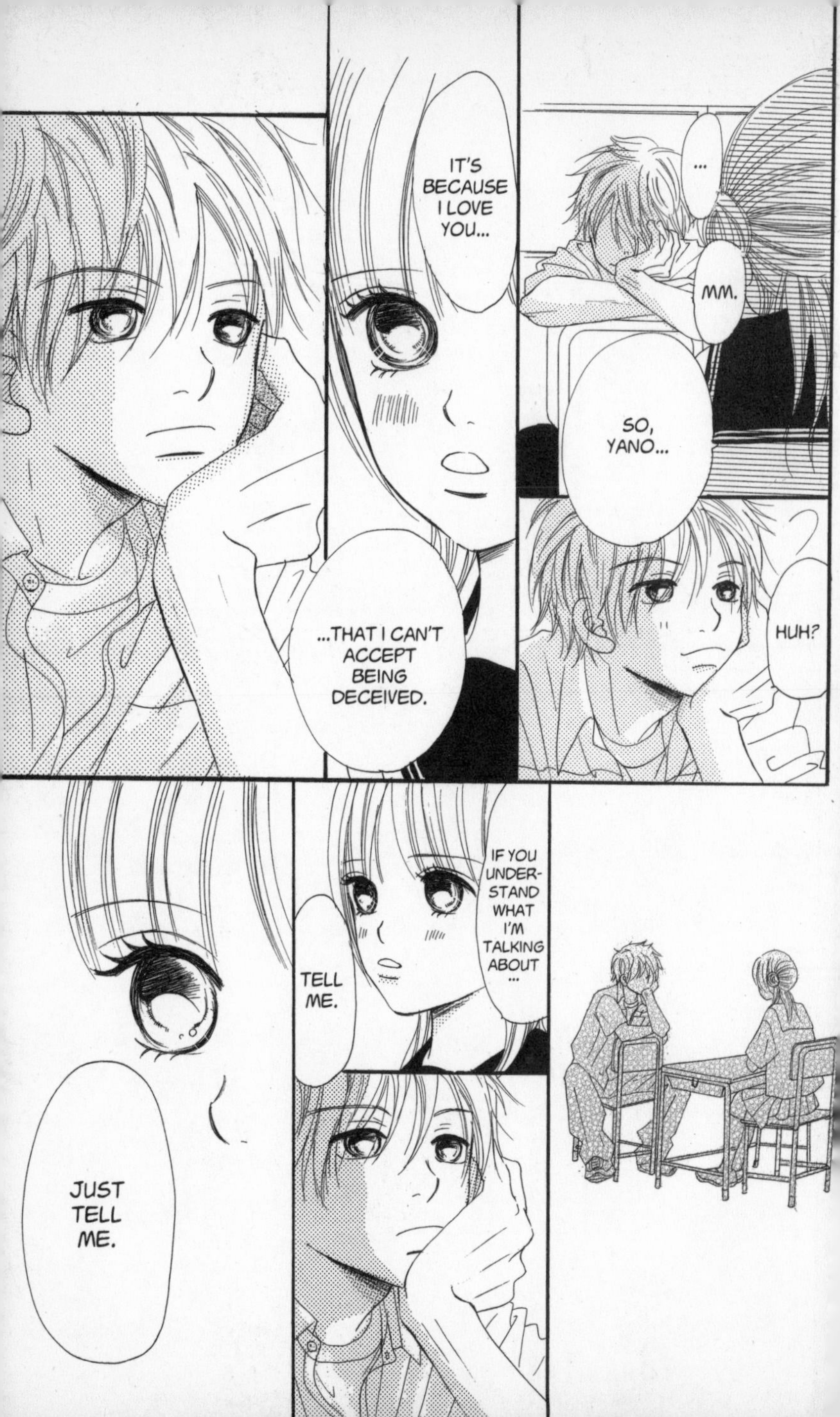
...
MM.
SO, YANO...
HUH?
IT'S BECAUSE I LOVE YOU...
...THAT I CAN'T ACCEPT BEING DECEIVED.
IF YOU UNDERSTAND WHAT I'M TALKING ABOUT...
TELL ME.
JUST TELL ME.

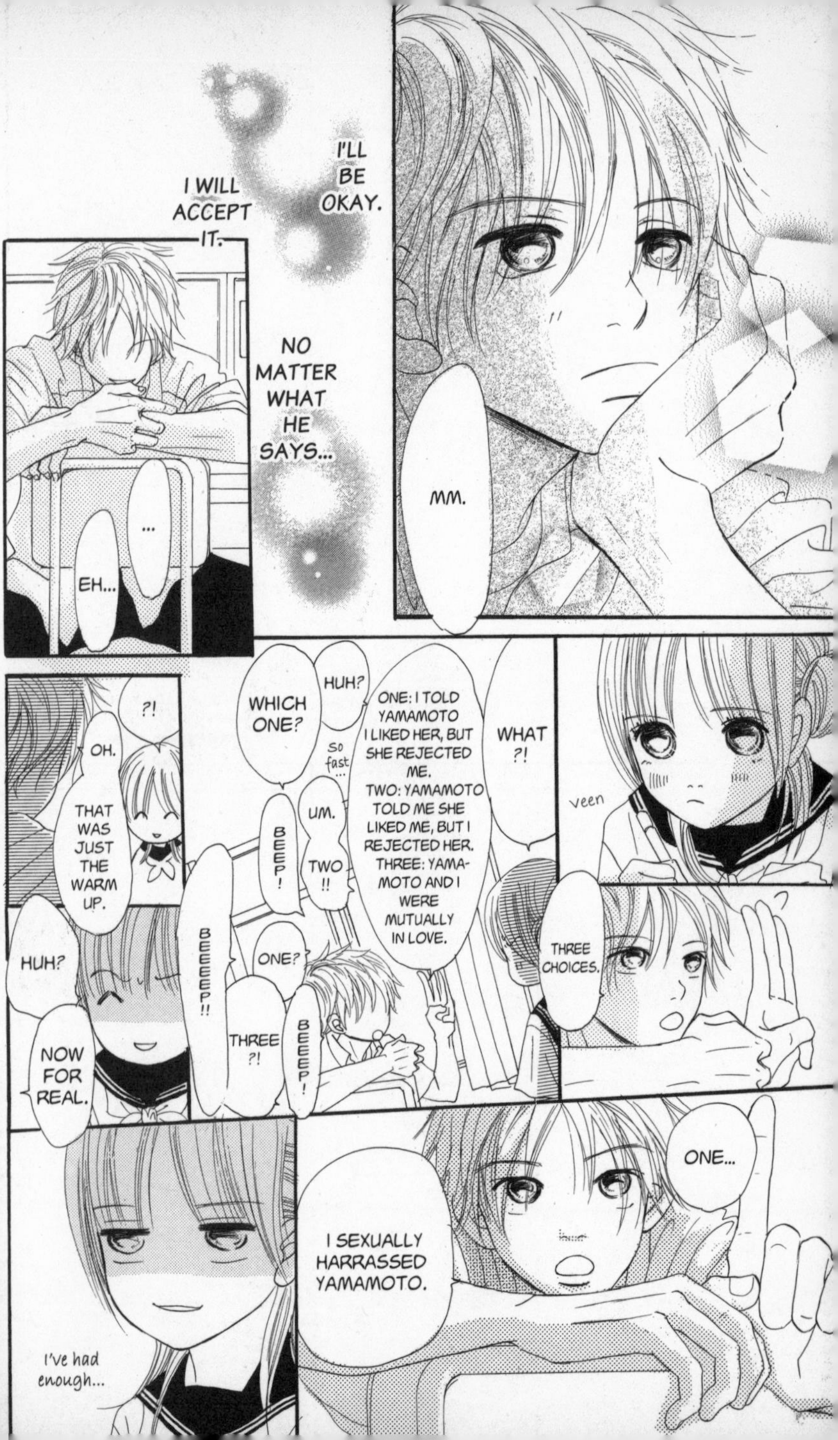
MM.
I'LL BE OKAY.
I WILL ACCEPT IT.
NO MATTER WHAT HE SAYS...
...
EH...
veen
THREE CHOICES.
ONE: I TOLD YAMAMOTO I LIKED HER, BUT SHE REJECTED ME. TWO: YAMAMOTO TOLD ME SHE LIKED ME, BUT I REJECTED HER. THREE: YAMAMOTO AND I WERE MUTUALLY IN LOVE.
WHAT?!
HUH?
WHICH ONE?
so fast...
UM.
TWO!!
BEEP!
ONE?
BEEEEP!!
THREE?!
BEEEEP!
?!
OH.
THAT WAS JUST THE WARM UP.
HUH?
NOW FOR REAL.
ONE...
I SEXUALLY HARRASSED YAMAMOTO.
I've had enough...

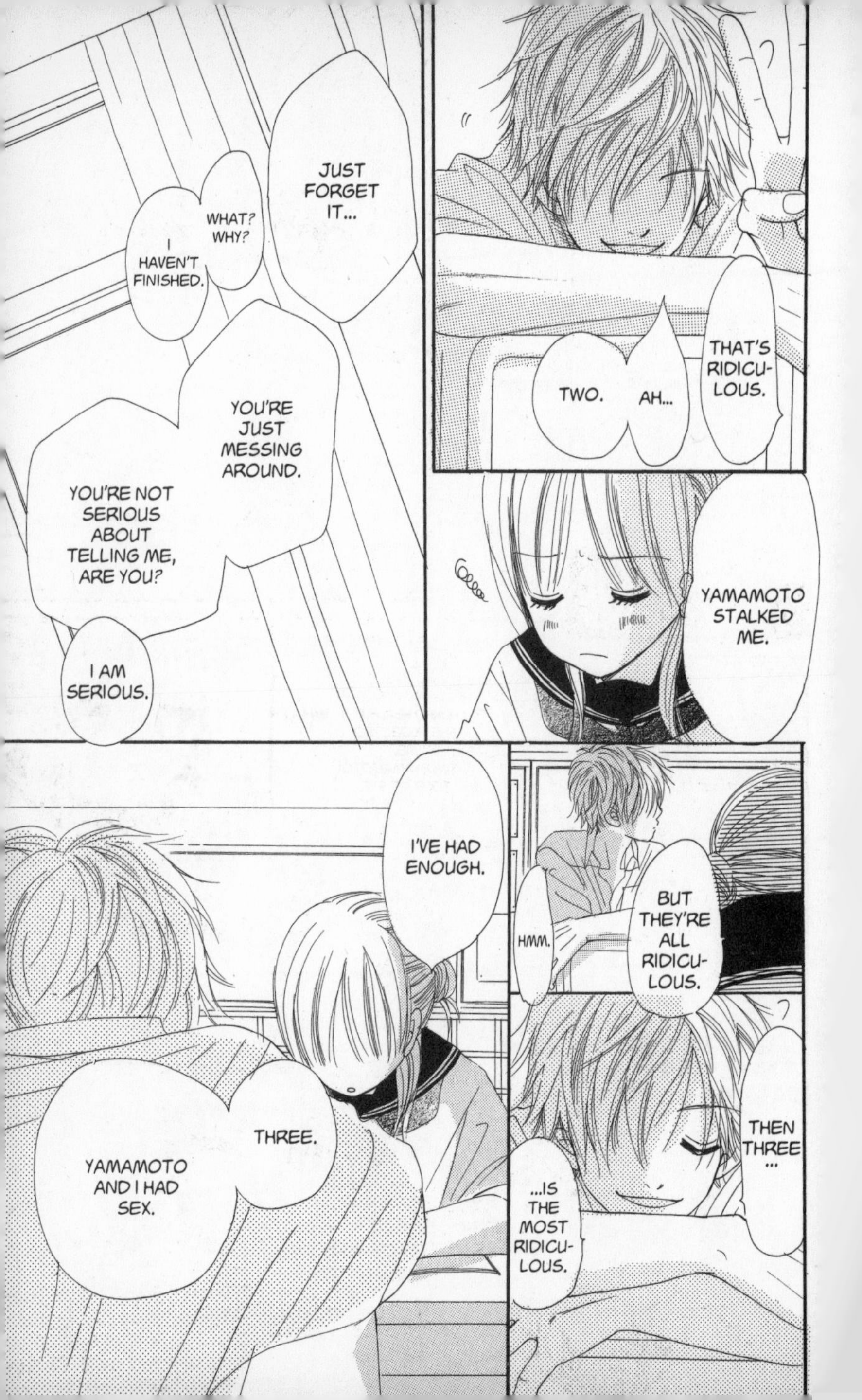
THAT'S RIDICULOUS.
AH...
TWO.
YAMAMOTO STALKED ME.
JUST FORGET IT...
WHAT? WHY?
I HAVEN'T FINISHED.
YOU'RE JUST MESSING AROUND.
YOU'RE NOT SERIOUS ABOUT TELLING ME, ARE YOU?
I AM SERIOUS.
BUT THEY'RE ALL RIDICULOUS.
HMM.
THEN THREE ...
...IS THE MOST RIDICULOUS.
I'VE HAD ENOUGH.
THREE.
YAMAMOTO AND I HAD SEX.

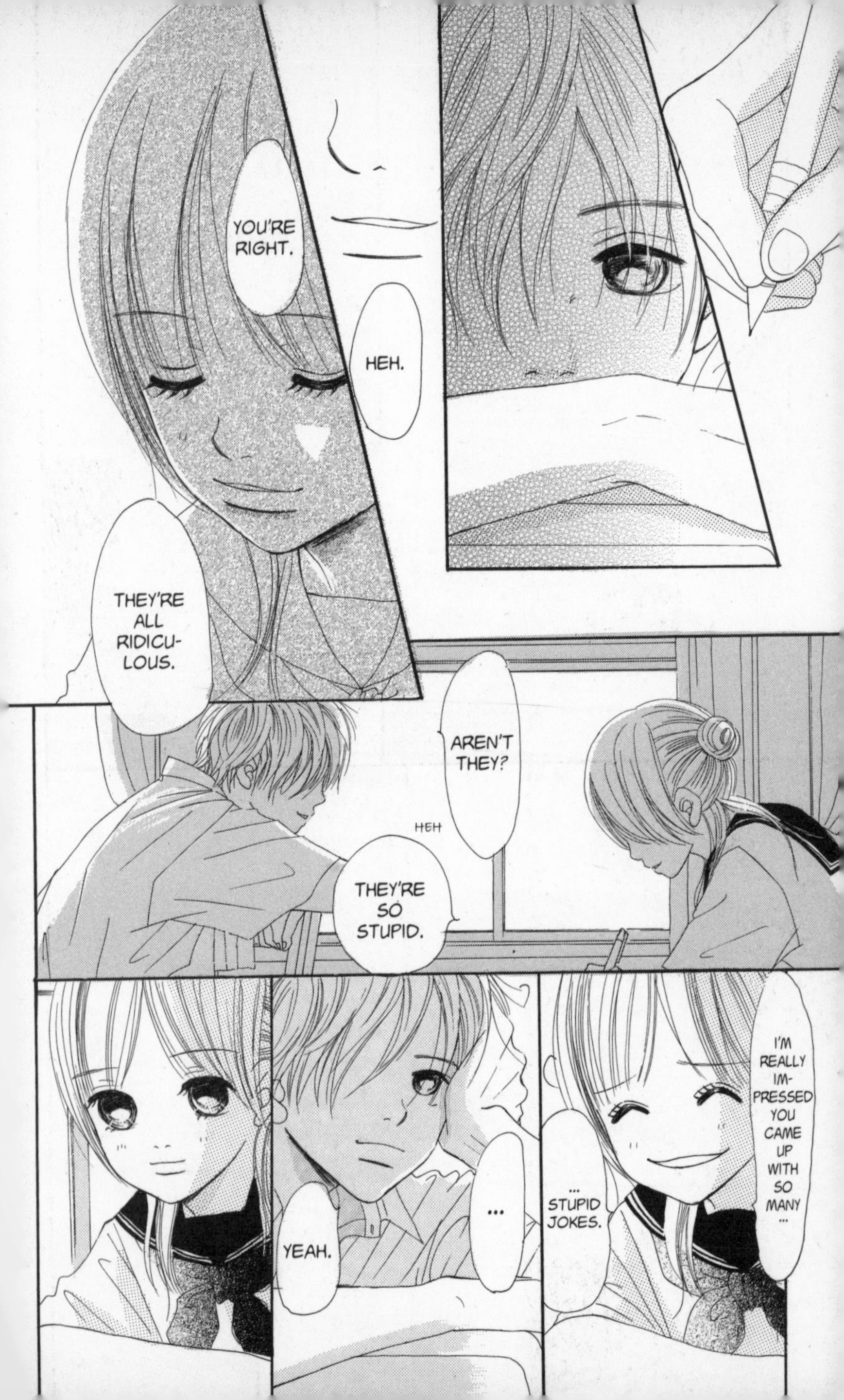
YOU'RE RIGHT.
HEH.
THEY'RE ALL RIDICU-LOUS.
AREN'T THEY?
HEH
THEY'RE SO STUPID.
I'M REALLY IM-PRESSED YOU CAME UP WITH SO MANY ...
... STUPID JOKES.
...
YEAH.

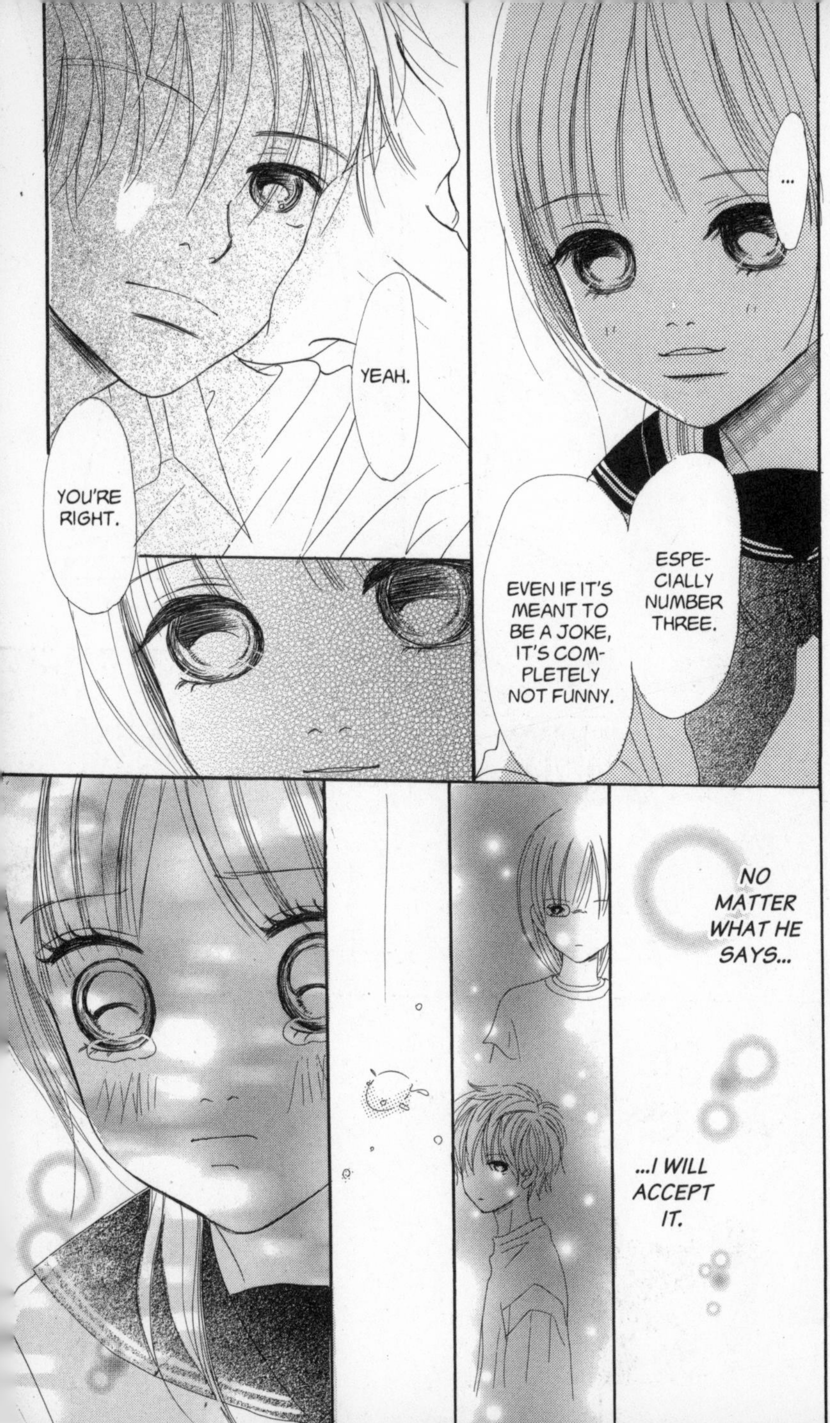
...
ESPE-CIALLY NUMBER THREE.
EVEN IF IT'S MEANT TO BE A JOKE, IT'S COM-PLETELY NOT FUNNY.
YEAH.
YOU'RE RIGHT.
NO MATTER WHAT HE SAYS...
...I WILL ACCEPT IT.

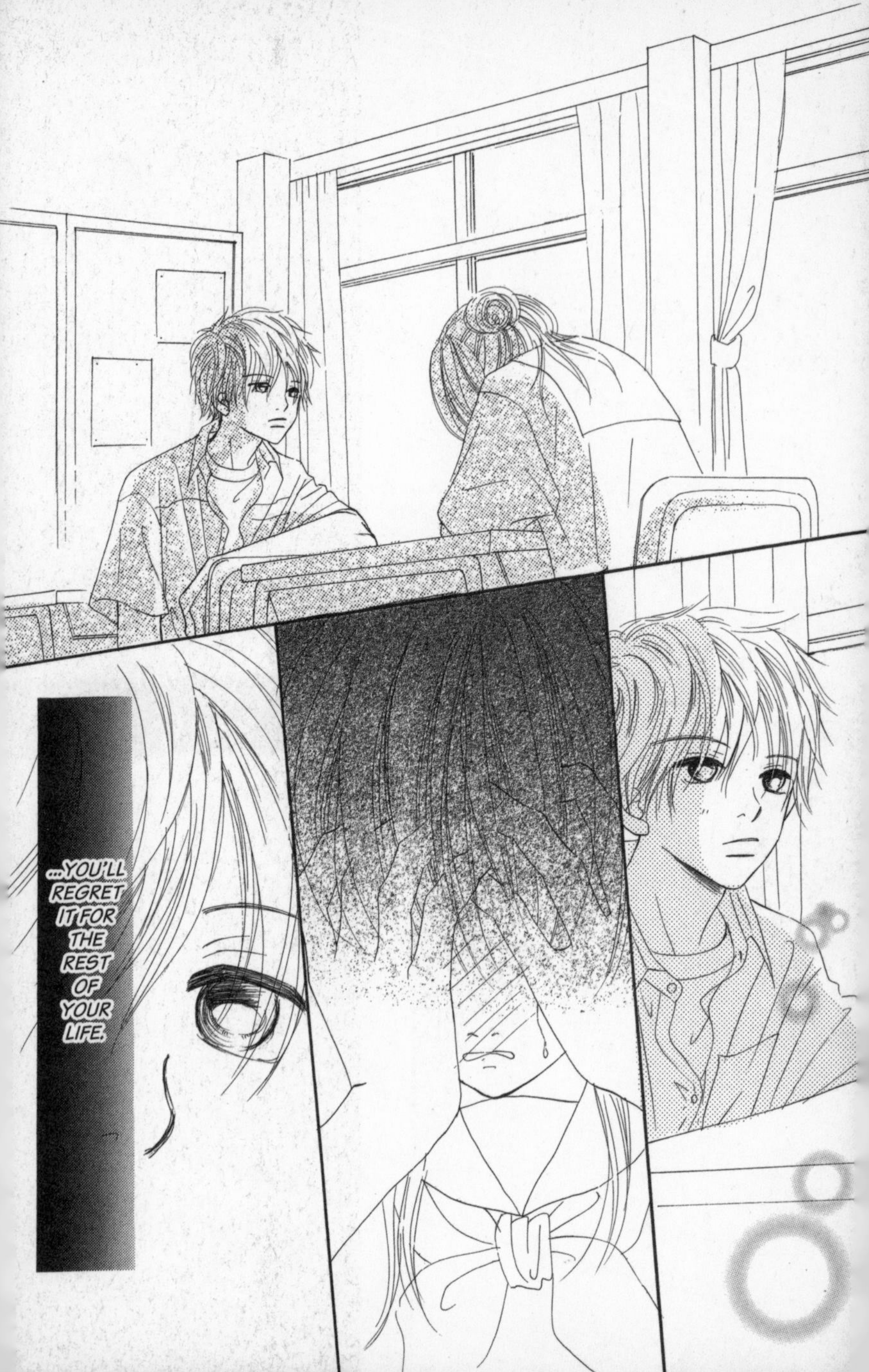
...YOU'LL REGRET IT FOR THE REST OF YOUR LIFE.

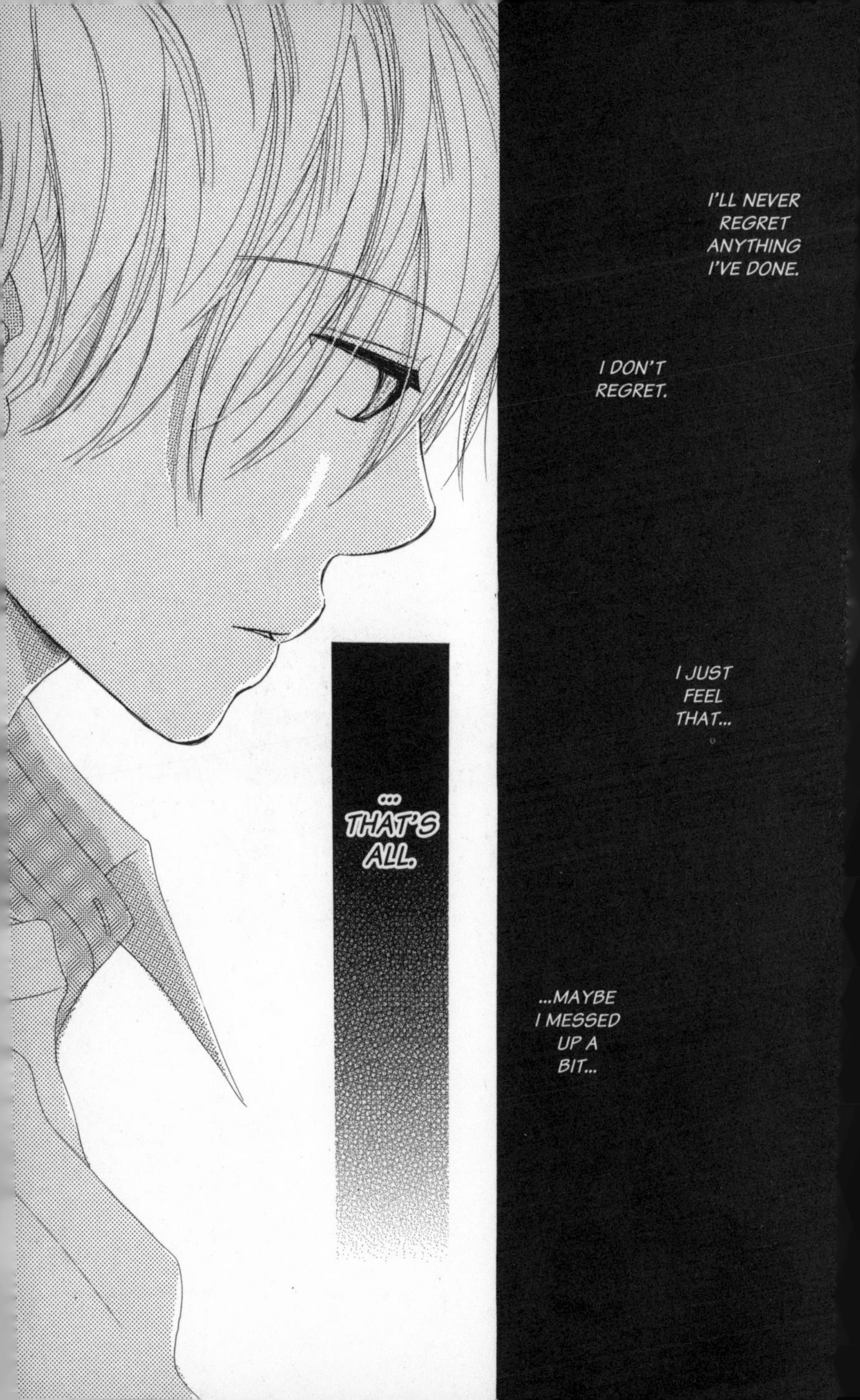
I'LL NEVER REGRET ANYTHING I'VE DONE.
I DON'T REGRET.
I JUST FEEL THAT...
...MAYBE I MESSED UP A BIT...
...THAT'S ALL.

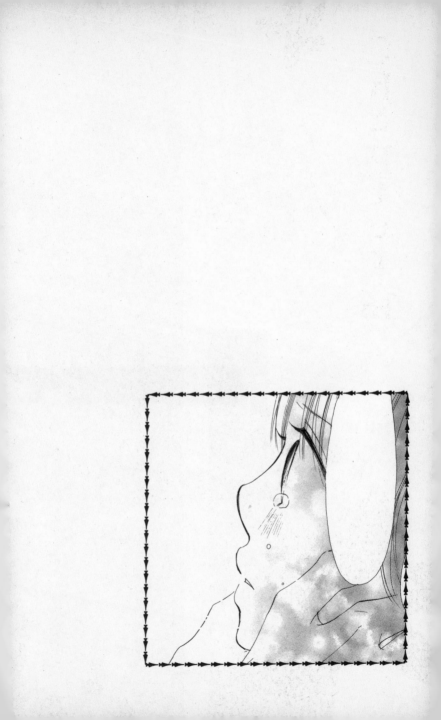

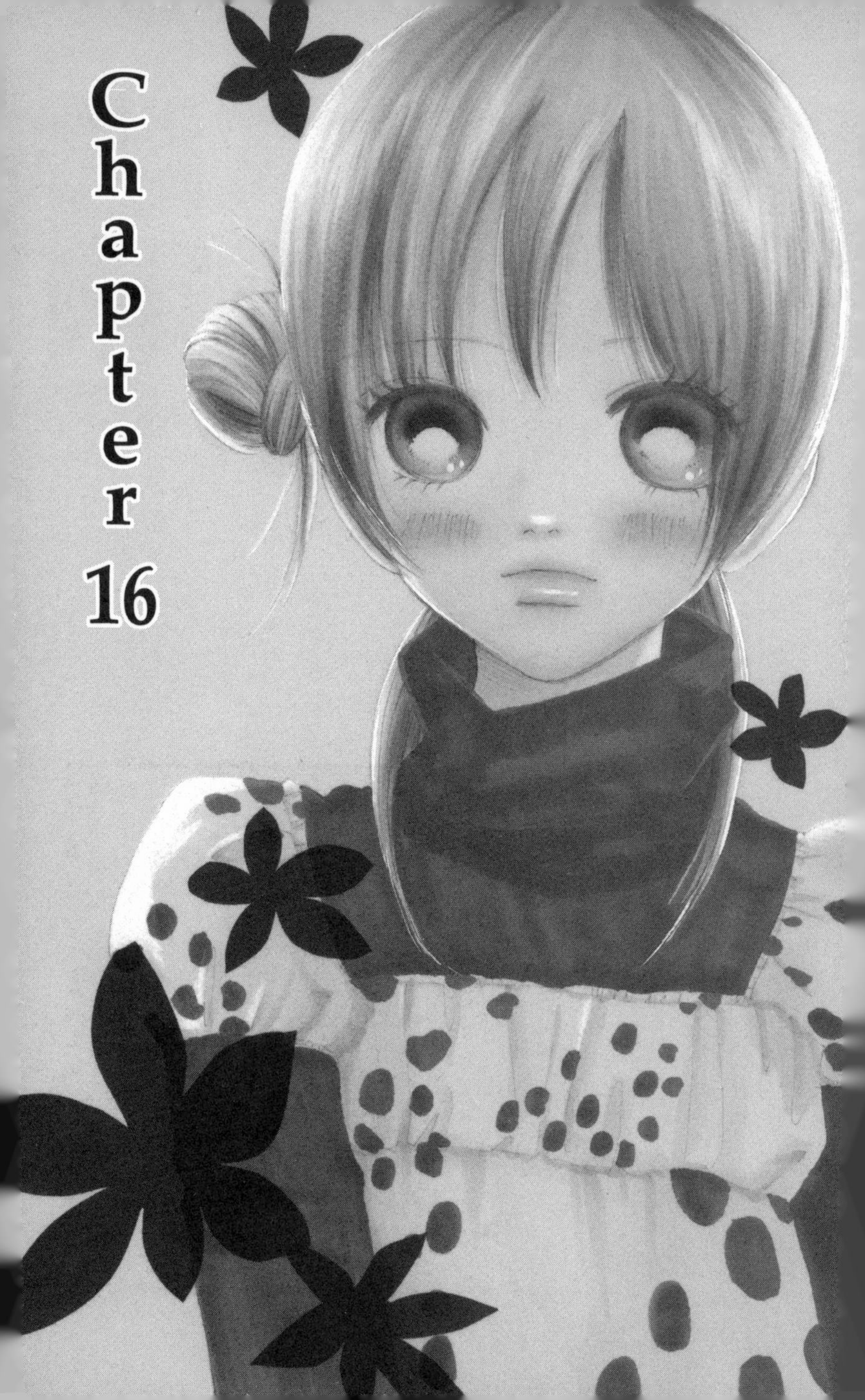
Chapter 16

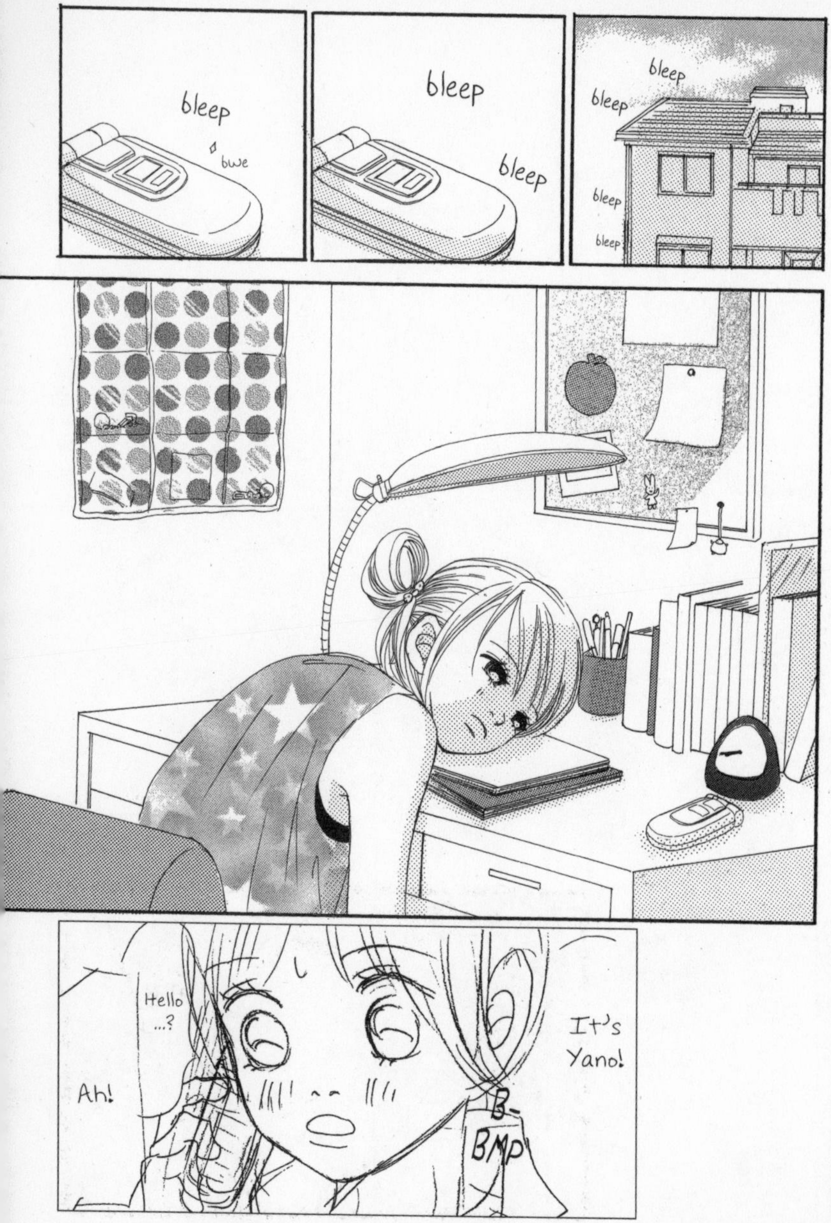

bleep
bleep
bleep
bleep
bleep
bleep
bleep
bwe
It's Yano!
Hello ...?
B-BMP
Ah!

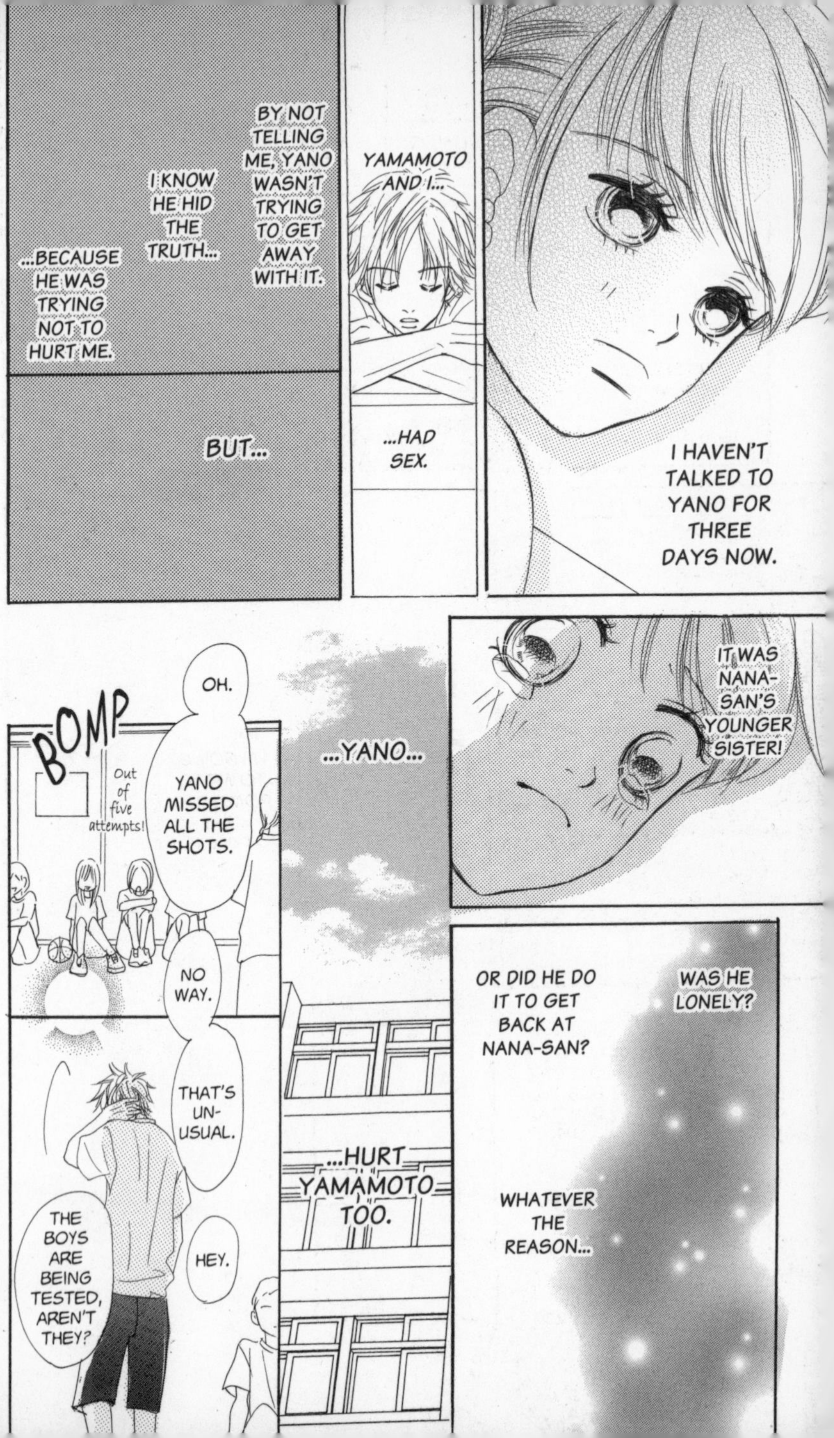
I HAVEN'T TALKED TO YANO FOR THREE DAYS NOW.
YAMAMOTO AND I...
...HAD SEX.
BY NOT TELLING ME, YANO WASN'T TRYING TO GET AWAY WITH IT.
I KNOW HE HID THE TRUTH...
...BECAUSE HE WAS TRYING NOT TO HURT ME.
BUT...
IT WAS NANA-SAN'S YOUNGER SISTER!
WAS HE LONELY?
OR DID HE DO IT TO GET BACK AT NANA-SAN?
WHATEVER THE REASON...
...YANO...
...HURT YAMAMOTO TOO.
OH.
BOMP
YANO MISSED ALL THE SHOTS.
Out of five attempts!
NO WAY.
THAT'S UN-USUAL.
HEY.
THE BOYS ARE BEING TESTED, AREN'T THEY?

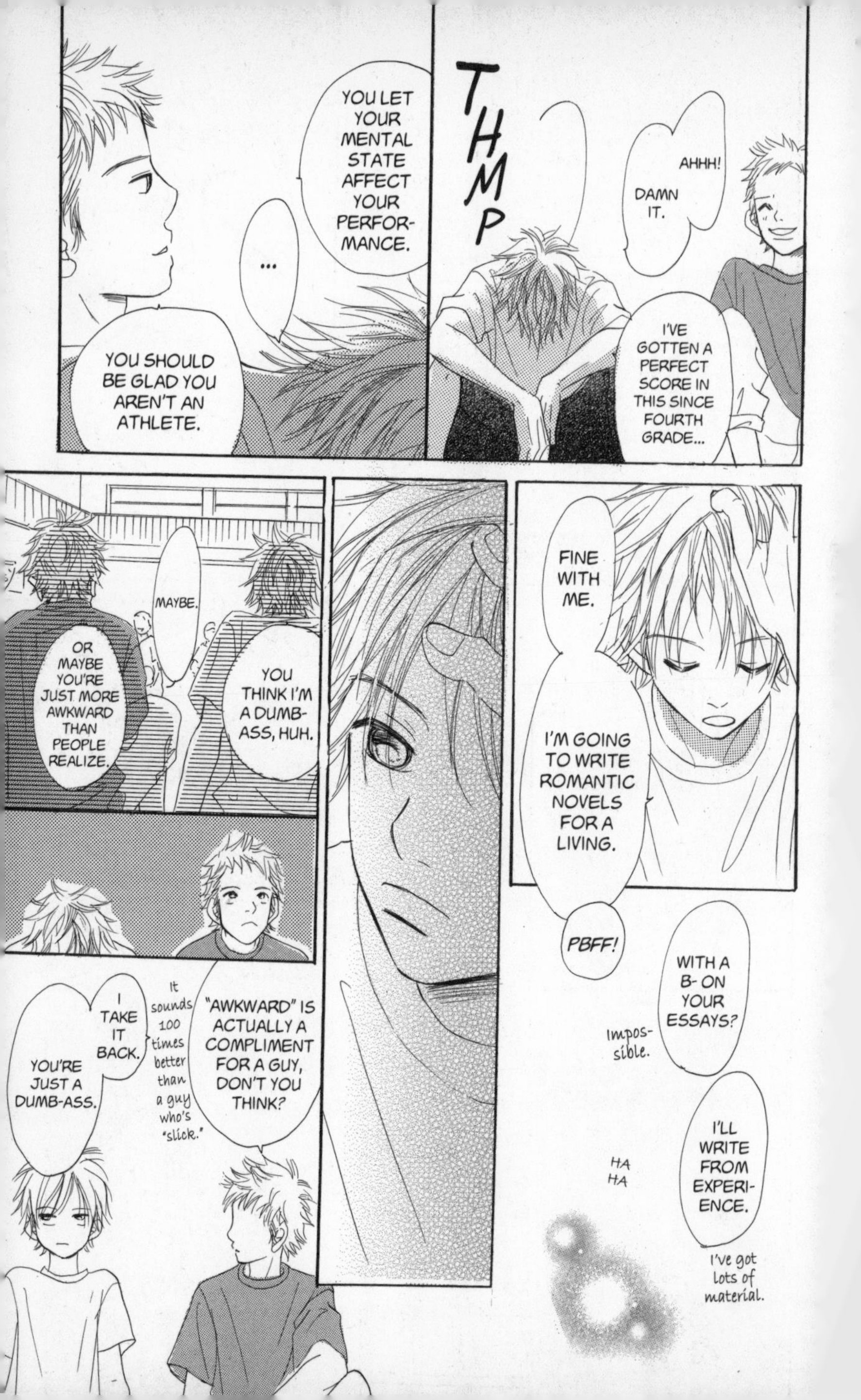
THMP
AHHH!
DAMN IT.
I'VE GOTTEN A PERFECT SCORE IN THIS SINCE FOURTH GRADE...
YOU LET YOUR MENTAL STATE AFFECT YOUR PERFORMANCE.
...
YOU SHOULD BE GLAD YOU AREN'T AN ATHLETE.
FINE WITH ME.
I'M GOING TO WRITE ROMANTIC NOVELS FOR A LIVING.
PBFF!
WITH A B- ON YOUR ESSAYS?
Impos-sible.
I'LL WRITE FROM EXPERI-ENCE.
HA HA
I've got lots of material.
YOU THINK I'M A DUMB-ASS, HUH.
MAYBE.
OR MAYBE YOU'RE JUST MORE AWKWARD THAN PEOPLE REALIZE.
"AWKWARD" IS ACTUALLY A COMPLIMENT FOR A GUY, DON'T YOU THINK?
It sounds 100 times better than a guy who's "slick."
I TAKE IT BACK.
YOU'RE JUST A DUMB-ASS.

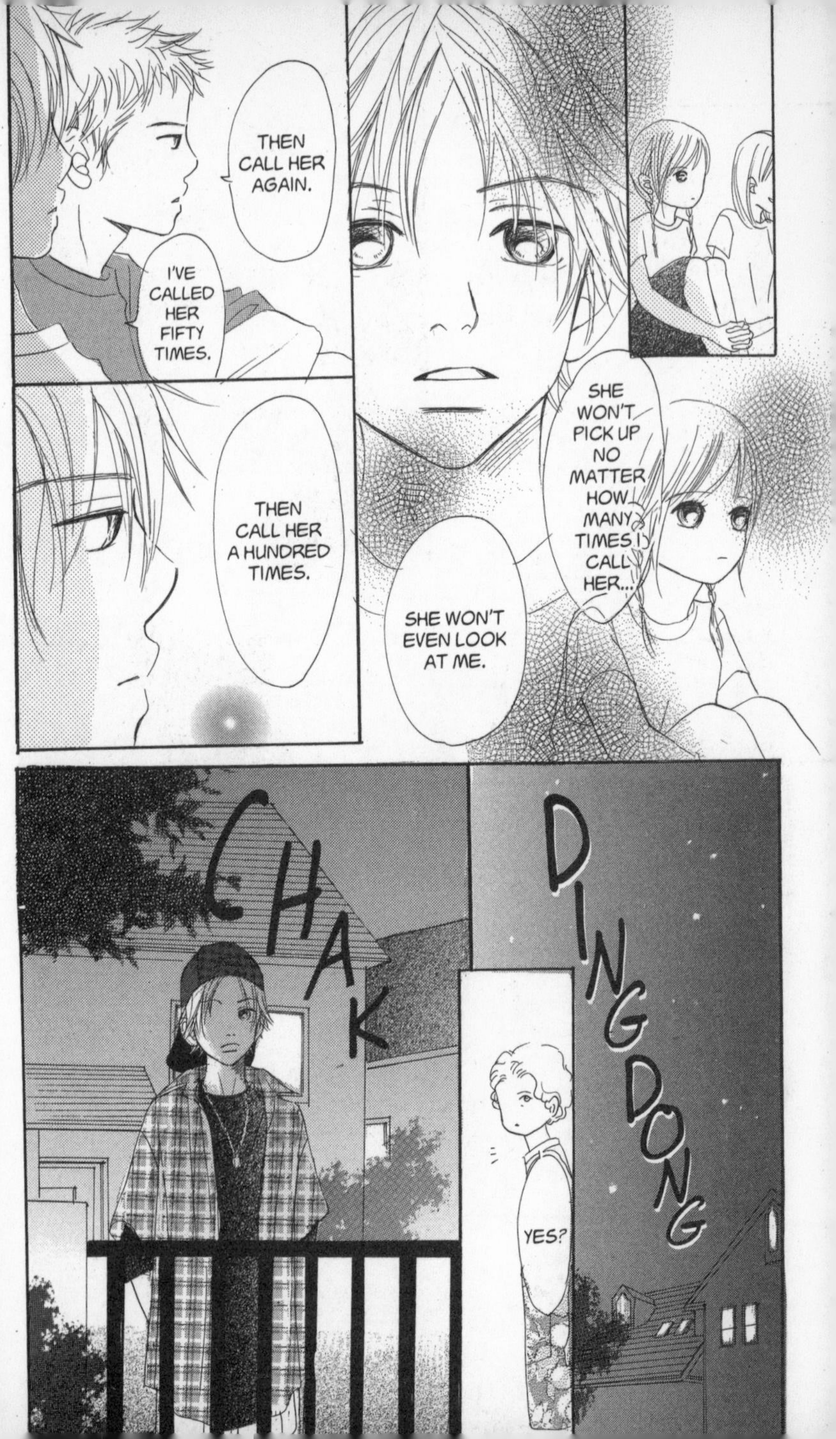
SHE WON'T PICK UP NO MATTER HOW MANY TIMES I CALL HER...
SHE WON'T EVEN LOOK AT ME.
THEN CALL HER AGAIN.
I'VE CALLED HER FIFTY TIMES.
THEN CALL HER A HUNDRED TIMES.
DING DONG
YES?
CHAK

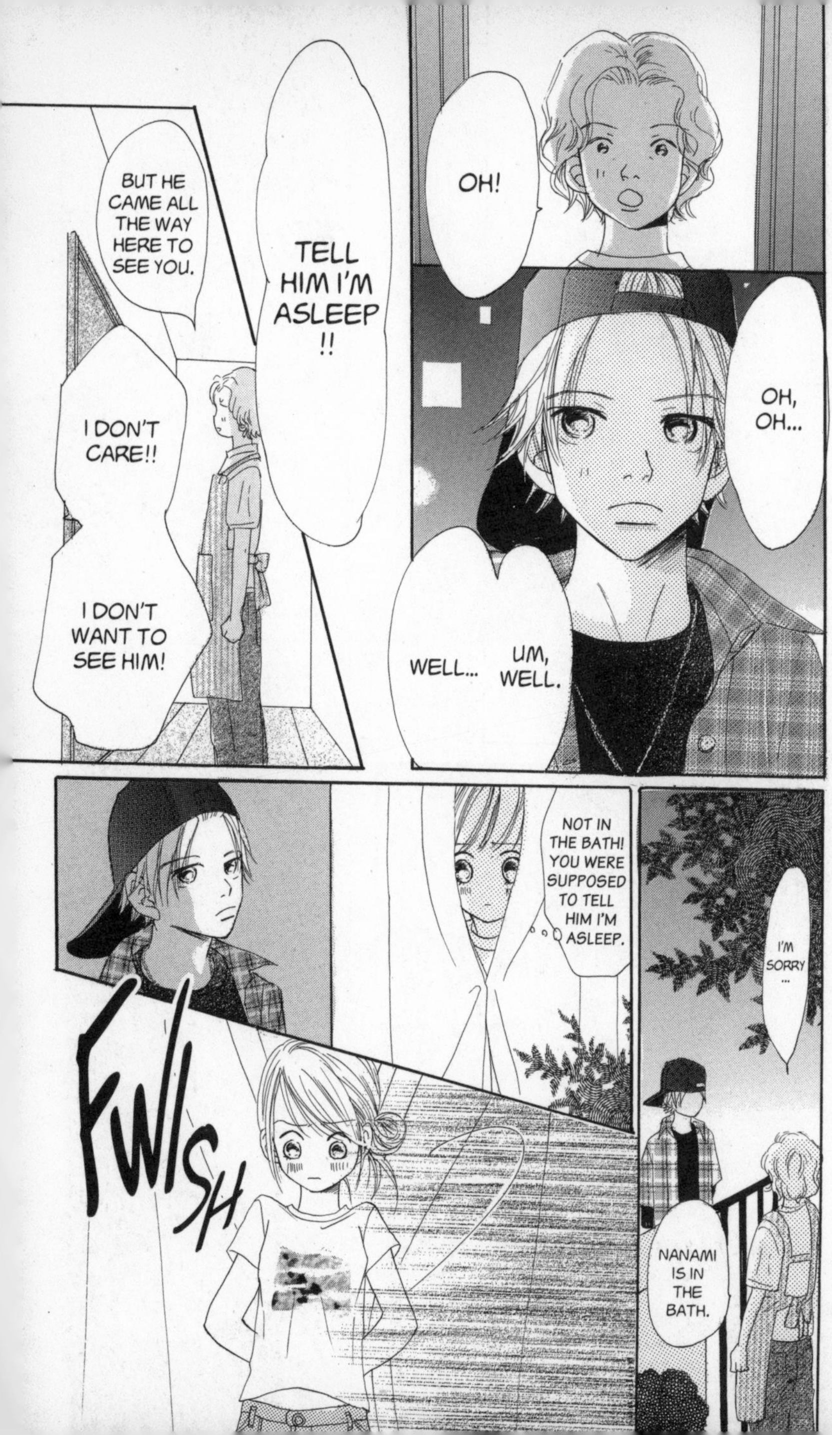
OH!
OH, OH...
WELL... UM, WELL.
TELL HIM I'M ASLEEP!!
BUT HE CAME ALL THE WAY HERE TO SEE YOU.
I DON'T CARE!!
I DON'T WANT TO SEE HIM!
I'M SORRY...
NANAMI IS IN THE BATH.
NOT IN THE BATH! YOU WERE SUPPOSED TO TELL HIM I'M ASLEEP.
FWISH

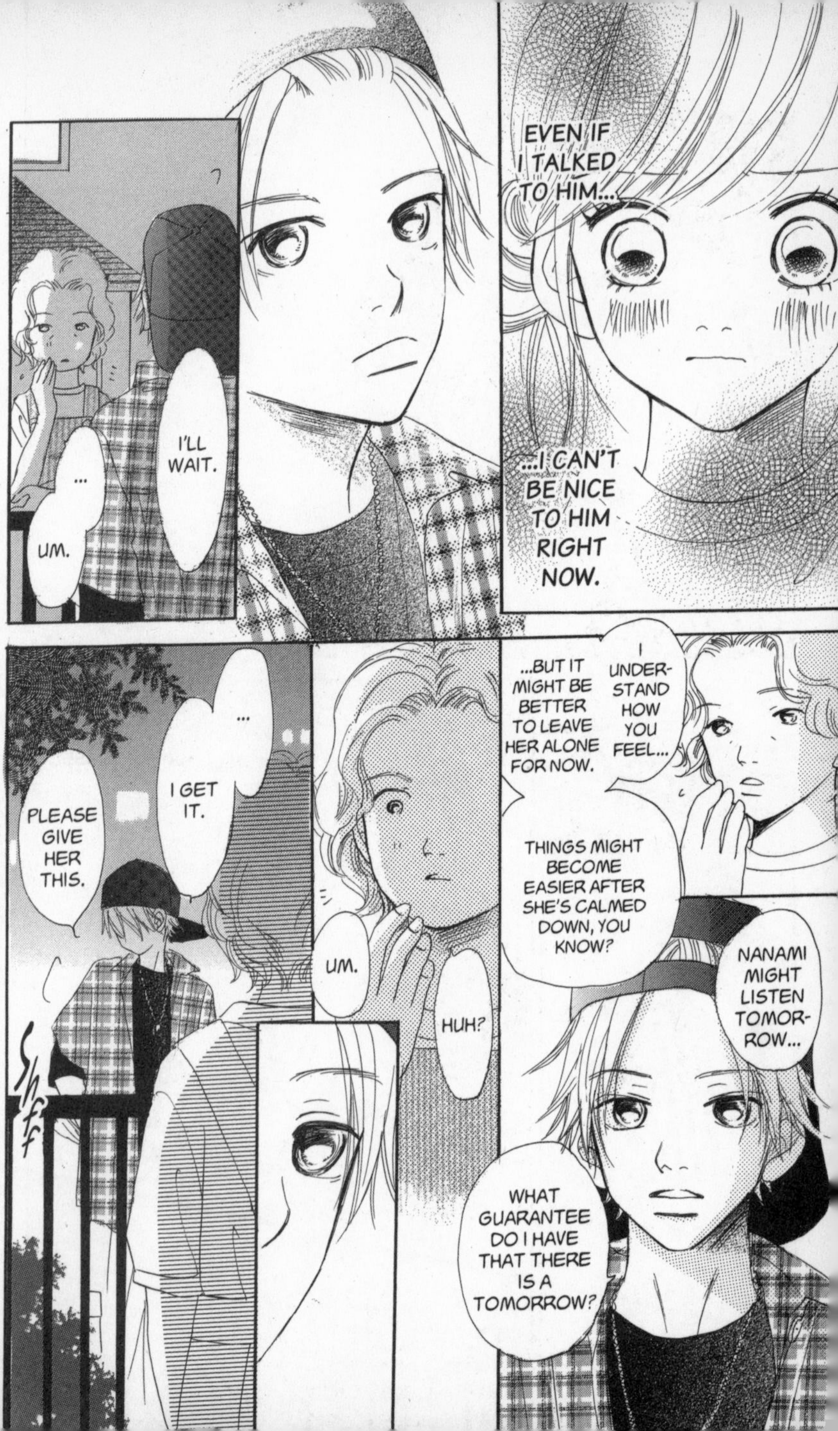
EVEN IF I TALKED TO HIM...
...I CAN'T BE NICE TO HIM RIGHT NOW.
I'LL WAIT.
...
UM.
I UNDERSTAND HOW YOU FEEL...
...BUT IT MIGHT BE BETTER TO LEAVE HER ALONE FOR NOW.
THINGS MIGHT BECOME EASIER AFTER SHE'S CALMED DOWN, YOU KNOW?
NANAMI MIGHT LISTEN TOMORROW...
WHAT GUARANTEE DO I HAVE THAT THERE IS A TOMORROW?
HUH?
UM.
...
I GET IT.
PLEASE GIVE HER THIS.
SHFF

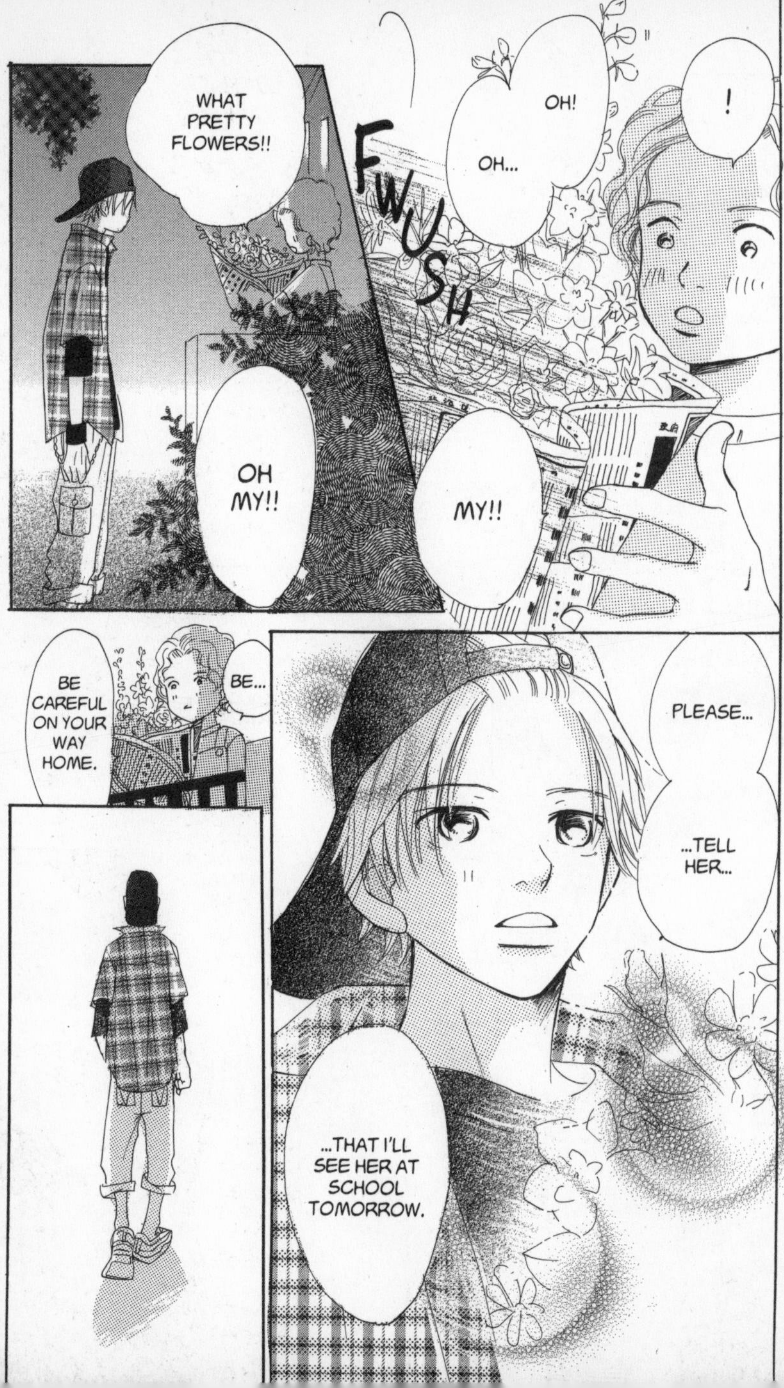
!
OH!
OH...
FWUSH
MY!!
WHAT PRETTY FLOWERS!!
OH MY!!
PLEASE...
...TELL HER...
...THAT I'LL SEE HER AT SCHOOL TOMORROW.
BE...
BE CAREFUL ON YOUR WAY HOME.

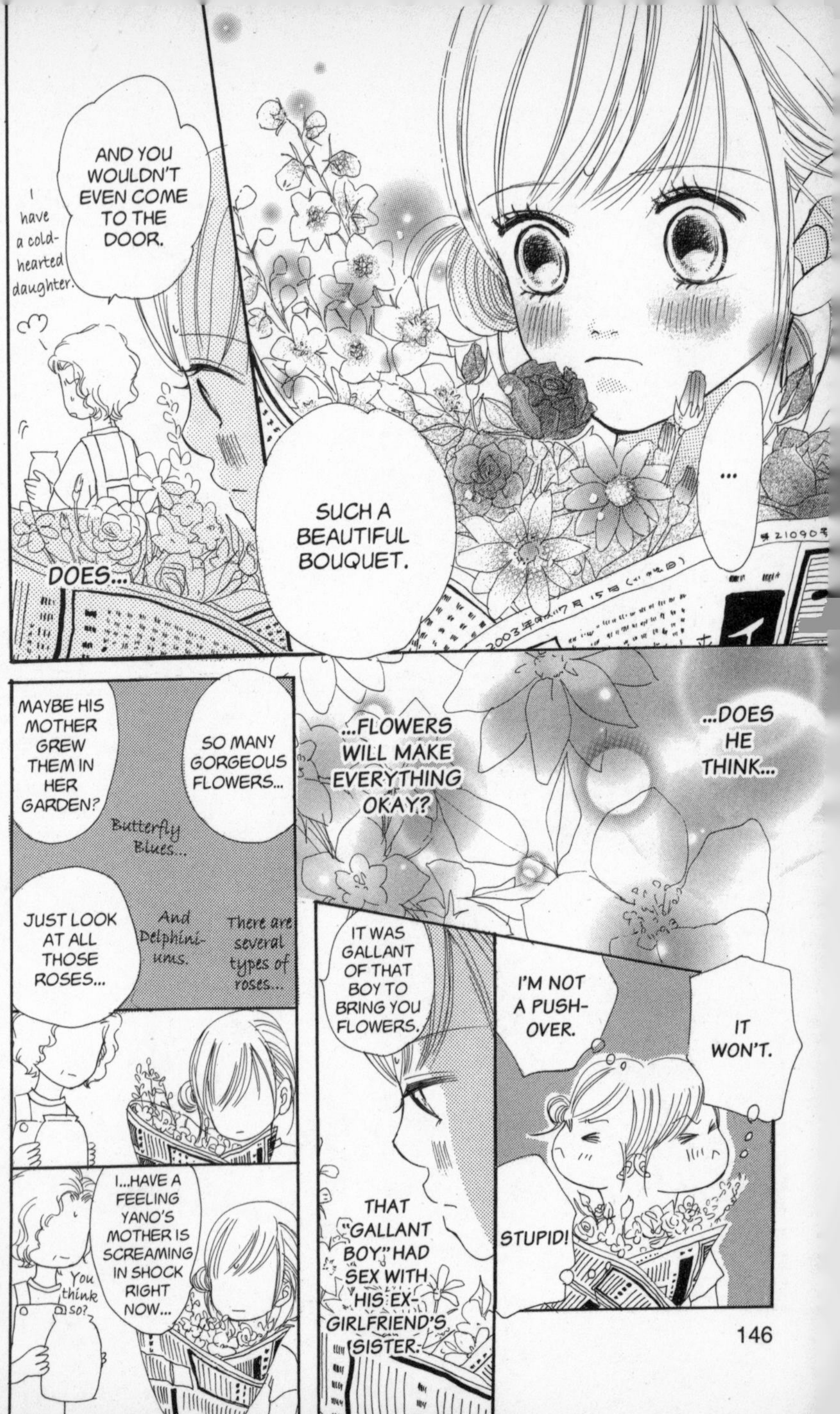
...
SUCH A BEAUTIFUL BOUQUET.
AND YOU WOULDN'T EVEN COME TO THE DOOR.
I have a cold-hearted daughter.
DOES...
...DOES HE THINK...
...FLOWERS WILL MAKE EVERYTHING OKAY?
IT WON'T.
I'M NOT A PUSH-OVER.
STUPID!
IT WAS GALLANT OF THAT BOY TO BRING YOU FLOWERS.
THAT "GALLANT BOY" HAD SEX WITH HIS EX-GIRLFRIEND'S SISTER.
SO MANY GORGEOUS FLOWERS...
MAYBE HIS MOTHER GREW THEM IN HER GARDEN?
Butterfly Blues...
There are several types of roses...
And Delphiniums.
JUST LOOK AT ALL THOSE ROSES...
I...HAVE A FEELING YANO'S MOTHER IS SCREAMING IN SHOCK RIGHT NOW...
You think so?

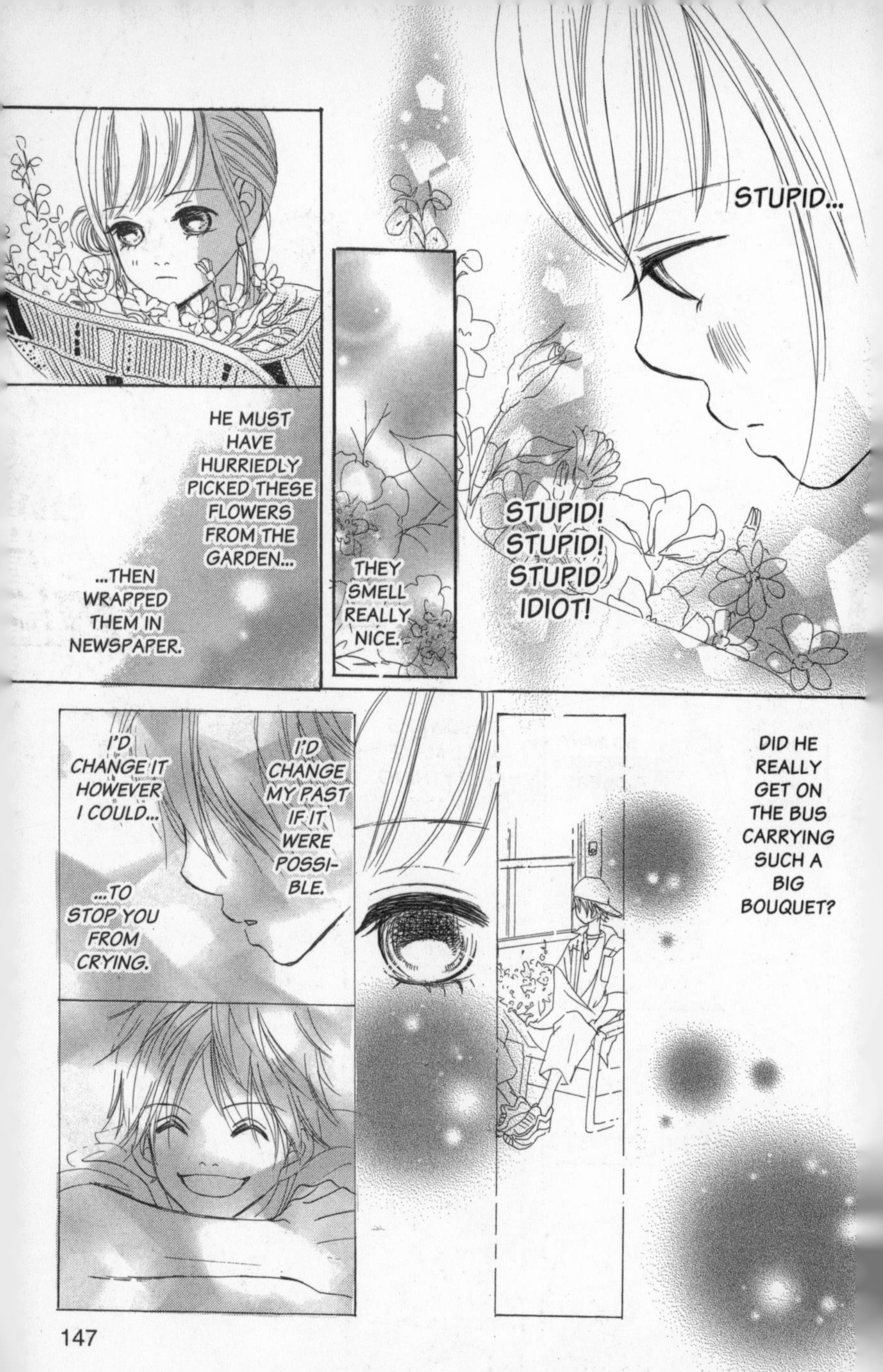
STUPID...
STUPID! STUPID! STUPID IDIOT!
THEY SMELL REALLY NICE.
HE MUST HAVE HURRIEDLY PICKED THESE FLOWERS FROM THE GARDEN...
...THEN WRAPPED THEM IN NEWSPAPER.
DID HE REALLY GET ON THE BUS CARRYING SUCH A BIG BOUQUET?
I'D CHANGE MY PAST IF IT WERE POSSI-BLE.
I'D CHANGE IT HOWEVER I COULD...
...TO STOP YOU FROM CRYING.

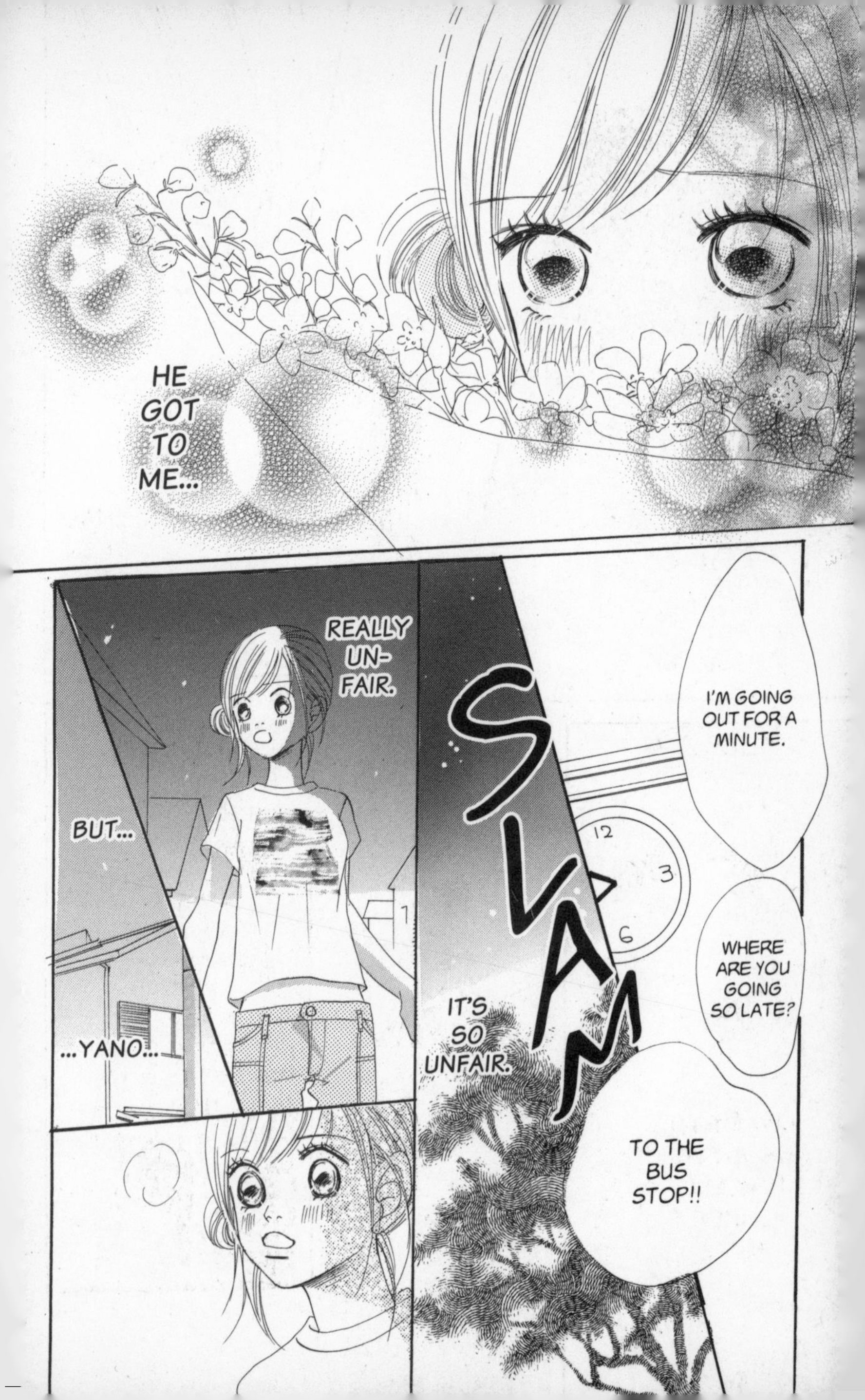
HE GOT TO ME...
I'M GOING OUT FOR A MINUTE.
WHERE ARE YOU GOING SO LATE?
TO THE BUS STOP!!
SLAM
IT'S SO UNFAIR.
REALLY UN-FAIR.
BUT...
...YANO...

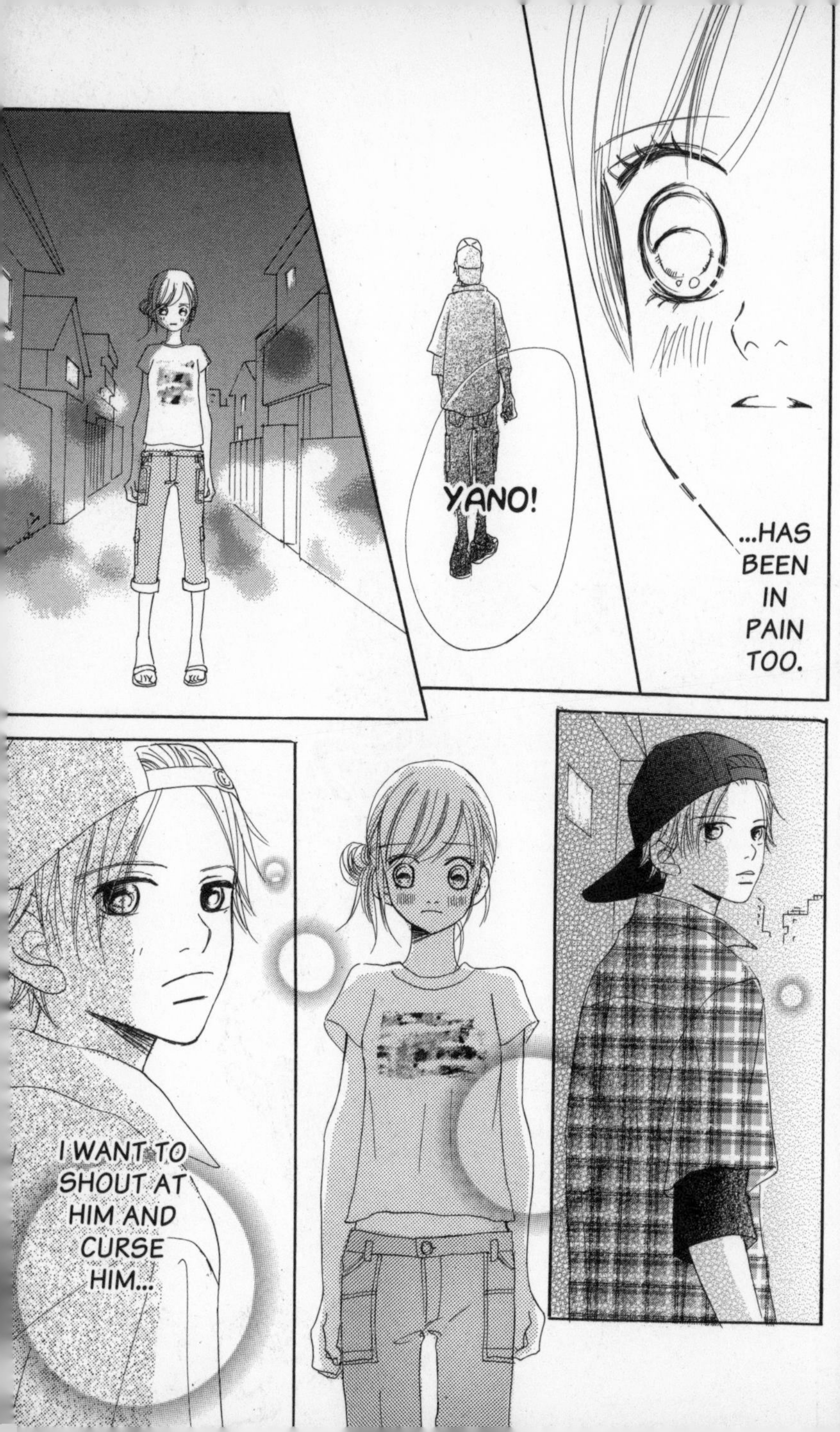
...HAS BEEN IN PAIN TOO.
YANO!
I WANT TO SHOUT AT HIM AND CURSE HIM...

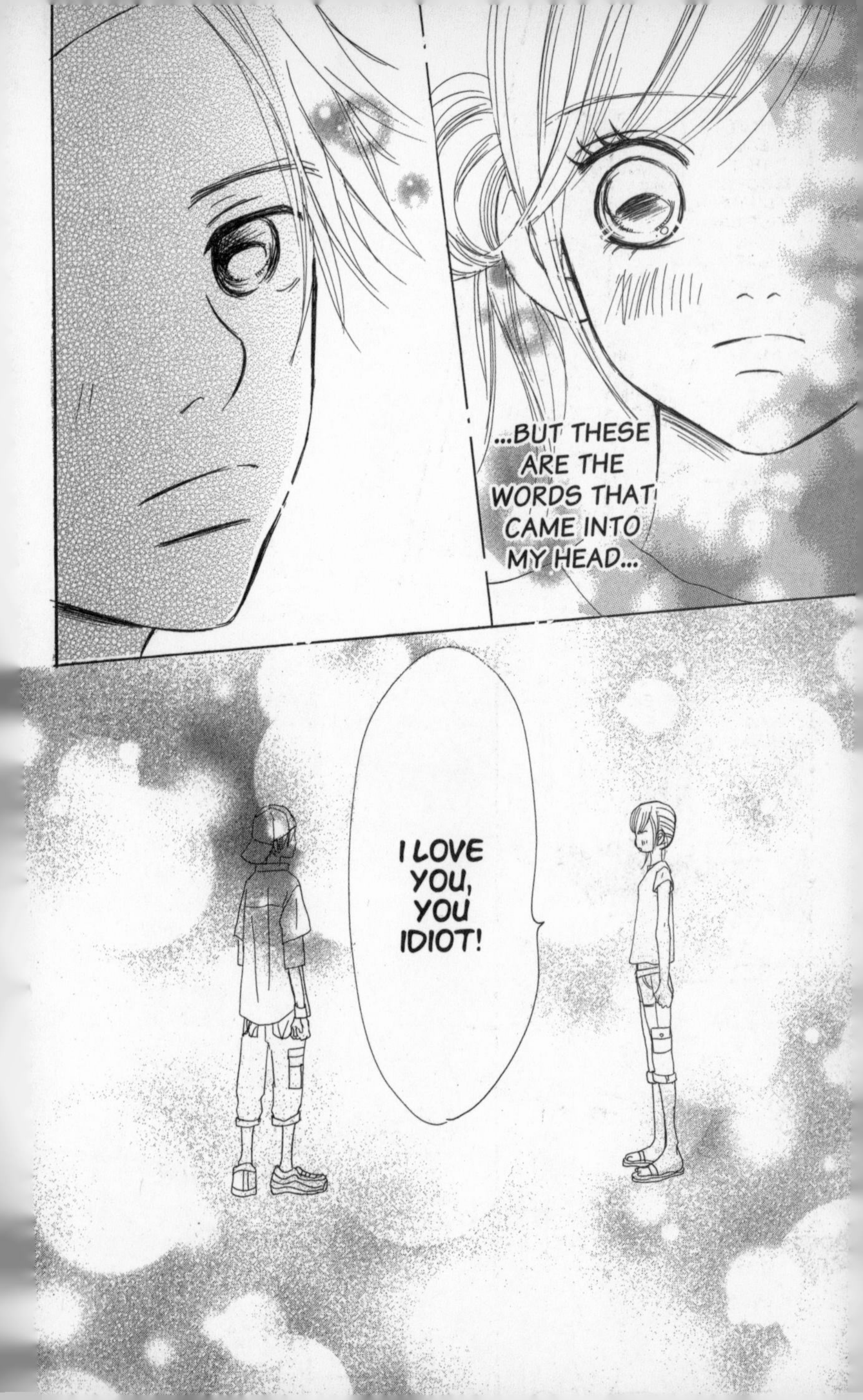
...BUT THESE ARE THE WORDS THAT CAME INTO MY HEAD...
I LOVE YOU, YOU IDIOT!

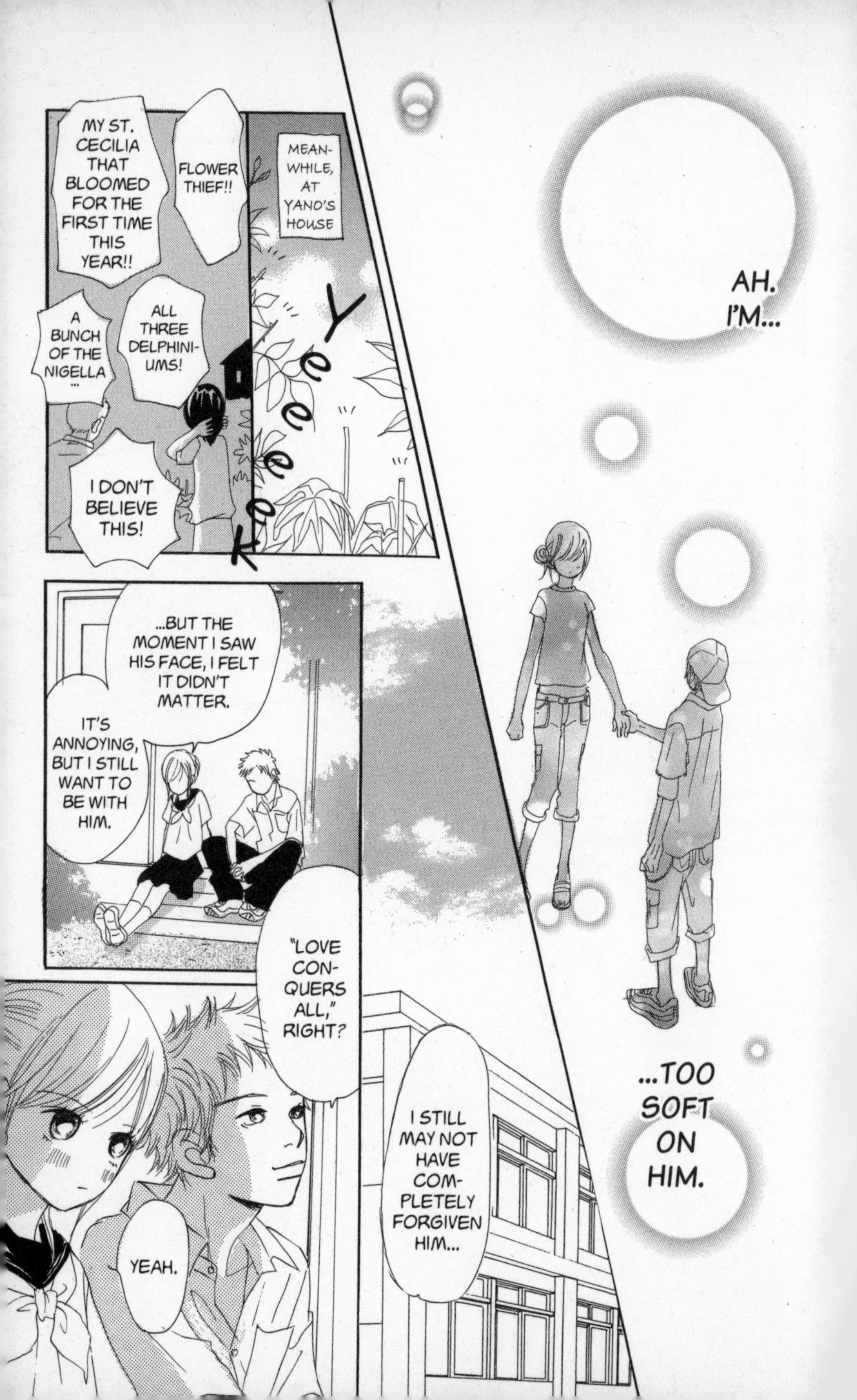

AH. I'M...
...TOO SOFT ON HIM.
MEAN-WHILE, AT YANO'S HOUSE
FLOWER THIEF!!
MY ST. CECILIA THAT BLOOMED FOR THE FIRST TIME THIS YEAR!!
ALL THREE DELPHINI-UMS!
A BUNCH OF THE NIGELLA...
I DON'T BELIEVE THIS!
Yeeeeek
...BUT THE MOMENT I SAW HIS FACE, I FELT IT DIDN'T MATTER.
IT'S ANNOYING, BUT I STILL WANT TO BE WITH HIM.
I STILL MAY NOT HAVE COM-PLETELY FORGIVEN HIM...
"LOVE CON-QUERS ALL," RIGHT?
YEAH.

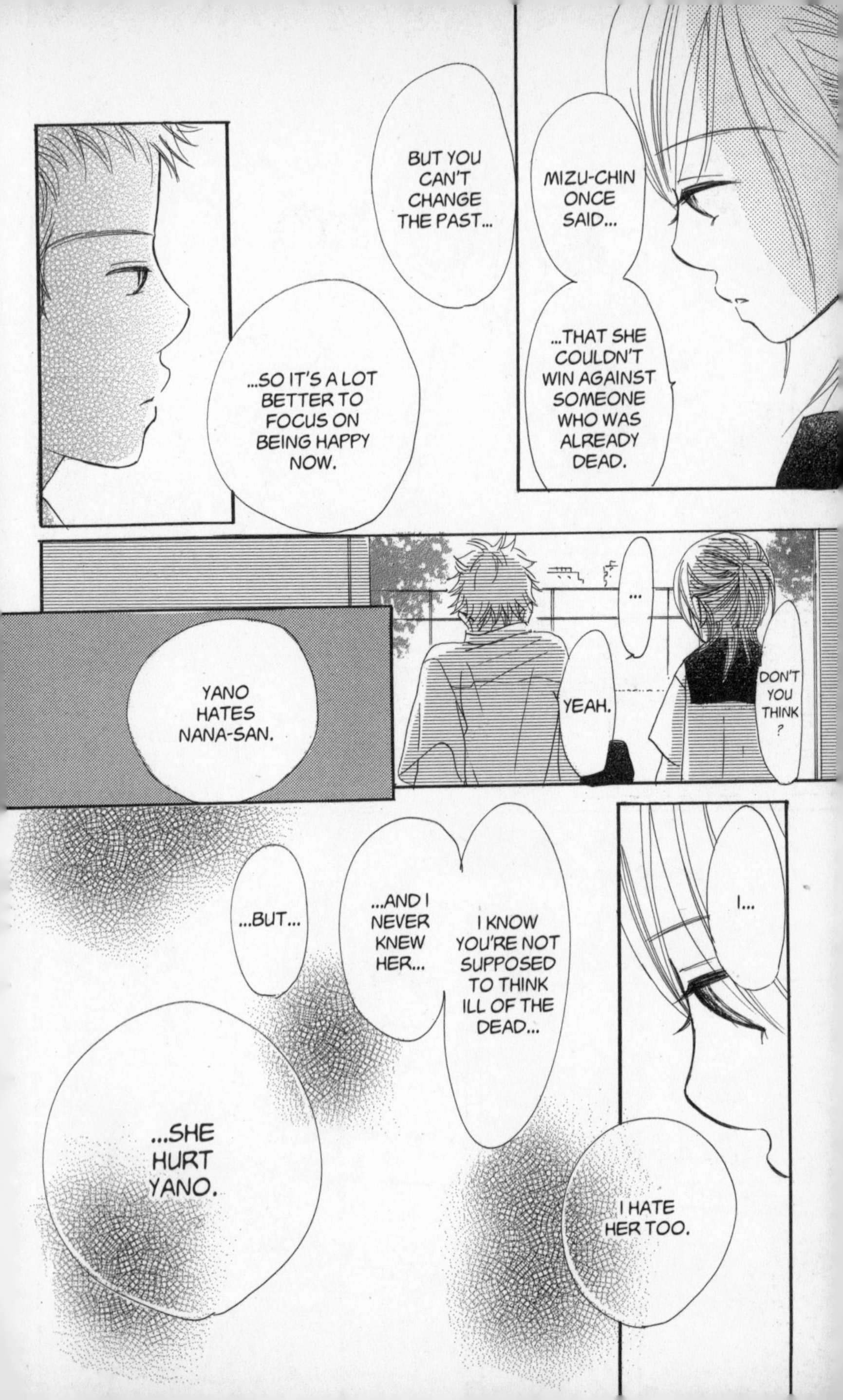
MIZU-CHIN ONCE SAID...
...THAT SHE COULDN'T WIN AGAINST SOMEONE WHO WAS ALREADY DEAD.
BUT YOU CAN'T CHANGE THE PAST...
...SO IT'S A LOT BETTER TO FOCUS ON BEING HAPPY NOW.
DON'T YOU THINK?
...
YEAH.
YANO HATES NANA-SAN.
I...
I KNOW YOU'RE NOT SUPPOSED TO THINK ILL OF THE DEAD...
...AND I NEVER KNEW HER...
...BUT...
...SHE HURT YANO.
I HATE HER TOO.

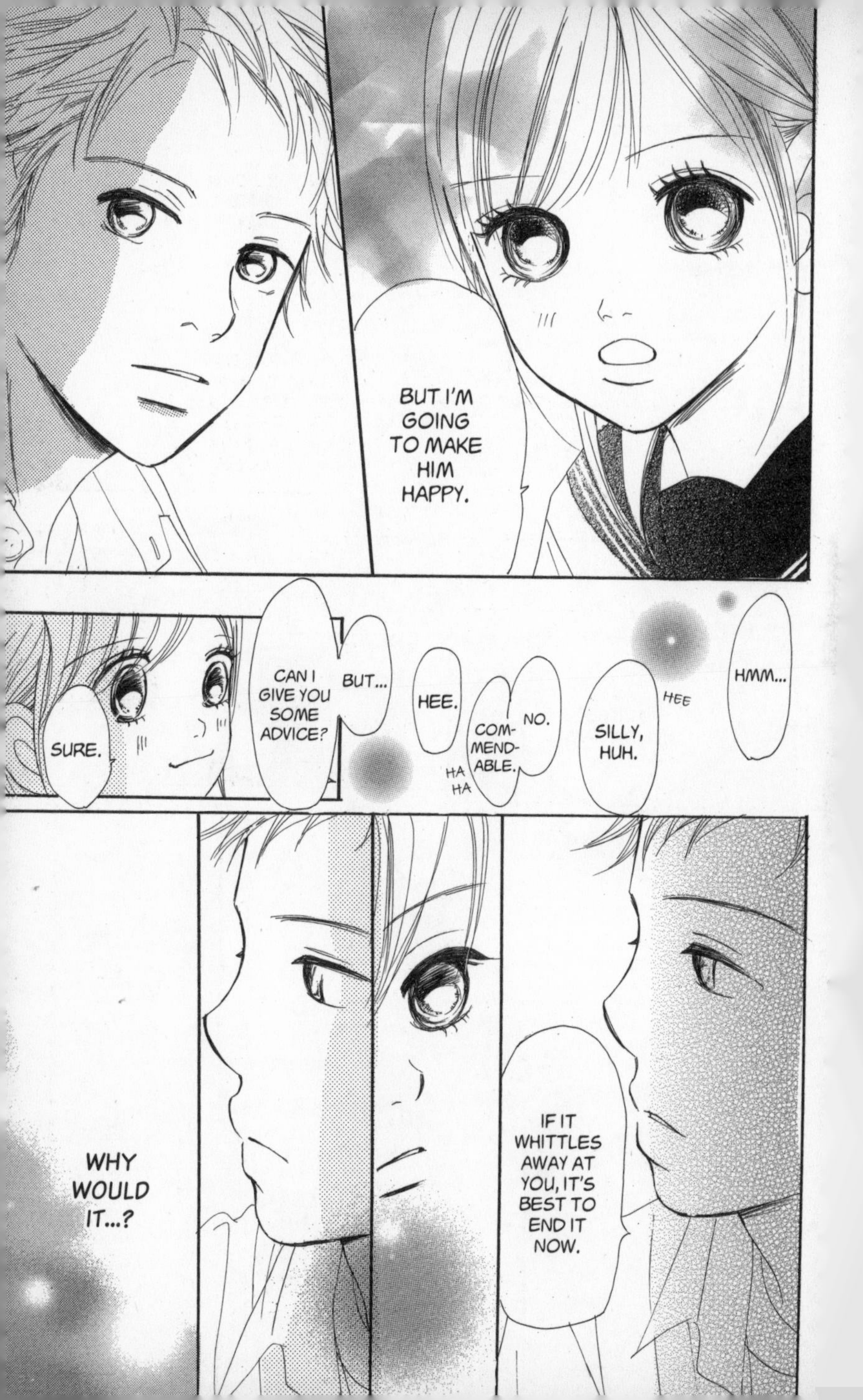
BUT I'M GOING TO MAKE HIM HAPPY.
HMM...
HEE
SILLY, HUH.
NO.
COM-MEND-ABLE.
HA HA
HEE.
BUT...
CAN I GIVE YOU SOME ADVICE?
SURE.
IF IT WHITTLES AWAY AT YOU, IT'S BEST TO END IT NOW.
WHY WOULD IT...?

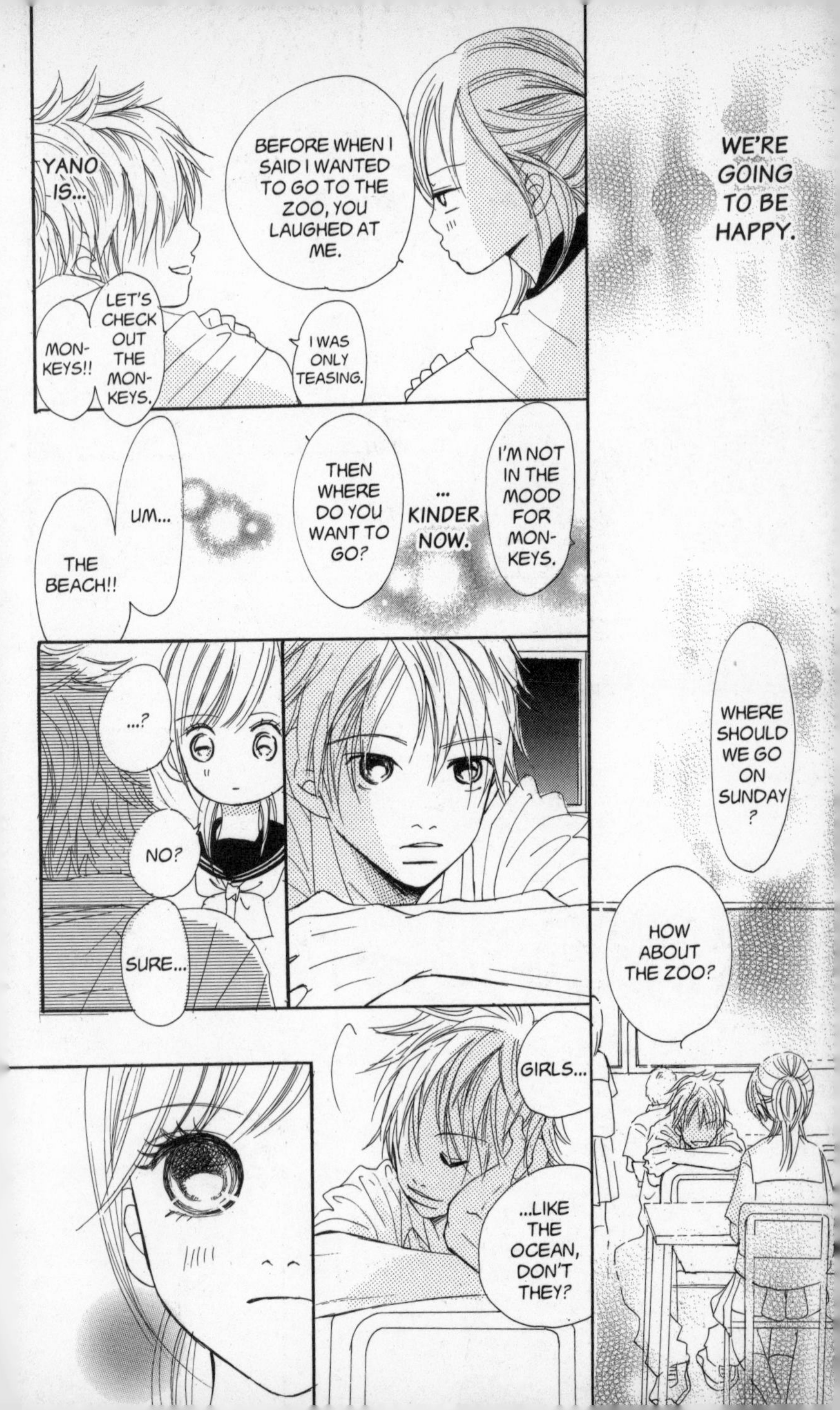
WE'RE GOING TO BE HAPPY.
WHERE SHOULD WE GO ON SUNDAY?
HOW ABOUT THE ZOO?
BEFORE WHEN I SAID I WANTED TO GO TO THE ZOO, YOU LAUGHED AT ME.
YANO IS...
I WAS ONLY TEASING.
LET'S CHECK OUT THE MON-KEYS.
MON-KEYS!!
I'M NOT IN THE MOOD FOR MON-KEYS.
...KINDER NOW.
THEN WHERE DO YOU WANT TO GO?
UM...
THE BEACH!!
...?
NO?
SURE...
GIRLS...
...LIKE THE OCEAN, DON'T THEY?

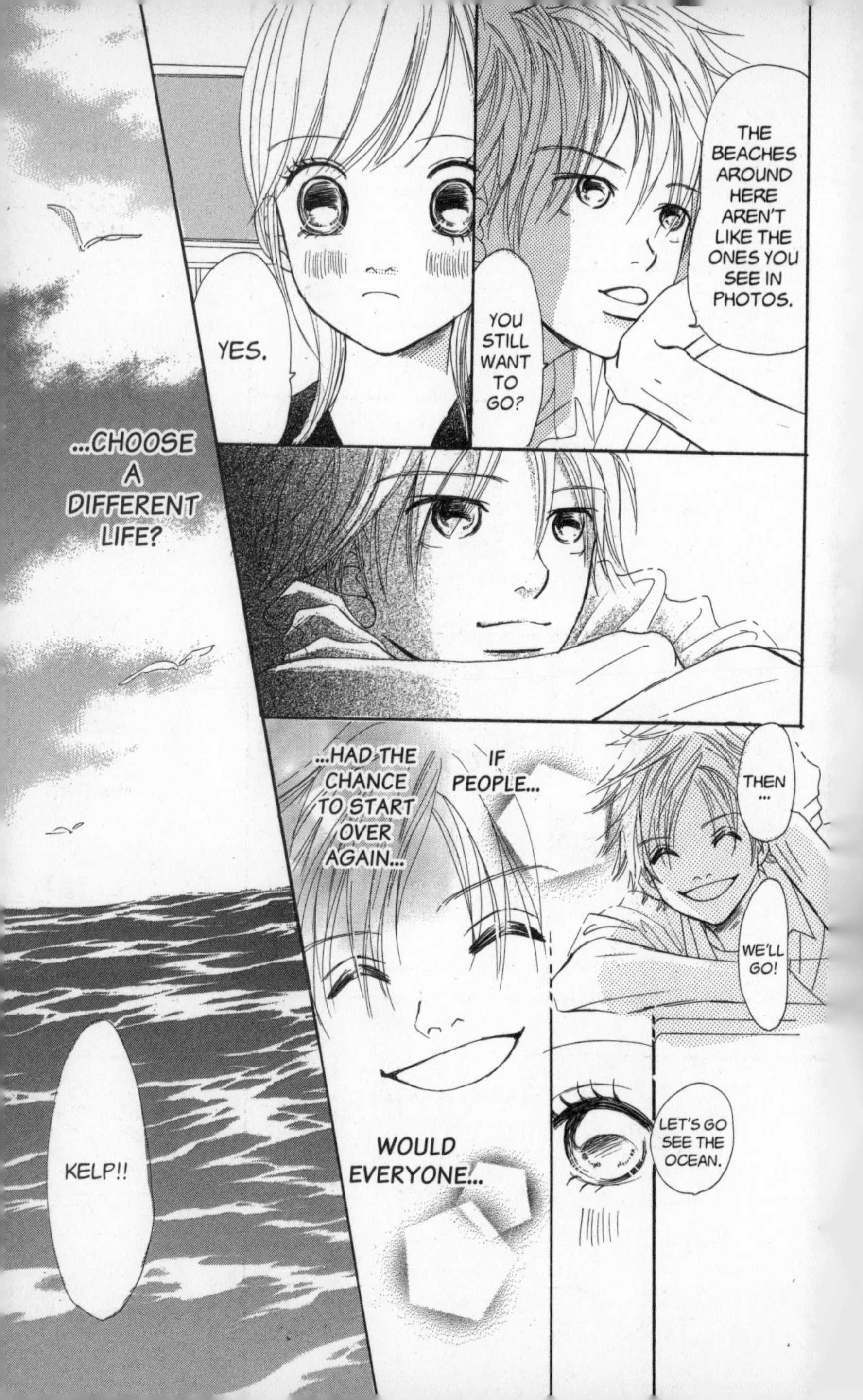
THE BEACHES AROUND HERE AREN'T LIKE THE ONES YOU SEE IN PHOTOS.
YOU STILL WANT TO GO?
YES.
THEN ...
WE'LL GO!
IF PEOPLE...
...HAD THE CHANCE TO START OVER AGAIN...
LET'S GO SEE THE OCEAN.
WOULD EVERYONE...
...CHOOSE A DIFFERENT LIFE?
KELP!!

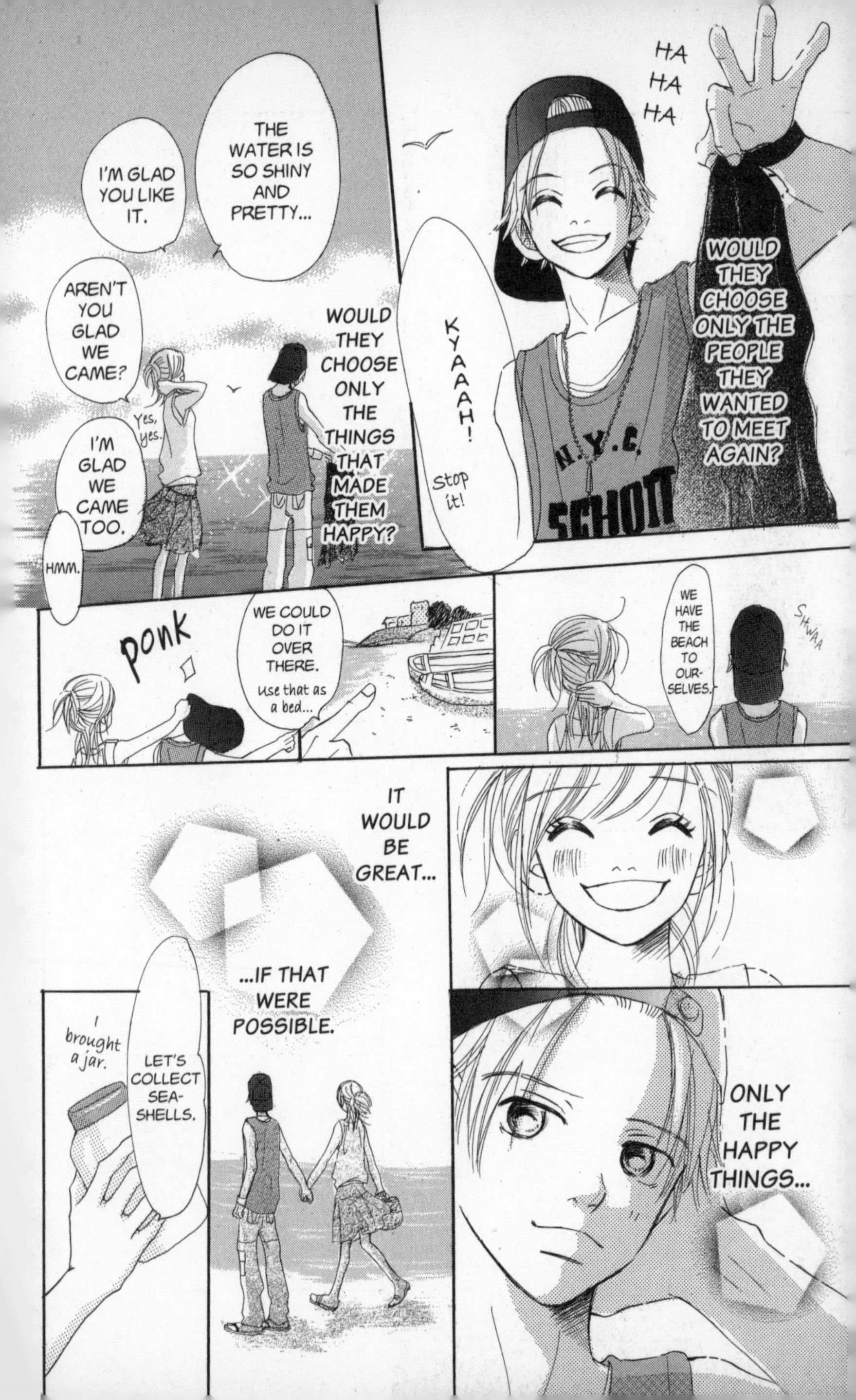
HA HA HA
WOULD THEY CHOOSE ONLY THE PEOPLE THEY WANTED TO MEET AGAIN?
KYAAAAH!
Stop it!
WOULD THEY CHOOSE ONLY THE THINGS THAT MADE THEM HAPPY?
THE WATER IS SO SHINY AND PRETTY...
I'M GLAD YOU LIKE IT.
AREN'T YOU GLAD WE CAME?
Yes, yes.
I'M GLAD WE CAME TOO.
HMM.
WE HAVE THE BEACH TO OUR-SELVES.
SHWAA
WE COULD DO IT OVER THERE.
Use that as a bed...
ponk
IT WOULD BE GREAT...
ONLY THE HAPPY THINGS...
...IF THAT WERE POSSIBLE.
LET'S COLLECT SEA-SHELLS.
I brought a jar.

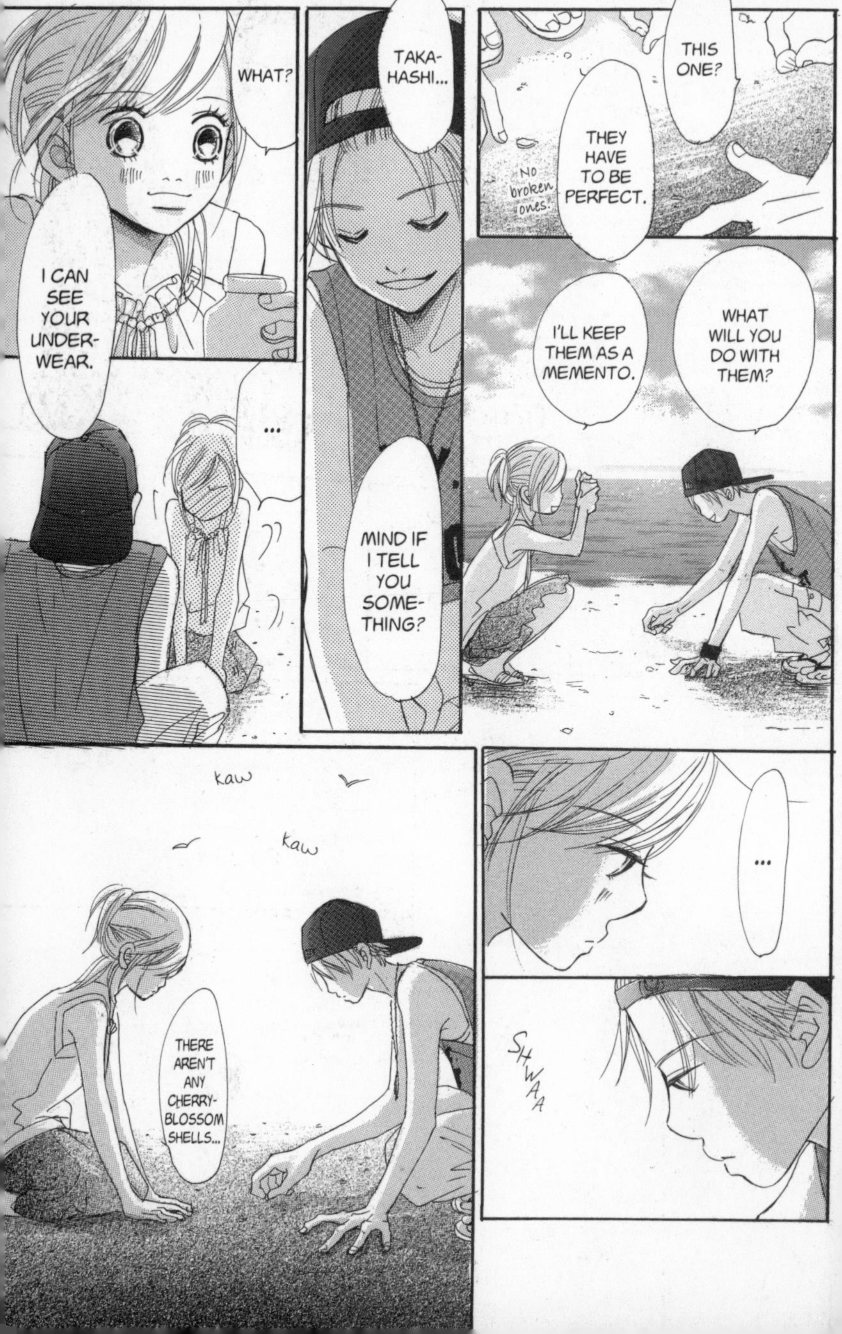
THIS ONE?
THEY HAVE TO BE PERFECT.
No broken ones.
WHAT WILL YOU DO WITH THEM?
I'LL KEEP THEM AS A MEMENTO.
TAKA-HASHI...
MIND IF I TELL YOU SOMETHING?
WHAT?
I CAN SEE YOUR UNDER-WEAR.
...
...
SHWAA
kaw
kaw
THERE AREN'T ANY CHERRY-BLOSSOM SHELLS...

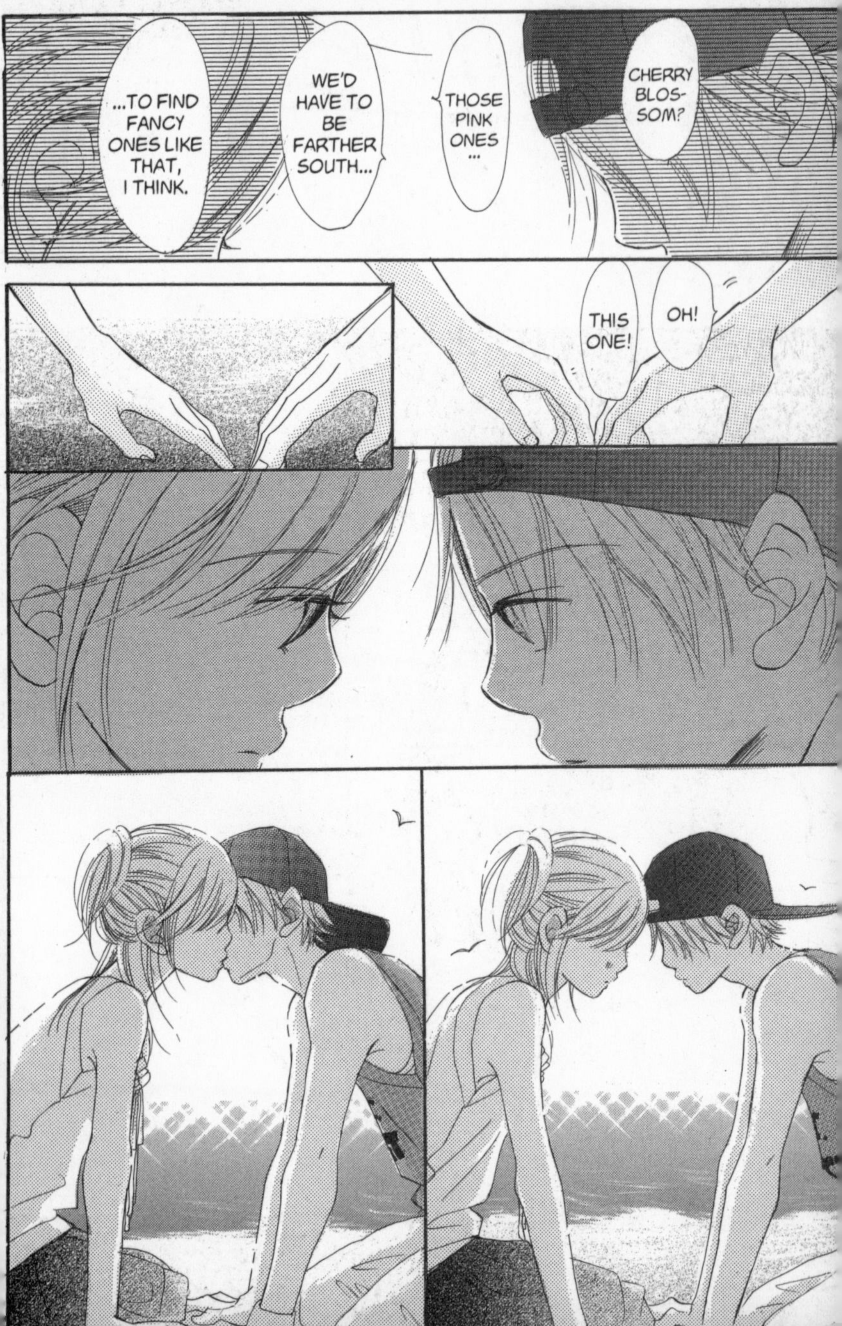
CHERRY BLOSSOM?
THOSE PINK ONES ...
WE'D HAVE TO BE FARTHER SOUTH...
...TO FIND FANCY ONES LIKE THAT, I THINK.
OH!
THIS ONE!

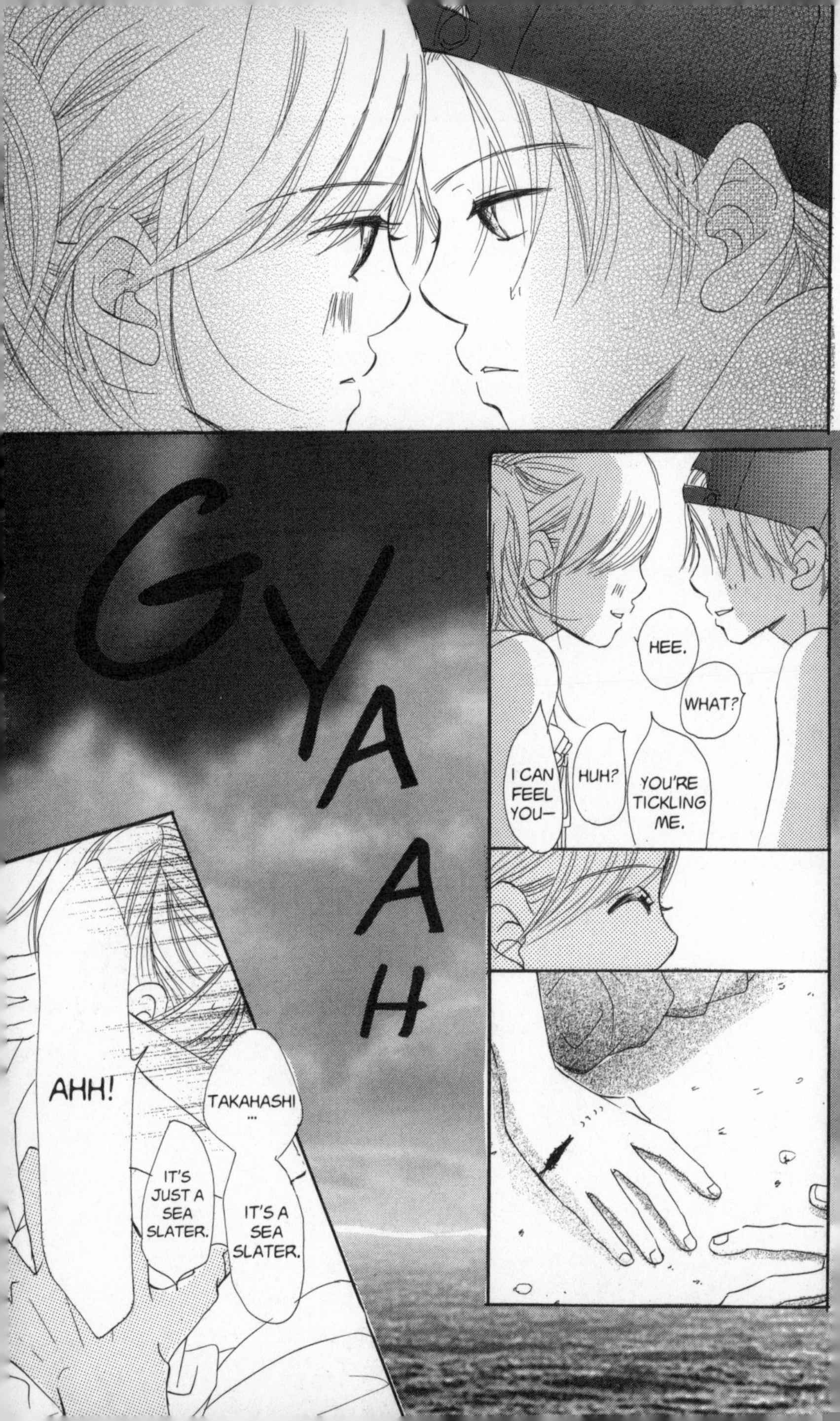
HEE.
WHAT?
YOU'RE TICKLING ME.
HUH?
I CAN FEEL YOU—
GYAAAH
TAKAHASHI...
AHH!
IT'S A SEA SLATER.
IT'S JUST A SEA SLATER.

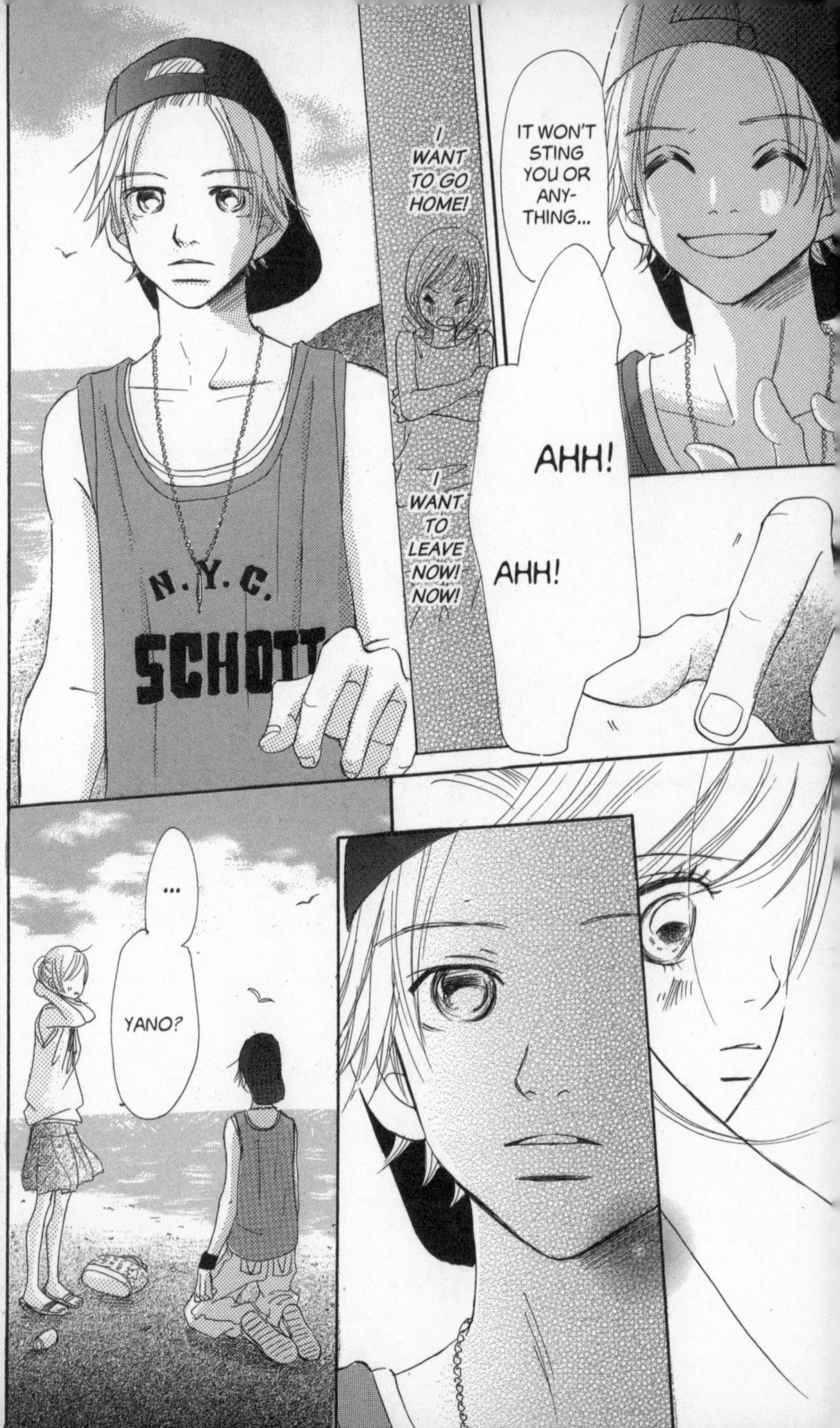
IT WON'T STING YOU OR ANY-THING...
AHH!
AHH!
I WANT TO GO HOME!
I WANT TO LEAVE NOW! NOW!
N.Y.C.
SCHOTT
...
YANO?

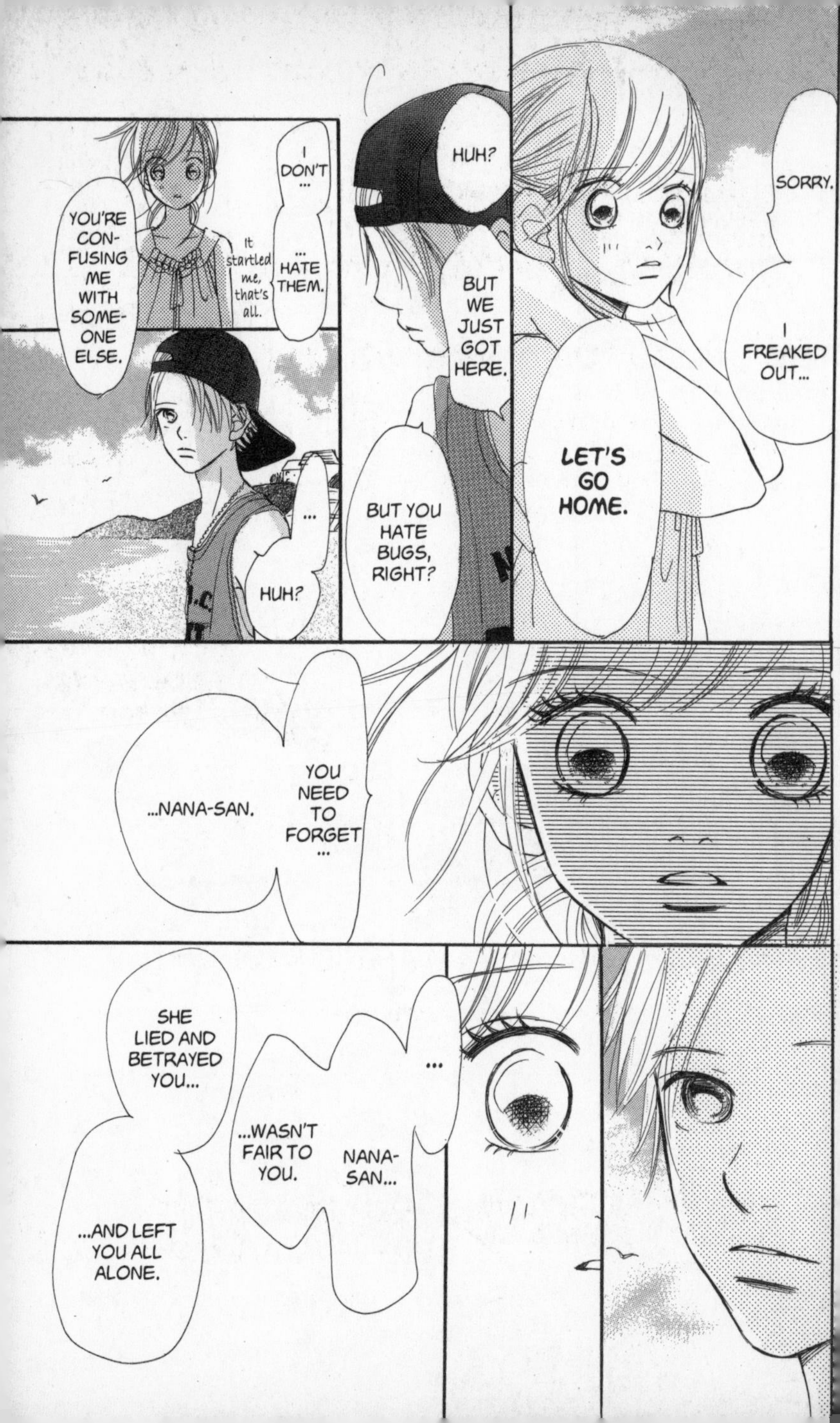
SORRY.
I FREAKED OUT...
LET'S GO HOME.
HUH?
BUT WE JUST GOT HERE.
BUT YOU HATE BUGS, RIGHT?
I DON'T ...
... HATE THEM.
It startled me, that's all.
YOU'RE CONFUSING ME WITH SOMEONE ELSE.
...
HUH?
YOU NEED TO FORGET ...
...NANA-SAN.
...
NANA-SAN...
SHE LIED AND BETRAYED YOU...
...WASN'T FAIR TO YOU.
...AND LEFT YOU ALL ALONE.

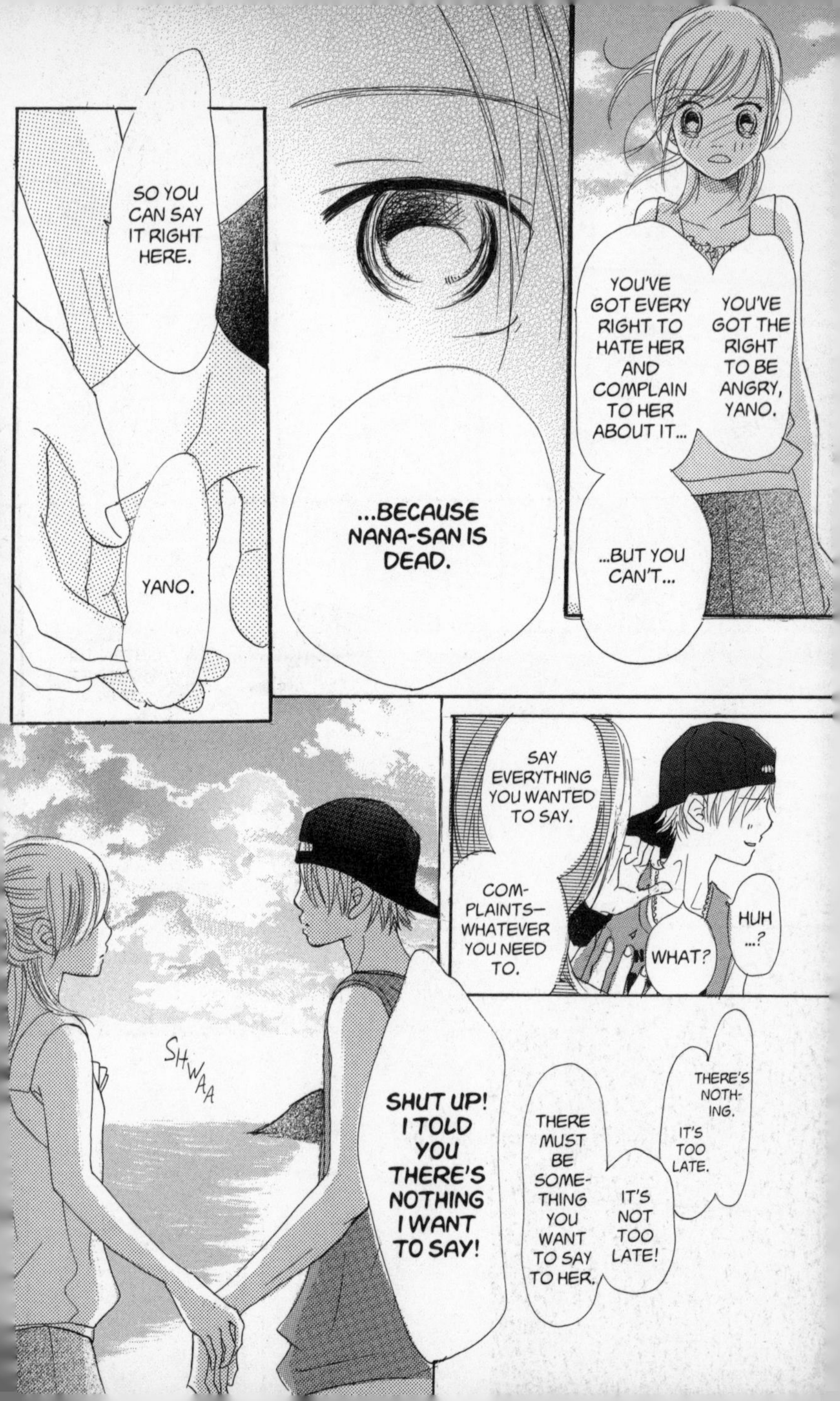
YOU'VE GOT THE RIGHT TO BE ANGRY, YANO.
YOU'VE GOT EVERY RIGHT TO HATE HER AND COMPLAIN TO HER ABOUT IT...
...BUT YOU CAN'T...
...BECAUSE NANA-SAN IS DEAD.
SO YOU CAN SAY IT RIGHT HERE.
YANO.
HUH ...?
WHAT?
SAY EVERYTHING YOU WANTED TO SAY.
COM-PLAINTS—WHATEVER YOU NEED TO.
THERE'S NOTH-ING.
IT'S TOO LATE.
IT'S NOT TOO LATE!
THERE MUST BE SOME-THING YOU WANT TO SAY TO HER.
SHUT UP! I TOLD YOU THERE'S NOTHING I WANT TO SAY!
SHWAA

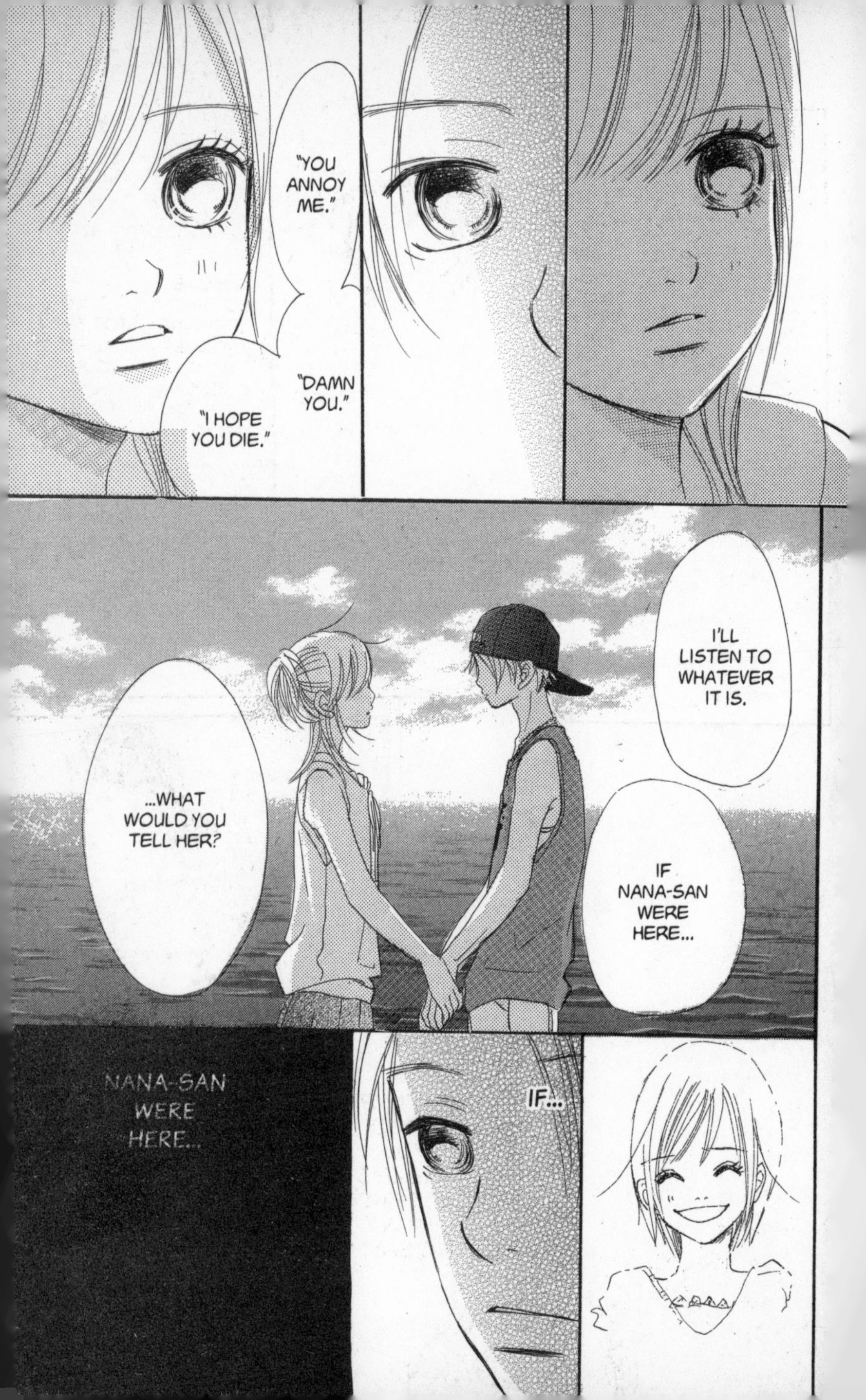
"YOU ANNOY ME."
"DAMN YOU."
"I HOPE YOU DIE."
I'LL LISTEN TO WHATEVER IT IS.
IF NANA-SAN WERE HERE...
...WHAT WOULD YOU TELL HER?
IF...
NANA-SAN WERE HERE...

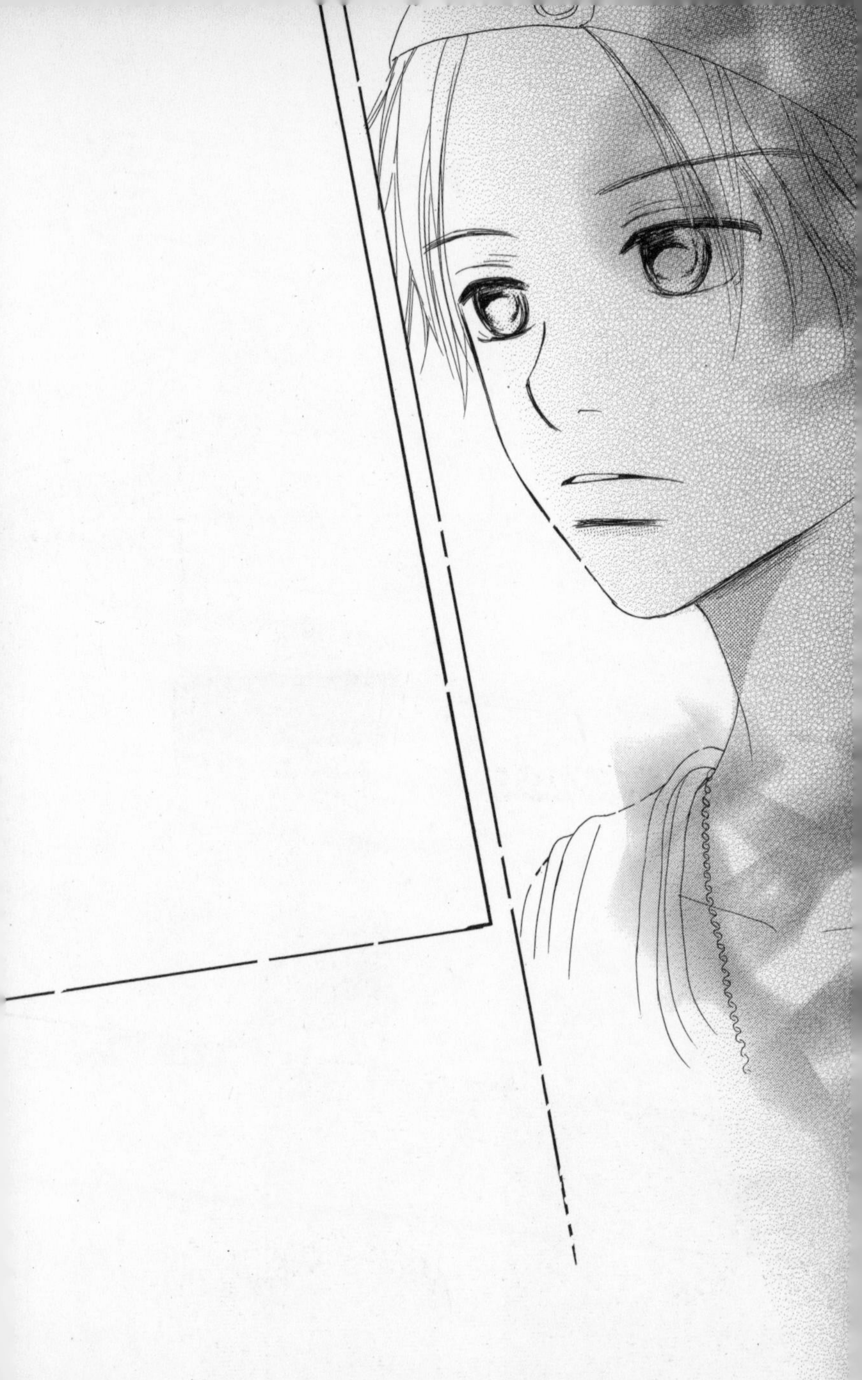

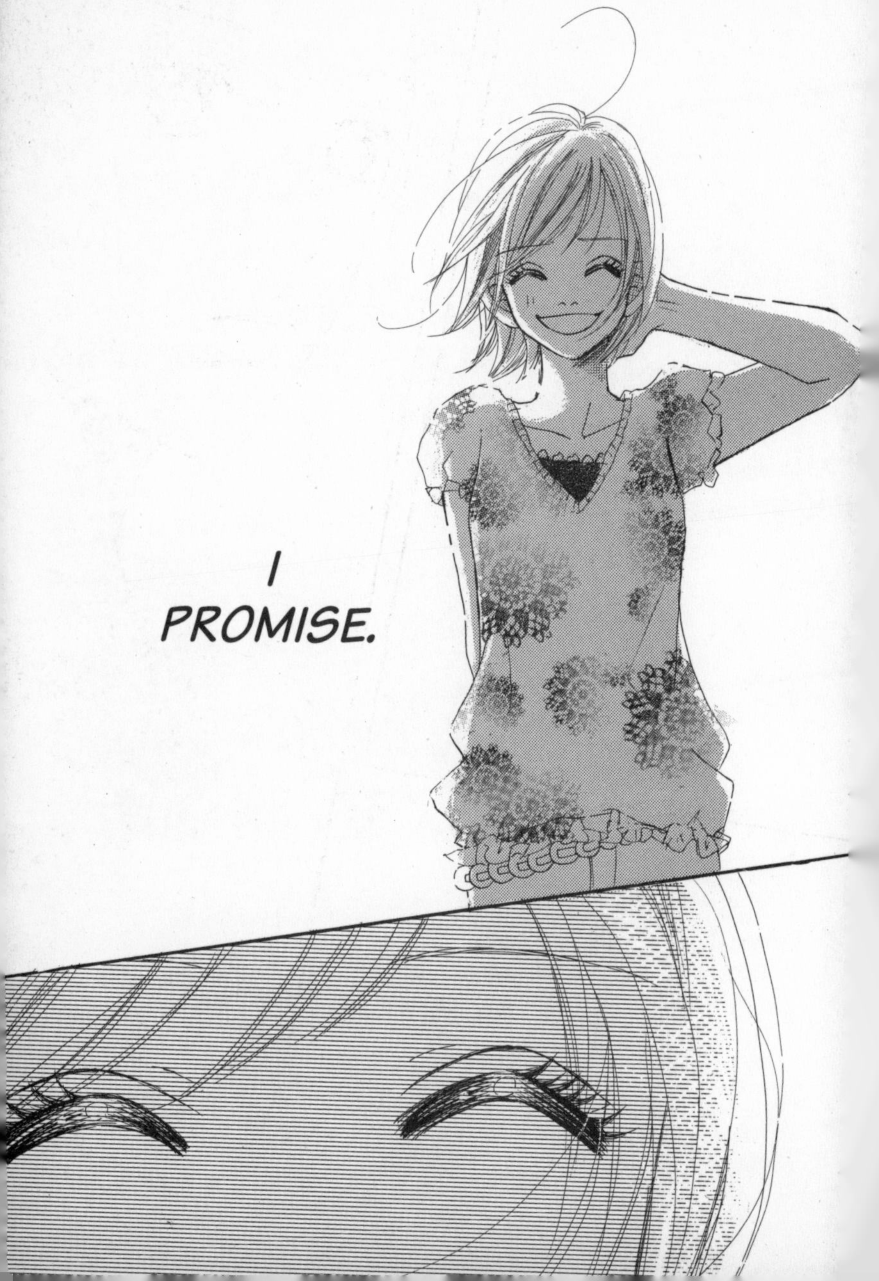
I PROMISE.

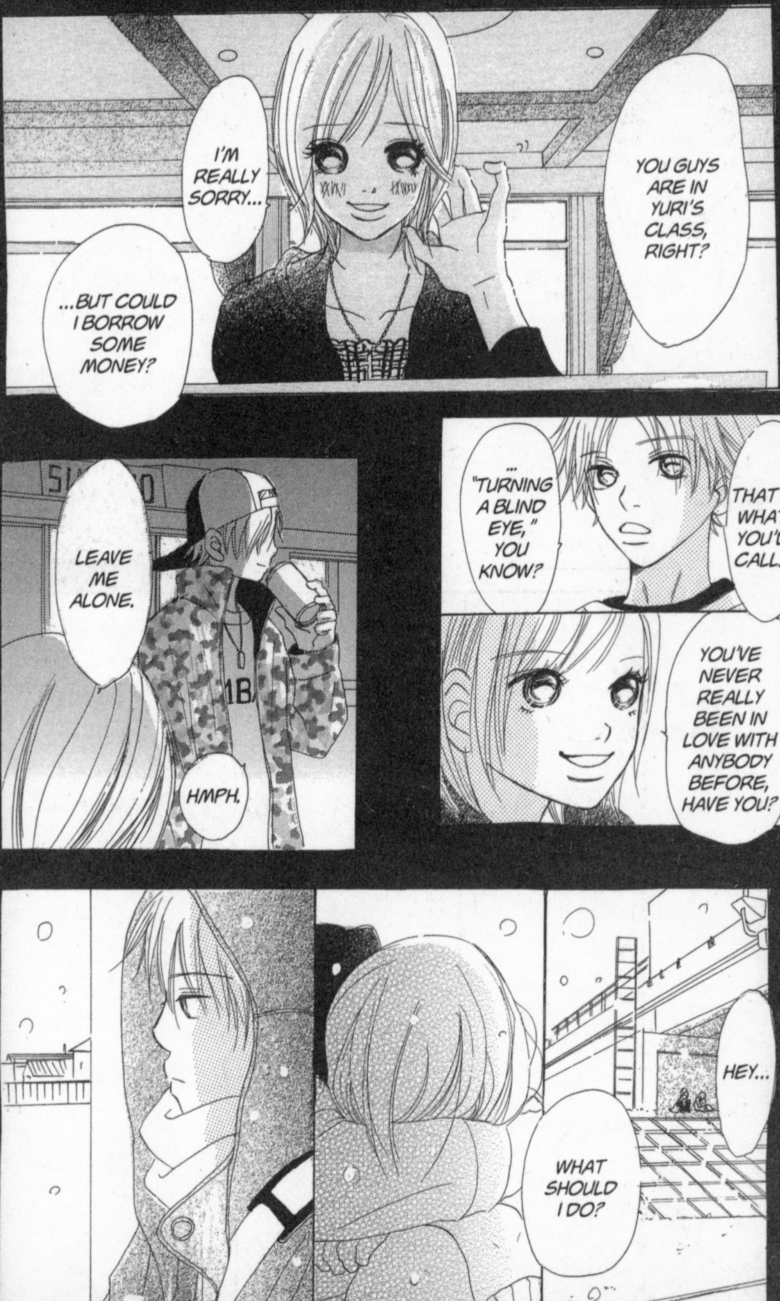
YOU GUYS ARE IN YURI'S CLASS, RIGHT?
I'M REALLY SORRY...
...BUT COULD I BORROW SOME MONEY?
THAT'S WHAT YOU'D CALL...
... "TURNING A BLIND EYE," YOU KNOW?
YOU'VE NEVER REALLY BEEN IN LOVE WITH ANYBODY BEFORE, HAVE YOU?
LEAVE ME ALONE.
HMPH.
HEY...
WHAT SHOULD I DO?

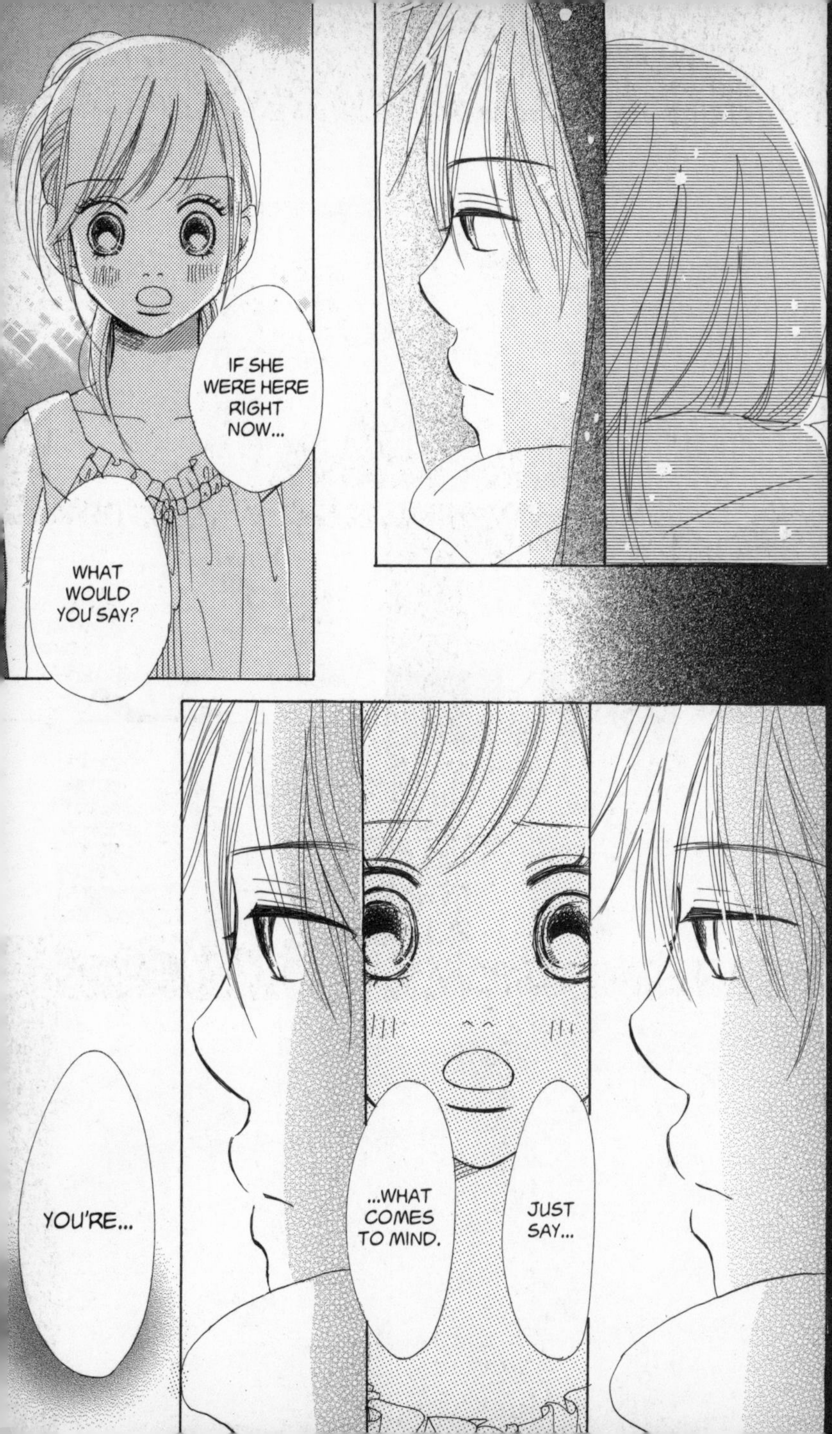
IF SHE WERE HERE RIGHT NOW...
WHAT WOULD YOU SAY?
JUST SAY...
...WHAT COMES TO MIND.
YOU'RE...

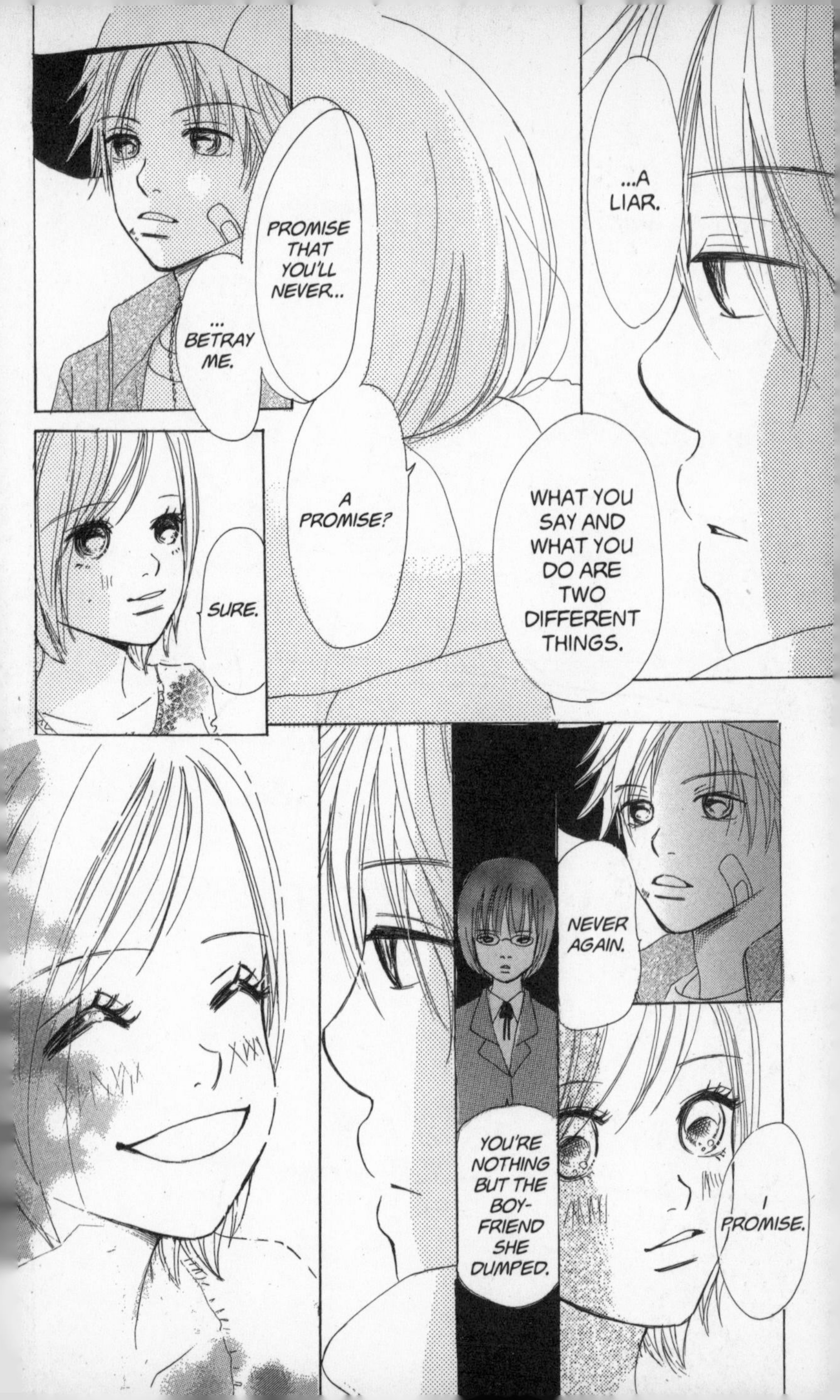
...A LIAR.
PROMISE THAT YOU'LL NEVER...
...BETRAY ME.
WHAT YOU SAY AND WHAT YOU DO ARE TWO DIFFERENT THINGS.
A PROMISE?
SURE.
NEVER AGAIN.
I PROMISE.
YOU'RE NOTHING BUT THE BOY-FRIEND SHE DUMPED.

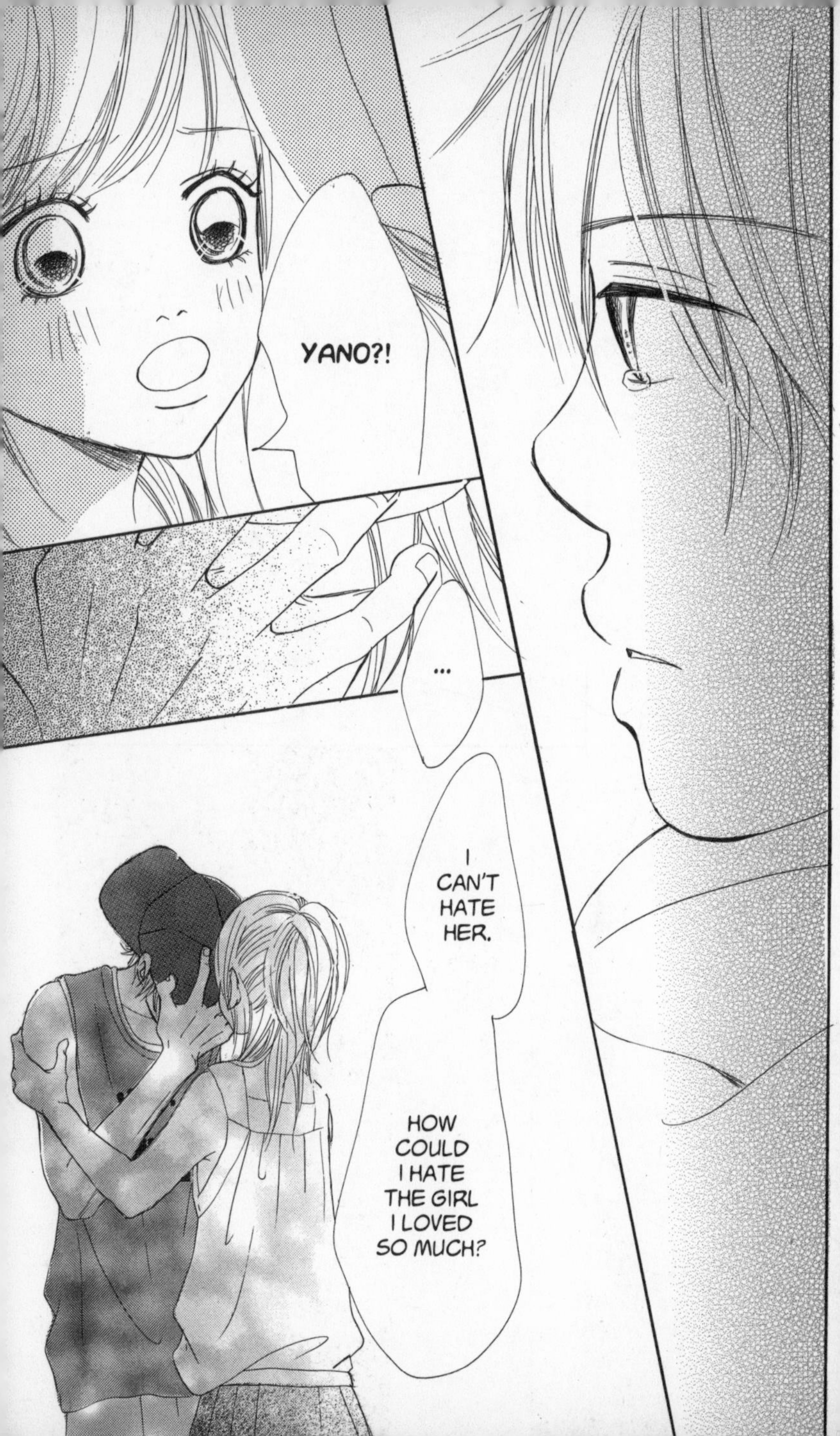
YANO?!
...
I CAN'T HATE HER.
HOW COULD I HATE THE GIRL I LOVED SO MUCH?

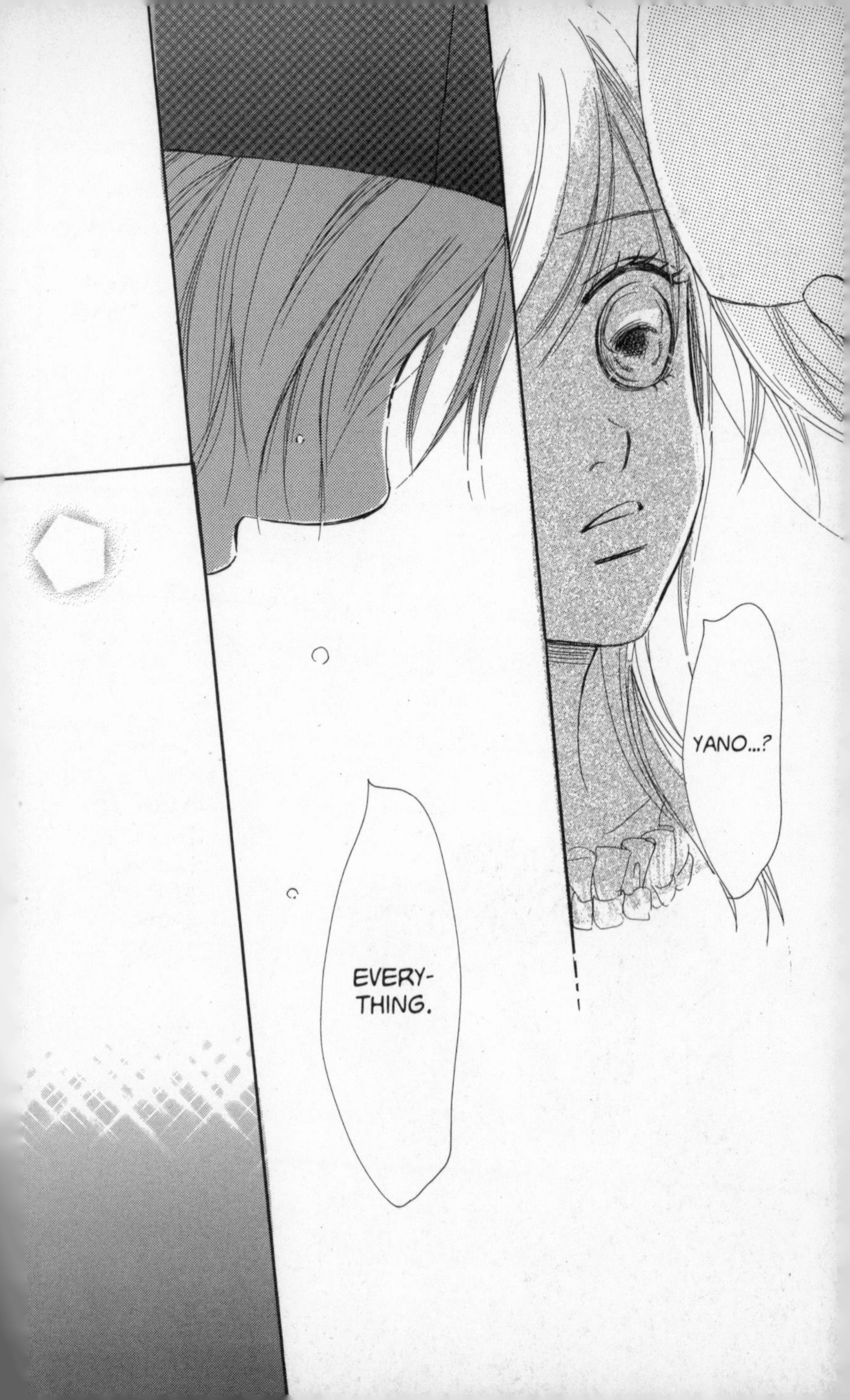
YANO...?
EVERY-THING.

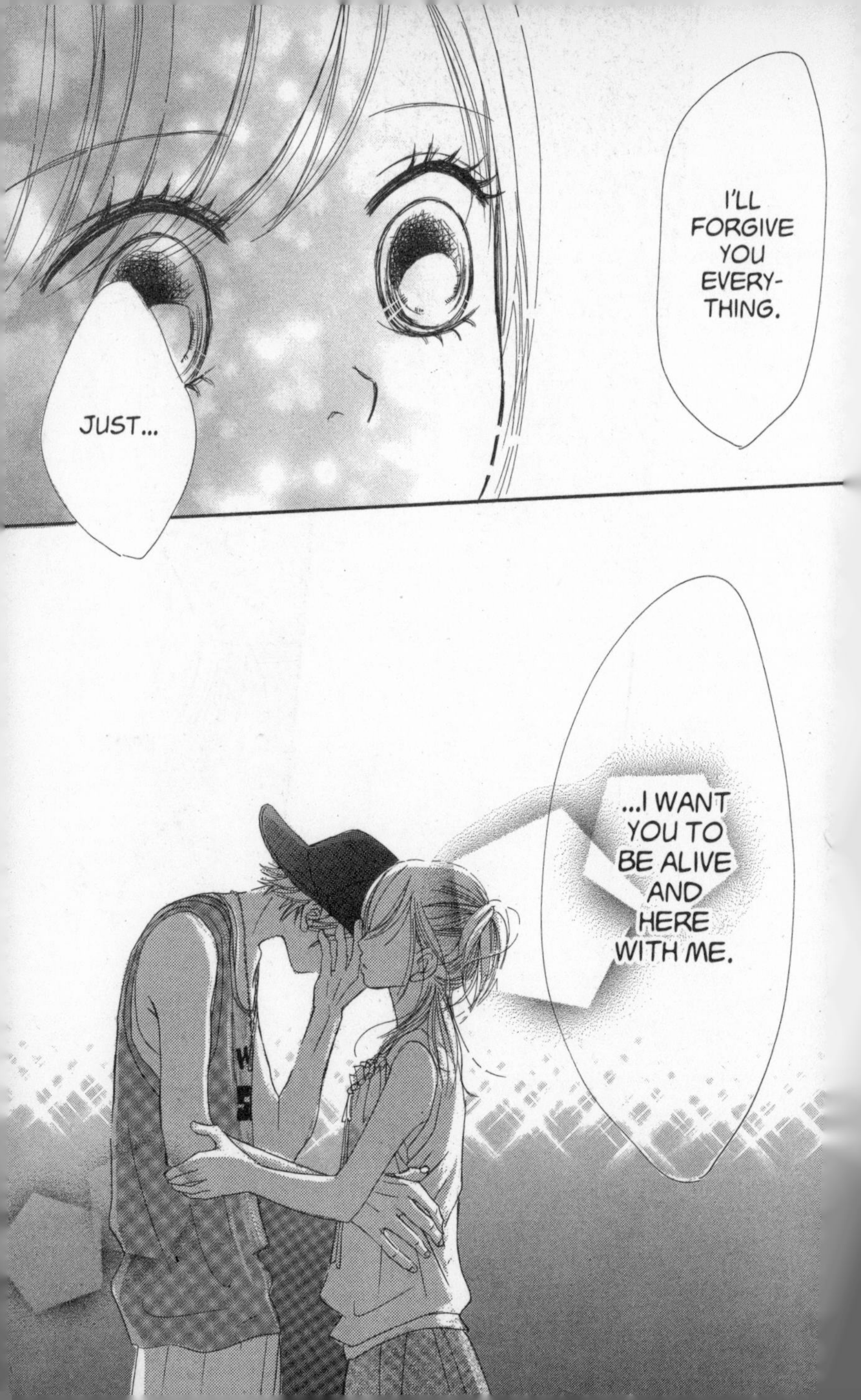
I'LL FORGIVE YOU EVERY-THING.
JUST...
...I WANT YOU TO BE ALIVE AND HERE WITH ME.

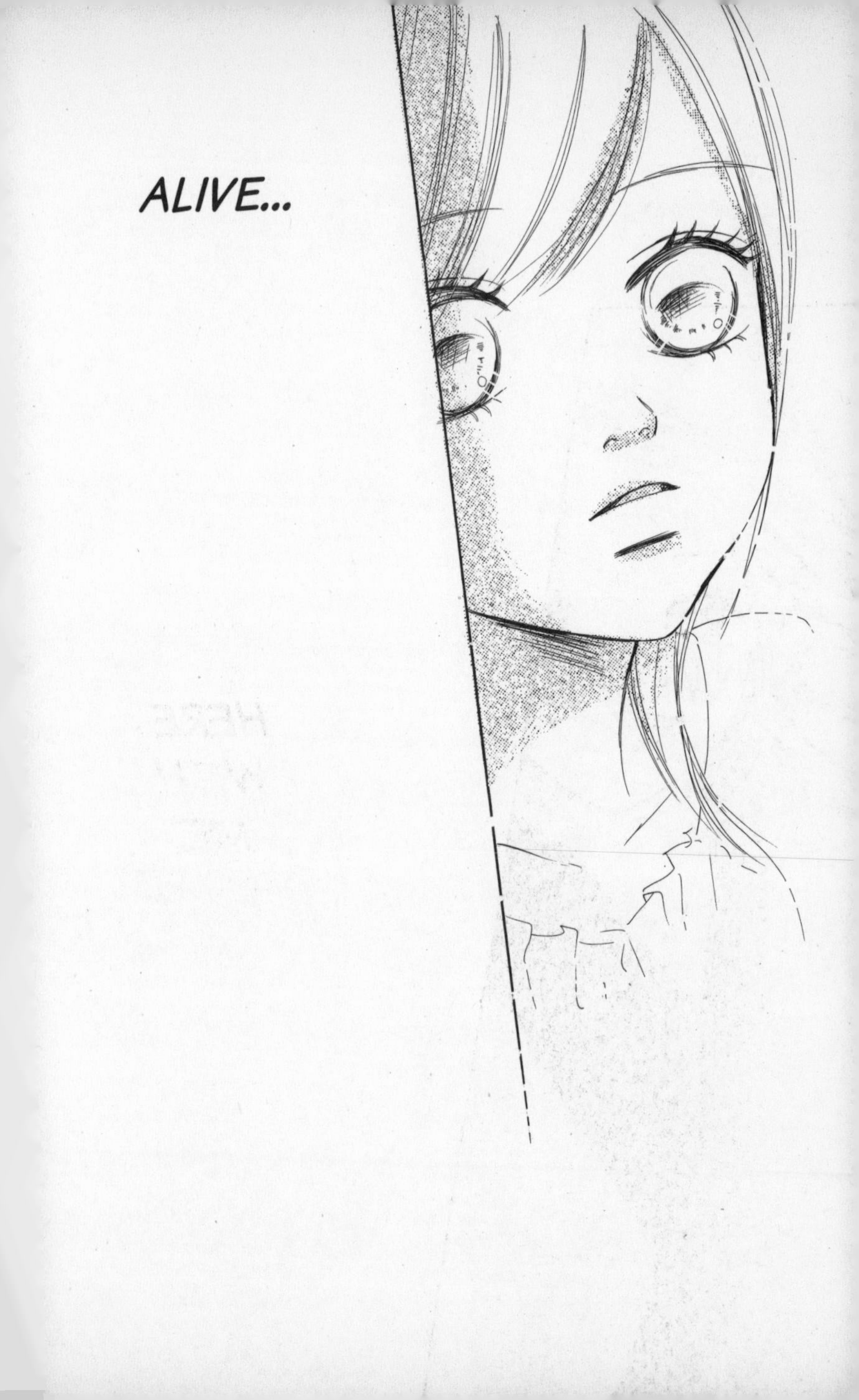
ALIVE...

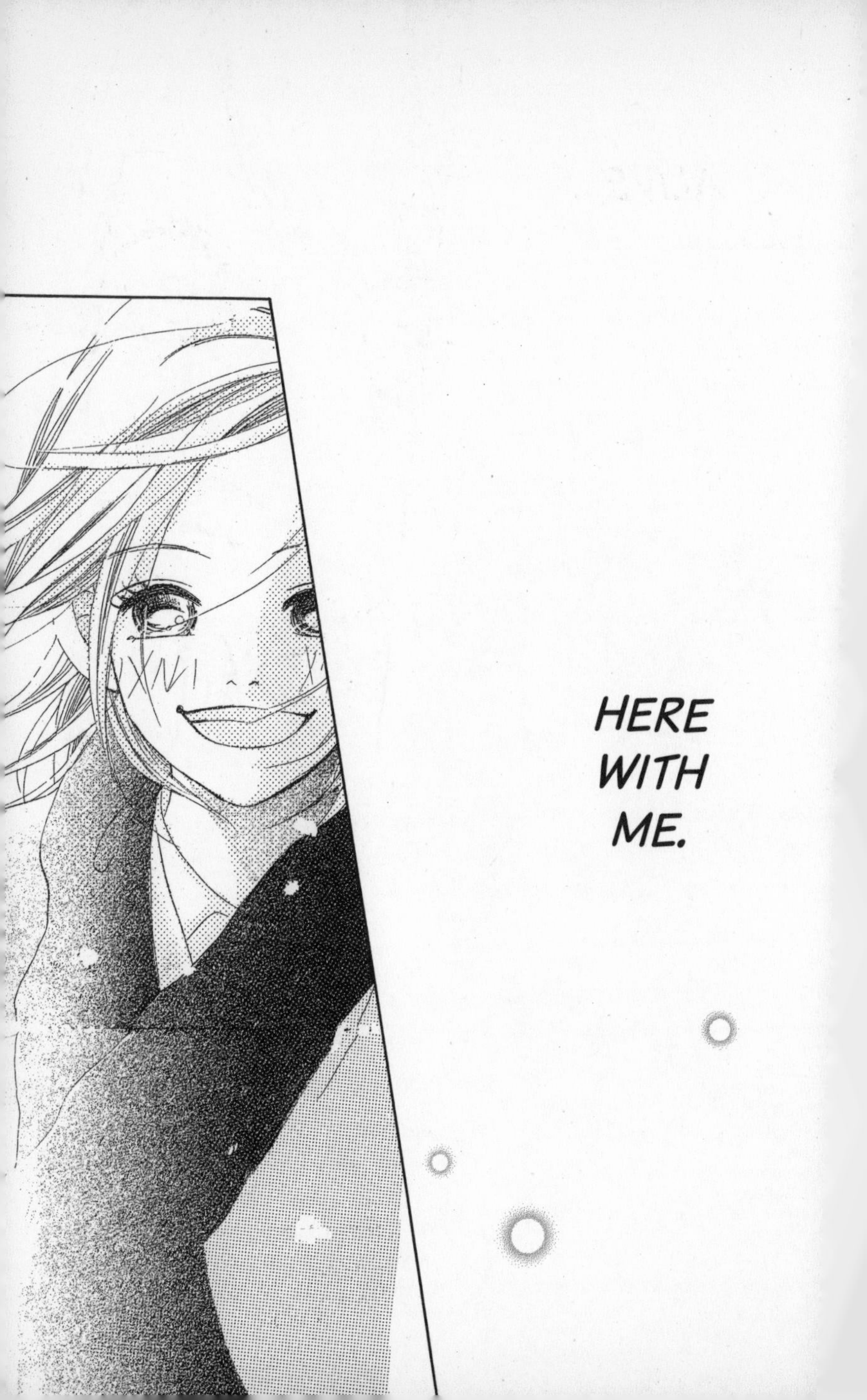
HERE WITH ME.

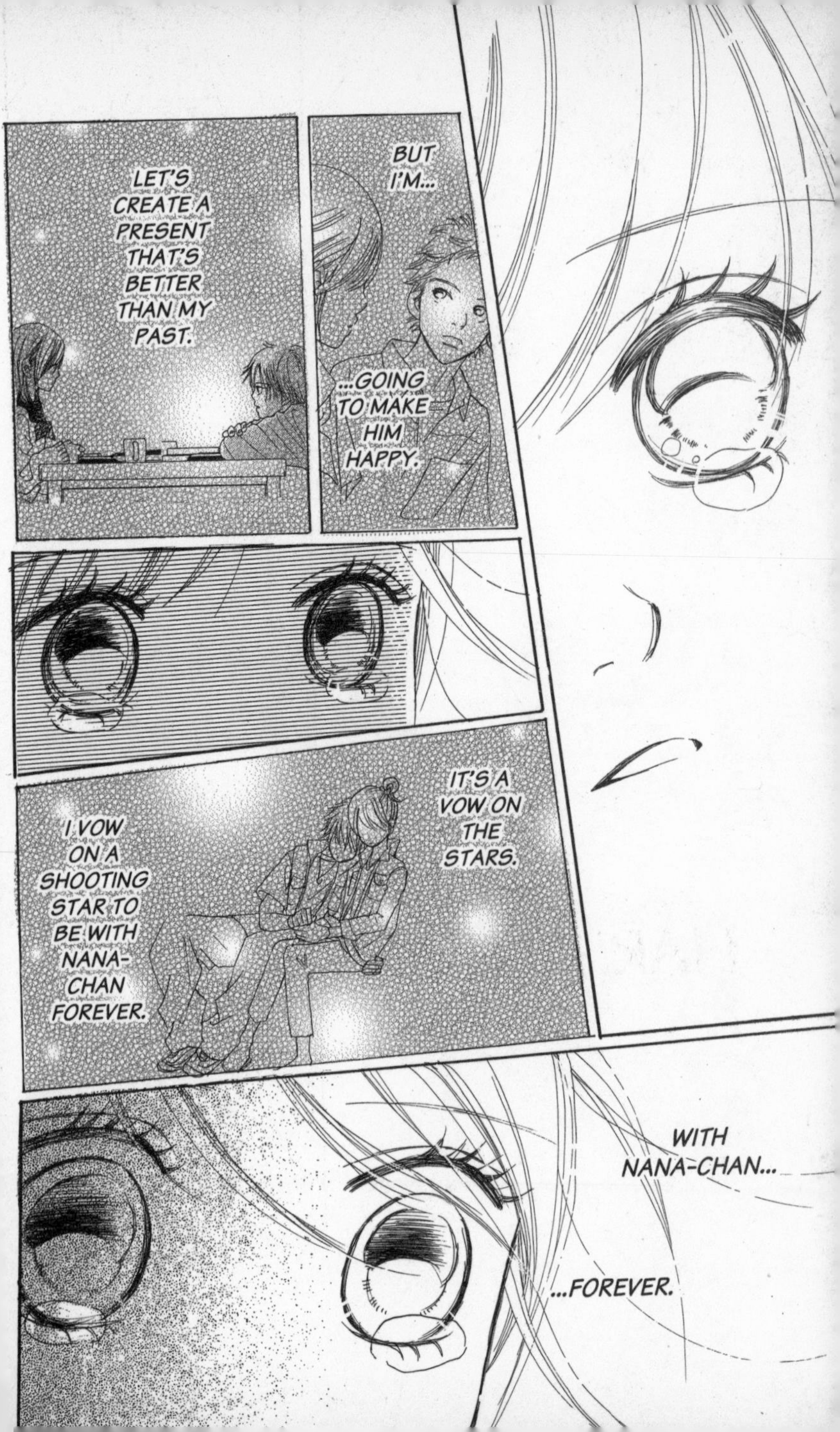
BUT I'M...
...GOING TO MAKE HIM HAPPY.
LET'S CREATE A PRESENT THAT'S BETTER THAN MY PAST.
IT'S A VOW ON THE STARS.
I VOW ON A SHOOTING STAR TO BE WITH NANA-CHAN FOREVER.
WITH NANA-CHAN...
...FOREVER.

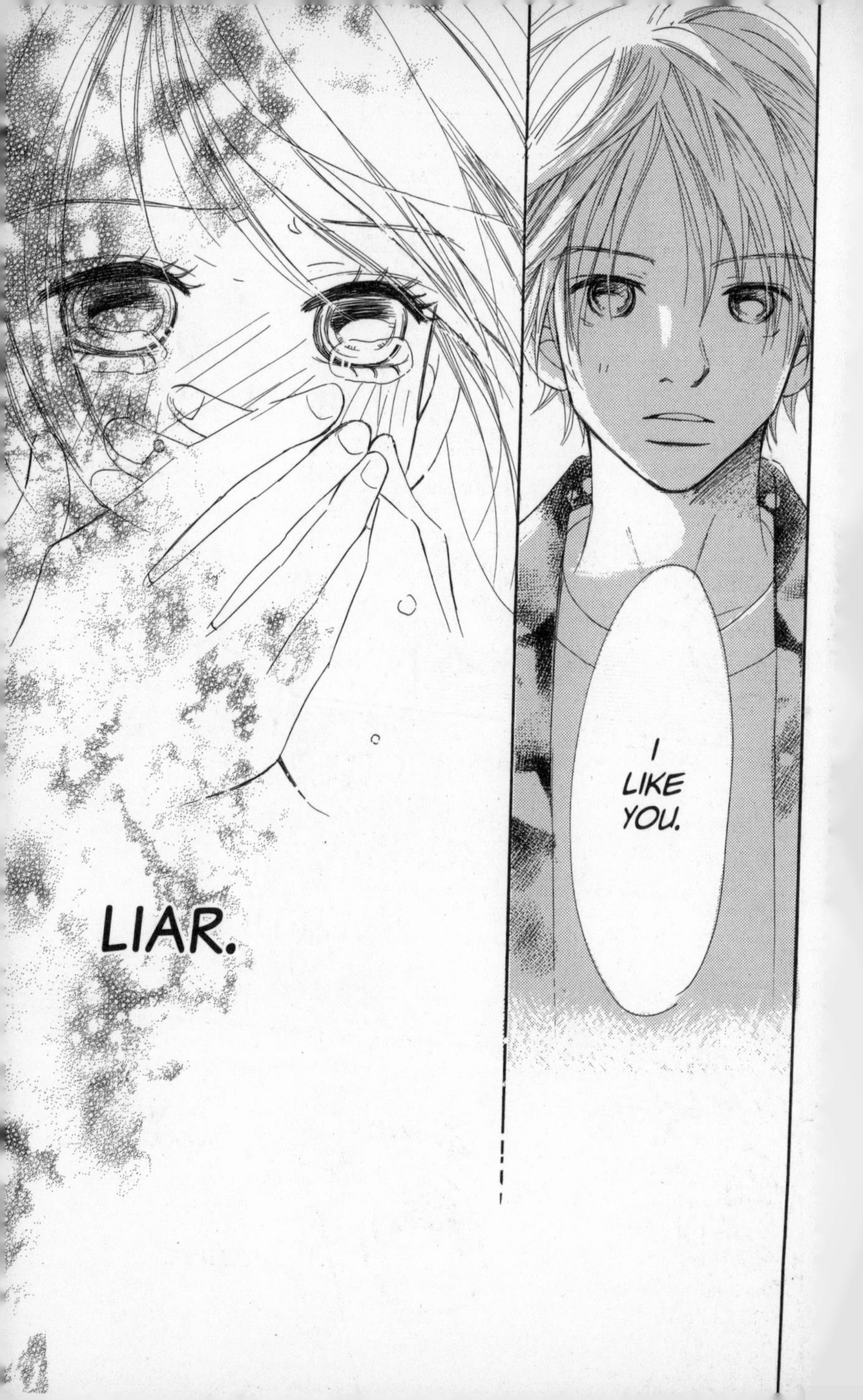
I LIKE YOU.
LIAR.

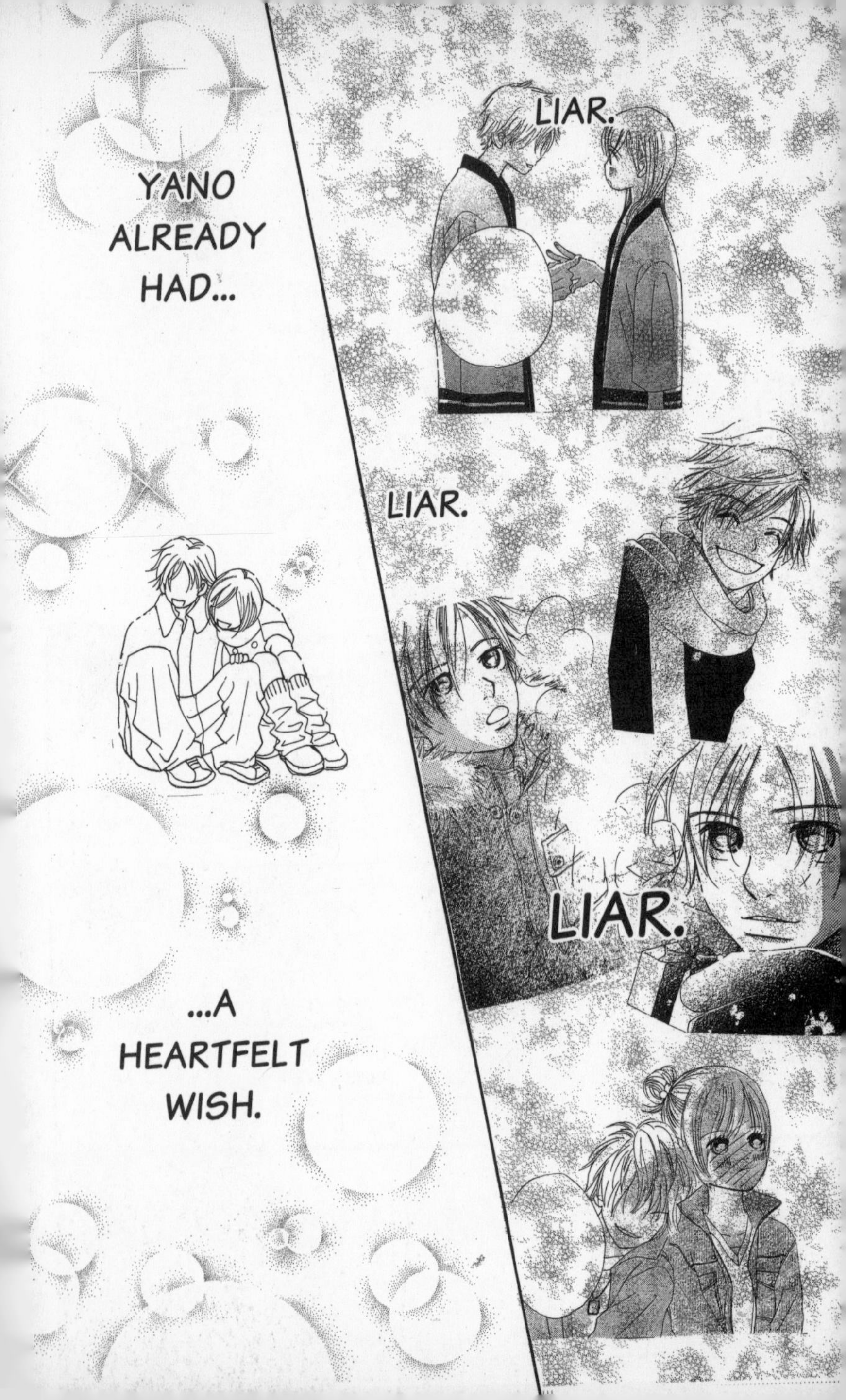
LIAR.
LIAR.
LIAR.
YANO ALREADY HAD...
...A HEARTFELT WISH.

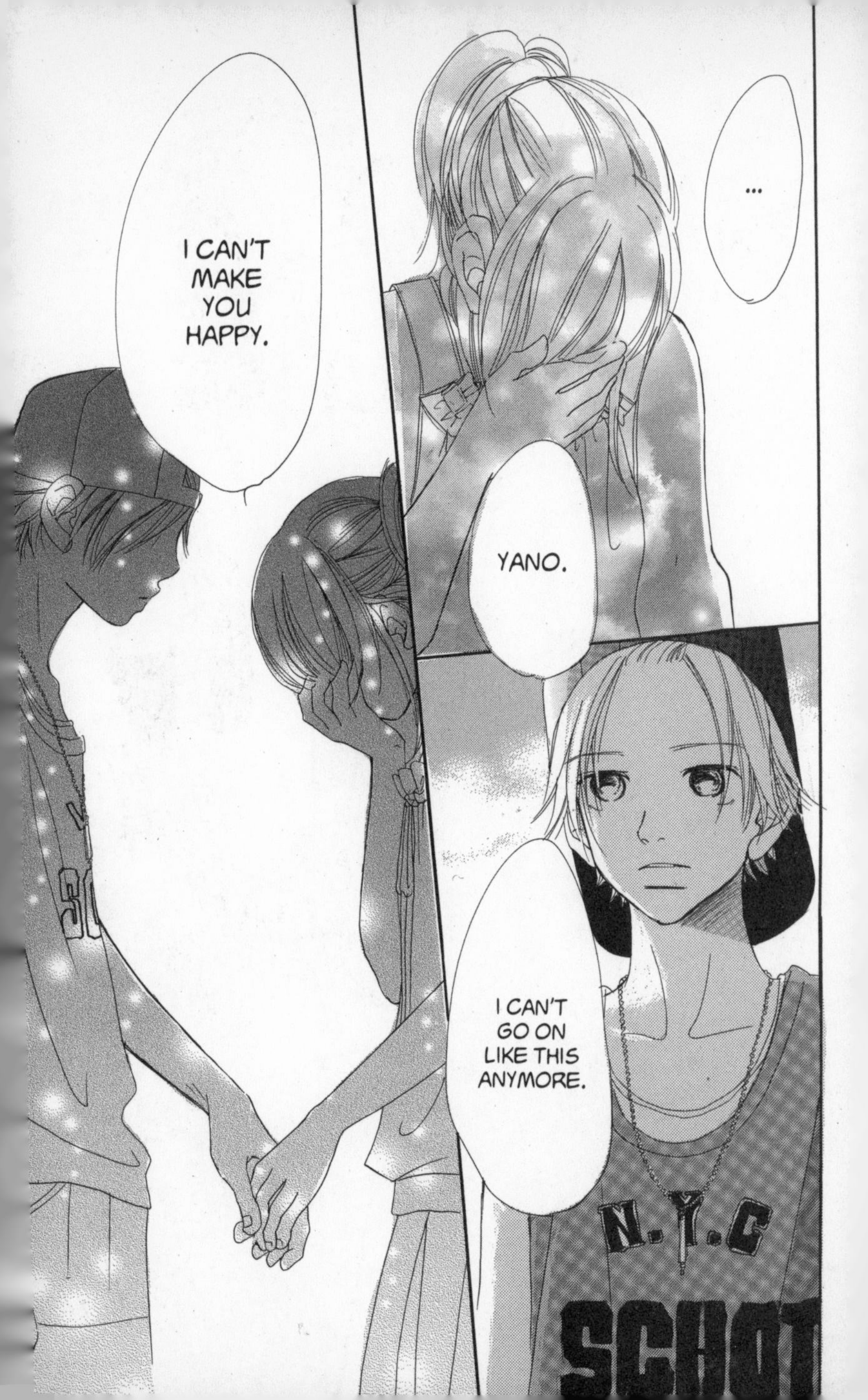
...
YANO.
I CAN'T GO ON LIKE THIS ANYMORE.
I CAN'T MAKE YOU HAPPY.

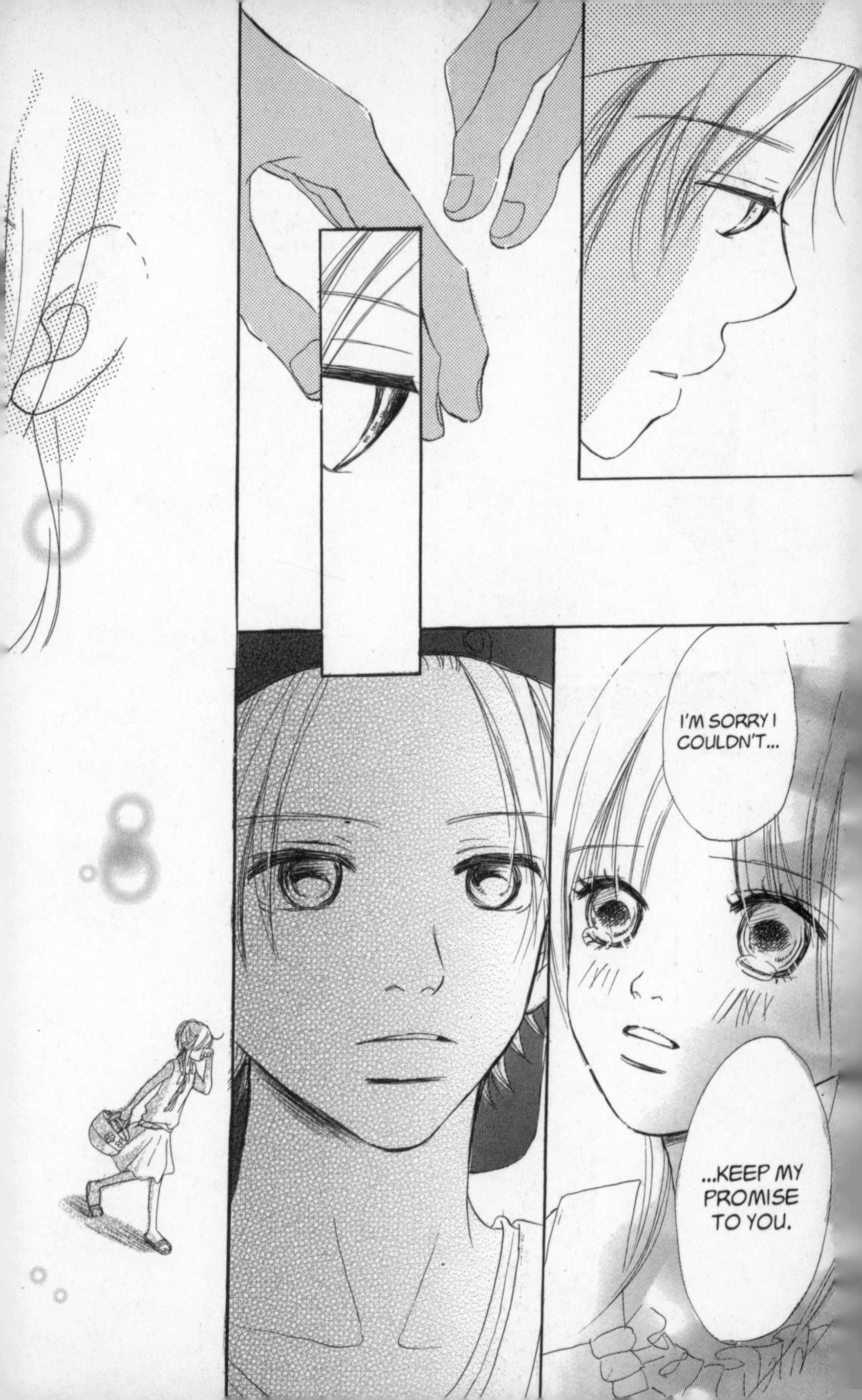
I'M SORRY I COULDN'T...
...KEEP MY PROMISE TO YOU.

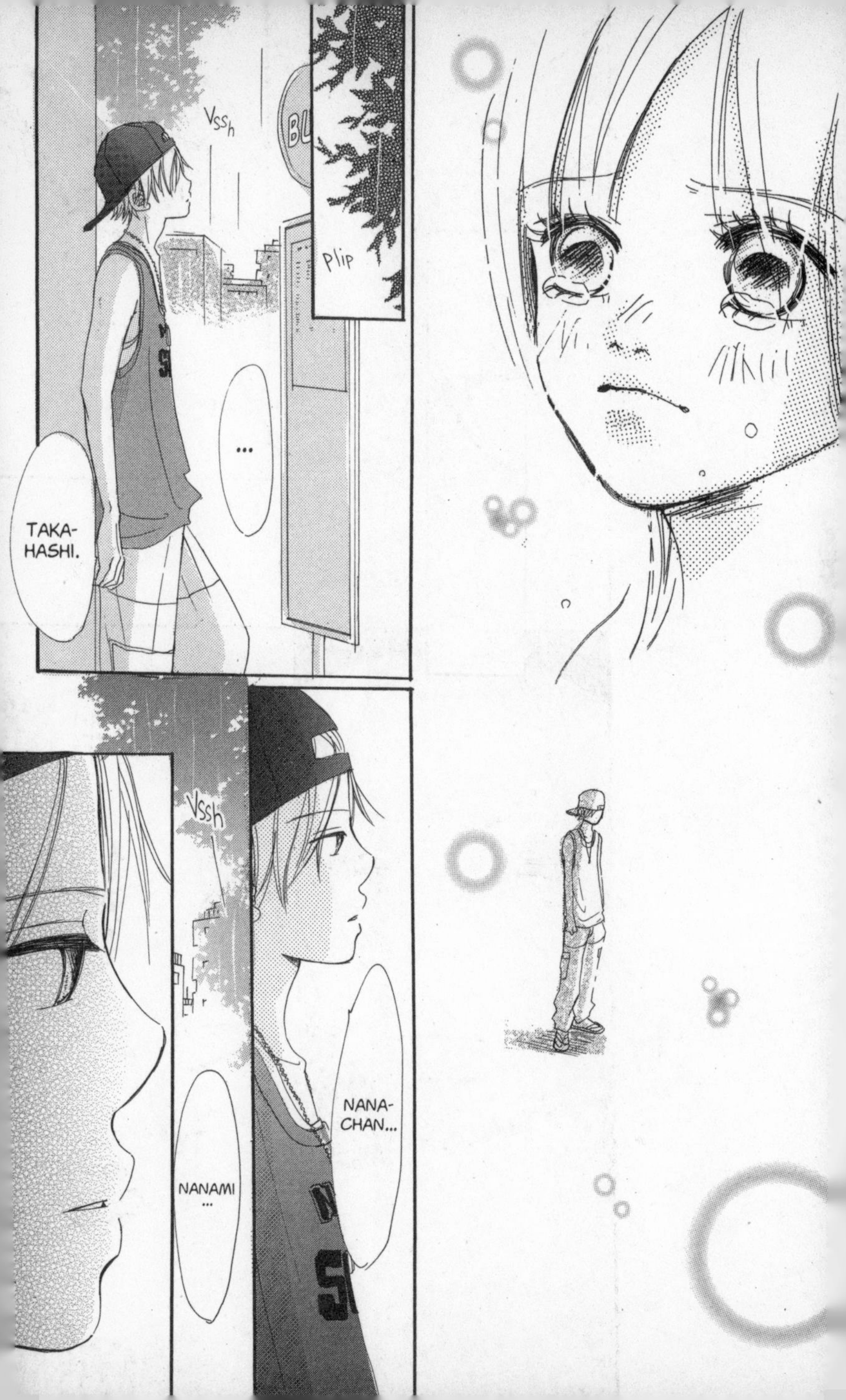
plip
Vssh
...
TAKA-HASHI.
Vssh
NANA-CHAN...
NANAMI ...

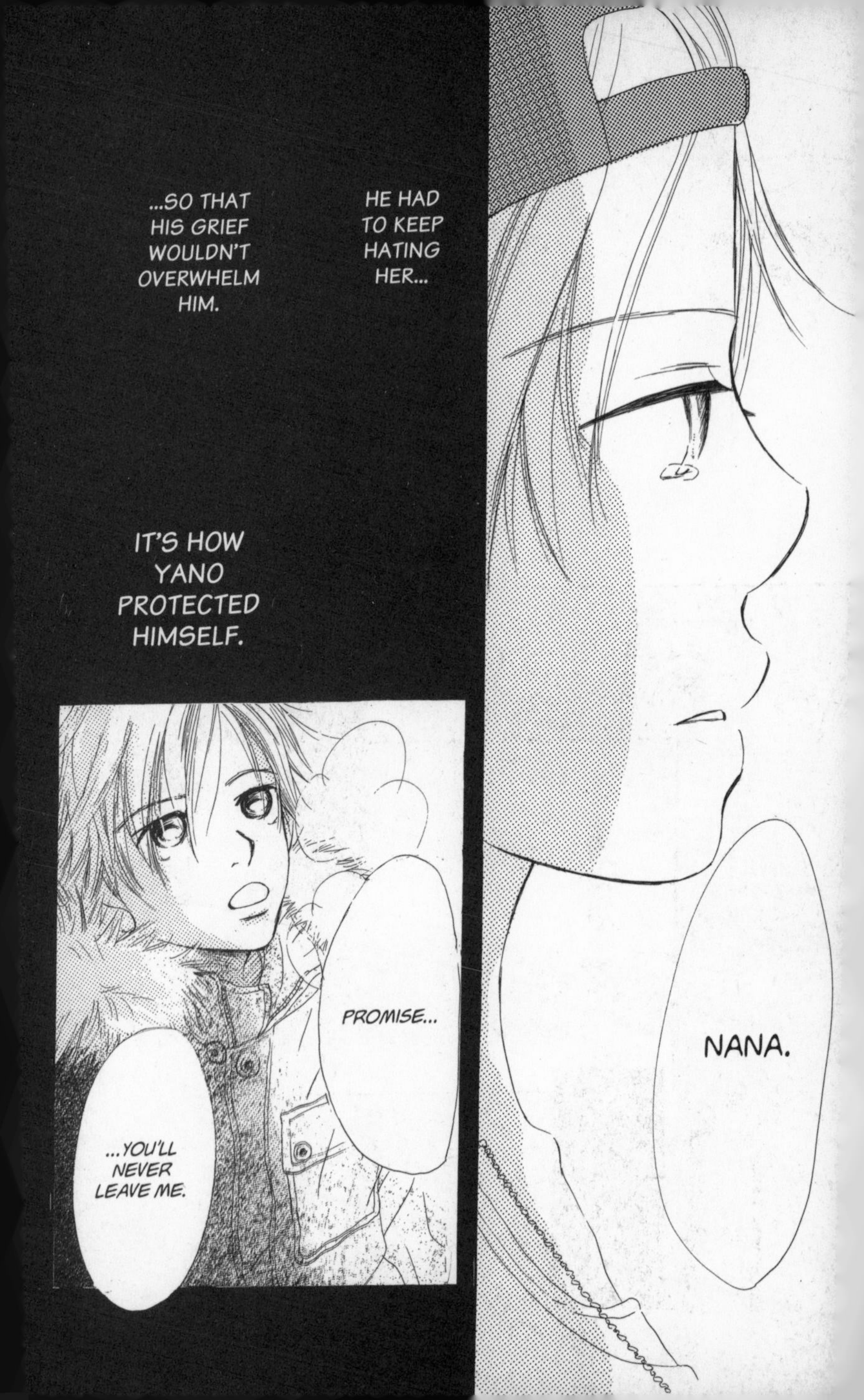
NANA.
HE HAD TO KEEP HATING HER...
...SO THAT HIS GRIEF WOULDN'T OVERWHELM HIM.
IT'S HOW YANO PROTECTED HIMSELF.
PROMISE...
...YOU'LL NEVER LEAVE ME.

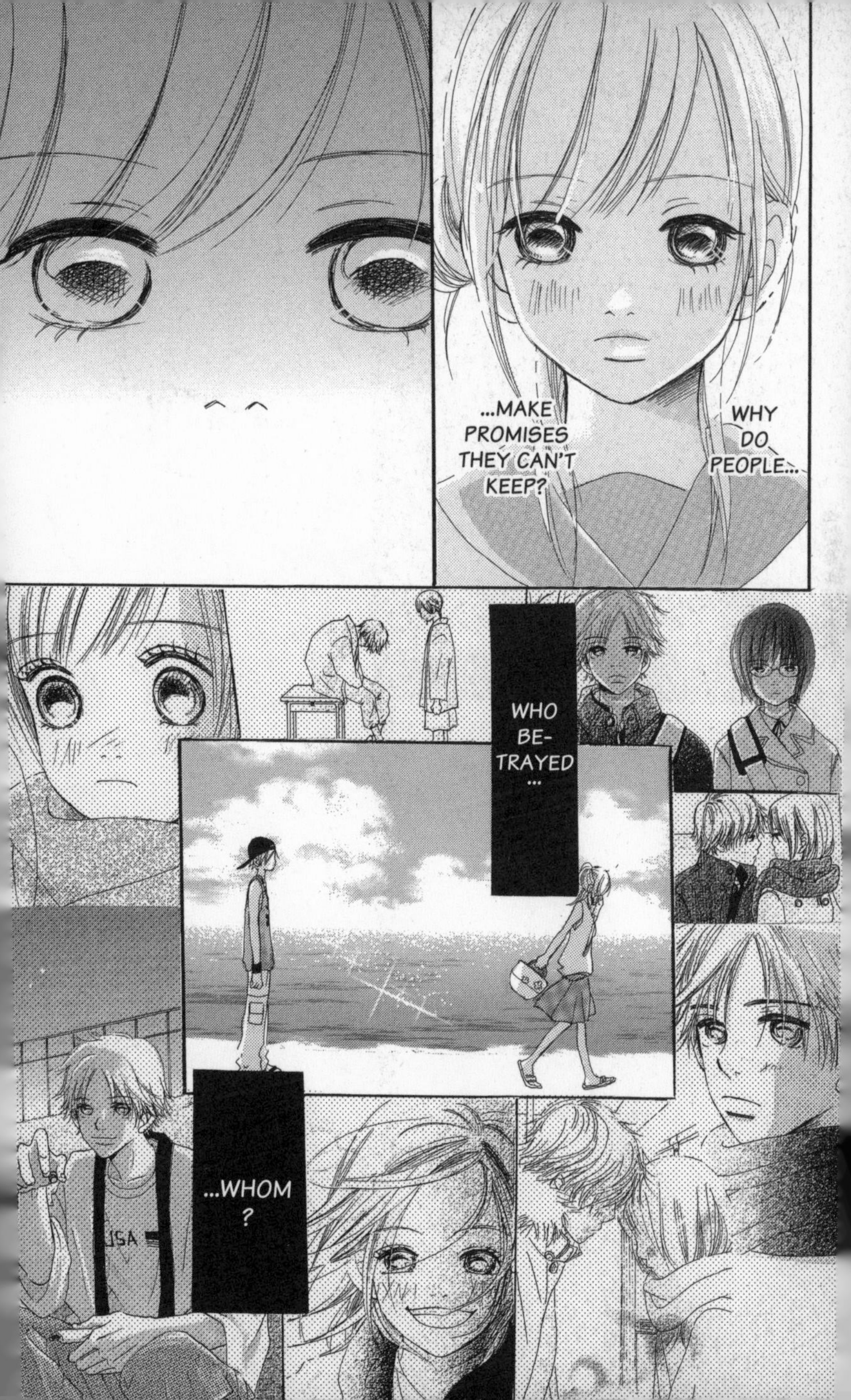
WHY DO PEOPLE...
...MAKE PROMISES THEY CAN'T KEEP?
WHO BE-TRAYED...
...WHOM?
USA

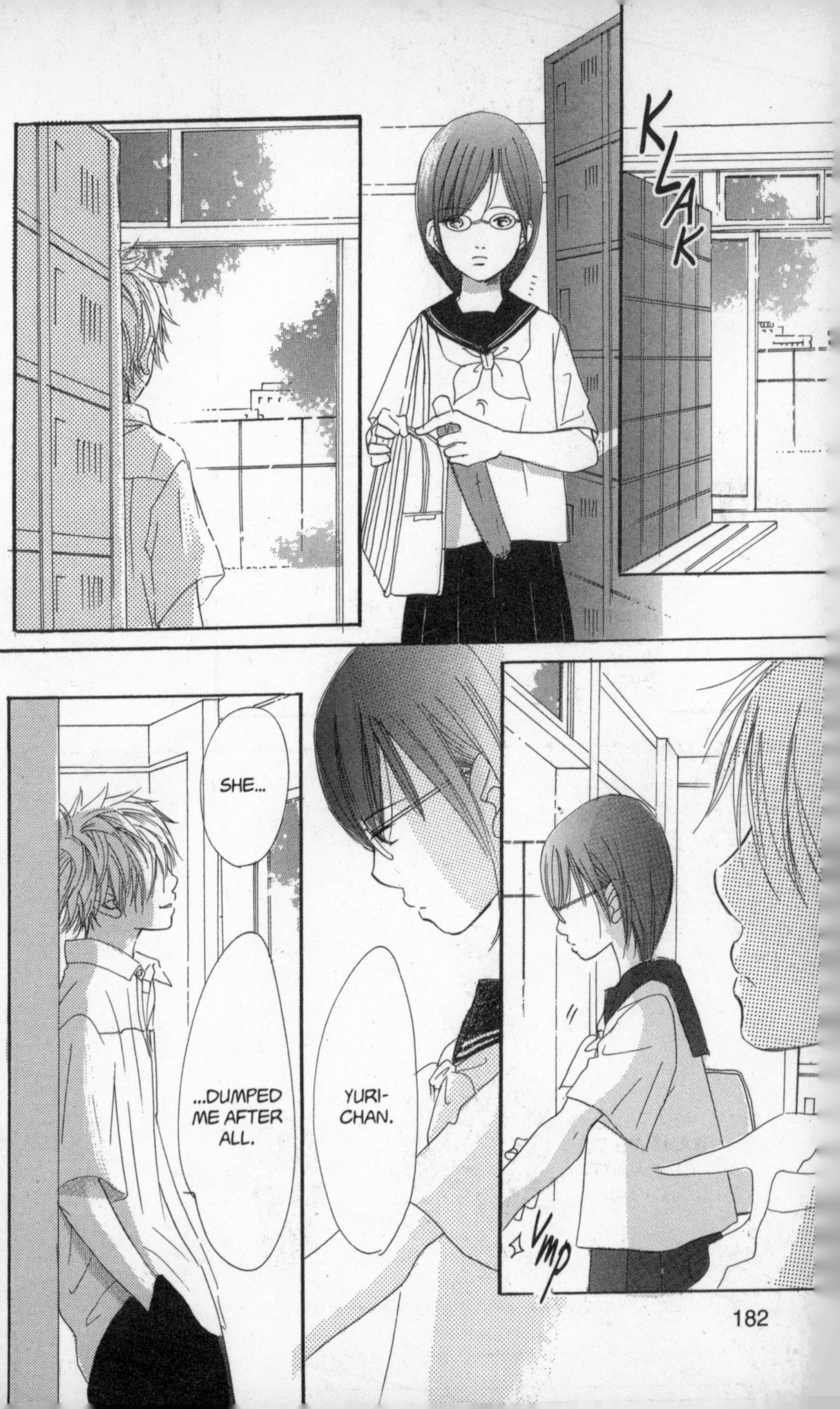
KLAK
VMP
SHE...
YURI-CHAN.
...DUMPED ME AFTER ALL.

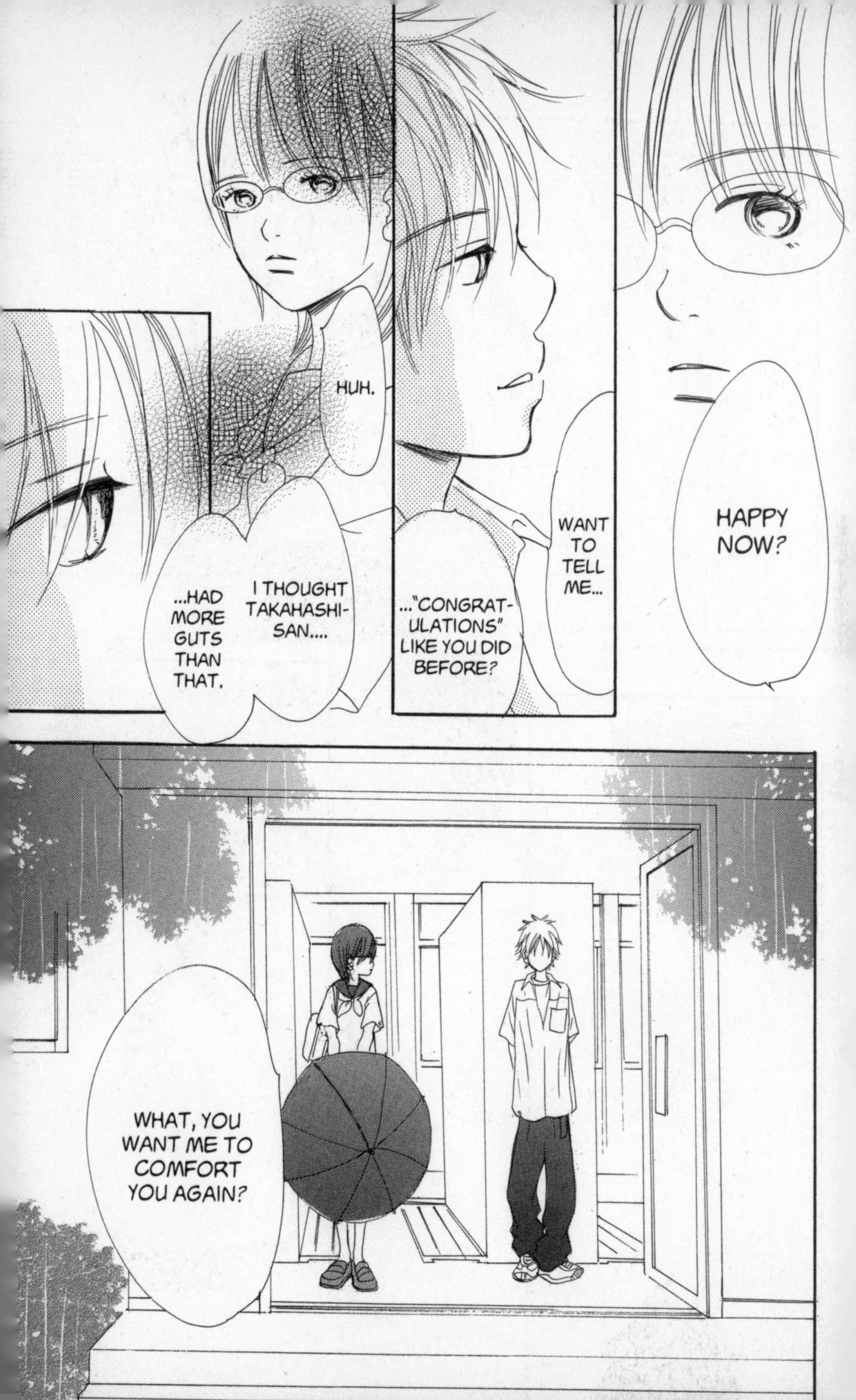
HAPPY NOW?
WANT TO TELL ME...
..."CONGRATULATIONS" LIKE YOU DID BEFORE?
HUH.
I THOUGHT TAKAHASHI-SAN....
...HAD MORE GUTS THAN THAT.
WHAT, YOU WANT ME TO COMFORT YOU AGAIN?

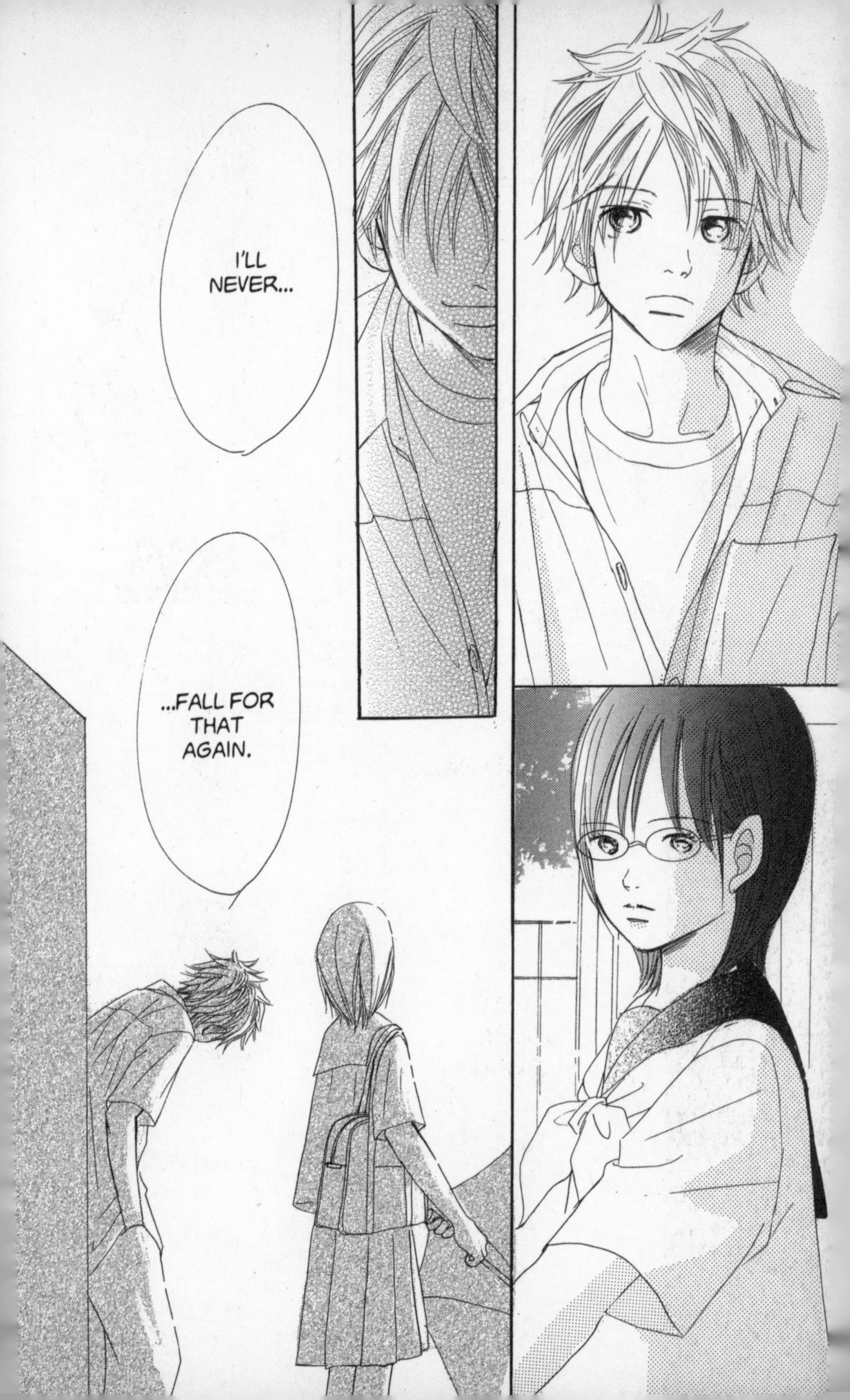
I'LL NEVER...
...FALL FOR THAT AGAIN.

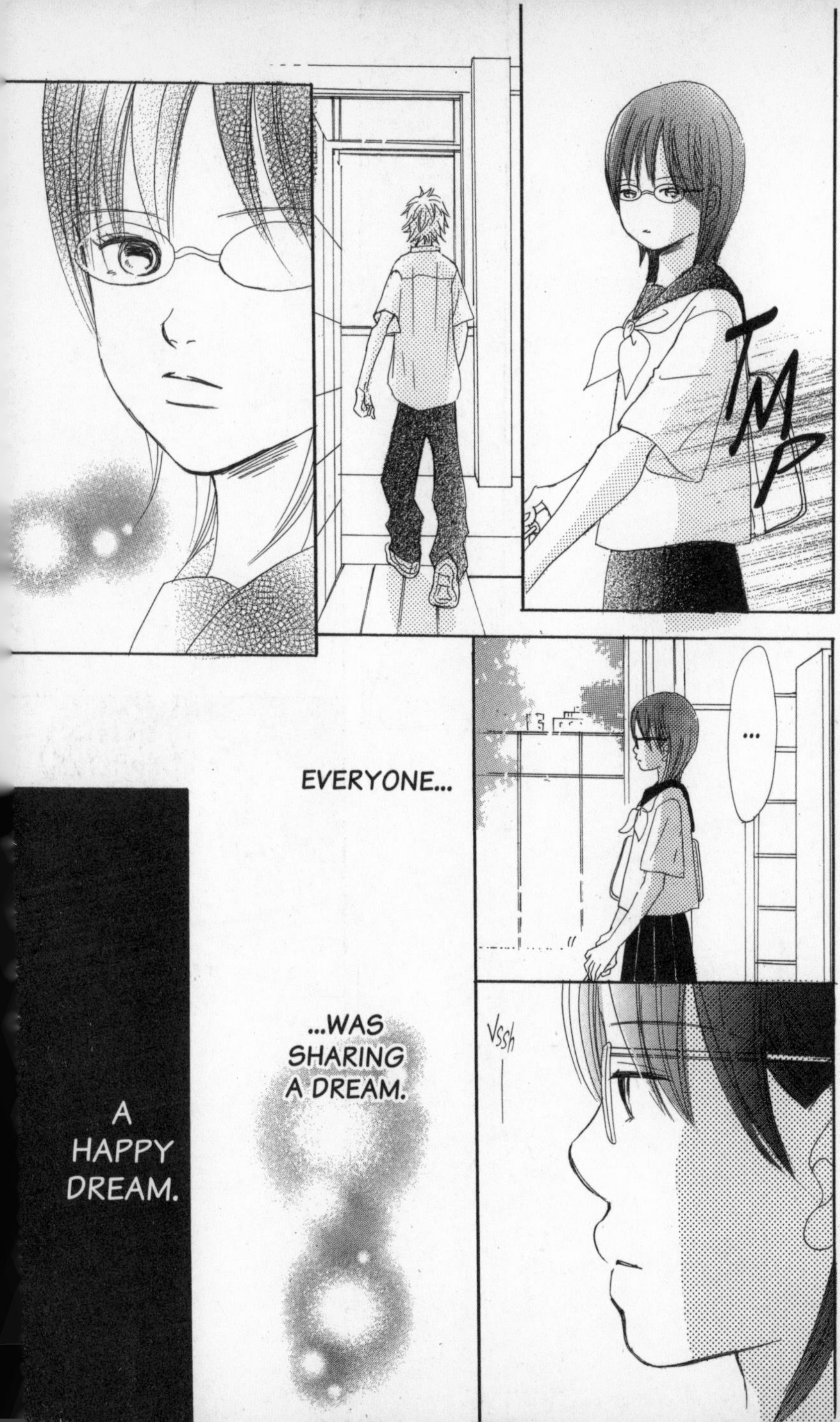
TMP
...
EVERYONE...
Vssh
...WAS SHARING A DREAM.
A HAPPY DREAM.

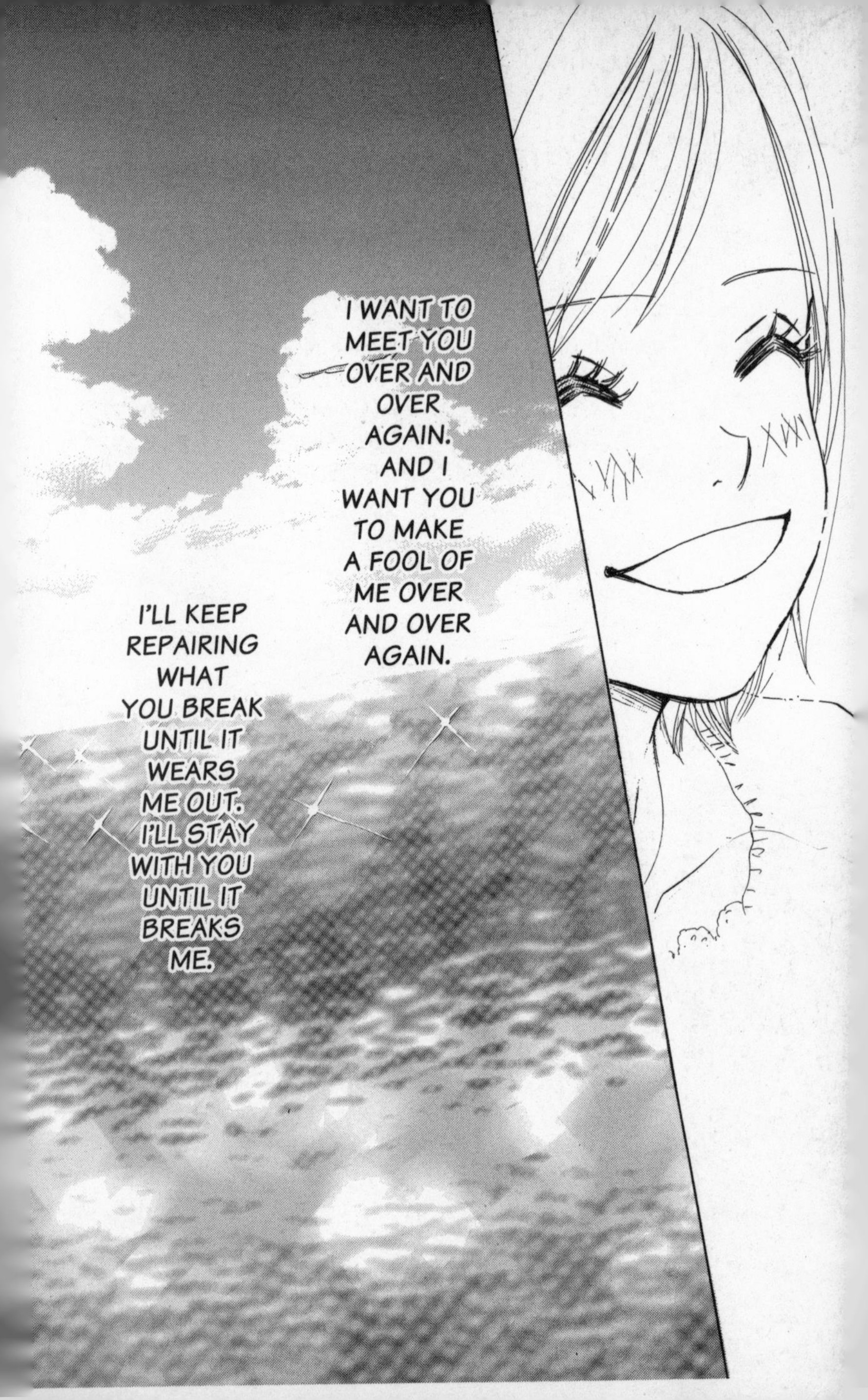
I WANT TO MEET YOU OVER AND OVER AGAIN. AND I WANT YOU TO MAKE A FOOL OF ME OVER AND OVER AGAIN.
I'LL KEEP REPAIRING WHAT YOU BREAK UNTIL IT WEARS ME OUT. I'LL STAY WITH YOU UNTIL IT BREAKS ME.

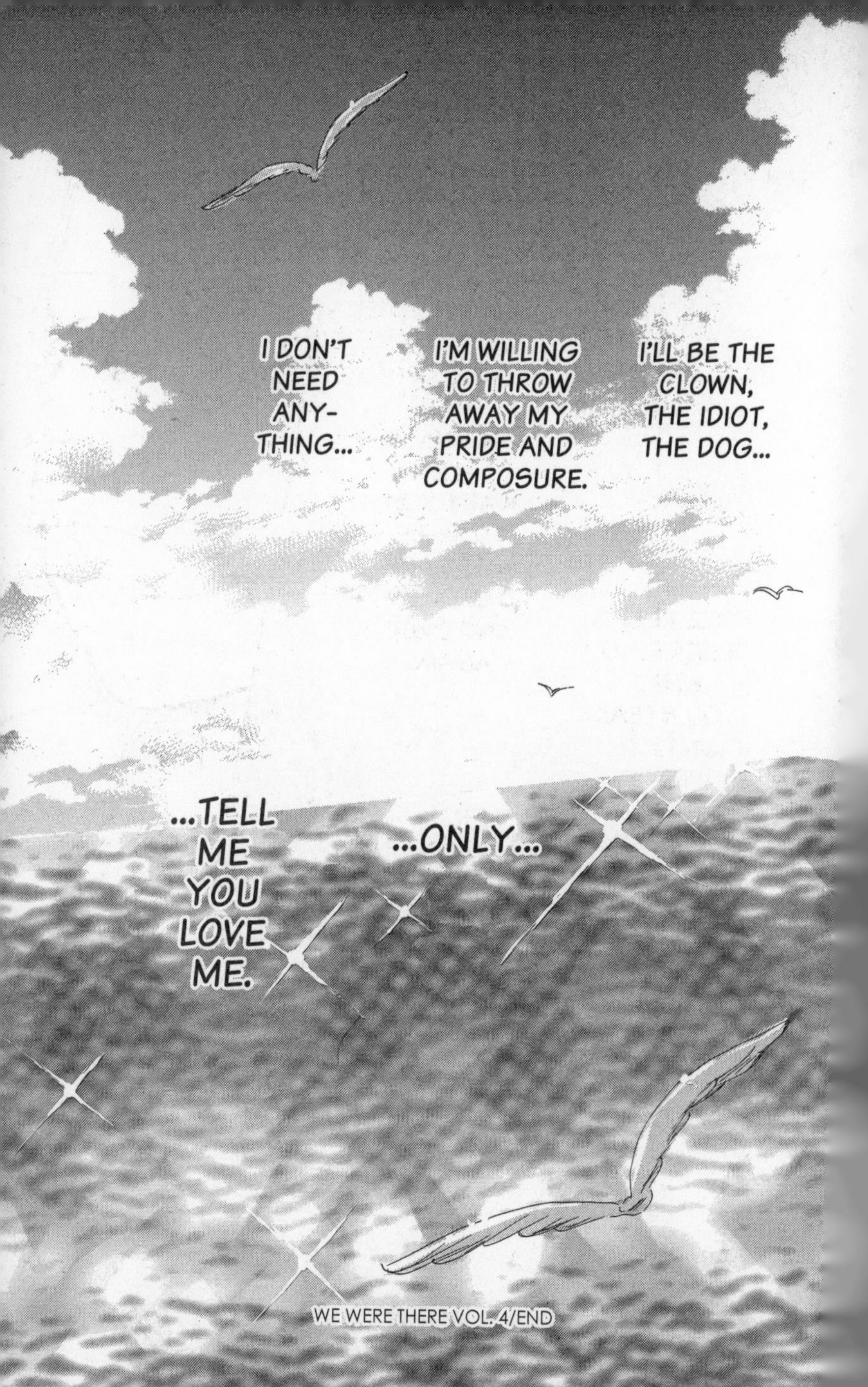
I'LL BE THE CLOWN, THE IDIOT, THE DOG...
I'M WILLING TO THROW AWAY MY PRIDE AND COMPOSURE.
I DON'T NEED ANY-THING...
...ONLY...
...TELL ME YOU LOVE ME.
WE WERE THERE VOL. 4/END

Notes

Honorifics

In Japan, people are usually addressed by their name followed by a suffix.
The suffix shows familiarity or respect, depending on the relationship.

Male (familiar): first or last name + kun
Female (familiar): first or last name + chan
Adult (polite): last name + san
Upperclassman (polite): last name + senpai
Teacher or professional: last name + sensei
Close friends or lovers: first name only, no suffix

Nana-chan vs. Nana-san

Nanami's nickname is "Nana-chan." Yano's ex-girlfriend
was a year older, so she was known as "Nana-san."

Terms

Eight thousand yen is about $75.
A Marimo Jelly Ball is a candy that looks like a ball of algae,
known as *marimo*.
A love hotel is a motel where people go to have sex.

I work really hard to keep up with the season in my
drawings for when the manga appears in *Betsucomi*
magazine. But it really is a tough thing to do...
–Yuki Obata

Yuki Obata's birthday is January 9. Her debut manga, *Raindrops*, won
the Shogakukan Shinjin Comics Taisho Kasaku Award in 1998. Her
current series, *We Were There* (*Bokura ga Ita*), won the 50th Shogakukan
Manga Award and was adapted into an animated television series. She
likes sweets, coffee, drinking with friends, and scary stories. Her hobby
is browsing in bookshops.

We Were There
Vol. 4
The Shojo Beat Manga Edition

STORY & ART BY
YUKI OBATA

Adaptation/Nancy Thistlethwaite
Translation/Tetsuichiro Miyaki
Touch-up Art & Lettering/Inori Fukuda Trant
Cover Design/Izumi Hirayama
Interior Design/Courtney Utt
Editor/Nancy Thistlethwaite

Editor in Chief, Books/Alvin Lu
Editor in Chief, Magazines/Marc Weidenbaum
VP, Publishing Licensing/Rika Inouye
VP, Sales & Product Marketing/Gonzalo Ferreyra
VP, Creative/Linda Espinosa
Publisher/Hyoe Narita

Printed in Canada

Published by VIZ Media, LLC
P.O. Box 77010
San Francisco, CA 94107

Shojo Beat Manga Edition
10 9 8 7 6 5 4 3 2 1
First printing, May 2009

www.viz.com

store.viz.com